SACRIFICE ON THE STEPPE

SACRIFICE ON THE STEPPE

The Italian Alpine Corps in the Stalingrad Campaign, 1942–1943

by
HOPE HAMILTON

CASEMATE
Philadelphia & Oxford

Published in the United States of America and Great Britain in 2011 by
CASEMATE PUBLISHERS
1950 Lawrence Road, Havertown, PA 19083, USA
and
10 Hythe Bridge Street, Oxford OX1 2EW, UK

Hardback Edition: ISBN 978-1-61200-002-2
Paperback Edition: ISBN 978-1-61200-392-4
Digital Edition: ISBN 978-1-61200-013-8

Cataloging-in-publication data is available from the Library of Congress and
the British Library.

Printed and bound in the United States of America

For a complete list of Casemate titles, please contact:

CASEMATE PUBLISHERS (US)
Telephone (610) 853-9131
Fax (610) 853-9146
Email: casemate@casematepublishers.com
www.casematepublishers.com

CASEMATE PUBLISHERS (UK)
Telephone (01865) 241249
Fax (01865) 794449
Email: casemate-uk@casematepublishers.co.uk
www.casematepublishers.co.uk

Cover design: www.mousematdesign.com

MIX
Paper from
responsible sources
FSC® C011935

CONTENTS

CONTENTS (*continued*)

Telling this story saves it from a definite death—
that of being forgotten . . .

PREFACE

During the Second World War, the Italian nation reaped the tragic results of years of Fascist rule under Benito Mussolini, who assumed dictatorial powers three years following the formation of the Fascist Party in 1922. Not only was Mussolini head of the Italian government, he was also responsible for Italian military policy for more than twenty years. Moreover, he was minister for all three armed services during 1925–29 and 1933–43.

Intent on maintaining an imperial image and emulating the glorious days of the Roman Empire, Mussolini clothed himself as a warrior by means of bellicose rhetoric combined with showmanship and propaganda; but the truth was that Italy was not nearly prepared for war. Nevertheless, Mussolini entered the conflict by declaring war against Great Britain and France in June 1940. He told his then Chief of the Supreme General Staff, Marshal Pietro Badoglio, "I need several thousand dead to be able to take my place at the peace table," as he justified his intervention.[1]

Various treaties bound Hitler and Mussolini together: the Anti-Comintern Pact, November 1936, the Tripartite Pact, 1940 (both of which included Japan), and the Pact of Steel signed in May 1939, yet neither dictator conducted foreign policy with much regard for the other, often giving little or no notice of their intentions to their ally. Such was the case when Mussolini invaded Greece in October 1940, and when Hitler invaded the Soviet Union on June 22, 1941.

Immediately upon hearing of Germany's attack on the Soviet Union (as troops of the Wehrmacht were already crossing the Soviet border), Mussolini declared war on Russia. In a matter of weeks, he sent a hastily organized Italian expeditionary force to join the Russian campaign even though Hitler discouraged such a move. Although entirely unprepared militarily, Mussolini meant to be at Hitler's side, partaking of the spoils that he assumed would follow a supposedly rapid Nazi victory on the Eastern Front.

The following year he offered even more Italian troops for Hitler's Soviet aggression. By early fall 1942, 227,000 soldiers of the Italian Eighth Army were aligned on a 270 kilometer front along the Don River; of these, 60,000 were alpini, Italian mountain troops serving in the Italian Alpine Corps.

The consequences of Mussolini's decision to send his troops to Russia were tragic. This story is complex and unsettling, often rising to the level of incredulity; but most of all, it is a human story about thousands of poorly equipped soldiers sent far from their homeland on a mission to wage war without a clear mandate against a people they didn't consider their enemy. Raw courage and endurance blend with human suffering, desperation and altruism in the epic saga of the withdrawal from the Don lines, the capture and imprisonment of thousands, and the survival of few.

Historical accounts concerning the Second World War exist in all languages, but the account of Italian troops sent to Russia has received scant attention in most books written in English. This little known story outside of Italy deserves telling in its entirety, shared with a wider audience.

Within this narrative, whenever possible, I have told the story of the alpini in Russia "from the bottom up," enabling those who participated in the campaign to share their experiences in their own words. Fortunately, a rich array of firsthand experiences written by Italians who served in Russia exists. I have relied heavily upon those sources. Translations from such texts are mine.[2]

On a personal note, I have included the experiences of my uncles Nello Corti and Veniero Ajmone Marsan, who served in the Alpine Corps in Russia.

Nello and I spent countless hours discussing the role of the alpini in the Russian campaign. I could only marvel at his keen memory of those days so long ago as he spoke about specific events in detail. Often his emotions were palpable as he recalled his experiences, in fact sometimes he even asked me to turn off my tape recorder as he spoke about painful events, especially those of battle. At other times his marvelous sense of humor shone, as did his sense of amazement and bewilderment. To this day, he asks, "How was it possible so many young men went off to Russia, possibly to die fighting against a people with whom they had no quarrel?"

We often discussed this issue. He remarked, "At that time, eighty percent of the Italian population was agricultural. Large numbers of soldiers who served in Italian infantry divisions were illiterate, especially those who came from southern Italy. Troops in the Alpine Corps consisted of men who came from hamlets, villages and small towns in the alpine valleys of northern Italy or the Abruzzi region. Many alpini were *contadini* (peasant farmers) or laborers. They were accustomed to a life of hard work, obedience, and sacrifice. For the most part these mountain dwellers had a limited elementary education, and it is entirely possible that most had no idea where Russia was located geographically. Just imagine—some men sent off to Russia had never even seen a tram or ridden on a train!"

Nello kept a small diary during the Russian campaign. Privileged to read his diary, I have quoted some of his writings within this narrative.

Veniero died in April 2007, a few weeks before his eighty-ninth birthday. By this time, we had worked together for four years. His memory of those times so long ago was keen, as was his great admiration and affection for the Russian civilian population. Although he experienced the tortuous withdrawal and horrific train transport to a prisoner of war camp, and hunger, disease, and suffering during the first months of imprisonment, I never heard him complain, never detecting anger or self-pity in his voice. Sometimes it appeared as though he was detached from all that he had endured. When he spoke about his association with Russian civilians while he worked in the countryside, there was warmth, understanding, and compassion in his words – he understood that they, the children, women, and elderly folks remaining in the villages were suffering almost, if not more, than the prisoners were.

It was clear when he spoke about his long separation from his wife, Lucia, that thoughts of her sustained his determination to survive all obstacles and challenges, to remain alive.

Veniero wrote several brief memoirs about his experiences in Russia. I have cited portions of his writings within this narrative.

During the Russian campaign, Veniero served with Gino Beraudi in the Cuneense Division. Their friendship endured until Gino's premature death in 1979 at the age of seventy-four. His book *Vaina` kaputt, guerra e prigione in Russia 1942–1945* was hailed as one of the best first-hand written accounts of imprisonment in a Russian prisoner of war camp.

In his preface, Gino tells the story of several encounters he had with elderly Russian peasants, either behind the lines on the Don, or later while he was held in several prisoner of war camps: "Realizing that I was not one who would betray them, they repeated the same formula— 'Mussolini kaputt, Hitler kaputt, Stalin kaputt: vaina`[war] kaputt.' If the three Caesars disappear, war will also disappear. And he convinced me."[3]

Gino wrote that it's a mistake to dress our warriors in hero's clothing. "The generations repeat that mistake, because whether before or after (if one loses or wins), inevitably there's fanfare, flowers, women's laughter, applause, and medals: but within the intermezzo there's mud, lice, anguish, fear (overcome or not, always fear), and the only thing that remains pure is blood.... But the price of wasting that purity...has too high a cost...."[4]

Once he returned from Russia, Gino resumed his life in Rimini with his family. He practiced law, and was an active participant in the civil life of his city. He remained a close friend, not only of Veniero, but also of our entire family. The Beraudi family has generously given me permission to include material from his book within this narrative.

During one of my trips to Italy, Veniero introduced me to Carlo Vicentini who served in the elite Monte Cervino Alpine Battalion in Russia. Carlo and I have also spent many hours discussing the role of the Alpine Corps during the Russian conflict. Material gleaned from interviews with him, as well as from his copious writings has added another dimension of depth and breadth to this story.

Carlo has generously shared many of his original maps and materials with me. The Italians relied on German maps for the most part. I have relied upon the Library of Congress transliteration tables for the correct spelling of Russian place names. Carlo has painstakingly altered his maps using these same transliterated place names.

On one of my last trips to Italy, I met Alarico Rocchi, a peasant farmer who lives in Anguillara, the town where I stay when I am in that country. Alexandra Petrova and her husband Valter Schiavoni, residents of Anguillara, introduced me to Alarico in October 2009. Alarico served in the Torino Infantry Division sent to Russia in 1941. It is a great privilege to include some of his firsthand recollections within this narrative.

PART I

ITALIAN TROOPS ARE SENT TO RUSSIA

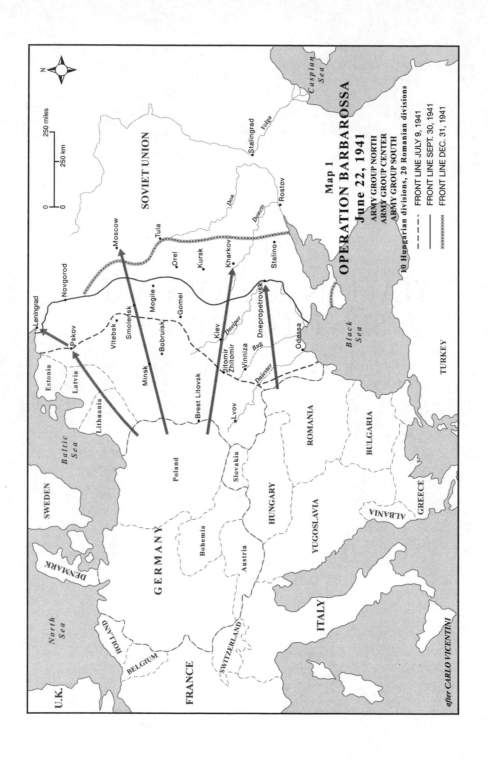

Map 1

OPERATION BARBAROSSA
June 22, 1941

ARMY GROUP NORTH
ARMY GROUP CENTER
ARMY GROUP SOUTH

10 Hungarian divisions, 20 Romanian divisions

- - - - FRONT LINE JULY 9, 1941
———— FRONT LINE SEPT. 30, 1941
ⱯⱯⱯⱯ FRONT LINE DEC. 31, 1941

after CARLO VICENTINI

Chapter 1

THE INVASION OF RUSSIA

OPERATION BARBAROSSA

In the early morning hours of June 22, 1941, Hitler broke the Nazi-Soviet nonaggression pact signed by the two nations August 1939, and launched a massive surprise attack against the Soviet Union. More than three million German and other Axis troops organized in three army groups moved across a thousand-mile front between the Baltic and Black Seas in attacks aimed at Moscow, Leningrad, and Kiev.

Hitler had declared his intention to invade the Soviet Union to his leading generals on July 31, 1940, making it clear that the acquisition of vast expanses of territory was not his only objective: "Wiping out the very power of Russia to exist! That is the goal!"[1]

He set the date for the start of the invasion for May 1941, stating that the campaign would last five months, and thereby implying it would be finished before winter set in. In April, due to preliminary operations undertaken in the Balkans, Hitler postponed the invasion's start-date to June 22, 1941.

Over the following months, meticulous planning for the destruction of the Red Army and the exploitation and mass murder of Soviet civilians and Jews took place. It was clear from Hitler's remarks in March 1941 that no restraints would stand in the way of the German onslaught against Russia, code-named "Operation Barbarossa." When the Nazi warlord spoke to leaders of the three armed services and key Army field commanders, he declared, "The war against Russia will be such that it

3

cannot be conducted in a knightly fashion. This struggle is one of ideologies and racial differences, and will have to be conducted with
unprecedented, unmerciful, and unrelenting harshness. All officers will
have to rid themselves of obsolete ideologies...."[2]

There then followed orders violating international law, including
the infamous *Kommissarbefehl* (Commissar Order): "The commissars
are the bearers of ideologies directly opposed to National Socialism.
Therefore, the commissars will be liquidated. German soldiers guilty of
breaking international law...will be excused. Russia has not participated in the Hague Convention and therefore has no rights under it."[3]

On May 13, at the behest of Hitler, General Wilhelm Keitel issued
additional directives. The "Jurisdiction Order" exempted members of
the Wehrmacht from prosecution should they commit crimes against
Russian civilians. It also eliminated a system of appeals on the part of
civilians suspected of a criminal offence. "Punishable offenses committed by enemy civilians do not, until further notice, come any longer
under the jurisdiction of the courts-martial..."

*"Persons suspected of criminal action will be brought at once before
an officer. This officer will decide whether they are to be shot."*

"With regard to *offenses* committed against *enemy civilians by
members of the Wehrmacht, prosecution is not obligatory* even when
the deed is at the same time a military crime or offense."[4]

Yet another directive, also signed by Keitel, placed Heinrich
Himmler in charge of "special tasks...tasks which result from the struggle which has to be carried out between two opposing political systems." As head of the Nazi secret police and the SS, Hitler entrusted
Himmler to act independently of the army, sealing off occupied areas in
order to complete his grisly work of extermination of Jews and other
undesirables.[5]

Former German ambassador to Italy (1932–38) Ulrich von Hassell,
an opponent of the Nazi Regime, had the opportunity to view copies of
the illegal Barbarossa documents. In a diary entry, he wrote, "It makes
one's hair stand on end to learn about measures to be taken in Russia
and about the systematic transformation of military law concerning the
conquered population into uncontrolled despotism—indeed a caricature
of all law. This kind of thing turns the German into a type of being
which had existed only in enemy propaganda."

In a following entry, he noted, "The army must assume the onus of the murders and burnings which up to now have been confined to the SS."[6]

Not many German officers protested the abandonment of international law in Russia. British historian Antony Beevor notes that perhaps this was due in part to the fact that "Nazi propaganda had so effectively dehumanized the Soviet enemy in the eyes of the Wehrmacht that it was morally anaesthetized from the start of the invasion." Even fewer officers raised objection to the rampant program of extermination of the Jews, owing to "the greatest measure of successful indoctrination... which was deliberately confused with the notion of rear-area security measures against partisans."[7]

Hitler assigned Herman Goering to develop plans for "exploitation of the country and the securing of its economic assets for use by German industry." Once military operations were concluded, Hitler declared that Russia was to be "divided up into individual states with governments of their own," and he appointed Alfred Rosenberg the Commissioner for Central Control of Questions Connected with the East European Region.[8]

Two days prior to the beginning of the attack on Russia, Rosenberg spoke to his underlings. He didn't mince words as he declared that Russia's production of food was to be sent to Germany. "The southern [Russian] territories will have to serve...for the feeding of the German people. We see absolutely no reason for any obligation on our part to feed also the Russian people with the products of that surplus territory. We know that this is a harsh necessity, bare of any feelings.... The future will hold very hard years in store for the Russians."[9]

FASCIST ITALY JOINS THE RUSSIAN CAMPAIGN

A military alliance between Nazi Germany and Fascist Italy was signed in Berlin May 22, 1939 by Italy's foreign minister Count Galeazzo Ciano (Mussolini's son-in-law), and Germany's foreign minister Joachim von Ribbentrop. The alliance, known as the "Pact of Steel," declared that either country would come to the aid of the other if attacked.

With the signing of the alliance and Italy's entrance into the war in 1940, Italian historian Giorgio Rochat noted, "Mussolini accepted a subaltern role to the politics of Hitler that translated into an increasing dependence…. An unequal alliance wasn't necessarily an unacceptable relationship per sè, if based on transparency and reciprocal loyalty…but [the Pact of Steel] was an alliance between a great power conducting a war of European domination with brutal confidence and a subaltern State holding on to its ally for its own survival, without the option of having any input whatsoever. It was an alliance based on mistrust and reciprocal deceit, and contributed to widespread images of the weaker ally as a loser and opportunist, in contrast to the arrogant and triumphal German."[10]

Underlining these facts, during the years of alliance, there was no joint military command structure of any weight, nor did political-strategic consultations or exchanges of timely information occur.

A few hours before the Russian invasion began Hitler dictated a long letter to his ally Benito Mussolini, informing him of his reasons to attack the USSR. At that moment, Mussolini was residing in his summer residence in Riccione. Awakened by a phone call during the early morning hours of June 22, he listened to his foreign minister Count Ciano read Hitler's "missive" over the telephone.[11]

Upon hearing the news of the invasion, however, Mussolini immediately declared war on the Soviet Union. Deluded into thinking the war in Russia would be victorious for the Germans, and more importantly of short duration, the Italian dictator offered military support to Hitler. Hitler was not keen to accept his offer to send Italian troops to Russia; in fact, he suggested that Mussolini should send more troops to strengthen his own forces fighting in Northern Africa.[12]

Il Duce[13] remained determined to come to the aid of his ally; he imagined he would be qualified to share a greater part of the spoils by assisting Hitler's troops on the Eastern Front.

Mussolini had entered the war in 1940 with an army of seventy-four divisions, but only nineteen of them were complete in terms of numbers of men and armaments. General Mario Roatta described the level of equipment and armaments of the Italian Army at that time: "Everything modern is missing."[14]

The army relied primarily on materiel from 1915–18, woefully inadequate for the kind of war being fought in Russia, which required rapid mobility, tanks, and modern weaponry, as well as tactical coordination between different branches of the military. Most Italian generals were not Fascists, owing their allegiance to the King, but they were inadequate, stuck in the past, lacking knowledge of "modern technologies and strategies." They were "fossils of the First World War."[15]

Although the Italian dictator was master of a grandiose repertoire of bellicose rhetoric, he possessed little knowledge of the materiel required to fight a modern war. Italian industrial preparedness as well as military preparedness was lacking; "Mussolini wants an imperial army, but he is educating it at the school of poverty.... He doesn't understand, behind the clang of armaments, you need the coverage of a large industry and the strength of technologies."[16]

Nevertheless, in August 1941, Mussolini sent 62,000 Italian troops to join the German offensive in Russia. He only worried that they might not arrive soon enough to join a triumphant German victory over the USSR.[17]

The Italian Expeditionary Corps, the *Corpo di Spedizione Italiano in Russia* [18](hereafter CSIR), under the command of General Giovanni Messe, joined the German invading forces in the Ukraine two months after the German offensive began. Although divisions sent to Russia were some of the best of the Italian army, there was a fundamental weakness of the force, because divisions were binary, composed of only two regiments, which meant they were slightly larger than reinforced brigades.[19]

Moreover, the CSIR was equipped negligently: airplanes lacked de-icing equipment, and the so-called "motorized divisions" (also called "self transportable divisions") were motorized in name only. In fact, since there weren't enough trucks to transport troops of the two infantry divisions, "this absurd euphemism was used to indicate they could be transported, but if trucks weren't available these troops could move from place to place on foot," which is what actually occurred.[20]

Soldiers left Italy that summer wearing lightweight uniforms and lightweight boots. When infantryman Alarico Rocchi (Torino Division), recalled the 500 kilometers he and his fellow soldiers traversed on foot to reach the Don River, he described boots issued to the infantry as being flimsier than *scarpe da ballerina* (ballerina shoes).

Troops of the CSIR were also poorly equipped in terms of individual and collective weapons. Rifles dated from 1891. Although they were sturdy and functioned, they were no match against the automatic rifles used by the Russians. Few sub-machine guns were available and Italian machine-guns functioned poorly in Russia's extreme winter weather.

Italian soldiers referred to their M-13 tanks as "sardine cans," realizing they would have little impact when confronted by monstrous Russian tanks.[21]

During the summer of 1941, Mussolini accepted an invitation from Hitler to visit the Eastern Front in the Ukraine. On August 28 the two Axis leaders, and several German and Italian dignitaries, met with the commander of the CSIR forces, General Giovanni Messe. Upon introducing Hitler to General Messe, Mussolini turned toward the General and said, "I am sure you deserve the trust which the Führer places in Italian troops."[22]

Later that same morning, in a private conversation with Mussolini, General Messe described the current conditions facing his soldiers, focusing particularly on the shortage of adequate transportation hampering the ability of his troops to keep up with German mobile divisions, as well as slowing the necessary flow of supplies from distant bases. Messe also referred to a shortage of fuel. Deliveries of fuel to Italian troops arrived late, causing a slowdown in the Italian advance. At the same time, the Germans were becoming increasingly impatient and frustrated with the pace of Italian units, which were unable to rapidly reach German forces on the front lines.[23]

Throughout Messe's report, Mussolini didn't respond; in fact, he spoke not a word. Messe noted he appeared "absent." Shortly after, several units of the CSIR forces arrived and proceeded to march in formation in front of the gathered dignitaries. Following a review of the troops, both Hitler and Mussolini expressed their pleasure at the "order and fine appearance" of the Italian units.[24]

The Soviets were not completely mobilized when the German offensive began, and were caught off guard, even though intelligence had indicated an impending German attack. German forces scored one victory after another, advancing rapidly. Russian forces attempted to gain time by withdrawing, "prepared always to sacrifice their inexhaustible assets—men and space."[25]

In his unpublished diary, Lieutenant Luciano Mela (Savoia Regiment) describes Russian tactics after the fall of the city of Kiev in September 1941. He claims the Soviets were imitating the withdrawal they conducted when Napoleon invaded their country: "They only leave ruins: they even wreck trails with an easy, practical method, causing movement of [our] trucks to be delayed. When leaving a village without bridges to blow up, or roads to wreck, but only trails like the ones they have here, tractors follow them with plows making large zigzag ruts on the trail. This doesn't seem like it amounts to much, but on such a trail [our] trucks can't go more than 8–10 kilometers per hour."[26]

At first, CSIR forces were under the command of Germany's Eleventh Army, then transferred to the control of General von Kleist's First Panzer Army, and in June of 1942, CSIR was subordinated to the German Seventeenth Army. Although the Italians performed well, both on the offensive and defensive in the Ukraine, they were plagued with logistical problems owing in large part to the fact they lacked adequate transportation for their troops and supplies.

Troops were running out of provisions, and their shoddy shoes were falling apart. Lieutenant Mela describes the situation in his diary: "*Non ne posso più*! ("I've had it!") I'm not afraid to say the person responsible for sending a division ahead in the condition in which ours finds itself is an assassin. We're without food, with broken shoes, uniforms in tatters, with just a little ammunition issued to each individual, since the rest is on trucks stopped without fuel at a distance of two-hundred kilometers...."[27]

Referring to words uttered by Mussolini, Mela writes, "In war it's the spirit that counts; it's enthusiasm that wins."

He continues: "To raise spirits and rekindle enthusiasm, soldiers are left with almost nothing to eat...without wool clothing, with broken shoes, and trousers falling to pieces. I talk to the soldiers, I live their life, and I listen to them."[28]

RELATIONSHIPS BETWEEN ITALIAN AND GERMAN FORCES AND THE RUSSIAN POPULATION

Mistrust, emanating from Hitler himself, colored relationships between the Germans and their Italian allies throughout the Russian campaign. For example, orders given to German Army Group South called for the use of maximum "precaution" when discussing allied participation or objectives of scheduled operations. The Germans gave the least possible amount of information to their allies, and most of it at the very last moment before an operation was to begin. In general, the behavior of German commands toward Italian troops was described as "arrogant" and "over-bearing."[29]

At the same time the Germans refrained from disclosing their detailed military plans to the Italians, they maintained careful surveillance of those forces. "Obliged by circumstances to collaborate and support each other, reciprocal resentment and contempt existed between them; paradoxically this wasn't the case between the Italians and the Soviet population."[30]

When German troops first arrived in Russia, many among the population, particularly those in the Ukraine and the Baltic, believed liberation from heavy-handed Soviet oppression was a possibility. Large numbers of Russian soldiers deserted in the Ukraine, where an independence movement had failed to be entirely crushed, as well as in the Baltics where Soviet occupation had existed for a shorter period. Many among these populations yearned for freedom from Soviet control—"even by the Germans."[31]

This initial acceptance soon faded, as the Germans became an occupying force bent on taking advantage of the territory and its people. Russian resistance to the German invaders gained strength as German brutality increased. Partisan groups (in some cases including women) multiplied. The civilian population suffered from hunger and abuse as Germans requisitioned their food supplies and human resources.[32]

The Nazis viewed Jews and the Slavic people as *Untermenschen*—sub-humans. Their very existence and right to live was to be subject to the needs of the Germans for their use as workers in the *Reich*. Some Slavs would serve as slave workers for Germany, but Jews were to be eradicated, as were the entire populations of large eastern cities such as Leningrad, Moscow, and Warsaw.[33]

Erich Koch, Reich Commissar for the Ukraine, gave voice to the Nazis' ethnic philosophy: "We are the master race and we must govern hard but just.... I will draw the very last out of this country. I did not come here to spread bliss.... The population must work, work, and work again.... We definitely did not come here to give out manna. We have come here to create the basis for victory."

He continued: "We are a master race, which must remember that the lowliest German worker is racially and biologically a thousand times more valuable than the population here."[34]

In a conversation between Rudolf, a German soldier on leave from the Eastern Front and his friends in Germany, he described the treatment of Russian civilians by German soldiers: "At first it was fine.... We swept on adding towns and villages by the score.... Do you know how we behaved to the civilians? We behaved like devils from hell.... We have left those villagers to starve to death behind us, thousands and thousands of them."

When asked if German troops left anything in the way of food, shelter or livestock for the villagers he replied, "Those are the orders.... Just to leave enough for the occupying troops...."

Rudolph claimed the Russian front was under control of the SS (*Schutzstaffel*): "I was one of those who marched in [to the Ukraine] to be received not as a conqueror but as a friend. The civilians were all ready to look on us as saviors. They had years of oppression from the Soviets. They thought we had come to free them.... What did we do? Turn them into slaves under Hitler. Worse, we deported their women for labor in Germany and did not bother if they were married or single, had children or not."

At the end of this conversation, when friends offered Rudolf a glass of wine, they began to hum an old German drinking song. Rudolf remarked, "You can take my word for it...if the Russians should ever knock at this door and only pay back one half of what we have done to them, you wouldn't ever smile or sing again!"[35]

The SS had "special task" forces, *Einsatzgruppen*, which were really mobile killing squads, working in zones occupied by the German Army. Deighton describes their brutal role: "Their task was the systematic murder of people for whom there was no place in the Nazi state."[36]

The Germans targeted political commissars, partisans, Jews, teachers, and religious leaders for execution. By the end of 1941, they had slaughtered half a million European Russian Jews, and approximately the same number of non-Jewish Russians. Hitler himself said: "We have a war of annihilation on our hands."[37]

Einsatzkommandos and *Sonderkommandos* were smaller units of the Einsatzgruppen. Their mission was the "organized, mass killing of Jews" which began a few days following the German invasion.[38] Einsatzgruppen usually followed German combat troops to carry out "one phase of the final solution." In the case of the USSR, five Einsatzgruppen with 3,000 men followed the Wehrmacht during the course of its invasion.[39]

Lieutenant Commander Whitney R. Harris, a member of the American prosecution staff at the Nuremberg Trials, interrogated Otto

Ohlendorf who had been commander of Einsatzgruppe D, operating in the Ukraine and Crimea in 1941. When asked how many Jews his Einsatzgruppe had killed in the Ukraine in 1941, Ohlendorf calmly confessed that 90,000 men, women and children had been liquidated.[40]

Arrigo Paladini who served with the CSIR forces, witnessed first-hand the brutality of the Nazis on an occasion when they executed 150 Jews. Stanislao Pugliese quotes an entry from Paladini's war diary (July 31, 1941): "Until now we thought this would be an easy war; instead today our eyes were opened."

Two weeks later, referring to the ferocity of both the Germans and the Russians, Paladini wrote, "...our Latin soul cannot accustom itself to what we must encounter every step of the way.... I never thought I would find myself before such brutality and gestures that are highly immoral. They preach 'civilization' but we become soiled by barbarism. I used to admire the German soldier but from today he presents himself in a different light: that of a strong but profoundly barbaric warrior."[41]

Generally, Italians in CSIR units established a respectful attitude toward the local population. In contrast to the Germans, the Italians had not come to the Ukraine inculcated with beliefs of racial superiority. If anything, they felt empathy and sympathy for the plight of Russian civilians as they observed the harsh, merciless behavior on the part of the Germans during their occupation.[42]

The Russian peasant population often displayed hospitality toward Italian soldiers, accepting them into their homes and sharing what little they had with them. Much later, during the tragic days of the withdrawal from the Don, many Italian soldiers probably owed their survival to the generosity of Russian peasants.[43]

One historian, General Libero Porcari, claims that the Italian soldier, far from his homeland, soon realized he was fighting a war for "a greater Germany" —for a cause he did not own. He wrote, "The Fascist drum could go ahead and beat Fascist propaganda, but the Italian combatant in Russia...couldn't tolerate the role of conqueror. It wasn't because he was more poorly armed and equipped than his adversary or ally. It was because he felt closer to the victims than to the rulers. He had no use for the Nazi longing for conquest, and could comprehend even less or justify their inhuman methods." Moreover, he adds, "...if the Germans judged Italians as 'weak conquerors,' in return Italians viewed the Nazis as 'stupidly cruel'."[44]

The Germans required the Italians to forward all Russian prisoners and deserters to German prison camps within thirty-six to forty-eight hours following their capture. Italian officers, aware of the brutal treatment of captured Russians by the Germans, attempted in every way to prevent sending prisoners to the "hell" of German camps. They took advantage of their own lack of available transportation for forwarding captured Russians, and often gave the Germans false figures with regard to the number of prisoners in their hands. In many cases, they put prisoners to work, doing useful odd jobs. Russian prisoners begged the Italians not to send them to the Germans because they knew they would leave a somewhat "dignified life" in exchange for one of "misery and suffering."[45]

With regard to treatment of Russian prisoners, General Messe claimed: "Nobody could ever impede any [Italian] soldier to manifest his kindness, innate generosity, and sensitivity toward the Russian population, and to reassure prisoners captured by us [of] treatment and conditions worthy of a civilized people, which often was in stark contrast to German orders."[46]

Lieutenant Bruno Zavagli (117th Transport Section) observed a German prison camp on the outskirts of Millerovo located in one of two circular valleys, which lay side by side. One valley was teeming with thousands of Russian prisoners and the other was completely empty. Zavagli observed prisoners standing in a line resembling a huge spiral, encompassing the width of one of the valleys. They held mess tins in their hands and were waiting for a portion of boiled millet cooking in huge pots. It was obvious their wait would last for hours. Above this crowd, a huge cloud of flies cast a shadow upon a scene of "putrefaction" where prisoners ate, slept, and existed with no shelter from the intense heat, surrounded by refuse, and stinking latrine pits. Every three days the Germans moved the prisoners to the second valley "for a change of air, and an exchange of filth."[47]

When CSIR forces were involved in rapid offensive movements, soldiers often needed to take advantage of local resources to supplement their meager food supplies, since their own provisions remained stuck for miles behind them. General Messe made it clear to his troops that provisions obtained from the local population were to be paid for in full and were not to be taken using any form of force.

"Right from the beginning," Messe writes, "I wanted to establish our relationships with these people who didn't know us, based on that [fundamental] principle...."[48] Even in critical moments, Italian soldiers requested very little from the population. General Messe preferred to reduce rations of his own troops rather than exploit the local villagers.[49]

The Italians asked the Russians to provide shelter for their soldiers, yet even in such circumstances military officials attempted to find suitable lodging in public buildings, schools, or offices rather than in private homes. It was expressly forbidden to requisition homes forcefully from the locals in the German manner.[50]

During the winter of 1941–42, the Russian urban population was on the edge of outright starvation. The Germans had requisitioned all local grain, and civilians traveled throughout the countryside searching for peasants who could give them a bit of precious flour. In return, the peasants wanted "things," not money, in exchange for their flour. "One could observe," Messe writes, "a procession of poor people who came from the cities with sleds, laden with the most varied objects...and then returning from this pilgrimage with a small amount of flour after walking kilometers and kilometers from house to house in the countryside." Hundreds tramped through the countryside in this manner. Italian military truck drivers picked up many of these exhausted civilians on the roads to "alleviate their fatigue," despite German orders forbidding transportation of civilians in military vehicles.[51]

The following summer, even the Ukrainian peasants remained without flour. Hundreds of hungry civilians tramped toward the Don regions where Russian troops had not yet destroyed all of the harvest during their withdrawal, and the Germans had not yet arrived to deplete supplies of grain with their system of requisitions. Italian soldiers picked up many civilians during this period, providing much needed transportation for those moving toward the Don on foot.[52]

The Germans were concerned about security to the rear of their lines as masses of civilians entered areas close to the front near the Don River. They ordered civilians without prescribed permits to be interned in prison camps. General Messe writes, "If those orders had been applied, prison camps would have been rapidly populated by the destitute, forced far from their homes by hunger." The Italians organized transportation for civilians who lacked documents, using empty trucks returning from the front to their supply bases: "Once more, good sense, pity, and understanding of human needs took precedence over German imperious categorical orders, giving the population more tangible proof of the kindness of the Italians."[53]

The Italian military had nothing to do with roundups of civilian workers sent to Germany for forced labor. The Italian "Office of Civilian Affairs" focused primarily upon assistance to the population.[54]

During the winter months, soldiers of the CSIR had more opportunity for contact with the local population. The troops had a period of quiet while in the zone of Stalino in the Donetz Basin, where their main battle was against the frigid weather. Soldiers frequently sought refuge in Russian homes where stoves offered welcome warmth. Women villagers often did the laundry for soldiers in exchange for part of their bread and rations. As villagers came to know the soldiers, they requested medical help for their children. Italian medical officers offered their assistance and even offered medicine. Numerous soldiers even gave blood for necessary transfusions. In Rikovo, officers of the Torino Division established free outpatient clinics, a rest house for the elderly, and even a clinic for pregnant women run by Italians with Russian personnel paid by the Italians. General Messe noted all activities were the result of "spontaneous initiatives by our commanders." Administration of the occupied territories was in the hands of the Germans, based on "the exploitation of every resource."[55]

Italian military justice was carried out "with severity" in cases when soldiers were found guilty of activities against the population. In most cases, folks who suffered any form of damages inflicted by an Italian soldier received support and compensation. Even minor acts were punished and not overlooked, such as stealing a chicken or goose from a peasant family. General Messe was resolute, believing the Russian population should not suffer at the hands of Italian troops.[56]

THE GERMAN OFFENSIVE CONTINUES: *CASE BLAU* (OPERATION BLUE)

The Germans had suffered over a million casualties by the end of winter and lacked enough troops to replace these losses. Hitler turned to Hungary, Romania, and Italy for additional troops to serve during his planned summer offensive.[57]

The launching of Operation Blue was to occur in June 1942. The original goal of the offensive was to drive south to the oilfields of the

Caucasus after destroying vital transportation lines along the Volga River (the route for transportation of oil from the Caspian Sea to central Russia), as well as Russian war production areas in the region of Stalingrad. Hitler wanted to seize the oilfields of the Caucasus not only to resolve his own shortages of fuel but also to disrupt the USSR's access to the fields.[58]

At the end of April 1942, Hitler met Mussolini in Salzburg, Austria where he obtained "the promise of more Italian cannon fodder for the Russian front."[59] Hitler reached out to his other allies and obtained the promise of "27 Rumanian, 13 Hungarian, 2 Slovak, and one Spanish division" to join German forces.[60]

Mussolini eagerly complied with Hitler's request for more Italian troops, and upgraded the Italian forces on the Eastern Front, forming the Italian Army in Russia *Armata Italiana in Russia* (hereafter ARMIR), integrated in the Axis forces as the Italian Eighth Army. Surprisingly, General Messe was not included in any preparatory discussions having to do with increasing the number of Italian troops in the Russian campaign.[61]

The Italian Eighth Army consisted of the following forces. The Thirty-fifth Army Corps (former CSIR force); the Second Army Corps, consisting of four infantry divisions: Ravenna, Cosseria, Sforzesca and Vicenza; the Alpine Corps, consisting of three divisions: Cuneense, Julia, and Tridentina (and the Monte Cervino Battalion which had joined the CSIR in January 1942), to complete a military force of 7,000 officers and 220,000 troops.[62]

Blinded by his own political ambitions and his fantasies of sharing the spoils of a German victory, Mussolini ignored a glaring reality. CSIR forces, already deployed in Russia for a year, and additional troops soon to be deployed, were inadequately equipped and prepared. Nor did he heed the continuous written warnings from General Messe from the Russian front, or warnings from his other military leaders. Even in October 1941, Chief of General Staff Marshal Ugo Cavallero had sent a memo to Mussolini indicating that six Italian divisions could be sent to Russia, but more equipment such as anti-aircraft and anti-tank guns and trucks needed to transport troops would not be forthcoming. The Germans, he noted, would have to to furnish such equipment.[63]

On May 30 1942, General Messe met with Cavallero in Rome. Basing his assessment on his own experience in Russia, he claimed it was a mistake to send more Italian troops to the Eastern Front. Cavallero patiently listened to his explanations, but when the general became more insistent, Cavallero cut him off abruptly: "These decisions have been made by the Duce on the basis of political considerations and it's useless to discuss them [any further]".[64]

General Messe, accompanied by General Magli, met with Mussolini on June 2. Mussolini praised the CSIR commander and his forces in this very brief encounter. Upon leaving, Messe requested a private meeting with the Duce, and later that same day he returned to Mussolini's office.

Once more Mussolini praised the general and the CSIR forces: "You have gained the respect of the Germans and they appreciate you. For this reason, we considered placing you in command of the Eighth Army. It seemed to me to be the most logical solution...but it wasn't possible."

The Duce then explained it was necessary to give the command of the Eighth Army to General Gariboldi, "who for some time was ready to assume a command."[65]

Messe chose not to discuss the issue of the command of the Eighth Army. Rather, he confronted Mussolini with regard to sending another army to Russia: "It's a grave error to send an entire army to the Russian front. If I had been consulted, I would have advised against [it]."

Mussolini replied, "I have to be at the side of the Führer in Russia.... The destiny of Italy is tied to that of Germany."[66]

Messe responded: "I am convinced an army of more than two-hundred thousand men will find itself in great difficulty in Russia." The general warned Mussolini that the problems faced by the 60,000 men of the CSIR during its year in Russia would only multiply for the Eighth Army. "Our meager, antiquated armaments, the absolute lack of suitable armored vehicles, the insufficient number of trucks, the grave problems of transport and supply, made more difficult by the lack of understanding and unyielding selfishness of the Germans, will create problems for the army that are really insoluble."[67]

Mussolini replied, stating the Germans had promised to "facilitate in every way" the needs of the Italian Army. He also noted that the Germans had signed new, "precise agreements" when they requested Italian troops at their side.

General Messe was not derailed: "The Germans have never respected the agreements signed by the two governments.... It was a continuous daily battle to obtain their compliance with signed agreements. It's important to realize, and not to forget, that it was a miracle the CSIR wasn't crushed and ground down in that terrible war of giants...."[68]

Mussolini dismissed General Messe's concerns with these infamous parting words based on his illusory conviction of a rapid German victory: "Dear Messe, at the table of peace the 200,000 soldiers of the ARMIR will weigh a lot more than the 60,000 of the CSIR."[69]

Chapter 2

SUMMER OF 1942

During the early summer of 1942, Italian soldiers of the ARMIR began to depart for Russia. They boarded trains surrounded by crowds of citizens bidding them farewell. In some cases, elaborate fanfare including military bands and waving flags added an air of festivity as the men left their homeland. Few in the infantry divisions had known up to the very last minute whether their destination was to be North Africa or Russia.

In large and small train stations throughout Italy there were similar scenes such as the following described by Ugo Magnani, an alpino serving in the Vicenza Battalion (Julia Alpine Division). "In the Udine station there began the harrowing scenes of goodbyes with relatives, friends, and fiancées who clung to the necks of their loved ones and didn't want to let them go, almost certain they wouldn't see each other again. There, among the crowd was my father, who came to hug me one more time, and for us the goodbye was also atrocious."

Years later, as Magnani recalled these anguishing scenes occurring repeatedly in each station along the route leading to the Brenner Pass, he writes, "I was sad then, but now even more so, because I realize almost all those young men [who left with me] remained up there [in Russia, and never came back to Italy]"[1]

In Mondovì, a crowd gathered around the train carrying alpini of the 4th Artillery Regiment of the Cuneense Division. As was the case in many train stations, groups of Fascist women distributed picture postcards to the departing troops, as well as small medals with the image of Mussolini on one side and that of the Madonna on the reverse.

Alpino Vicenzo Cucchietti, departing with the 12th Battery of the 4th Artillery Regiment of the Cuneense Division, recalled the mood of the troops and the folks surrounding them: "Some cried, some were drunk, even the strongest appeared shattered; it was a pitiful scene." When the train whistle blew, crowds refused to move away from the rail cars, causing guards to intervene. As the train slowly left the station and passed by small villages in the vicinity, relatives stood beside the tracks shouting and crying while alpini within reached out of the windows waving and shouting their last goodbyes.[2]

Troops of the ARMIR serving in infantry divisions, transport, and service units, were recruited from every corner of Italy, even Sicily, whereas soldiers in the Alpine Corps came primarily from specific Italian alpine regions. In the case of the 8th Regiment of the Julia Division, for example, soldiers in the three battalions came from the provinces of Friuli and Carnia, whereas those in the 9th Regiment hailed from the provinces of Vicenza, Treviso, Feltre, and provinces in the Abruzzi (a mountainous region in central Italy). The system of recruitment of alpini from specific provinces had many advantages, yet, as the future conflict unfolded, the price paid in losses from these localities would be devastating.

Ninety percent of officers in the Alpine Corps were not career officers; moreover half of these were twenty-something second lieutenants, former university students from all parts of Italy, who, like the soldiers, had been drafted. Second Lieutenant Veniero Ajmone Marsan, who had recently celebrated his twenty-fourth birthday, left Italy for Russia with the Cuneense Division on July 29. On the platform of the station in Cuneo, his family gathered to say goodbye to him. This was a wrenching moment for all of them; none suspected what was ahead.

When asked how he felt when he left Italy, he recalled he was very unhappy, especially because he was leaving his wife Lucia and his family. Then he said, "The real question that should be asked is why didn't I try to avoid going to Russia? Of course, I was ready to fulfill my duty to serve in the military, but I could have requested a transfer to a military post within Italy. Alpini under my command had no such option. They were all mountain men from alpine valleys, and the last thing they wanted to do was to go fight a war against the Russians. These soldiers were my responsibility. I had been living with them in the mountains of Piedmont during their training; they were fathers, sons, and brothers.

How could I let them go to Russia, and use my own status as an officer to remain behind in Italy to serve in a different branch of the service? In my mind, there was no clear alternative other than staying with my men.

"Furthermore, although my family was anti-Fascist, we weren't in touch with the anti-Fascist underground movement at that time. It was very much underground during those days, and even though some family friends were connected, nobody spoke about it openly until later."

Shortly before leaving for Russia, Marsan transferred from his post in the Saluzzo Battalion (Cuneense Division) to the Headquarters of the 2nd Alpine Regiment of the same division. His new assignment was that of "I Officer," Information Officer of the 2nd Regiment. The role of the I Officer was that of monitoring and observing positions and movements of the enemy. For this task, Marsan had a dozen alpini under his command. In addition to that role, and because he could speak a smattering of Russian, he was given the assignment of interpreter for the regiment. Colonel Scrimin, Commander of the 2nd Regiment, was indeed eager to have Marsan on his staff; his service as an interpreter would be a valuable asset once the regiment reached the East.

Marsan traveled to the frontier of Germany on a regular civilian train. Once in Germany, his unit transferred to a troop train. In Poland, he and his men began to question their role in the war as they witnessed a number of previously unknown disturbing and distressing realities of the Nazi regime. The first of these occurred when their train stopped in the Warsaw station for a few hours. They observed German soldiers with rifles at the ready, pointed at a group of civilians carrying railroad ties. These wretched looking people were dressed in rags, staggering under the weight of their burden. To their horror, the alpini realized the patch of yellow material on their ragged clothing indicated they were Jews.[3]

Shortly after leaving Warsaw, the troop train stopped out in the countryside. Soldiers observed a group of about twenty civilians walking toward the train in single file under guard. Among the group, there was a pretty young girl with long blonde hair. As she passed by the train, an alpino offered her a small pocket comb. Marsan recalled her words of thanks: "*Ago tibis gratias*" ("I say thank you, to you"). The group continued on its way: "We asked our medical officer where these people were going. He told us they were probably being taken to a large pit [mass grave] a short distance from here at which, with one shot to the nape of the neck, they would end up next to the hundreds, maybe thousands shot in the same way."[4]

Shocked by this response, Marsan asked for an explanation. He recalled that the medical officer told him he had seen similar incidents while traveling back and forth from Italy through Poland. The officer said, "It was quite possible some of these civilians were Jews, or perhaps they had had some role in the resistance to the German occupation."

While the troop train was still traveling through Poland, it stopped out in the countryside once more. Marsan said, "Women immediately came to the train offering eggs to the soldiers in exchange for bread. Each alpino had a mess kit containing two large biscuits (hard tack) called *gallette*. They were not supposed to eat their hard tack unless they found themselves in circumstances in which there was no other available food, such as combat or some other kind of military engagement. As women crowded around the train, many alpini gave them portions of their hardtack, but declined to accept the eggs because it was obvious these people were very, very hungry."

Lieutenant Nuto Revelli, who served in the 46th Company of the Tirano Battalion, Tridentina Division, was also on his way to Russia in a troop train that summer. When the train arrived at the Brenner Pass, it remained stopped on a sidetrack for some time. A German train, loaded with tanks on flat cars also remained stopped on a parallel track. It was a very hot day; German soldiers were sitting in the sun, bare to the waist leaning on their tanks, whereas the alpini were sweating in their uniforms and alpine hats. Ninety mules transported along with the alpini in rail cars at the end of the train were suffering from the heat and began to kick at the sides and floors of the rail cars, making an "incredible racket." Wide-eyed German soldiers stared in wonder. Revelli recalled that "humiliating moment," as he compared the two sets of troops: "We had one mule for every four alpini, whereas the ratio was one tank for every four German soldiers."[5] Comparing the two sets of soldiers, Revelli writes, "We were the ancient [warriors]; they were the soldiers of modern warfare."[6]

Revelli noted the general mood among the alpini of the battalion was "resigned rather than dejected" as they traveled toward Russia. Italy was at war and there seemed no way out: "If, following the war on the Albanian-Greek front, another war was to be fought on the

Russian front, so be it." Then too, Fascist propaganda had been rampant during the month prior to their departure. The general gist was, "the ragged, confused Russians" were being captured by the thousands and didn't want to fight. They advanced like sheep, with political commissars at their backs. Even the population is tired of the war and fraternizes with the Axis liberators; it's a primitive population, a bit like the natives of Africa...." Soldiers were advised to bring postcards for purposes of bartering: "It's recommended to bring postcards with pictures of the Duce or the King, because they have double value [over picture postcards]." Revelli notes it was difficult to believe this propaganda, but exposure to it on a daily basis meant some resonated, and was bound to have an effect.[7]

In the middle of July, an "odd memo" circulated among the alpine units; it didn't refer to superior Russian weapons or tanks: "Rather, it reiterated the same old story; the Russians were tired of fighting, they were disorganized, and dying." Included in the memo were references to the Russian climate and the water: "...the winter is very cold, so cold the Russians don't sleep in beds, they sleep on top of stoves. The water is dreadful...."[8]

As alpini of the Tirano Battalion passed through Austria they were impressed by the "order" they saw as they viewed the countryside. The same was true as they traveled through a portion of Germany. In Poland, they saw vast expanses of uncultivated land and fields of grain ready for harvesting. Alpini in the Tirano Battalion were for the most part mountain peasant farmers accustomed to their own small terraced plots of land in Italy's northern alpine valleys. As they gazed at these immense lands, some remarked, "If we were here, we could cultivate that land." As an aside, Revelli notes that the men didn't realize (or know) Poland had been occupied by the Germans since 1939. As they traveled further into Poland, they saw evidence of the war; rail stations destroyed by bombardments, and then the vast destruction of Warsaw.[9]

When the train stopped in a small station somewhere between Brest-Litovsk and Minsk, the troops were told to get off the train since it would remain in the station for some time. On the platform, they encountered a group of sixty to seventy people. Women, children, and elderly men were "in an indescribable condition, barefoot, covered in rags, and barely able to remain upright." A young girl passed by the alpini: "Without stopping and in a warm voice, she repeated a prayer in

Latin, asking for bread...at times she modestly adjusted the rags covering her."[10]

Twenty meters from this ragged group, three young SS officers dressed in elegant uniforms were standing guard with guns at the ready. It appeared they didn't seem to mind the fact that these "down and out" people joined the Italian soldiers on the platform.

Referring to the Germans, Revelli spoke to his fellow officers: "They must be crazy to permit us to see a terrifying spectacle like this; it's astounding. What's the point?"

Soon he realized the Germans were purposefully exposing the Italians to this scene, and he wondered if this was an isolated event.

"Holy Mother of God," Revelli exclaimed. "If this is the German war I want no part of it, it's not my war."[11]

Taking advantage of this long stopover, Revelli and his men prepared a hot meal, their first since leaving Italy. Once their minestrone was ready, the alpini shared it with those starving wretches who held up dirty rusted cans they had retrieved from the rail beds for their portion.[12]

That summer, a medical officer, Second Lieutenant Italo Serri,[13] also traveled to Russia along with 230 alpini and 160 mules of the Julia Division. These troops knew their destination was the Caucasus. Although the region was definitely an unknown, once told that the Caucasus was a zone with mountains, the explanation seemed satisfactory; after all, mountains were "a suitable place for alpini."[14]

As Serri reached the Ukraine, the train stopped in a station in a small village. Groups of ragged children ran to the train shouting, "*Viva Italia, vive Mussolini, vive Re, vive Duce, dare piccolo gallette.*" ("Long live Italy, long live Mussolini, long live King, long live Duce, give a little hard tack.") The lieutenant recalled he would have never imagined soldiers coming to fight in Russia putting bread into the small hands of begging children.[15]

On August 23, in a letter to his family, alpino Romano Gallo (Cuneense Division) wrote, "If you could see the population of these regions, [you would realize] it's extremely poor, they even eat sunflower seeds, just imagine how hungry [they must be]. In the stations, they came to ask us for food, we had little to spare, yet out of pity, we gave them something...."[16]

Marshal Antonio Votero Prina, a career officer serving in the

Dronero Battalion of the Cuneense Division, described the face of hunger in a letter to his wife on August 9: "Lisa, I have traveled through miserable places.... I thank God knowing you and our little ones are in our beautiful Italy, where in comparison to so many others we can consider ourselves living a life of one hundred percent luxury. There's a scarcity of many things [in Italy]; but there isn't the terrible hunger I recognize in the many faces of those I have met along my journey...."

His letter contains his firm belief that the Italians were in Russia "on a mission, a holy crusade, to save a people who have renounced God, from the miserable conditions in which they live. We hope to offer our honest effort [to achieve that result]." [17]

Twenty-year old Alfonso Di Michele, an alpino in the Aquila Battalion, Julia Division, left Italy in August 1942. Di Michele came from a small town on the slopes of the *Gran Sasso* Mountain in the Abruzzi, a region of recruitment for many alpini in the Aquila Battalion. Di Michele and most of his comrades had never crossed the frontiers of Italy. The cleanliness and order of the Tyrolese rail stations and the large green fields fascinated them as they passed through Austria.

Once in Germany they began to see the effects of the war—semi-destroyed railroad stations, piles of rubble, and masses of German troops on the move. In a railroad station in Poland they also saw emaciated men and women working around the station. Each had a large yellow Star of David on their filthy ragged clothing. As this sorry group worked, they glanced at the Italians in the train. Eventually, realizing they were not German soldiers, a few came close and timidly asked for something to eat. Alpini quickly gave them food and attempted to speak to them using gestures and the few foreign words they could think of. Hollering German soldiers interrupted their attempts, ordering the Jews to get back to work.[18]

This experience left an indelible mark on the troops. Di Michele writes, "One could tell these people were normal people, not delinquents. We couldn't understand why those women were so degraded and why those people were subject to such humiliation. In reality we didn't realize or couldn't even imagine the immense tragedy lying in wait for the [Jewish] population."[19]

From the window of his rail car, Lieutenant Gino Beraudi (17th Company of the Dronero Battalion, Cuneense Division) observed the passing scenery. He described the features of the flat plains of

Belorussia. "Scorched by the July sun, they didn't seem to be made by the same God who created the hills of Val Maira [Italy], now covered with green meadows and vineyards."[20]

Beraudi continues: "Don Oberto celebrated a Mass at a small out-of-the-way station. A group of silent peasants stood at a slight distance from the alpini surrounding the chaplain. It seemed as though they wanted to say to us they were together with us in God, yet were separated from us by the inhuman barrier dividing the victors from the defeated."[21]

Later that same morning, Captain Chiaramello played a record on a gramophone in Beraudi's train compartment. At a certain point, Chiaramello took the record off the turntable and threw it out the window. Beraudi wasn't surprised; he realized the captain was distressed because he hadn't married his fiancée before leaving Italy.

Beraudi then recalled the moment of his departure from his own wife: "We parted at the entrance to our home—no going to the station together; that is awkward and uncomfortable—and anyway the children were still sleeping. Smiling after a chaste kiss, we parted. A firm handshake sealed a pledge, one I didn't have the courage to express out loud: I will return!"[22]

As troop trains advanced into the Ukraine, alpini observed evidence of heavy fighting that had occurred during the previous summer. "Tracks, locomotives, and railcars were overturned and burned. The crossing of temporary railroad bridges proceeded at a snail's pace. Not far from the rail lines, destroyed trucks, cannons, and tanks were already rusting...." As trains entered the industrial area of the Ukraine, soldiers could see ruins of factories and on their gates a few remnants of Soviet symbols of the hammer and sickle. "The inevitable statues of Stalin were either smashed or decapitated."[23]

In the case of the Cuneense Division, it took twenty-five days to transfer the 18,500 alpini of the division to the Ukraine; the journey for each individual train took approximately thirteen days. The final destination of the entire division had originally been the zone of Rikovo, northeast of Stalino. Later, orders called for the Cuneense to proceed to the zone of Uspenka, about 100 kilometers from Taganrog on the Sea of Azov. Owing to priority given to German troop movements in the region, various trains transporting the division proceeded south to Uspenka, while others redirected north to Izyum, which meant 400 kilometers would separate the various units of the division.

General Emilio Battisti, commander of the Cuneense Division, arrived in Uspenka on August 9. The following day he was informed the Alpine Corps was now under the command of German Seventeenth Army, part of Army Group A (General Ewald von Kleist) operating in the Caucasus. [24]

On August 13, Marsan's unit arrived in the Izyum zone. He recalled that moment: "We spent that first night camped out on the grass in the middle of nowhere. The next day we began to walk in a southeasterly direction, convinced we were headed to the mountains of the Caucasus."

The original objective of the German 1942 summer offensive (Case Blau, or Operation Blue) had been to destroy arms factories along the Volga River in the region of Stalingrad, as well as river transportation routes, before moving on to capture vital oil fields in the Caucasus. On July 23, 1942 in Führer Directive 45, Hitler enlarged the goals of Operation Blue abruptly. Instead of achieving both objectives sequentially, as originally planned, orders now called for them to occur simultaneously. Namely, German Army Group A (in April Army Group South had been split into Army Groups A and B), was to advance through the Caucasus to seize oilfields at Maikop, Grozny, and Baku, while Army Group B was to seize Stalingrad on the Volga River and then proceed to Astrakhan on the Caspian Sea. [25]

In the middle of August, the Alpine Corps received orders to change course. Diverted from their original mission to proceed to the mountains of the Caucasus, the three divisions were to join the armies of Hungary and Romania, and the Italian infantry divisions of the ARMIR to defend the western side of the Don River, the left flank of the German assault on Stalingrad. [26] General Battisti received this information August 19 and redirected alpini of the Cuneense, already marching from Izyum toward the Caucasus, to the east, whereas those in Uspenka redirected to the northeast. Both groups were to join forces in the zone of Starobelsk and then move on to Rossosh together. [27]

Alpino Vicenzo Cucchietti recalls the words of General Battisti as he spoke to units of alpini of the Cuneense Division in Uspenka while standing on top of a small truck.

"Come close, I want you all to hear, I have some important things to tell you. We will go to the Don, on the plains. When we left, we all had the desire to go and fight in the mountains, in the Caucasus. Instead, superior orders say that we alpini will have to fight on the plains. The geographical configuration of the front we must reach is similar to this: low hills, inserted among stretches of plains."

"Are you pleased?"

"I'm not pleased."

"Our ropes, our ice axes, our hobnail boots, and our mules won't be needed where we are going. We are equipped for the mountains, but we have to obey superior commands. There on the Don we will uphold our motto, '*di qui non si passa*' ('none shall pass through here')."

"Alpini, put on your vest of steel....We will remain on the defensive, but when orders arrive to advance, we'll advance."[28]

Mussolini was responsible for the decision to increase the number of Italian troops sent to Russia, however, the specific choice of which troops to send was up to superior Italian commands, primarily Chief of Staff General Ugo Cavallero.

Alpini had left for Russia on a mission to the mountains of the Caucasus with "tons of alpinist equipment," yet, as historian Giorgio Rochat has noted, it was never clear as to why these particular troops were selected. That decision, he claims, based primarily on their "fine reputation," took place months before their possible deployment in the Caucasus was even a consideration. Furthermore, there is no evidence to suggest that operational planning for such a mission with the Germans ever took place since the Germans had their own fine mountain troops.[29]

Italian commanders made the "thoughtless suggestion...of making the Caucasus the objective for the alpini, a proposal initially accepted overall by the Germans but quickly discounted owing to their lack of transportation and dependence upon slow-moving mule trains."[30]

At approximately the same time the alpini received notice to change course and move to the banks of the Don, the Germans sent 10,000 troops of the LXXIX Jäger Corps (German mountain troops) to the mountains of the Caucasus. In mid August, a group of German and Austrian alpinists climbed Mt. Elbrus, the highest peak west of the Himalayas, and planted the Nazi flag on its summit.[31]

The very structure of the Alpine Corps "was the exact opposite of what was required for fighting on the Russian plains." Alpini were mountain troops, trained for combat in rugged, mountainous terrain, and presented a "strong and formidable force to be reckoned with." Two particular features formed "the basis of their moral and material strength," namely the makeup of the Corps and its small fighting units.[32]

Alpini were mountaineers, possessing enthusiasm and commitment and a "tradition of glory and valor."[33] Their allegiance was to the "honor of their valleys from whence their battalions recruited, where their school friends were, where their families, cousins, and brothers of their sweetheart lived. Feelings of solidarity and pride gave units cohesiveness and contributed to their earned reputation as magnificent fighters."[34] Their small units "had their own definite moral and tactical features, and special tradition which buttressed the fundamental unity of the men in battle. In mountain warfare, where one fights in a harsh and uneven environment which frequently separates the forces, it is always the small unit, equipped and accustomed to this type of warfare, that occupies the preeminent position...."[35]

Divisions of the Alpine Corps were structured to be autonomous and self-sufficient. Every company had a unit of *salmerie* (a train of pack animals consisting of mules, mule handlers, and a few horses). Obviously, the slow-moving mules, an indispensable part of an alpine division fighting in the mountains, were not suitable for rapid defensive or offensive maneuvers.

Carlo Vicentini described the pack mule units: "Each alpine division relied on approximately 5,000 pack mules with their handlers (sometimes referred to as mule skinners or mule drivers). Since alpine troops move on foot, pack mules were responsible for all transportation needs for the division, carrying weapons, ammunition, food supplies, mountaineering gear, and all other equipment needed to maintain the combat and survival needs of the division.

Vicentini noted, "In the mountains there are roads, paths, and mule trails. Mule trails are narrow and often very steep, and mules are well suited to carry heavy packs in such rugged terrain." When asked if mule handlers received training for combat, Vicentini said mule handlers were armed, but generally not trained for combat. Nonetheless, on numerous occasions during the Russian campaign, soldiers from mule outfits fought alongside combat units.

Many mule handlers came from Calabria, in southern Italy, since almost all transportation in that region proceeds on foot with mules. These Calabrese drivers knew how to behave with the animals and how to care for them. Vicentini emphasized it was absolutely absurd to send mules to Russia, where transportation needs called for trucks to cover the long distances, and where rapid mobility was necessary as opposed to dependence upon slow-moving mule trains. He also pointed out that "a mule has to eat and drink every day, whereas a truck only uses fuel when it's running."

Most Italian weapons were relics of World War I. The alpini had no antitank weapons. Revelli refers to this deficiency: "As usual, the anti-tank weapons available to us consisted of the 1891 rifle, some hand grenades, and the agility of our legs. After two days, I already had a Russian parabellum,[36] model 1942 [probably obtained from a Russian prisoner]. From a single shot from my rifle I changed over to a burst of 72 firing bullets."[37]

Radios were lightweight and mobile, designed for high mountains, not for long distances such as those of the steppes, where they failed to function properly. It was often easier to send a runner from unit to unit rather than rely on communication by radio.[38]

Hitler's new orders that summer had far-reaching consequences, causing commanders of the Alpine Corps to evaluate their effect on the ability of their men to engage in combat.[39] Dismayed by the sudden change of their mission, the alpini were well aware they were not prop-erly equipped for other than mountain fighting; they had no heavy artillery. Their weapons consisted only of rifles (no automatic assault rifles), and light artillery weapons. They could not imagine how their troops could defend themselves with their limited, mostly antiquated weapons, against the motorized Russian army. They wondered how any commander would want to place them in a position where they literal-ly could face extermination.

Written records exist of two officers of the Julia Division who expressed their disapproval over the decision to divert the Alpine Corps to the Don. Colonel Pietro Gay, commander of the 3rd Alpine Artillery Regiment, wrote a letter to the president of the Senate, Giacomo Suardo, in which he stated it was "beastly and criminal" to send troops trained for mountain combat to the Don.[40]

Lieutenant Colonel Rinaldo Dall'Armi, commander of the Gemona Battalion, Julia Division, wrote to Mussolini, August 27. "We arrived in

Russia, destined to go the Caucasus, where our training, armaments, and equipment, and our deployment would be natural, where we could have competed sportingly with the best German and Romanian mountain troops. Suddenly, we were redirected to the Don in flat territory and denied [proper weapons] (1891 rifles and 4 laughable small cannons of 47/32, harmless against Russian 34-ton tanks)."[41]

In conclusion, Dall'Armi wrote: "There are only a few alpini—this is not human materiel with which one can play lightly; a day could come, in this same war, when one might weep bitter tears for having ruined and actually destroyed the alpini."[42]

Orders to advance to the Don proceeded despite verbal and written opposition. Far from their homeland, poorly equipped in comparison to their ally and their adversary, the alpini followed Hitler's new orders. Unlike the Germans, the Italians had not come to Russia on a quest for *Lebensraum* (space for living). Uneasy with the Nazi-Fascist alliance, and Nazi appetite for conquest, and unable to comprehend the aggressive, inhuman treatment of civilian populations by the Germans, the alpini abandoned their mission to the Caucasus and began their long trek to the Don.[43]

Chapter 3

THE TREK OF THE ALPINI

It took almost a month for soldiers of the alpine divisions to traverse the plains of the Ukraine. As they set off on foot for the Don, the mood among officers and troops was one of "mounting anger and disappointment" for being sent on what they viewed as an "absurd and dishonorable" mission. Trained and outfitted for mountain combat, they now would deploy in an environment where, as they scanned the limitless horizon, the highest visible objects were telegraph poles.[1]

The trek across the plains was slow going, as alpini loaded with their heavy packs trudged past vast fields of sunflowers and grain—kilometers and kilometers of "a monotonous vision."[2]

Dust clouds rose from the tracks, mixing with their sweat as they advanced, and by evening, alpino Vincenzo Cucchetti writes, "We were unrecognizable...we always arrive dead tired and have to fix something to eat, one of us goes to search for a cabbage, another for a tomato, the luckier ones captured a chicken along the trek..."[3]

From time to time, the alpini passed by small villages scattered here and there along their route; each seemed to resemble the one before, nothing seemed to distinguish one from another. In some cases, children came out to greet them. Alpino Di Michele describes such a moment: "The children had learned a few Italian words," probably from CSIR troops who had camped near the village in the past. They shouted, "*Viva Italia*; *dare galletta, dare pasta.*" ("Long live Italy, give hard tack, give pasta.")

"They were so nice and so amusing and we did everything we could

32

to please them, also because they gave us the gift of a few moments of family life, which we already missed."[4]

Sometimes the men camped for the night close to an inhabited area. The alpini enjoyed interacting with the local peasants who came out to greet them in a friendly manner. Although they couldn't speak Russian, they managed to communicate with gestures for the most part. Some of them attempted to explain their various trades to the locals. Most alpini were ordinary folk: "peasant farmers, shoemakers, bakers, iron workers; in short, representatives from all manners of labor."[5]

Of course, the Italians were attracted to the Ukrainian girls who were friendly and "spontaneous." The girls seemed particularly fascinated by articles alpini carried with them, namely their combs, and the needles and thread used to mend their clothing.[6]

On some days the alpini never saw a living soul as they marched by the seemingly endless fields of rye and sunflowers, but one day during their march, alpini of the Aquila Battalion faced a gruesome sight: "Two Russian civilians hung swaying from a pole.... Rumors among our troops blamed our German allies. The possible reason was lack of help given by inhabitants of that small village to the Germans. In other words, the inhabitants hadn't given enough information, provisions, or shelter for their troops. For that reason, as an example for the population, the Germans committed this macabre slaughter for all to see."[7]

Di Michele notes that he didn't witness the actual hanging of the two Russians, therefore he couldn't prove the Germans were responsible: "All I can say, as far as the Germans were concerned, even though we were allies, our relationships were not idyllic. They were real soldiers." He recalled that, when Hitler was mentioned in a conversation, "they leapt to their feet." When peasants spoke about the Germans, they generally used gestures and "words of contempt"; some said, "Italians are good, Germans are not." Di Michele admits that a few Italians acted improperly with the local population. When this occurred, "it was severely reprimanded, and dealt with severely."[8]

Units marched daily from sunup to sundown in blistering heat with temperatures reaching more than 40° Celsius.[9] The unpaved tracks they followed were not much wider than a path, covered with layers of fine, dust-like powder kicked up by hoofs of the mules and boots of the marching men. Marsan noted it would have made sense to march during the night when it was cooler, "but practically every day, in the late afternoon, torrential downpours caused the roads to become impassable until about midmorning of the following day. When it rains in this region, soil turns to mud, several feet deep, impeding the movement of transport on wheels. The Russians call this phenomenon *rasputitza*, the period of mud; the Germans called it *Zeit der schlechten Wegen*, period of bad roads."

Lieutenant Serri and his men were caught in such a storm. At first, the soldiers believed they would gain some relief from the scorching sun as they observed clouds gathering in the sky, but soon an intense cold wind began to blow and menacing dark clouds appeared to touch the ground. Then the rains began, and in minutes the soil transformed into a quagmire. The alpini and their mules sank up to their knees into this slimy, sticky, black muck. Lightning bolts frightened the mules. They became agitated and bucked, losing their loads. Soldiers, soaked to the bone, had to retrieve fallen packs and pull and tug the mules out of the muddy mess. At a certain point, the men thought it would be easier to walk on the side of the tracks where some vegetation could support their weary steps. As they trudged forward, the only evidence of any other human existence amid that desolation were signs posted along the route warning all who passed: "*Achtung Minen!*" ("Watch out for mines!")[10]

Alpino Ugo Magnani describes his frustration as he and his unit became engulfed in mud. It was exhausting to attempt to walk, and dealing with the overloaded mules was an ongoing drama. The animals dropped to the ground, unable to walk, and no amount of cajoling could make them get up on their own without removing all gear and packsaddles. "We began to walk again, but after a while another mule fell and we began all over again. One of my comrades became so exasperated with the mule that he bit its ear, hoping to get it to move, but it remained impassive. I would have liked to have cried out in pain, fatigue, and anger against the one who sent us here to die, but there wasn't even time for tears."[11]

Eventually Magnani and his fellow alpini arrived in a deserted village. By now it was dark as the soldiers unloaded the exhausted mules. Magnani entered an empty *izba* (peasant house). Too tired to remove his pack, he sat down on the floor. Water and mud oozed from his clothing and shoes. Before attempting to change, and because he was famished, he opened his pack to find his daily ration of hard tack and can of meat.

The gallette were soaked and had increased in size ten-fold![12]

Lieutenant Gino Beraudi (adjutant to Major Guaraldi, Dronero Battalion, Cuneense Division), recalled being immersed in the endless days of marching: "Most of all it means cutting oneself off from the memory of sweet and clean things, one's wife, children, and running water; in short, it means disengaging from one's own personality.... It's an effort to write home at night; one can only speak of daily events because already our languages are different."[13]

Lieutenant Revelli had left Novo Gorlovka in the middle of August, with 342 Alpini, 8 officers and 90 mules. He describes the experience of the daily marches: "Like an immense tribe of gypsies, we began the march.... Thirty, forty kilometers a day, loaded like pack animals, with shoes that spewed [hob] nails." The men walked in single file along the unpaved tracks in two columns. Each soldier marched holding his mountain *Alpenstock* (alpine walking staff); "It was a spectacle from another time." German troops moved along the same route. Their vehicles churning up dust resembling dense fog forced the alpini to the sides of the track: Venting his frustration, Revelli writes, "One couldn't curse out loud at them, we had to curse silently, within."[14]

On August 24, alpini of the Tridentina Division were loaded on trucks and taken to the Don front lines in order to support units of the Sforzesca Infantry Division attacked by the Russians. By the time alpini of the Tridentina took their defensive positions further north on the Don with the other two alpine divisions at the end of October, they had covered 1,300 kilometers on foot.[15]

During their long trek across the dusty plains of the Ukraine, the alpine troops encountered numerous logistical difficulties. Since the region east of the Donets River was sparsely populated, there were long distances between villages, therefore fewer resources for shelter, fresh food supplies, and water. Obtaining fresh water presented a huge problem, not only for the men, but also for the well-being of the hundreds of quadrupeds accompanying the divisions. Scarcity of fresh water, and time needed to search for water sources, caused repercussions all along the line, which in turn delayed the troops and contributed to deterioration of the animals' physical condition.[16]

The overall nourishment of the marching troops was insufficient in quantity and quality. Daily rations were short, often only amounting to two gallette and a small can of meat. It was impossible to conserve fresh meat for any length of time due to the intense heat, as well as the great distances between supply centers and locations of the troops along the route. Vegetables, grown in the region, requisitioned by the Germans for their supply bases, were not available for Italian troops.[17]

The Alpine Corps depended upon the Germans for supplies of fuel and oil for their few trucks. Deliveries of these supplies were always in quantities less than what was required and often arrived late. Frequently trucks loaded with supplies remained stopped for several days to wait for fuel and oil. When this occurred, supplies needed for immediate use were transported by means of carts obtained from local peasants and pulled by mules.[18]

Another major problem facing the alpini during the march across the plains was the difficulty of linking up with each other by radio. As noted earlier, the troops had radios designed for communication over short distances in mountainous regions. Vicentini noted that in his platoon, alpini had mobile phones. It was possible to transmit voice messages for distances of one kilometer and Morse code messages for approximately five kilometers. Furthermore, certain times to communicate between units had to be prearranged; radios did not remain turned on all the time. When, for example, the Cuneense Division began marching across the plains, various units of the division remained separated by 400 kilometers. General Battisti noted, during this period that the only way the various units of the division could communicate with each other was by sending couriers (in pairs), back and forth, from unit to unit, on motorcycles.[19]

Units of the Cuneense Division walked between 300 and 700 kilometers to reach their assigned positions on the Don. By the time the Julia Division reached the Don (having left from Izyum), they had marched 300 kilometers.[20]

Chapter 4

ON THE DON LINES

ARRIVAL ON THE DON LINES

The Cuneense and Julia divisions arrived at the Don River toward the end of September 1942, and the Tridentina arrived in October, joining its sister divisions to complete the deployment of the Alpine Corps. German troops of the 294th Infantry Division had previously occupied the section of the Don lines taken over by the Cuneense Division. Troops of the Hungarian 23rd Division had deployed in the sector the Tridentina occupied, whereas both German and Hungarian forces had occupied the sector taken over by the Julia Division.[1] The Alpine Corps was now between the Hungarian army, on their left, and the rest of the ARMIR and then the Romanian Third Army on their right, all protecting the left flank of German Sixth Army farther east at Stalingrad.

While Captain Reitani camped out with his unit of the Julia Division, preparing for the transfer of his troops forward to the Don front lines, two German artillery officers, a captain and a lieutenant of the 294th Division, arrived to discuss details of the transfer. The German captain reported that, at least for now, their section seemed calm. However, he warned Reitani they had been hearing "incessant movement" across the river at night, and believed the Russians were up to something.

The captain said, "I am proud to transfer this section [of the front] into your hands. Now we're in dire need of rest, we've been fighting uninterruptedly for over a year, and last winter was terrible."

The officer then spoke about losses in his artillery unit, which had been reduced to 245 soldiers: "Near Moscow last winter, on two consecutive mornings we found almost three thousand of our soldiers still in their tents, frozen to death...."

"It's the Russian front," the lieutenant remarked. "Do not delude yourselves. May God save you from what we've suffered."[2]

Marsan noted: "The exchange of German troops with the alpini was a delicate one. If the Russians became aware of this maneuver, they might attack when both German and Italian troops would be highly vulnerable. For this reason, Germans in the section taken over by the Cuneense Division decided to cover the exchange operation by sending a company of soldiers, supported by light artillery, on a mini-raid in the thick woods across the Don where they suspected locations of Russian strongholds existed."

Since Marsan was the Intelligence Officer of his regiment, he requested permission to join the mission to gain a sense of Russian positions across the river. Both German and Italian commanders accepted his request: "The German lieutenant told me I couldn't go on the mission dressed in an Italian uniform, because the Russians might become suspicious." Describing the outfit he was required to wear, Marsan said: "I wore a German jacket and helmet, both gray-black. My pants were those of my regular Italian uniform, gray-green.

"At four o'clock the next morning, a small group of Germans and I crossed the Don in rubber boats. Everything was very quiet as we crossed and then began to walk through the forest on the other side. The soldiers fired off a few rounds as they walked. Altogether, we only came across one Russian outpost near the riverside. After an exchange of a few shots, the Russians who were there surrendered. Eleven Russians were disarmed and taken back to regimental headquarters when we returned across the Don. Other than this brief encounter, there seemed to be very few Russians hiding out in the forest, at least very few were visible. Our group walked for several more hours. At a certain point, I became a target. A bullet whizzed by the side of my head, missing me by an inch.

"Around two o'clock, we arrived at a clearing in the forest near the river. It was then that a barrage of heavy artillery began. The Russians, hiding in the wooded area, had obviously informed the heavy artillery stationed far behind them there were enemy soldiers at the periphery of the forest. Shells began to fly! At that very moment, I was standing inches apart from a German officer, waiting for the boats to take us back across the river. As we were conversing, a shell hit the ground and exploded very close to us, causing the immediate death of the officer and several soldiers. Fortunately, on that day of my baptism by fire I was spared from a similar fate."

The day before the Germans left the Don lines, Italian officers invited German officers to a farewell luncheon under a large tent. Marsan, who could speak some German, conversed with one of them and asked his opinion of the Russians. In his opinion, the officer remarked, the Russians were primitive, at the same level as natives in Africa. Shocked by this disparaging remark, Marsan said he felt the Germans probably expressed similar unflattering opinions about the Italians.

At the command headquarters of the 2nd Regiment of the Cuneense Division, located a short distance west of the Don, Marsan had decent accommodations in an izba. While carrying out his assignment as I Officer he deployed the alpini under his command in small groups south of Staraya Kalitva, near Novaya Kalitva, where the Don bends toward the east. From this position, they could easily monitor and observe Russian activity across the river.

Soon after his arrival, Marsan spent some time with several units of the Cosseria Infantry Division (the point of juncture with the Cuneense Division) in order to exchange information relating to observed activity of the enemy. He had lunch with some officers that day and noticed they were eating soup consisting of broth with a few small bits of meat floating around in it. He was surprised, because when officers in his division ate soup, it was so thick with meat and vegetables their spoons stood straight up in their mess tins. He knew alpini periodically went to Rossosh to load their mules with ample provisions for the troops: "For some reason the infantry wasn't as well organized or as aggressive as the alpini when it came to getting provisions for their men. When I returned to my unit, I told my fellow officers the real heroes on the front were those men in the infantry."

Marsan also noted that the alpini had another advantage over the infantry. Coming from alpine regions, they were accustomed to cold weather, therefore the climate on the front was somewhat acceptable to them. Men in the infantry came from southern Italy for the most part and were utterly ill-equipped for the coming Russian winter.

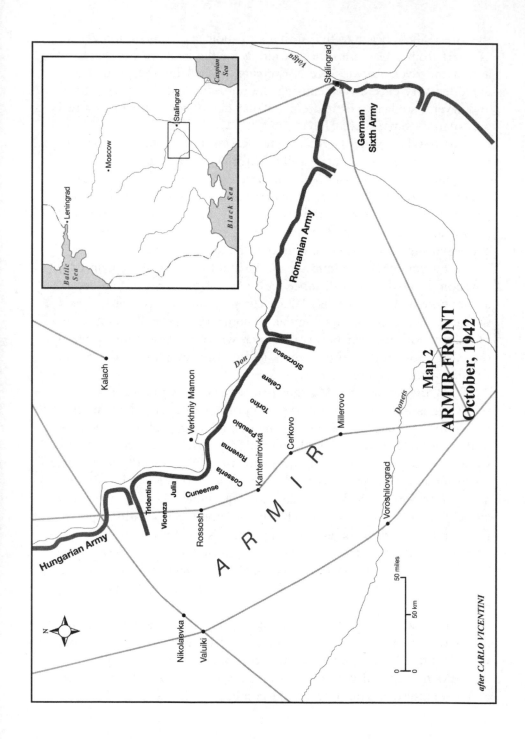

Map 2
ARMIR-FRONT
October, 1942

after *CARLO VICENTINI*

DEFENSIVE POSITIONS OF THE ALPINE CORPS

The Italian Eighth Army (ARMIR) occupied a stretch of approximately 270 kilometers along the Don River. The northern wing of the ARMIR consisted of three divisions of the Alpine Corps: Tridentina, Julia, and Cuneense. The southern wing comprised seven Italian infantry divisions: Cosseria (reinforced by the 318th Regiment, German Grenadiers), Ravenna, Pasubio, Torino, Celere, Sforzesca and Vicenza (the last two as reserves). The German 298th Infantry Division was interspersed between the Pasubio and Torino Divisions. The Romanian Third Army was to the southeast of the ARMIR holding the area between Serafimovich and Kletskaya; the Hungarian Second Army occupied positions to the north of the three alpine divisions.[3]

The total length of the defensive line allocated to the Alpine Corps was approximately fifty kilometers as the crow flies, but in actuality, it was more than eighty kilometers in length owing to the natural course of the river. Each division occupied approximately 30 kilometers of the Don front.[4]

Alpini of the Cuneense Division took over their 30-kilometer section of the Don lines on a long flat ridge running north to south from the village of Karabut to that of Staraya Kalitva. The ridge was approximately 100 meters above the river; below the ridge the Don was approximately 100 meters wide. Although the current was relatively weak, there were no fordable areas. Across the river, the terrain was flat, covered with dense forests for the most part, and the shore inclined slightly toward the river. At both ends of the sectors held by the division there were two valleys rising slightly to the west. The valley to the south ran between the villages of Novaya Kalitva and Staraya Kalitva. It was five kilometers wide containing flat meadows with two small clusters of trees in the middle. The narrow, deep Kalitva River ran along the southern portion of the meadows and was the point of juncture between the Cuneense and the Cosseria infantry division. To the north, the Karabut Valley was approximately two kilometers wide. Slightly north of the valley was the junction with the Julia Division.[5]

Once the Tridentina Division arrived on the Don lines, it occupied a stretch of approximately 28 kilometers between the villages of Basovka and Karabut further north at the juncture of the division with the 23rd Hungarian Division.

Shortly following their arrival on the Don front, a Russian airplane dropped leaflets over the lines held by the Julia Division: "Welcome to the Don, Alpini: too bad none of you will see beautiful Italy again." The leaflet was signed, "Command of Soviet Forces of the Don."[6]

When the alpini arrived at their respective locations on the Don, they found only rudimentary trenches, and a few bunkers built by the Germans or Hungarians. General Reverberi, commander of the Tridentina Division writes, "The battalions and groups set to work with indomitable willingness, tenacity, and superhuman effort to create a defensive system guaranteeing protection against attack, not only by the enemy but also from the rigors of the Russian winter."[7]

Alpini, artillerymen, and engineers approached this massive undertaking starting from scratch, constructing bunkers, communication trenches, gun emplacements, observation posts, command bunkers, barbed wire fences, anti-tank trenches, and minefields.[8]

Shelters for the mules, food supplies, and equipment were also constructed. Throughout this period temperatures continued to decline, and often there were incursions by enemy patrols attempting to test the strength of the alpine defenses. Moreover, most of the work took place at night due to the danger of enemy snipers. The soldiers quickly began digging using their shovels and pickaxes, creating "underground villages," excavating mountains of earth by the light of the moon. Before dawn, the men camouflaged the fresh mounds of earth with brush and straw. [9]

In some cases, troops finished their work at a designated site, but received orders to move to a new location where they had to begin all over again. Bedeschi claims that he and his unit of the Julia Division had to move from their first stronghold to another area further north near the devastated village of Kuvshin, almost directly on the river. The new site was in a bare clearing without a tree, open to the view of airplanes, and already pocked with large craters made by mortars and cannons and covered with wild thistles. When the men asked their captain why they were supposed to build a stronghold in that exact spot, he said: "When the Don freezes the Russians will attempt to cross it with their tanks."[10]

The first snow began to fall in October as these alpini set to work once more, building new underground bunkers and connecting trenches, racing against the onset of winter. In this case, the men dug seventeen pits close to each other, three meters deep, four meters wide and seven meters long; "the subterranean refuges." They also dug more than 1400 meters of communication trenches linking all the various sections. The trenches were three meters deep and one meter wide. During the day, the men cut down trees in a forest to their rear. Mules dragged the huge logs to sites to reinforce and line the sides of the excavated pits, and for roofs on the underground bunkers. Once a layer of light snow covered the ground, the men had to increase the speed of their work. Since only a few mules remained on the front lines, alpini hitched themselves to ropes and pulled logs from the forest along the icy ground for a distance of nine kilometers. Half a meter of straw with a layer of soil on top covered the roofs of the bunkers. The alpini built tables, chairs, and beds, and made bricks out of clay from the steppe, with which they built wood-burning stoves. By the end of October, seventy centimeters of snow covered the well-built, snug, and camouflaged bunkers.[11]

Sergeant Mario Rigoni Stern of the Vestone Battalion (Tridentina Division) recalled that when he and his men excavated their communication trenches through the ruins of an abandoned Cossack fishing village, they found potatoes, carrots, cauliflower, and cucumbers buried by the former inhabitants in the now destroyed gardens. When those vegetables were in good condition, the alpini added them to their *minestrone*.[12]

During the day, other than doing sentry or observation duty, the alpini generally remained inside their bunkers resting after their sleepless nights of guard duty. Frequently they attempted to deal with the plague of lice, throwing them on top of their wood burning stoves where "they'd go white all over and then explode." At night, the men cut brush and undergrowth which they placed in front of the barbed wire fences strung along the shore of the river, creating yet another obstacle for Russian patrols.[13]

In some stretches along the Don where a few outposts of the 3rd Alpine Regiment were situated, the river was approximately thirty meters wide. Occasionally Soviet troops communicated with the alpini across this short distance using a megaphone. One evening a bugler by the name of Casasola gave a particularly stirring performance. Lieutenant Eraldo Sculati writes, "The Russians responded with a chorus of applause amplified by a megaphone, and invited the alpini to cross the river and fraternize with them."[14]

Alarico Rocchi of the Torino Infantry Division also recalled times when soldiers in his unit heard Russians singing on the opposite side of the river. The Italians returned the favor by singing their own folk songs.

In October, the Alpine Corps received a shipment of German anti-tank and antipersonnel mines. Up until this point, the Italians had had no experience with mines, and required clear instructions. The shipment of mines came with instructions written in German. No one, according to Lieutenant Pasquale Grignaschi of the 124th Engineering Company, could translate the highly technical instructions. Captain Cozzani resolved the problem by inviting a German lieutenant from a nearby Pioneer Company to a luncheon. The officer in question arrived, "perfectly groomed," dressed in a splendid uniform. He clicked his heels and exchanged the usual courtesies with the alpini, "who were not at all turned out as well as he was." Following a pleasant, satisfying lunch, the German officer carefully explained the directions for the placement of the mines. Grignaschi couldn't remember the German officer's name but he recalled the officer was probably a "baron or a count or something like that; he was cordial and well-behaved."[15]

While German and Hungarian troops had occupied these same sites, they had laid mines along the shore of the river and at other points they considered vulnerable, but left no mapping system of these minefields. Consequently, there was no way to know what types of mines (antipersonnel or anti-tank) were in the area, nor their location. This posed a tremendous danger for the alpini, especially for those on patrol. Therefore it was necessary to define and map the mined areas, an extremely dangerous task, since most of the work had to be done at night to avoid being fired upon by Russian snipers across the river. As this delicate work proceeded, some mines did explode killing or wounding a number of soldiers. Once minefields were located and mapped, the alpini added new mines, especially in the recently excavated antitank trenches, and along the barbed-wire barricades.[16]

Placement of units of the Cuneense and Julia divisions initially conformed more or less to that of the Germans and Hungarians during their occupation of the same lines. At that time, the deployment was appropriate since there were few enemy forces across the Don and the river offered a certain degree of protection. Nevertheless, right from the beginning, the ability of the alpine divisions to defend themselves was somewhat compromised.

In the first place, three battalions were on the front lines and three deployed to the rear. Later on, two battalions deployed either directly on the banks, or on a ridge overlooking the river, while one battalion was slightly to their rear. This meant three to five hundred meters separated alpine strongholds.

Second, the length of the actual front precluded placing one of the divisions to the rear of the other two, which would have been the normal procedure in order to create a proper defensive line.

Finally, the Vicenza Division, an infantry division consisting of approximately ten thousand men, was placed to the rear of the three alpine divisions to serve as a reserve. Soldiers in the Vicenza were, for the most part, elderly, in poor shape, and poorly trained for any kind of sustained action. They were poorly outfitted and equipped in terms of armaments and vehicles, and the division had absolutely no artillery. Therefore, in essence, the Alpine Corps had no real reserves it could rely upon: "A front, therefore, absolutely out of proportion to their forces and most of all for their means of rapid transport; that is to say it was twice as long as it should have been in order to permit an efficient defense."[17]

When the German 294th Division withdrew from the Don line and deployed between the valley of Rossosh and the Meshonka River to the rear of the Cuneense Division, it came under the command of the Italian Eighth Army (ARMIR). Although the division had no tanks it served as a quasi reserve force, but after November 15, the division transferred further south.[18]

Since there were virtually no real reserve troops, on November 15, commanders of the Alpine Corps decided to form a "rapid response group" for the corps, taking one battalion and a battery from an artillery group from each division. A nucleus of engineers completed the tactical unit which was ready to move immediately when needed.[19]

As winter approached, along with an observed gradual reinforcement of enemy deployments across the river, more activity by the Russians was expected. Once the Tridentina Division took over its designated section, commanders of the Julia and Cuneense divisions hoped they could shorten the length of their defensive sectors and increase the density of their deployment. This hope soon evaporated. Once the Tridentina assumed its position, the front held by the Alpine Corps actually lengthened. Increased activity of enemy patrols caused General

Battisti to occupy the meadows surrounding the Kalitva River since the river ran along the junction with the Cosseria Infantry Division, and once the Don froze, the meadows offered a favorable point of penetration by enemy forces. The Saluzzo Battalion of the Cuneense took position in that zone, occupying positions three to five kilometers from the Don. Thus, the length of the front lines of the Cuneense Division increased to thirty-five kilometers, and lines of the divisions to the north of the Cuneense also lengthened.[20]

These modifications designed to reinforce the front lines meant positions of resistance to the rear of the front almost vanished. With only one battalion in reserve, especially in the winter months, the divisions would not be in a position to repulse an enemy attack of large magnitude aimed at any one point along their defensive lines.[21]

A series of activities commenced designed to reinforce the front lines as much as possible. General Battisti noted, "More weapons were scrounged wherever they could be found; automatic weapons, small cannons, light and heavy mortars, and even a Russian cannon." The alpini also began building a series of fortifications, including a continuous triangular-shaped barbed wire fence along the front lines. They placed hundreds of anti-tank mines and several thousand antipersonnel mines at the most sensitive areas of the front. The alpini also excavated enormous anti-tank trenches, one along the five-kilometer length of the Kalitva plain, and a second one at the entrance of the Karabut valley.[22]

A German general in command of the liaison section of German Army Group B and the Alpine Corps came to inspect the front lines held by the Cuneense Division in early November. Although he commended the Italian commanders for the work they had accomplished, he told the battalion commanders to deploy their companies right on the banks of the Don.[23] Following his inspection, the German general met with General Battisti of the Cuneense Division. He insisted having his suggestions carried out by battalion commanders. Specifically, he wanted all artillery deployed directly on the riverbanks.

During his conversation with Battisti he remarked, "The Russians actuate the principal—where a man can pass so can a battalion—they are skilled at using the tactic of infiltration. Therefore, it is necessary to have a continuous line of fire so that even if the smallest enemy patrol is sighted it is driven back before it crosses the river, especially when the river is frozen."

The general also told Battisti "not to be concerned" if the Russians should break through the Italian lines at some point: "German divisions, which are about to arrive on the Eastern Front will drive them back and stop them. What is essential is for you to give the enemy the impression that every meter of the front is held by at least one rifle."

General Battisti tactfully let the German general know he could not agree with his suggestions and, in any case, he was not going to make any modifications of the front lines without specific orders from Italian superior commanders.[24]

Four to five days later, an order from headquarters of the ARMIR ordered the modifications suggested by the German general to take place. In the case of the Cuneense Division, carrying out these orders meant increasing the length of the front lines to not less than 55 kilometers, which obviously meant weakening the defensive capability of the front. Furthermore, it also meant the work of developing fortifications would require numerous modifications. In actuality, only slight modifications occurred, regardless of the orders.[25]

From the middle of November on, commanders of German Army Group B ordered alpine divisions to carry out intense patrols "to stimulate an aggressive spirit in units and to give the enemy the impression they were in front of active and courageous troops." Battisti writes, "Factors of general order (essentially a mistrust created by the manifested inferiority of our individual weapons), as well as the necessity to evade unnecessary losses, precluded following these orders. Enemy activity in the zone near the river could be monitored fairly well from our positions at a higher altitude, and the steady flow of deserters gave us sufficient information about the enemy in front of us...."[26]

RELATIONSHIPS WITH RUSSIAN CIVILIANS

In November, the Germans handed the Italians the job of organizing and administering zones behind the lines of the alpine divisions. Most civilians in villages near the river had moved to inhabited areas at some distance from the front lines, or lived in bunkers they had built within the rear zones of the alpini. Battisti acknowledged there probably was a network of spying and propaganda (referring to damages attributed to the troops), but generally, "the behavior of civilians toward our troops was fairly benevolent." The Italians helped civilians in the occupied zones within possible limits, especially with health services.[27]

Lieutenant Rocco G.B. Carbone was a doctor serving in the Monte Cervino Battalion, deployed in a small village near Rossosh, quartered in an izba with a Russian family. In a letter written in November 1942 to his sister Angiolina, he said, "In my whole life I have never found people who are as kind and hospitable as the Russians; the Russian fighter is courageous and fierce, but as soon as he is deprived of weapons he becomes tame and gentle as a lamb. This kindness amazes me even more since the Russian people don't consider us as liberators but only view us as an invading and usurper army; the population is firmly convinced of a final Russian victory and proclaims openly that one day the Red Army will chase us back to Italy which will be occupied by red troops (??!!)...."

Carbone served as a doctor for the alpini, as well as civilians in the village and surrounding countryside. Civilians in need of medical attention offered eggs, honey, milk, and sometimes chickens as payment for his services. He wrote, "It's useless to speak of money because it has no value here."[28]

Units of the three alpine divisions established supply bases to the rear, and Russian civilians living in those zones soon established friendly relationships with the soldiers. Upon finishing their daily work, the locals often spent the evening chatting with the alpini. Bedeschi notes that the Russians learned to speak Italian easily. In the evening whole families would surround the Italians: "They never tired of asking about Italy and all things that weren't Russian."[29]

Bedeschi described them as "good folk, primitive and generous." They invited the soldiers to use their izbas for their quarters. "That way," they whispered, "the Germans can't requisition them."[30]

Vicenzo Cucchietti and thirty-nine alpini remained behind the front lines along with mules of the Cuneense division at the periphery of Rossosh. Two to three men quartered in izbas along with the local residents. Cucchietti lived with a mother and daughter; two sons were serving in the Soviet army. In order to converse with the family, Cucchietti made use of a Russian-Italian dictionary.

In the beginning, the villagers appeared somewhat distrustful of the Italians, but Cucchietti claims their demeanor changed quickly. He was amazed at how quickly the locals, made up of the very young and the elderly, learned the names of all forty alpini. The alpini noted the

Russians had no matches or salt. They wrote letters to their families in Italy asking them to send matches in their packages from home. Asking for salt was out of the question as there was a scarcity of it throughout Italy.

The alpini spoke to the Russians about their life in their villages in Italy: "We speak about private property, of our land bequeathed from father to son. These are all things they deem impossible...."[31]

In the evenings, young men arrived in the izbas. Cucchietti writes, "They are sons of the peasants who are sheltering us; they come home searching for cigarettes. We don't realize these young men live in hiding and are all partisans. One day I attend a party and a few officers of the partisans arrive and take part in the dancing. Not one of them makes a move [against us]. They tell us, 'we are Russian soldiers [who have] escaped from the Germans.' The mayor of the village, who hears this, says to us, '*Italiani bravi*' ('Italians are good')...."[32]

A few German soldiers remained stationed near the Italian supply bases behind the front lines held by the Julia Division. In general, Bedeschi noted, one-on-one encounters between Germans and Italians were cordial, yet "their manner of resolving certain situations was disconcerting" in the eyes of the Italians, causing them to seriously question their relationship with their ally. On the one hand, alpini admired the Germans' "organization and discipline," but their behavior toward the local population was at times incomprehensible when, for example, the following incident took place in Popovka.[33]

When several German soldiers occupied an izba in Popovka, they turned out the two inhabitants, an old man and his twenty-year-old granddaughter. The two dislodged folks dug a small bunker close to their izba. As the old man went about preparing the bunker for the coming winter, he removed a small door of an unused pigsty located next to his izba. He wanted to use the door to close the opening of the bunker. A German soldier, noticing the man carrying the door away from the pigsty, ran toward him shouting and subsequently grabbed him. In the ensuing tussle, the old man refused to let go of the small door. The soldier slapped him across the face, causing him to fall to the ground.

At this point, the granddaughter came on the scene, screaming at the soldier to stop, placing herself between the soldier and her grandfather. The German shoved her to the side as he moved toward the old man still on the ground. The young girl threw herself on the soldier attempting to stop him from hitting her grandfather. During the course of the struggle, she scratched him, raising several bloody marks on his bare arms. At that moment, several other German soldiers intervened and broke up the fight.

Unfortunately, this was not the end of the story. The next day the Italians found the old man and his granddaughter hanging from a tree in the village square.

Witnessing this ghastly scene, a distraught Bedeschi asks, "Was it unleashed bestiality? Was it contempt of life over won populations? Was it owing to a horrific presumption that victors are untouchable?"[34]

Lieutenant Vittorio Trentini also witnessed an act of brutality as he arrived to the rear of the Julia lines at a base where mules of the division sheltered. Hanging from a tree next to an izba, he saw the body of an elderly Russian man: "The Germans had hung him in front of the eyes of a little girl because he didn't want to reveal the place where he had hidden his stash of potatoes."[35]

Many years after the war was over, Nuto Revelli interviewed Battista Candela, a butcher by trade, who recalled his experiences while serving with a unit of alpini in charge of provisioning the 2nd Regiment of the Cuneense Division, located in a village thirty kilometers from Rossosh. When the alpini first arrived, they used a few buildings in the village as warehouses for supplies and provisions for the regiment. Candela was in charge of organizing a "warehouse for meat" in a building filled with grain. The Germans had locked and sealed the doors to the building. At first, once the doors were unsealed, the alpini thought they would give the grain to their mules, but upon re-thinking this idea, they decided to offer it to the local population.

Candela explained: "Folks [in the village] live on charity because the Germans have taken everything from them; they are friendly, good people. We give them a loaf of bread and in exchange, we receive milk. With the distribution of grain to each family the population becomes our friend."[36]

Candela became acquainted with Katia, a forty-five year old woman, and her daughter Dusja who lived in the village. Like most families in the area, Katia and Dusja lived in an underground bunker; the military had requisitioned their home. Candela frequently spent time in Katia's underground home. In one corner, a table was reserved for him, where he kept photographs of his family and other possessions.

One evening he entered the bunker in the dark; Katia confronted him crying, begging him not to hurt her. Dusja was also crying. A young man with a parabellum on his shoulder stood near Katia. Candela asked Katia what the man was doing there.

Still crying, Katia said, "My husband is away in the war and I haven't had any news from him. When the Russians abandoned the village, my son was too young to enlist. Because we were afraid the Germans would deport him, I hid him in the lower zone of the village.... Every night Ivan comes here in the dark to get food. Please, I beg you, don't denounce him to your headquarters."[37]

Candela told Revelli that whenever the Italians took Russian prisoners they were required to turn them over to the Germans. "If I could have been certain Ivan wouldn't end up in German hands, if I could have been certain Ivan would remain in Italian hands, perhaps I might denounce him. However, my conscience prevented me from handing him to one of the Germans. I smiled at Ivan, and he smiled as well...Katia and Dusja stopped crying. Right away we had a new pact of friendship."[38]

Candela told Katia and Ivan he would bring three steaks to their home every night instead of two as in the past. From then on, Candela saw Ivan every evening. Ivan never spoke about the war or politics, but he did warn Candela about the Russian winter. "Escape before the cold and ice come, because if you wait it will be too late, and it will be all over for you."[39]

RUSSIAN PRISONERS

When German troops left the lines occupied by the Cuneense Division, they left approximately 600 Russian prisoners. The Germans required the prisoners to work for them, even on their front lines. The Italians forwarded approximately half of these prisoners to prisoner of war camps behind the lines. The alpine regiments divided the remaining prisoners amongst them for services generally to the rear of the front lines.[40]

The prisoners had done heavy work for the Germans. The Italians soon discovered these men were in very poor physical shape. It was obvious they had been given too little to eat, and so were half starved.

Marsan spoke about the thirty prisoners who worked for the alpini of the 2nd Alpine Regiment. "The alpini in my regiment wanted to find a way to give the prisoners decent rations, yet using our provisions for prisoners was forbidden. Helping these men regain their strength was in the interest of both the prisoners and the troops. A captain of the 2nd Alpine Regiment made a special requisition for more provisions, declaring a Russian bomber had destroyed part of the supplies, and provisions were needed to replenish those supplies. In this manner, *alla italiana* (in the Italian way), we resolved the problem of obtaining more rations for the prisoners in our sector."

General Battisti described the condition of Russian prisoners assigned to the Cuneense Division, claiming that not only had they been poorly fed, they were also poorly dressed; many of them had no shoes. Battisti noted that the Germans had ordered a reduction in rations for Russian prisoners. He realized the prisoners were fulfilling their work requirements, and he responded to the German order by providing rations equivalent to those of the alpini. Furthermore, in order to give decent clothing and shoes to the prisoners, Battisti decided to outfit an entire company of alpini with new uniforms and shoes. He then gave the prisoners all the used clothing and footwear.[41]

Following a prescribed interrogation process, alpini of the Julia Division also retained captured Russian prisoners to work for them. Prisoners quickly adapted to the daily routines of the soldiers, willingly working at jobs assigned to them, even taking care of the mules. They also scavenged through the destroyed village nearby, bringing back window glass, window and doorframes, and even sacred icons for the alpini to use in their bunkers. Bedeschi notes that the Russians had a "weakness for wine and liquors, but they also drank denatured alcohol." They particularly liked toothpaste, devouring it as they liberally squeezed the paste out of the small tubes.[42]

In many cases, Russian prisoners worked side by side with alpini without guard surveillance, especially during the period when the men were building their bunkers and communication trenches. Although orders emanating from German commands forbid Italian soldiers to fraternize with the local population or Russian prisoners, these orders were observed lightly or ignored, even by the higher Italian commands.

Lieutenant Pietro Marchisio of the 3rd Alpine Regiment writes, "Russian peasants...possessed the same characteristics as our alpini.... They were accustomed and tempered by the many difficulties of farming." Although it would have been easy for the prisoners to escape, they remained with the alpini. In the evenings, they slept in their tents and appeared in the morning on time and ready for work. The Italians soon learned a few Russian phrases and conversed with the prisoners as best they could. Marchisio asks, "How could the Italian soldier fail to fraternize with the Russian prisoners from whom they received help building their winter refuges? The alpino, instinctively fraternizes with those who suffer and most of all with those, like him, who have a profound sense of family and human solidarity; in any case, he is always ready to assist those who are in need both in peacetime and in war."[43]

In December, alpini of the Cividale Battalion, Julia Division, captured two Russian women attempting to cross the frozen Don. Although German orders dictated that Russians captured during attempts to infiltrate the front lines were to be shot immediately, General Ricagno ordered the women forwarded to his headquarters.

Several weeks later, Information Officer Lieutenant Angelo Damini, who would have been responsible for the execution of the women, accepted an invitation to a luncheon given by the general where he observed these same two women happily working in the officer's mess.[44]

When Lieutenant Giorgio Gaza assumed command of the 253rd Company of the Val Chiese Battalion of the Tridentina Division, he decided to inspect the lines held by his company along the river; most of all he wanted to get to know the men under his command. Gaza carried out his inspection during the middle of the night. At a certain point, the lieutenant entered the bunker of a squad of riflemen. To his surprise, he saw a Russian soldier in a Russian uniform standing at attention along with the Italians. Gaza writes. "I was dumbfounded."

One alpino spoke: "Lieutenant Sir, don't hurt him, he's a good man." The alpino told Gaza the men had captured the prisoner several nights before. He had remained with them taking care of their daily chores. He cut the wood to keep the stove burning, cleaned the bunker, and took care of providing the squad with water from the river, a difficult task during the winter.

Gaza describes his reaction to this unusual situation: "These blessed alpini captured a prisoner, and instead of handing him over as required, they've kept him and turned him into their orderly. Naturally, he eats and smokes like them and they treat him with kindness and care as if he were one of them. It's incredible. I remained stunned. I thought to myself, these men are supposed to be the ferocious Fascists. In a few days, they might be capable of dressing him in a uniform of the alpini and even sending him out to take his turn at guard duty, as if he had been born in Vestone [Italy] or the vicinity."[45]

Of course, Gaza had to follow orders, forwarding the prisoner to headquarters of the battalion. "Yet," Gaza writes, "In my heart I can only admire the behavior [of the alpini] even though it is completely against military regulations, but it is, on the whole, in line with the principles of humanity, which make those who practice them noble and great. Thanks to them goodness can sprout, even within the horrors of war."[46]

Russian deserters frequently presented themselves at the Italian lines. Regimental information officers forwarded them to the headquarters of the Alpine Corps following interrogation.[47]

While the Tridentina Division was fighting in the zone held by the Sforzesca Division (late August and September), chaplain Don Gnocchi recalled a day in August when a small patrol of alpini ran in to a large Russian patrol commanded by a political commissar. Russian soldiers captured and disarmed the alpini. Following their capture, the commissar drove away in his car. As soon as the commissar disappeared, Don Gnocchi writes, "The Russians returned our weapons, got in line, and entered our lines as prisoners."[48]

While Marsan was on the Don front he received mail, and he knew how much letters from home meant to him and his comrades. One day he asked Russian prisoners working in his section if they wanted to write to their families. He believed their circumstances were much like his. The prisoners were eager to send letters, but few knew how to write; in fact, most were illiterate. Literate prisoners wrote for those who were unable to. Marsan took the small package of letters to his headquarters for further processing and mailing, and was told that all mail had to be sent to German headquarters. Marsan noted, "I suspected the Germans would never mail those letters. Sure enough, an officer in divisional headquarters, who contacted the German command, soon confirmed this very fact."

NOVEMBER

Troop trains continued to travel between Italy and Russia bringing additional men, supplies, and mail. Second Lieutenant Nello Corti had barely turned twenty-one when he arrived in Millerovo November 12.

Following the completion of officer's training, Corti had taken advantage of an Italian government decree permitting officers formally enrolled in a university in the faculty of medicine or veterinary science to continue their studies at a university located near a a military base. He was able to carry on with his studies at the University of Turin and perform various military duties at the headquarters of an artillery regiment of the Alpine Corps.

Corti had no doubts about taking advantage of this opportunity. This coincided with the period his father had been condemned to five years of internal exile (*confinato*) by Mussolini's regime because of his anti-Fascist political opinions.[49] Professor Alfredo Corti had lost his professorship at the University of Turin, as well as his salary. Returning to Turin gave Nello Corti the opportunity to be close to his family and to attend to their needs. His two sisters and younger brother were still living in the family home during this period.

In November 1942, the government revoked the decree permitting officers to continue their university studies, and Corti returned to full active duty. He traveled to Bologna where he joined other troops departing for the Russian front on November 4, 1942.

Corti recalled this period: "My decision to return to Turin to continue my studies didn't present a problem for me. But now, looking back, I wonder if I had had sufficient reasons to go to war somewhat voluntarily—to go to fight in a war that was the fruit of the politics of a dictatorship that had taken away every civil liberty, affecting the whole population, and in the case of my own family, condemning my father to internal exile. Now, looking back at this issue after so many years it is obvious that as a twenty-year-old I probably couldn't really grasp the full scope of the tragedy in which my family, country, and the whole world was involved.

"The family environment in which I grew up was clearly anti-Fascist, but any overt act against the regime was not a part of our family culture that was liberal and, in a sense, still tied to national principles derived from the First World War. The condemnation of my father to five years of internal exile came about for reasons little more than his expressing contrary opinions, which really demonstrated that the Fascist regime was nothing other than a piece of buffoonery.

"Although I could have requested a transfer to the Medical Corps because I had been a medical student before I changed my course of study to veterinary science, I refused to take advantage of that option because I felt it would have been a way out, a cowardly act on my part. The alpini were for the most part simple people of the mountain valleys. They had no options when sent off to Russia to fight. They never would have even considered saying 'no' to the system. I couldn't respond in any other way other than to express solidarity with the soldiers in my care, to do the best in my relationships with the men under my command, to take care of them as best I could, and also not to push them, or force them to do something that might be wrong.

"Perhaps, if I had had contact with some underground clandestine organization fighting the Fascist regime, I could have participated, finding in this way, a response to my own moral compass. I was definitely opposed to the Fascist system."

By November 17, Corti was on the front lines of the Don with the Julia Division, serving in the Val Cismon Battalion, 9th Regiment. During the first days, he spent most of his time building communication trenches and a new underground refuge. Inside the refuge, the alpini transformed a large gas canister into a wood-burning stove; there were beds, benches, and a table, all skillfully built by the alpini. This bunker was "home" for Corti and his colleague Lieutenant Capparella. Corti and Capparella occupied the most northern stronghold of the Julia Division. The Edolo Battalion of the Tridentina Division occupied the adjoining zone.

Corti described his surroundings: "The Russians were situated in a dense forest across the river. Occasionally they fired artillery rounds across the river at us; otherwise, we only heard a few isolated shots— ta-pum, ta-pum. Now and then a Russian sniper shot at our sentries, killing several of them, and sometimes a few small parties of Russians managed to infiltrate through our lines. I only saw four Russians across the river through my binoculars while I was on the Don. In the distance, I could see the windmills of the city of Pavlovsk to the northeast."

When alpini of the Val Cismon had first arrived on the Don, they had relieved a battalion of Hungarian soldiers. While those troops had occupied the zone, they had placed mines around the outskirts of their positions, yet like the Germans they had not left any maps of the mine-fields. Corti had a firsthand look at them a few days after he arrived on the Don, when he paid a visit to Lieutenant Gamba, who commanded a platoon farther south. Gamba was known as *un tipo con molto carattere* (a real character). He told Corti to get out of the trenches and to walk around the area separating the stronghold from the river in order to observe the wires connecting the mines (in his case the river was fairly close to the refuges, in comparison to the layout of Corti's stronghold). Corti recalled this incident: "It was broad daylight at the time. Gamba said: 'Don't worry about the Russians across the river, they are probably sleeping, they won't try and shoot you.' I, somewhat hesitatingly, followed my friend's orders, realizing he was testing me. As I jumped out of the trench, I could see the wires on the ground connecting the mines to each other."

Corti continued, "Soon the Don began to freeze. Once it snowed, wires connecting the mines were no longer visible! The alpini had established a safe path through the mines, yet they didn't want to venture outside of their immediate lines because of the inherent danger, particularly at night. At a certain point, an officer from the Corps of Engineers came to the area to attempt to improve and expand the mine system and to create some sort of map of its layout. He was an expert on bombs and mines, yet while performing this duty (by moonlight in order to escape detection by the Russians), one of the mines exploded and injured him severely. By chance, once I returned to Italy, I ran into this officer sitting in a café in Bologna. His face was horribly disfigured, and one of his legs had been amputated."

Corti had three squads under his command (forty-five alpini ranging in age from nineteen to thirty-one). Within each squad, he divided the men into families, making the eldest of the group "head of family." Each head of family was responsible for the welfare of five to six men. It was very important to keep all of the weapons in prime condition. It was also important to make sure the soldiers had clean, dry socks and intact boots to prevent the onset of frostbite in the below-zero temperatures. Corti double-checked to be sure his men's boots were in good shape. The boots were poorly manufactured, and pieced together with numerous seams. If he saw a seam unraveling, or a deteriorating sole, he insisted on immediate repairs. Fortunately, a shoemaker was in one of the squads and he took care of all necessary repairs. Of course Corti knew once his men were involved in any kind of combat, there would be no time for any of these preventive measures.

Corti was an experienced alpinist and skier, accustomed and well prepared for winter weather. To protect himself from the cold, he wore a wool undershirt, a regular military shirt, two sweaters his mother had made for him, a jacket, and a great coat with a removable sheepskin lining. On his head, he wore his alpino hat or his balaclava. His boots were well-made ski boots with Vibram soles. They were slightly over-sized, permitting him to move his feet within his boots, an important factor to prevent the onset of frostbite.

Chapter 5

GENERAL CONDITIONS ON THE DON FRONT

Distribution of winter equipment to the alpini occurred toward the middle of November. Although uniforms and boots were inadequate for rigorous winter weather, manufactured poorly, out of shoddy materials,[1] the alpini were better equipped for the cold weather in comparison to soldiers in infantry divisions. Some alpini had jackets with removable sheepskin linings, but they only covered the men from the waist up. They were cumbersome and tended to hamper movement, especially during combat.[2]

General Battisti describes the quality and characteristics of the standard boots issued by the military to the alpini: "Once these leather boots became wet, they lost their resistance to water and became hard as wood. The heavy hobnails [on the bottoms of the boots]...only served to allow the formation of a permanent crust of ice under the sole, thus keeping the bottom of the boot frozen." So many cases of frostbite occurred due to this factor, not only during the days of the withdrawal but also while the alpini were on the Don front. Woolen socks issued by the military shrank when they became wet, contributing to cases of frostbite. "All in all our equipment was rich in terms of quantity, but not adequate in terms of quality, especially with regard to footwear, which was fine for the summer, but once it froze should have been substituted with the type of footwear similar to Russian felt boots (*valenki*)."[3]

In general, Russian soldiers were well equipped for cold weather, particularly as the war went on. They wore waterproof down pants and jackets over their uniforms. These insulated outfits permitted them to remain well protected in frigid weather and enabled them to lay out in the snow for hours with no ill effects. On their heads, they wore a fur-lined hood closed with a zipper, and on their feet, they wore valenki. Made of fused felt with no seams, they kept feet warm and dry, even without socks. Flexible and elastic, they covered the foot and lower leg up to the knee. When men's feet would swell after they had walked for long periods, valenki perfectly accommodated the swelling and did not impede circulation. Even the best-made alpine boots lacked this feature. Soldiers who removed their boots after hours of walking were unable to put them on again due to swelling. This often meant certain death once the withdrawal from the Don began. Corradi believes the commander of the Julia Division, General Ricagno, ordered the manufacture of valenki, and about half of the troops in his division received them. The distribution of valenki to all troops of the ARMIR might well have saved thousands from the agony of frostbite. Corradi recalled that it hurt to see how poorly equipped the infantry was in terms of their footwear. They had small, lightweight boots, designed for warmer weather, not at all like the heavier albeit inadequate ones of the alpini.[4]

Carlo Vicentini addressed the issue of the lack of adequate winter clothing for soldiers of the ARMIR. From a list of distributions of fur coats issued to the infantry and alpine divisions, it could be determined, for example, that fewer than half of the men in most divisions received fur coats, whereas troops in service and command units (behind the front lines) received 100 percent of the much needed fur coats. The Cuneense Division should have received 17,000 fur coats; 3,000 were distributed. The Ravenna Infantry Division received 7,000 fur coats for a force of 15,000 men.

Vicentini said, "It was absurd! Instead of distributing winter coats to those men on the lines, soldiers in command centers were complete-ly outfitted." When questioned about the scarcity of coats Vicentini facetiously said, "Maybe the Fascists in Rome thought the war would be over before the onset of winter." Vicentini noted that alpini in the Monte Cervino Battalion were equipped with outfits similar to those of the Russians, but his battalion was the only alpine unit properly outfit-ted for the rigorous Russian climate.

While Lieutenant Nuto Revelli was recuperating from a wound in his arm in Voroshilovgrad (the seat of the central hospital facility of the

ARMIR), he was astonished to observe the existence of a flourishing Italian black market. "In the bazaars, in the shops, one could buy Italian cigarettes... [mountain] boots, and [knee-high] boots. All equipment of the Italian Army was for sale for incredible prices." On the front lines, there had been rumors about "Italian officers dealing out in the open to make money. But to see these truths was searing."[5]

Railcars full of clothing, shoes, and equipment had left Italy for the front. All such supplies should have been distributed to the fighting troops; "instead," Revelli writes, "in a matter of fifteen days, Italian gangsters in Voroshilovgrad discovered a shorter and more profitable route, selling to Russian civilians at inflated prices. It seems the guilty ones were under investigation. Will they end up against a wall, or will they be promoted?"[6]

Lieutenant Bruno Zavagli was also shocked to see brand new Italian military fur-lined leather gloves for sale in a bazaar in Rikovo. He writes, "The black market has achieved full legitimacy in Rikovo.... One freezes and trembles on the front and here, behind the lines, there's everything, but everything doesn't go further: the supplies remain here for some time, passing through predatory clutches that choose and plunder, reducing the amount; [eventually] only the leftovers arrive at the front."[7]

The distribution of food supplies to the troops also became deficient as time wore on. "Rations would have been sufficient for living and working in normal conditions, but were actually reduced due to the almost complete absence of fresh vegetables and potatoes. Comfort foods (chocolate, sugar, candies, vitamins, cognac) were rarely distributed and in insufficient amounts." General Battisti notes, owing to the size of the front, that "every night *all* men of every company were required to perform guard duty, or went on security patrols."[8]

Although there are records of the amount of food supplies sent from Italy to Russia, there are no records of provisions forwarded from supply centers to the front lines.[9]

In letters written by alpini serving on the Don front in the Cuneense Division, the theme of hunger became increasingly insistent. Many wrote to family members saying they were "tightening their belts." On September 24, 1942, alpino Romano Gallo wrote, "When I finish eating my rations I feel like sitting down at table for a dinner.... On October 8 he wrote, "With regard to food, it's scarce: a little pasta in beet and cabbage soup; instead of one bread roll I need two...." On October 30 he wrote, "Of course if I had a little of your bread I would eat it the same way we ate sweet pastries once upon a time."[10]

On October 16, 1942, alpino Francesco Tortone wrote, "With regard to food there's little, but as you know, at home I ate little so it doesn't hurt much, but on the other hand, here there are some alpini who eat a lot, and what they get isn't enough, and they are hungry and also here the kitchens are far behind us, and when rations arrive on the lines they are always cold, even the coffee in the morning which would be nice to drink hot is always cold."[11]

On October 10, 1942, alpino Giacomo Origlia wrote, "As soon as you can send a package from Centallo, you will send me some bread and if you can, something to eat, but the most important is the bread and then you will send other stuff." On October 15 he wrote, "As soon as you can send a package send me something to eat, mostly bread." On October 21, Origlia also asked for woolen clothing as well as food.[12]

On October 2, 1942 alpino Stefano Rosso wrote, "If by chance you can send something out of wool it would be good, especially socks and a small sweater if you have an extra one, otherwise if there isn't one I'll remain the way I am; oh well, if there isn't one send some chestnuts...."[13]

On October 19, 1942, alpino Spirito Gonzo wrote, "As far as food goes, we can't say we have enough, because we grind rye to put in our soup to make it thicker, but you don't need to worry because in one way or another we search to find something to satisfy our hunger.... If you can send me some dried chestnuts, I have a grand desire to eat them...."[14]

On September 2, 1942, alpino Giovanni Gonzo wrote, "....if by chance you can send something, a pair of socks and gloves and put in a few heads of garlic with some salt, and I would also like some ink, send some garlic because it's good [for me] here the water is unhealthy...."[15]

On November 14, 1942, alpino Bruno Viale asked his wife to knit heavy socks for him, and a pair of gloves. "If you can't send anything else, send a package of two kilos of dried or white chestnuts...." [16]

Thousands of packages mailed to alpini on the Don from villages and hamlets in the province of Cuneo contained kilos of chestnuts, flour, and bread. "Meanwhile," Revelli writes, "other packages from Russia reach Italy: they are the packages of the thieves in the rear lines, and contain cigarettes, sugar, coffee, 'comfort foods,' and rations of the soldier who is on the lines...."[17]

On November 18 when Lieutenant Revelli returned to his unit, now deployed in Belogory, he noted his impressions of the alpini in his company. They looked like "strangers" they had aged so much.[18] They had also gained weight. "They were heavier because to compensate for the poor rations" they were eating many potatoes they had discovered in fields surrounding their outposts. They had also discovered stores of grain they ground up in improvised grinders they had built.[19] Rations were scarce on the front lines. "Four tubes with meat in the morning, four tubes without meat at night. Once a week pasta with little sauce; twice a week, a glass of wine....We never saw cognac."[20]

Revelli continues: "The worst sin of Fascism isn't that it betrayed the generation of Fascism, that it betrayed us who shouted '*viva la guerra, viva il duce*' ('long live the war, long live the Duce'). It's having betrayed these poor souls on whose shoulders the war has fallen, like an epidemic...." He observed how poorly equipped the alpini in his company were, wearing worn out inadequate clothing. Some only possessed a summer uniform and a fur coat while others had their broken shoes resoled with "pieces of rubber pulled off abandoned Russian trucks, and others lost their shoes, piece by piece."[21]

Most weapons issued to the alpini were not suitable for the climatic conditions of the Russian winter. When temperatures dropped, mechanisms froze. The alpini devised various ingenious methods for keeping their rifles and machine guns warm to prevent them from jamming. Revelli notes that alpini in his unit kept their machine guns inside the bunkers close to the stoves; the weapons only functioned when they were warm; there was no more oil to lubricate them.[22]

Sergeant Major Mario Rigoni Stern of the Vestone Battalion (Tridentina Division) recalled, that alpini in his unit kept heavy machine guns functioning in cold temperatures by placing helmets full of hot coals beneath them.[23]

When temperatures dropped, mechanisms of heavy artillery weapons also froze. Technicians came from Italy to adjust the artillery, using oil designed not to freeze in subzero temperatures, but changing the oil failed to yield favorable results and many weapons were ruined as a result.[24]

One serious problem needing to be resolved was the sheltering of hundreds of quadrupeds belonging to the alpine divisions. Shelters on the front lines for some mules and a few horses were constructed, and alpini built a few sleds that one or two mules could pull. In this manner, they were able to take care of their immediate transportation needs by keeping only a few mules on the front lines and sending the majority to villages behind the lines, where it was easier to shelter and feed them. Some of these villages were more than fifty kilometers from the front. In the case of the Cuneense Division, for example, most pack mules and drivers went to zones between Rossosh, Mitrofanovka, and Rovenki. It would take four days for these units to reach their respective units on the front lines if, as was the case during the withdrawal, the division was required to move.[25]

The mules represented an enormous burden in the winter. It was difficult for them to walk in deep snow and consequently they were only used on cleared roads, whereas the local Russian horses were able to pull sleds off the beaten track. Furthermore, the health of the mules deteriorated because of the consistent cold temperatures and scarcity of food for them.[26]

Each alpine division had approximately 500 motor vehicles (trucks of various sizes, and motorcycles). Traveling on roads in the summer and autumn was extremely difficult, since the unpaved roads had a clay surface. As noted, when it rained, roads were impassable. When roads were dry, vehicles could only proceed at a slow pace since surfaces were full of huge potholes, causing wear and tear on vehicles, drivers, and transported materiel. Few roads remained cleared of snow during the winter, therefore transportation by means of truck or motorcycle was severely limited.[27]

Most Italian vehicles designed for the milder climates of Italy were poorly adapted for subzero temperatures in Russia. For example, when Lieutenant Egisto Corradi was with the Julia Division south of the Kalitva River in December, he and his men had to keep two small fires burning under the trucks (one under the motor, and the other under the differential). It was necessary to drive the vehicles for five to ten minutes every hour. Even with all the attention given to maintenance, many trucks simply stopped running.[28]

A scarcity of fuel, especially diesel fuel, was another problem the alpini faced. Before leaving for the Russian front, the Germans had told the Italians they had more supplies of diesel fuel than gasoline, so the Italians sent diesel trucks to Russia. Once in Russia, they found the exact opposite was true. The Germans had less diesel fuel and more gasoline. Furthermore, the Germans were stingy when supplying the Italians with fuel. Italian trucks received three liters of oil for every hundred liters of diesel fuel, but Italian trucks required five liters of oil for every hundred liters.[29]

Some vehicles originally camouflaged for the African campaign were sent to Russia. When the alpini were already on the Don and the snow began to fall, General Ricagno put in a request to have the camouflaged vehicles painted white. After the first hard freeze, paint on the vehicles peeled off, and the sand and yellow colors of the camouflage were visible once more. Trucks without camouflage were painted white as well. The white paint peeled off these trucks as well, revealing the original dark green color, which meant they stood out starkly against the snow.[30]

During the first weeks the alpini deployed on the Don, the number of Russian troops on the opposite side of the river lacked sufficient strength to initiate any significant offensive action. On the other hand, they were very active when it came to sending small patrols across the river to infiltrate between strongholds and penetrate deeply to ascertain the location and consistency of artillery positions and to take prisoners. When skirmishes with Italian surveillance units occurred, well-armed Russians, possessing superior automatic weapons, were able to either escape or have the "upper hand."[31]

Lieutenant Angelo Damini was in charge of observing enemy activity across the river in the sector held by the Tolmezzo and Gemona Battalions of the Julia Division. In September, Damini was keeping an eye on a building within a small village across the river, believing the Russians had established a headquarters for a command post. The building in question was the only structure in the village built out of bricks, surrounded by the usual Russian izbas.[32]

The divisional command decided to conduct a surprise attack on the suspected building, which was only 300 meters distant from the alpine lines. Colonel Cocuzza of the Udine Group was to direct the operation. As the first four salvos destroyed a corner of the structure, alpini observed three children and two women fleeing precipitously from the building. Colonel Cocuzza immediately suspended the attack fearing civilians had been harmed. Following this episode, the alpini never fired on the brick building again, even though future intelligence indicated it actually was the headquarters of a Russian command, yet also housed a family of women and children.[33]

In another sector of the lines, Lieutenant Damini had been observing an area called *Isola* (Island), held by the 70th Company of the Gemona Battalion, to determine if the Russians were fortifying their positions opposite the embankment of the small island in the river. In that location, there was an outcropping of rocks jutting out into the water for approximately thirty meters, forming a sort of natural dam or breakwater. After several days of observation, Damini noticed that the dam had lengthened by several meters. Apparently, under cover of darkness, the Russians had pushed more rocks to the end of the dam and camouflaged their work with algae, thus diminishing the distance between the dam and the embankment of the island facing them. Alpini of the Val Piave artillery group moved a cannon on to the island during the night. The following morning they easily destroyed approximately half of the dam. Although the Russians responded to this attack with violent firepower directed at the island, all alpini reached safety along with their mountain cannon.[34]

Russian sniper activity was a continuous menace. At first it seemed as if the snipers were invisible because it was impossible to spot them. The alpini soon discovered that the snipers, well camouflaged, hid themselves in treetops. In turn, the alpini positioned their crack shots in well-camouflaged positions and thus were able to eliminate their share. Now and then, alpini patrols crossed the river, capturing prisoners and weapons. In addition, from their own surveillance and from information they were able to obtain from captured Russians, it became clear that the Russians were moving large columns of vehicles at night toward the south.[35]

DECEMBER 1942

Russian reconnaissance planes frequently flew over the lines held by the Italians. At one point, hundreds of small leaflets written in Italian and Russian dropped from one. The leaflets "invited" the Italians to give themselves up as prisoners. None accepted the invitation, though it was not necessarily because most soldiers gave credence to Fascist propaganda, which accused the Soviets of atrocities against prisoners. "Rather, it was for a much simpler reason. Namely, no combatant easily throws down his weapon in order to be taken prisoner, even when he is not completely convinced of the reason for which he is fighting the war."[36]

Soldiers on the front lines and command centers looked out over the snow-covered landscape and hoped that the winter would pass "without any great surprises, even though by now the Don which lay directly in front of them, was completely frozen and no longer represented a natural obstacle for enemy movement."[37]

"Ignorance of many facts suffocated any serious concern for the immediate future." No one, had a realistic awareness of the superior automatic weapons of Soviet soldiers, and no one realized that the Italian 47/32 anti-tank gun couldn't damage a Russian T-34 tank. No one really realized that one night out of doors could wipe out an entire unit from combat owing to poor quality uniforms, gloves, headgear, and lightweight boots supplied by the military. "But, most of all, who could imagine that the spectacular fireworks glowing to the south...were those of a circle closing around the Germans in Stalingrad?"[38]

Other than an occasional death caused by sniper fire, mortar fire, or a skirmish with a reconnaissance patrol, life on the front was relatively quiet and "monotonous" during the first ten days of December. In a few sectors, there were increased Soviet patrols and one could hear the persistent noise of running motors across the river during the night.[39]

On December 12, Soviet *katyushas*[40] began firing on the lines held by the Tridentina Division in Belogory. "The sky became red, on fire; following four bursts of [rocket] fire, our village was in flames." [41]

Katyusha rockets made a terrifying, screaming sound leaving a long trail of flame as they came screeching toward their target, inflicting a considerable amount of damage. The katyusha ("Little Kate") had "sixteen 132mm rockets, fired from two rows of rails on the back of a truck.... Because of the sound the rockets made, as well as the arrangement of the sixteen rails or 'pipes,' the Germans called it 'Stalin's organ.'"[42]

Belogory was a vulnerable point on the Don. The surroundings were flat for the most part and Russian tanks might attempt to traverse the frozen river. Italian mortars dated from 1881, and in order to fire them it was necessary to obtain permission from the regimental command; shells were counted. Revelli writes, "The greatest danger was that the Russians would attack us with tanks. Headquarters baptized our section of the line as 'the door of Belogory'—it was an 'open door' without a doorbell."[43]

Alpini of the 46th Company, mule drivers and artillerymen, feverishly dug an antitank trench as rumors of a Russian offensive circulated. They believed it was only a matter of time before an attack. At a certain point, each company was to designate four alpini to form a platoon of "tank hunters." Their orders were to attack advancing enemy tanks with bottles of gas and hand grenades! "We knew the situation was serious", writes Revelli. "We knew it wasn't enough to work day and night on the anti-tank trench of Belogory to save the front…. We didn't want to think about the worst because we didn't want to give up."[44]

On the night of December 23, the ground trembled as katyusha shells streamed above the alpini lines. Revelli notes, "We shot until dawn…. Disaster was in the air…. Now mule handlers and artillerymen came to help with the excavation of the antitank trench…."[45]

Around Christmas, more leaflets dropped from Russian planes: "The Soviet Union possesses the greatest general—General Winter. We invite you to surrender individually, by platoons, by companies. Surrender before the end arrives for you."[46]

Chapter 6

THE SOVIET WINTER
OFFENSIVE BEGINS

On August 23, 1942, tanks of the 16th Panzer Division, the spearhead of Germany's Sixth Army, had reached the Volga River near Stalingrad. Also on that day, the first major Luftwaffe bombing raid of "2,000 sorties" attacked the city itself, and over 40,000 people perished with 150,000 others wounded.[1]

In the following weeks the rest of Sixth Army along with parts of Fourth Panzer Army arrived at Stalingrad, and on September 14 launched a concentrated assault. Left behind in the now-shattered industrial metropolis was Soviet 62nd Army, which had orders to hold out till the last. Fighting raged among the rubble from block to block and from building to building. On September 27 the Germans sprung another full-scale assault and again met heavy resistance. Although Hitler was determined to take Stalingrad, by October 29, his victory continued to remain elusive despite ferocious fighting and massive loss of life on both sides.[2]

At the end of August and during the first few days of September, Russian troops attacked several infantry sections of the Italian Eighth Army's front southeast of Novaya Kalitva. In the course of those attacks, the Soviets increased the number of their troops deployed on two bridgeheads. The bridgehead of Verkhniy Mamon in front of the Ravenna Division (twelve kilometers deep and eight kilometers wide) had a small bridge connecting it to the left side of the Don. The second bridgehead, that of Veshenskaya, was in front of the Sforzesca Division.[3]

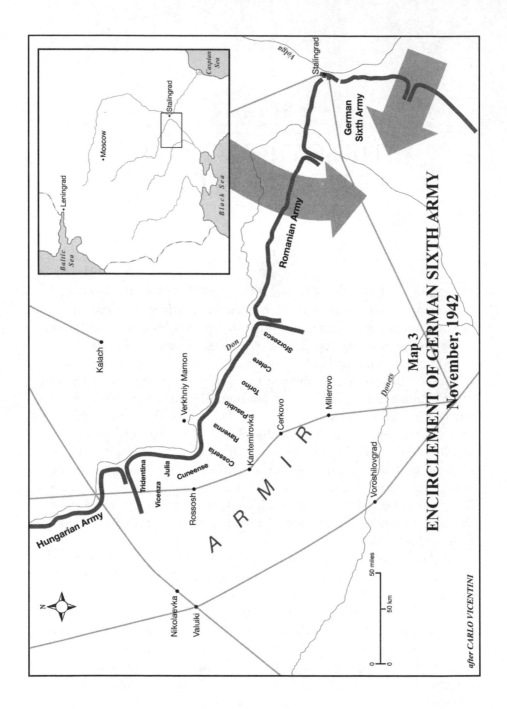

Map 3
ENCIRCLEMENT OF GERMAN SIXTH ARMY
November, 1942

after CARLO VICENTINI

Vicentini notes it would have been wise for the Italians to clear these bridgeheads, but under the circumstances, it wasn't possible since the only troops available for such an offensive were already on the front lines. A strong defensive line in front of these sensitive positions with a second defensive line to the rear would have been ideal. There would have been enough time to create such a line since the Italian divisions had arrived in August.

"Unfortunately," Vicentini writes, "our soldier [in the infantry] was not at all equipped to take advantage of the terrain, nor did he have the necessary tools to do it; pickaxes, shovels, saws and hatchets were rarely found in our units, barbed wire was handed out in ridiculous quantities, sacks to be filled with earth to protect trenches were an unknown...." Vicentini contrasts the infantry with the alpini, who on their own initiative had constructed a strong fortified defensive line to the north of the infantry, utilizing their own "ingenuity."[4]

Moreover, Vicentini writes, "[in the infantry] there was minimum technical or psychological preparation for combat [especially] by very small units...for individual initiative, for the hard work and rigor of responding to the unexpected, or setbacks. One cannot blame the ordinary soldier, the blame rests with the criteria of training, which favored specialized corps and considered the infantry as inferior, deployable in a casual manner."[5]

Already in mid-September, Soviet General Georgi Zhukov and Aleksandr Vasilevsky, the Red Army's Chief of Staff, had begun planning a Soviet counteroffensive. "Operation Uranus" would be the first part of a three-phase offensive carried out over a three-month period, designed to encircle German forces in and around Stalingrad, as well as those in the Caucasus. The Soviets realized that German Army Groups A and B were over-extended with fragile supply lines. The most obvious points of weakness in the Axis lines closest to Stalingrad were the two flanks of Sixth Army held by the Romanian Third and Fourth Armies.

The Soviets required time to prepare for their winter offensive. Any attack, in order to be decisive, would have to be massive and would need a buildup of men and materiel; all planning and related activity would require utmost secrecy. Furthermore, it was necessary to keep the Germans focused on the battle in Stalingrad while the buildup of forces and materiel for the offensive took place. Throughout this period the Russians stepped up operational security measures, including a reduction of radio transmissions, and substituted person-to-person communication in place of written orders. They also engaged in deceptive maneuvers near Moscow and along the Voronezh front, both of which were not part of the impending offensive.[6]

On October 17, inhabitants living close to the eventual front lines received orders to evacuate by October 29. The purpose was to use the civilians' houses to shelter and hide advancing troops during daylight hours as they moved toward the front.[7] Russian deserters arriving on the Alpine Corps' front lines told Italian officers that houses on the opposite side of the Don were filled at night with troops who were under orders not to come out of the izbas during the day for any reason (under the threat of being shot). When the Germans received this information, they didn't appear to be overly concerned. They gave more credence to their own reconnaissance by air.[8]

The Russians launched the first phase of their winter offensive on November 19. The grand design of Operation Uranus was to encircle German Sixth Army in Stalingrad in a giant trap, cutting its troops off from the rest of the Axis front. Over a million Red Army troops waited for the signal to move across the steppe in a multi-pronged advance.[9]

Soviet forces attacked the Third Romanian Army (the left flank of Stalingrad) from the Serafimovich and Kletskaya bridgeheads, while from the southwest of Stalingrad, forces attacked the Fourth Romanian Army to Stalingrad's right. In three days, the Soviets destroyed fourteen German and Romanian divisions. On November 22, the Russians secured the vital bridge over the Don River at Kalach (Kalach-na-Donu), eighty-five kilometers west of Stalingrad, and by November 23, the two pincers of the attacks met at Sovietsky to the east of Kalach to complete the encirclement of German Sixth Army in Stalingrad and cut off German supply lines.[10] Map 3

OPERATION LITTLE SATURN

On December 11, preliminary movements of the second phase of the Soviet winter offensive began, code named "Operation Little Saturn." The Soviets had amassed a huge, well-equipped army for their strike against Italian and German divisions deployed southeast of the Alpine Corps, as well as remaining forces of the Romanian Third Army, positioned southeast of these divisions.

Soviet forces included the following units: First Tank Army, with thirteen brigades and over 700 tanks, the Sixth Infantry, with 10 divisions and 4 motorized brigades, and the Third Red Guard with 10 divisions and 4 motorized brigades. Between December 12 and 14, large Soviet units of infantry supported by artillery began attacking the Italian infantry lines without respite. The purpose of this phase was to discover the weakest points in the defensive lines of the Cosseria, Ravenna, and Pasubio infantry divisions. The presence of Russian-occupied bridgeheads in front of the Ravenna and Pasubio divisions gave Russian troops a great advantage during this preliminary phase.[11]

By now the Don was completely frozen, permitting tanks and motorized units to cross with ease. On December 14, after a massive barrage of artillery, followed by large columns of tanks and armored vehicles, supported by motorized infantry as well as cavalry, and accompanied overhead by aircraft, the Russians smashed through the center of the Ravenna, Cosseria, and Celere infantry divisions. With a "six to one" superiority of troops and artillery, and a "frightening imbalance" of armored vehicles, Russian forces carried out this assault with 750 tanks poised against the three divisions. The Italians faced this formidable force with only 47 tanks, loaned to them by the Germans.[12]

Despite fierce resistance by units on the front lines of the Cosseria Division, enemy forces increased their hold on the western shore of the Don and seized terrain immediately behind the river, reaching several villages and small rises, the so-called "*quote*" (elevations designated by meters above sea level).[13]

The command of the Alpine Corps, concerned about what was happening on its immediate right flank, ordered the transfer of the Monte Cervino Battalion to move behind alpini of the Saluzzo Battalion (Cuneense Division) who were engaged in a vigorous defense of the mouth of the Kalitva River. The Monte Cervino Battalion transferred by truck from Rossosh on the morning of December 14, arriving at noon to support infantry units of the Cosseria Division defending Novaya Kalitva.[14]

On December 16, Russian forces initiated the final phase of their attack following three hours of shelling, breaking through the remaining lines of the Cosseria, Ravenna, and Pasubio infantry divisions with waves of tanks and strafing aircraft. Strongpoints of the Cosseria and Ravenna continued to resist, yet weakened by four days of assaults and

Map 4
OPERATION LITTLE SATURN
December, 1942
Routes and Dates of the Withdrawal
of the Torino and Pasubio Divisions

••••••••••• 20   ROUTE OF THE PRINCIPAL COLUMN
              AND DATE OF TRANSIT IN LOCALITIES

——————→ 20   DIRECTION OF RUSSIAN ADVANCING UNITS
              AND DATES OF OCCUPATION

after CARLO VICENTINI

counterattacks were unable to regroup after heavy losses and were forced to yield more and more ground.[15]

The Soviets soon encircled the Torino, Pasubio, and Sforzesca divisions, forcing them to abandon their lines. These infantry divisions fought valiantly to open a way through the area now completely controlled by enemy forces. As the Russians rapidly moved into zones behind the Italian front, they created havoc with communications, supply bases, and command centers of the ARMIR. As infantry units withdrew, they encountered hundreds of disorganized, leaderless groups of Italian soldiers, burning warehouses, and the total destruction of what had been their former headquarters and sites of command. The majority of officers in withdrawing infantry units lacked maps of the areas behind the lines as they attempted to guide thousands of men out of the Russian encirclement to save them from annihilation. Essentially, they were "abandoned, on their own, without orders, ammunition, or provisions of food." By now, in a matter of only three days since crossing the Don, the Russians had occupied Cerkovo, almost 100 kilometers distant from the point where they had first broken through the Italian lines.[16]

The withdrawal of Italian infantry troops followed three different directions. Some soldiers of the Cosseria and Ravenna divisions to the immediate right of the Cuneense Division were able to withdraw behind the alpini. A portion of the Torino and Pasubio divisions marched toward the south or southwest. Soviet ground troops, tanks, planes, and partisans attacked them repeatedly. The Italians fought many battles as they attempted to break out of the encirclement and escape capture, but few were able to save themselves. Those reaching Cerkovo remained encircled until mid-January when liberated by the Germans. Survivors of the Sforzesca and Celere Divisions and some from the Pasubio Division who fought and marched in a southerly direction, reached German lines on the Donets River at the end of December, a march of 250 kilometers.[17]

Of the thousands captured during these withdrawals, hundreds died in the freezing temperatures during forced marches across the Don to various railheads where they were loaded on trains bound for prisoner of war camps. "By December 25, 1942, infantry divisions of the ARMIR ceased to exist."[18]

Chapter 7

TRANSFER OF THE JULIA DIVISION

Lieutenant Egisto Corradi served with Operations and Services of the Julia Division. On December 17, the division's commander, General Ricagno, sent him on a mission to reach the headquarters of the Italian Second Army Corps (Cosseria and Ravenna divisions) in Taly. Corradi was to inform the command that a "rapid response group" was on its way and the whole Julia Division would follow shortly. The Lieutenant was also bringing various maps of the region to officers of the Second Army Corps.

Once he arrived in Taly, he saw a city engulfed in flames. While searching for the headquarters of the Second Army Corps, Corradi discovered that it had transferred to Kantemirovka. Corradi traveled to Kantemirovka, but once there, officers informed the lieutenant that the Second Army Corps had moved its headquarters further north to Mitrofanovka, approximately 50 kilometers away.[1]

As Corradi carried out his orders, he witnessed the chaos of those days as withdrawing soldiers from the Ravenna and Cosseria divisions arrived near Mitrofanovka. He described the scene as "*uno spavento*" ("a frightful sight"). Now in flames, the city was under attack by low-flying enemy fighter planes firing machine guns at hundreds of fleeing Italian soldiers resembling an "unending herd," moving forward, ignoring the carnage around them. Blankets covered their heads and some men had their feet wrapped in torn pieces of blankets.[2] Map 4

It was clear that once the front lines of the Cosseria and Ravenna divisions were overwhelmed, Russian forces could launch another attack through that breach to penetrate deep into the territory and encircle the whole of the Alpine Corps from the south. On December 16 and 17, the command of German Army Group B was faced with the choice of either sending troops to the area to launch a strong counteroffensive, or ordering the Alpine Corps to withdraw from their lines in order to avoid encirclement. For strategic reasons, the Germans wanted the Alpine Corps to remain on the Don as a defensive bulwark on the left flank of their forces engaged in Stalingrad. General Battisti claims the command of Army Group B decided "to plug the [aforementioned] breach as best it could, throwing already exhausted German units into the area and moving the entire Julia Division from the central section of the Alpine Corps to the zone south of the Kalitva River."[3]

Carlo Vicentini spoke about the transfer of the Julia Division: "The overriding factor was one of urgency to halt the Russians from advancing north. Taking account of the frigid temperatures, four major factors complicated planning for the impending move.

"In the first place, there were not enough trucks to transfer all of the division along with necessary equipment needed for survival and combat. The trip south was approximately 150 kilometers. The division only had one hundred trucks. If trucks could have made a round trip in the course of twenty-four hours, commanders calculated it would take about eight days to transport all 15,000 alpini of the division, but that figure would not have included the transfer of necessary services needed by the division. The Alpine Corps was able to obtain some trucks from headquarters of the ARMIR, but not enough to complete the mission. For this reason, most troops of the division would have to to make the transfer on foot.

"Second, a total lack of communication existed between units of the Julia Division once they began moving south. Communication difficulties plagued the other two alpine divisions still on the Don, and communication between headquarters of the Alpine Corps and headquarters of the ARMIR was fraught with difficulties. There was no communication between scattered infantry units to the south of the alpine divisions."

Vicentini continued: "The third major problem, faced primarily by those units heading south by truck, was the poor condition of the roads. During the short daylight hours, roads were somewhat recognizable, but at night, traveling without lights, it was an entirely different matter.

In some stretches, roads resembled canals with snow piled up high on either side. Drivers were unable to turn to the right or left and most were not familiar with the roads. Driving at night, in unfamiliar territory, without lights and overloaded trucks, made the going slow and treacherous. Accidents occurred, and sometimes drivers took the wrong roads. For example, the 143rd Company of the Aquila Battalion (one of the first units to move south by truck) took thirty hours to cover the 150 kilometer distance. Only five of the twelve trucks traveling south on this occasion returned to Rossosh.

"Russian planes bombed and strafed the convoys. The alpini were unable to defend themselves from low-flying planes, sometimes only fifty meters above them. Mules and trucks were lost, and there were casualties." In conclusion, Vicentini said, "The transfer south of the Julia Division turned out to be a terrible, terrible event!"

A rapid response group had formed with units of the Julia Division, consisting of the Aquila and Tolmezzo battalions, two batteries of the Third Alpine Artillery Regiment, and a battery of anti- aircraft artillery.[4]

On December 16, Captain Ugo Reitani of the Conegliano Group received orders to be ready to proceed on a mission "for an 'unknown destination' with three officers, one hundred men, thirty-six mules, twelve sleds, mountain cannons, two machine-guns, plus ammunition, various armaments, and food for one day." Once he got underway, he was told that a courier would meet his group with further orders.[5]

The rapid response group, which included Medical Officer Lieutenant Italo Serri, left the Don at 1700 and headed south on foot to a small village where the men spent the night. The next morning, men, mules, armaments, and sleds were all loaded on trucks. Once the trucks arrived in Saprino, three hundred more alpini joined the 26th Battery. At this point, Major Amerri took command of the rapid response unit.[6]

Major Amerri ordered truck drivers to turn off their lights and follow his car. He informed the alpini they would not stop for any reason; the convoy had to reach its destination no matter what. He also told the men he could not tell them where they were going. As the soldiers traveled south, they suffered dreadfully from the intense cold, in trucks which for the most part only had tarpaulin covers. The temperature dropped to -38°. The mules soon began braying loudly because of the extreme cold. Many of them went crazy in the back of trucks, stomping frantically. A few broke through the bed of the trucks with their hoofs, fracturing their legs. Mules in other trucks began to bray in response to the agonized sounds of the injured animals. Several trucks slid off the road and remained stuck in snow banks. By the time the convoy passed Rossosh, it had thinned out, since several drivers, overcome by frigid temperatures, lost control of their vehicles, causing them to overturn. Men and mules were hurt and precious equipment was lost. If a truck remained stuck or crashed, officers were to transfer to another vehicle and were ordered not to stop. At a certain point, the convoy was bombed for more than an hour by low-flying Russian planes.

Tortured by hours of sitting in the cold, alpini struggled to keep from freezing to death. They moved their feet and hands, and massaged their bodies. Eventually the mules became silent; many had succumbed to the cold. On December 18, the convoy arrived in Mitrofanovka in the early morning. The terrible cold night had reduced the 26th Battery to sixty artillerymen and nine mules. Overall, there were only two hundred able-bodied men. Trucks with food supplies had been lost and some men dispersed.[7]

While the men rested and warmed up in izbas, Captain Reitani and Lieutenant Serri searched for the headquarters of the Italian Second Army Corps. Once located, Major Amerri joined the other two officers and spoke to an unnamed colonel of the General Staff. Major Amerri asked the colonel to brief them about the general situation. The colonel, amazed that the officers knew nothing about the current situation, brought them up to speed and then said, "We don't know exactly where the Russians are and what objectives they want to reach.... In any case, here there is no line [of defense]; we fear the Russians are getting ready to launch more forces across this area.... It's your job to plug the leak."[8]

Major Amerri reported that he only had two hundred men. The colonel informed Amerri the whole of the Julia Division was transferring to the area on foot. At that point, the major requested supplies for his alpini. The colonel said he had nothing he could offer; all warehouses and supply depots had been set on fire to prevent them from falling into the hands of the Russians.[9]

Later that day, Major Amerii and his officers were to proceed with the alpini to Ivanovka, which was an unsecure zone. Their mission was to prevent the Russians from passing through Ivanovka, and to resist any Russian attack with their last bullets. The colonel informed Amerii that his units were now under the general command of the German

XXIV Panzer Corps, and eventually they would meet up with the Germans. Gas for their trucks, and only one hundred bread rolls were distributed.[10]

A dozen trucks loaded with alpini began to move northeast. The men attempted to split the frozen bread rolls in half. The only way to divide them was to cut them with a bayonet. Once they were distributed, it was impossible to eat them because they were hard as rocks. Bedeschi writes, "This is the way things are in Russia: one has to remain hungry with bread in our pocket."[11]

The alpini proceeded on their mission, aware of the possibility of a Russian attack at any moment. Eventually they arrived in Krinichnoje and then Ivanovka. While there, they encountered a number of soldiers from the Cosseria Division who were in terrible shape. They also encountered a unit of the Monte Cervino Ski Battalion, a company of the Aquila Battalion, and a unit of the 68th Battery, thus completing the rapid response group. Approximately 100 Germans also arrived under the command of a colonel. The Germans had several vehicles, a rocket launcher with a few shells, two tanks (one out of commission), and no ammunition. The alpini had had virtually nothing to eat for three days. In Ivanovka, they found some abandoned provisions in a church that had previously served as a warehouse for the Cosseria Division. There was enough for all the men, including the Germans.[12]

The next morning, the Russians began to attack. Three hundred alpini, along with several mountain cannons and the German rocket launcher with its few remaining rounds, deployed on a defensive line in order to defend Ivanovka. One soldier deployed every five meters on that line extending for approximately two kilometers. A furious battle ensued as the men held the Russians at bay. That night, alpini of the 26th Battery moved north toward Novaya Kalitva. On the way, they were able to gather up provisions and ammunition from one of their overturned trucks. They marched on during the night, carrying the supplies on their backs, until they reached an abandoned village where they rested in a few izbas.[13]

The following day, Captain Reitani led his men to the top of a low-lying hill and told them this was where the 26th Battery would remain as per orders. Immediately the alpini began to attempt to dig rudimentary shelters. The snow was three meters deep and the ground frozen. The wind blew unmercifully. The temperature was -32° and falling.[14]

The Russians attacked the positions on the hill repeatedly. It seemed the end was near; it was at this point when the rest of the Julia Division arrived on foot from the north.[15]

At 1400 on the afternoon of December 17, Lieutenant Eraldo Sculati (17th Battery, Udine Group, 3rd Regiment, Julia Division), was told that all remaining batteries of the 3rd Regiment were to be ready by ten that evening to transfer on foot to the south. He also received orders to build enough sleds for his unit. Sculati calculated his unit would need twenty-five sleds. All together, his men only possessed four axes. The lieutenant divided his men into four squads of twenty and gave the following order to the alpini who were, in his opinion, "the greatest woodcutters in the world." He said, "The axes must never stop." The alpini proceeded to walk into the forest behind their lines in single file, selecting the best trees. The man at the head of each line chopped the trunk of a tree ten times "in just the right place," and after passing the axe to the next man in line, moved to the end of the line. This efficient, revolving method continued until enough trees were readied for the job at hand. By 1900, all twenty-five sleds were completed; the 17th Battery left their lines on the Don at 2200.[16]

On December 18, Lieutenant Corti wrote the following in his diary while on the Don with the Val Cismon Battalion of the Julia Division: "Last night the order came to prepare to leave. This morning we still don't know who is going to relieve us, nor do we know where we are going...to the Caucasus...to Stalingrad...to Italy?"

On December 19, the Vestone Battalion (6th Regiment, Tridentina Division) relieved the Val Cismon Battalion. That same day, alpini of the Val Cismon began marching south. Corti recalled that day: "I remember that day so well because of an event which evidently was of great importance to me at that moment and also in the years that followed. On the first day we left our lines to march south, somebody organized a hot meal for us along our route. We were in a small clearing in a forest. Soon our mess tins overflowed with boiling hot minestrone. One of my alpini approached me holding his mess tin full of soup.

"Speaking in his dialect, he said, '*Lu, Sior c'el ga studia`, me diga, cosa semo vegnu a far qua noialtri?*' ('Lieutenant Sir, you who have studied [at the university], tell me, what have we come here to do?')

"This was a difficult question to answer at that moment. I really didn't have a good answer for him, or for myself. Later, during our days of battle, this question came back to haunt me. Why were we here fighting the Russians, invading their country? We had no quarrel with the Russian people. Many of us were asking ourselves the same question. At that moment though, I told the alpino I would make sure his socks and boots were dry, that he would be fed properly, and I would do everything I could to keep him safe.

"A few days later, after a particularly fierce battle, I reflected on this answer of mine. I certainly couldn't have given the alpino a revolutionary response to his question, even though I was beginning to feel a certain degree of understanding and empathy as I saw the Russians fighting for their motherland with such tenacity and bravery against us, the invader. After all, the Russian people were resolving their problem. What I had said was the truth. What else could I have said? I suppose I could have said, well, let's get rid of our commanders and just go home, but that was ridiculous. I knew the character of these mountain people. They were accustomed to a hard life, a life of sacrifice, of poverty, of carrying forward and doing their job obediently. Within the Alpine Corps, there was a strong bond of solidarity between the men within a unit who all came from the same mountain zone, and an equally strong bond between the troops and their officers, who acknowledged the value of this solidarity. Soldiers did address officers as 'Sir,' but that was just a formality. There was a real feeling of trust between soldiers and officers, a true esprit de corps.

"On some level we all knew we were involved in a dirty war. Moreover, there were rumors, probably based on Fascist propaganda, that if the Russians captured us they would kill us. None of us wanted to be taken prisoner, or surrender. What we all realized was that we were just plain stuck—stuck in a terrible situation! The only thing we could do was try not to freeze to death, to avoid hunger when we could, try not to be killed, and to do a minimum of killing ourselves.

"I thoroughly despise—even then I began to feel this way—those who used and exploited the esprit de corps and elementary sense of duty of the alpini, involving them in dirty operations like the war against Albania, against Greece, and the war against Russia."

The forty-five men under Corti's command marched south on foot with the entire Val Cismon Battalion: Corti recalled the long column of men trudging south in the snow. "It took us four days to arrive at our destination. At first we walked during the day, but the Russians strafed and bombed us from airplanes, causing some casualties and general confusion among the units as they stopped and searched for protection. After that, we began to march during the night hours. We walked all night, sometimes for more than thirteen hours straight. We were carrying very heavy packs loaded with ammunition, weapons, and other equipment. Sleds, built by the alpini, transported the heavier weapons. If we stopped for any reason, the men dropped down in the snow, exhausted. Sometimes, when it was time to get going again, officers had to shout and even resort to a few kicks and shoves to get them moving once more.

"Actually, I remember very few details of that long march, except for the two following incidents when we encountered some Germans. My overriding concern at the time was to keep the men moving.

"The first incident occurred one morning after we had marched all night. We stopped by some large stables, which were part of some kind of Soviet agricultural establishment. German troops with horses had been occupying the place, but at that particular moment, it was vacant. Many alpini went inside and stretched out. The stalls reeked of horse manure, but it was better for us to rest inside rather than sleep out in the cold. At a certain moment, a German marshal appeared. I remember the unfamiliar, dazzling insignia on the shoulders of his uniform; I surmised he might be a high-ranking officer. He started hollering at us like a lunatic. One of my men could speak some German and told me the marshal wanted us to leave. I tried to explain why we had stopped to rest, but to no avail. The marshal continued to yell like a crazy man; his demeanor was contemptuous. So I told the alpino, who above all wanted to be sure that he was translating my exact words correctly, to tell the German to fuck off. The German officer became very red in the face after my alpino translated my words. He continued to yell at us as he distanced himself, but that was the end of that episode.

"Although we generally marched during the night hours, the next night a decision was made to take a break for a few hours. We arrived at a village where there were a few izbas. German soldiers, who were already there, told us they were expecting some Panzer units in the morning, and we couldn't enter the izbas. Once more, a German began shouting at us: '*Nein! Nein!*' I told them I was an officer and I wanted to speak to one of their officers. At that moment, a young German officer arrived. Fortunately, he spoke French and I was able to converse with him. He told us of course we could stay since we were planning to leave in the morning. In the meantime, I noticed one of my men was holding a piglet in his arms and I realized he had stolen it from some village. There was no way to return the piglet to its rightful owner, but I reprimanded him sternly. Then I walked away from the izbas for a few minutes with the German officer, who actually was very polite.

"When I returned, my men were waiting for me outside of the izbas with German soldiers who continued to shout at us. An alpino spoke to me: 'Lieutenant, Sir, walk away for a while, we will take care of this situation.' I did what he asked me to do. When I returned, my alpini were in an izba roasting the piglet! I have no idea how they managed to get inside that izba, and I never asked."

Corti noted most of the men in the battalion came from the zone of Feltre. Their fathers, who were also alpini, had fought in World War I. Unfriendly feelings toward the Germans remained in the minds of their sons.

Once the Val Cismon Battalion reached the zone the Julia Division was to defend, Corti's company moved to Kholkhoz Stalina, the Val Cismon's command post. A new, continuous front formed between Novaya Kalitva and Belovodsk, with the Julia Division, the Monte Cervino Battalion, and units of the German XXIV Panzer Corps.

The front converged with the southern tip of the Cuneense Division, extending in a wide semicircle from the right side of the Kalitva River to the southwest, as far as the Derkul River. The weakest area was the portion of the front held by the German 27th Panzer Division at the southwesterly end of the semicircular front, whereas the most threatened section of this new front was between Novaya Kalitva and Derezovka. It was there the Russians continued to attack, attempting to break through that sector and push toward Rossosh. Alpini of the Julia along with units of the German 385th Infantry Division were entrenched along that line.[17] Corti's unit deployed between Derezovka and Ivanovka.

The terrain in the area was agricultural, dotted with haystacks and devoid of trees or shrubs. To dig any kind of trench or refuge, the alpini would have needed tools suitable to break frozen ground. Even if they had had such tools, there would have been little time to engage in such work owing to the frequency of violent Russian attacks. Therefore, the men lived and fought without any kind of shelter. The equipment issued to the alpini was not suitable for such long periods of exposure; consequently, they sustained many cases of frostbite. Even though some valenki, extra blankets, and warm clothing were distributed, there was little relief from the unrelenting winds and subzero temperatures.[18]

It was challenging to provision the alpini on the lines. During their transfer and first days on the new lines, the men relied on hard tack and canned meat with no chance of having a warm meal or drink. Even when the rudimentary kitchens of the various units began to function in abandoned villages behind the front, meals were prepared out in the open and transferred to the lines, usually at night. By the time rations arrived, they were frozen. The alpini had to use their hatchets to cut their pasta, bread and wine.[19]

Regular deliveries to the battle lines of ammunition, armaments, and rations occurred once the full Julia Division was in place. There was no water; the men ate snow to satisfy their thirst. In just a few days, Bedeschi observed the toll of biting winds and temperatures registering -40°: "The intense cold, sleeplessness, and fighting caused haggard expressions of suffering on the faces of the alpini." Yet the 10,000 men held their lines, "devouring ammunition and food" brought to the front by mules and their drivers.[20]

Alfonso Di Michele served in the Aquila Battalion as a telegrapher, deployed directly behind the machine-gunners of his company. His job was to transmit orders to the battalion's command post indicating enemy targets. On December 23 the Aquila battalion was under constant fire from katyusha rockets and artillery fire causing many losses and an infernal racket, making it almost impossible to send or receive messages. It was necessary for Di Michele and his men to move to a position at a slight distance from the front lines. From there, Di Michele could observe Russian troops advancing toward the line held by the alpini: "A mass of men advanced toward our lines yelling, '*Ura! Ura!*'[21] Without fear, they threw themselves frontally assaulting our positions...these soldiers fortified with vodka were drunk. Alcohol had taken away any sense of danger; they pushed forward without hesitation. Commissars behind them urged them on and incited them to attack...."[22]

Following this assault, the alpini had to withdraw to reestablish a line of defense and regroup. Di Michele and his men, unable to rejoin their company, became isolated at this point and were quickly under enemy fire. Soon Russian soldiers attacked them with hand grenades.

As the Russians advanced, one of the alpini yelled to the others, "We have to give ourselves up as prisoners, these Russians will kill us all; they will kill us!"

This same alpino rose up with his hands in the air, but the Russians didn't seem to realize he was surrendering and continued firing. Then, this same alpino broke off the antenna from one of the transmitters and wrapped the first piece of clothing he could find around the top. He raised it and waved it back and forth to make the Russians understand the men were surrendering: "In the blink of an eye a multitude of men surrounded us, and pointing their bayonets, they indicated we should drop our weapons and raise our arms."[23]

The soldiers, who were Mongolians, quickly searched the Italians. One alpino still had his pistol in its holster. A Russian pulled it from its holster and pointed it at the alpino's throat. He attempted to pull the trigger two or three times but nothing happened; fortunately, he didn't realize the safety lock was on. Angered by his inability to make the weapon fire, he pistol-whipped the alpino in the face.[24]

Shortly thereafter, the Russians herded the captured alpini across the battlefield, pushing and shoving them with rifle butts and pricking them in the back with the tips of their bayonets.

Di Michele describes the field of battle: "It was a harrowing scene; a field covered with grey-green or brown uniforms scattered on the snow surrounded by red stains.... The real anguish was seeing all our wounded comrades who begged us for help, asking us not to leave them there on that battlefield." Self-preservation ruled: "The hearts of the survivors remained deaf to those laments. We were terrified. We didn't even have the courage to lower our arms and extend a hand to our companions.... This is war!"[25]

On Christmas Day, Corti wrote the following in his diary: "Yesterday the Russians attacked us violently with many supporting troops. My company left for a counterattack. I remained at the headquarters of the battalion with my platoon and others, ready to intervene.

"I shall never forget that day", Corti recalled. "As the Russians attacked they yelled, '*Tikaj! Tikaj!*' ('Run away, run away'), 'Ura! Ura!' When they reached the alpini, they killed many. We could see what was happening, and that's when Captain Valenti, commander of the Val

Cismon Battalion, told me to take my group into action.

"As the thousands of Russians attacked in wave after wave, Captain Valenti ordered a German officer to get his tanks moving. The tanks were lightweight and the Germans didn't want to take them into the raging battle. When the officer refused to move his tanks, Captain Valenti shot him. Then we left with Valenti and those tanks and threw everything we had at the Russians.

"I went up the hill. I could see all the dead soldiers lying on the snow; Russians and Italians—it was a terrible scene. I still have that vision before my eyes. The Russians had automatic rifles with 70 rounds. We had our ridiculous antiquated rifles! I saw my men killed or wounded, all around me. One of my alpini hollered, 'Lieutenant, Sir, they are going to kill us all. Let's go slowly, find a defensive position, a place we can defend.' I told my men we had to move forward. I felt such rage and anger; to see this butchery around me was just terrible.

"The Russians finally began to retreat. Near me there was a Russian soldier, face down in the snow; he had a parabellum. I kneeled down to reach for his rifle, thinking he was dead, but he was still alive, poor man. He raised his head, I could see his dark eyes; maybe he was a Mongolian. He lobbed a hand grenade toward me and I threw myself backwards to avoid the explosion in front of his head; then I shot him. He probably was already dead; in any case, he was wounded badly. It hurts my heart to recall this moment; it weighs on my conscience. I still remember his black eyes."

In a diary entry, Corti wrote, "During the attack Lieutenant Sanguinetti was killed and is buried here; Lieutenant Montanari was seriously wounded, so was Lieutenant Gamba (later he died in a hospital in Italy). Lieutenant Castabile wounded slightly, died a few days later after returning to the front lines. Many alpini are dead, maybe more than fifty, there are many wounded. One platoon of the company doesn't exist anymore."

Lieutenant Capparella, Captain Valenti, and Corti were the only officers who survived this attack. Capparella died a few days later. Many years later, his brother, with the help of local peasants, was able to find his remains and return them to Italy. Captain Valenti died during the withdrawal in January 1943.

The Val Cismon Battalion had relieved the Monte Cervino Battalion on December 24. Alpini of the Monte Cervino battalion, including

Lieutenant Carlo Vicentini, walked all night from Krinichnoje to Rossosh, arriving there on Christmas day. Vicentini was looking forward to a few hours of rest and warmth in an izba after so many days of battle. Captain Lamberti, commander of the Monte Cervino Battalion, asked Vicentini to accompany two ambulances to the front lines near Krinichnoje to evacuate a group of badly wounded soldiers. Both ambulance drivers were new and unfamiliar with the roads leading to Krinichnoje. Although Vicentini had not slept for days while on the front lines, he followed Lamberti's orders.[26]

While riding in the cab of one of the ambulances, slipping and skidding on the icy road, he noticed the young, inexperienced driver was becoming increasingly anxious as he attempted to control the vehicle. When he removed his gloves, Vicentini admonished him, reminding him to be aware of frostbite. As the ambulance moved closer to the front, evidence of the battle ahead became visible. Although Vicentini attempted to reassure the driver, the young man became more and more agitated as explosions thundered, and fire and smoke rose on the horizon.[27]

Once both ambulances reached Krinichnoje, they were directed to the road leading toward Derezovka where the wounded were being held in a shed. Upon arrival at the shed, which Vicentini surmised had once been the garage of a kholkhoz, he noted it had no windows and the door was wide open: "The dirt floor was covered with wounded men; bandaged heads, legs, hands; dead men covered with greatcoats; pale faces, feverish eyes; [there were] Italians, but also many Germans. In a shed at some distance, two doctors covered with blood were working around a table." Vicentini was told by the doctor to take away as many wounded as possible, excluding any with abdominal wounds. Not knowing how to choose, Vicentini asked the doctor to point to the ones who required immediate evacuation. The doctor let it be known he couldn't offer any assistance, he was feverishly attempting to save lives.[28]

Each ambulance could hold two stretchers comfortably. Realizing he could only evacuate four wounded and despite protests of the second ambulance driver, Vicentini managed to load six more soldiers in the back of the ambulances and two more in the cabs. It was difficult to choose which soldiers to evacuate. "Once the soldiers realized what I had come to do, a real row ensued.... Since I only chose Italians, the Germans hollered and swore; some grabbed my pant leg and wouldn't let go, others able to stand up besieged the two ambulances, and it took a great deal of strength to impart any sort of order." Before the ambulances departed, Vicentini promised he would return and make as many trips as required to evacuate all of them.[29]

Once in Rossosh, the ambulances were required in another zone. Vicentini pleaded with the authorities to permit him to return to evacuate more wounded. Authorized to take one ambulance, two hours later he was back on the road to Derezovka: "I will never be able to forget what we saw as we drove around the bend in the road. The shed didn't exist anymore. Fragments of wood and sheet metal were scattered all over the place, along with body parts, and burned rags containing shapeless objects. There was an enormous black mark on the ground.... A group of alpini sought in vain to find any signs of life in that apocalyptic scene." Katyusha shells had hit the area. By some miracle, doctors operating in the izba close by survived the shelling. Once more, the ambulance was quickly crammed full of wounded men. Vicentini recalled his young driver "hid behind the ambulance, vomiting."[30]

Returning to Rossosh, Vicentini spoke to his driver: "Today you have learned what war is all about!" During both trips to evacuate the wounded, Vicentini had been rather brusque with his driver, attempting to diffuse the young man's fear and anxiety. Now, overwhelmed by the impact of the ghastly scene just witnessed, both men began to "weep uncontrollably." The ambulance contained the wounded, but as Vicentini writes, "it also carried two men, each with a terrible wound that would never heal. And every Christmas that same wound reopened...."[31]

On Christmas Eve and Christmas day, alpini of the Julia remained on alert; the Russians didn't attack in Corti's section. In a diary entry he wrote, "We had a calm night, now we are on alert. The Aquila fought very well. Many alpini are dead. The situation is not good. I wrote to Carlo, Lucia, Mother and Papà to reassure them, but they will read about what's going on here in the newspapers. They say the Aquila and Monte Cervino battalions were mentioned [in newspaper articles]. I am especially sorry about Montanari, our fine new commander."

Corti wrote to his parents, telling them not to worry, he was fine and all was well. However, in his diary he noted he had written to his sister Lucia telling her things weren't going very well but the alpini were hoping for the best.

"I realized things were not going well for us where we were," he said. "I remember this very well. I looked around and asked myself what might happen, what could actually happen. Could we withdraw, with all this snow? We could walk for one hundred kilometers, but then we would fall to the ground dead! I might be killed or the Russians could wound me. I had so much to do, to command and to take care of my men, but I decided to write to my friend Carlo Vallerini. I wrote on one of those military postcards given to us. I wrote: if you hear that I am dead, please go to see my parents to console them."

Continuing with the diary entry of December 25, Corti wrote, "I am feeling all right: sometimes I think that it won't be easy for me to return home. Turin most likely is partially destroyed. Now it is better to think about making sure the men are all right. To get here, there were nights of hard marching. The alpini did really well, and their spirit is also good, in spite of our losses."

As the daily battles raged along the front, every day claimed its dead and wounded, but as Bedeschi writes, "The intense cold was the worst long-lasting enemy; all of the Julia suffered under its implacable assault.... Forced to remain immobile in their frigid emplacements, the alpini remained vigilant under the sights of Russian machine guns and hourly threats of assaults." The numbers of alpini suffering from frostbite multiplied the longer the men remained in those bitterly exposed positions.[32]

When the medical officer of the Tolmezzo Battalion died, Lieutenant Italo Serri, medical officer of the 26th Battery, assisted on the lines held by the Tolmezzo. He observed the suffering experienced by the men. As he moved along the lines, he could see alpini with rudimentary bandages around their wounds; they frequently failed to leave their positions even when gangrene threatened. Serri attempted to convince them to go to the camp hospital: "One couldn't reason with them; they only knew they wanted to remain with their comrades." However, out of pity and concern for their condition, their comrades secretly made it known to the medical officer that specific soldiers were in need of medical help. In one case, they pointed out an alpino who operated a machine gun, and told Serri the man's feet were probably frostbitten. An alpino spoke to the lieutenant: "For a week now he leaves his hole [in the snow] only at night, just to go to the bathroom and is forced to crawl on all fours like a dog, he can't stand up."

Serri spoke to the soldier and asked him to remove his shoes so he could look at his feet but the alpino stated he couldn't take his shoes off.

"My shoes are frozen and I can't untie them."

Serri said he would notify the commander of the company to have the soldier sent to the hospital.

"Oh, don't do that doctor, Sir...."

Pointing to another alpino he continued, "He is frostbitten as well, and as long as he is staying here [the commander] can't send me away."[33]

In another case, an alpino pointed out a soldier who hadn't slept for three days because his feet were hurting so badly; in fact, he had thrown his shoes away. Serri ordered the soldier to remove his socks. At first, the alpino refused, saying his feet didn't hurt anymore:

"Thank you Lieutenant Sir, but I don't need anything."

The officer insisted. As he removed the soldier's sock impregnated with ice, the color of the man's foot was black; his big toe and the toe next to it had fallen off and remained in the sock.

"The alpino looked at his two toes, turning them over in his palm. He then wrapped them carefully in his handkerchief, placed it in his pocket, and said, 'I have to remember to bury them, otherwise on the Day of Judgment if I don't have these two I'll be in trouble.' He then added, 'If I forget, my mother will hit me on the side of my head when I get home.'"[34]

In a camp hospital located near the headquarters of the 8th Julia Regiment, Lieutenant Angelo Damini (34th Battery, Udine Group) was summoned to interrogate a wounded Russian officer.

Medical Officer Giannetto was tending the officer who lay nude on a stretcher. Damini asked the Russian if he was able to speak, and the officer replied in Italian that he was. "He told me he was an officer. I asked him if he would like some cognac and a cigarette. He took a small sip of cognac and a cigarette, thanking me politely. Encouraged, I asked him if he could tell me to which unit he belonged and the location of the headquarters of that unit. Smiling, he asked me how I would have responded had I fallen into enemy hands." He continued to smile and his eyes shone, owing to high fever. "He wanted to demonstrate his honor that continued to sustain him during these last moments of life. I told him I admired him and that he should ask me for anything he needed. I didn't ask him any more questions having to do with military matters. He continued to smile as I offered him another cigarette."

As the Russian left the camp hospital aboard a sled destined for a hospital in Rossosh, he reached out for Damini's hand, thanked him, and then fainted. "The officer died during the trip; the medical officer explained he couldn't be saved—eight bullets had perforated his chest and abdomen."[35]

Between January 8 and 11, 1943, in a military hospital in Kharkov, Corti wrote an entry in his diary, recalling the events occurring December 28 while still on the front lines: "I was with the platoon at the kholkhoz headquarters of the battalion. Around two in the morning, I received the order to go reach the 264th Company at the famous quota (elevation) of 200.5 meters. I left with my men and presented myself to Captain Bertolotti positioned within a large haystack. When he emerged, his face was purple due to the atrocious cold."

Corti recalled that while climbing uphill his men asked to slow down so they wouldn't sweat, because once they stopped, the freezing effect against the moisture on their skin could be fatal.

"The Captain told me a burned haystack [further away] was in the hands of the Russians, and that Lieutenant Sigle was on the move going toward it—the Captain gave me the order to join up with Sigle and to organize an attack to reoccupy it. We went, but Sigle had already reached that point, and some of his men occupied several positions to the right. Sigle had actually moved right into another haystack to protect himself from the cold."

Corti noted Sigle was exhausted because he hadn't slept for days. Both officers stretched out on the ground where another stack had burned because the ground was still warm.

"At dawn we heard shooting but we didn't know where it was coming from. On the right, we caught a glimpse of an outpost the Germans were supposed to have held, but it seemed they had left during the night. We decided to go and have a look. The men, placed badly, were too visible on the snow. We didn't have white camouflage snowsuits like the Russians; we were easy targets. At that moment, while preparing to leave, Sergeant Romanini arrived. He wanted me to take a squad to join the captain. I said a few words to Lieutenant Sigle and turned to leave. After a few steps, a bullet hit my upper left arm throwing me to the ground. My attendant Candido De Luca immediately threw himself on top of me to protect me.

"We didn't move for a few moments. By now it was daylight, and we spotted a Russian patrol on skis; they were moving toward Derezovka. We gathered they had moved forward to occupy the outpost the Germans had abandoned without advising the alpini they were leaving."

Corti spoke of his wound: "I could see my arm was twisted and I thought it was broken. I didn't have any other thought at the moment, but I realized immediately it wasn't serious." He recalled he could feel blood running down his arm toward his hand, but he wasn't exactly sure of where he was wounded because of all the heavy clothing he was wearing. The string around his neck holding his gloves served as a makeshift support for his arm.

In his diary entry written in Kharkov, Corti wrote, "I took the squad to Company Headquarters. Captain Bertolotti was sorry to see I was wounded. Lieutenant Corvino, wounded just before me, is with me in the hospital. The captain told me to place the squad at two haystacks, more to the north. At the stacks, I met up with my company— Lieutenant Assanelli who took over from Lieutenant Montanari, and Lieutenants Facchini and Capparella, with whom I served at the Don outpost. I left them and went to battalion headquarters where I presented myself to Captain Valenti and told him what had occurred. Our medical officer, Lieutenant Aldo Follis, treated my arm. Lieutenant Ettore Annone was there, a wound in his chest and death in his eyes. After a while Bono, one of my corporals, arrived with a wound to his head, and many other alpini." Corti said he heard that Lieutenant Sigle, shot in the heart, died the following night.

Corti and other wounded alpini were in an izba serving as a camp hospital with straw spread out on the floor. The medical officer Follis remained with the men. Corti recalls that he was a nice man from Turin, who didn't return from Russia. He never found out how the officer died. Corti's friend Ettore Annone was also in the izba with him. Ettore had commanded the ski platoon in the Val Cismon Battalion. Corti had known him in Turin and had gone skiing with him in Aosta while they were both draftees.

Lieutenant Follis told Corti the bullet had damaged the nerves in his arm. While being treated, Corti had been distracted, focusing on his friend Ettore near death, lying next to him in the izba, and didn't realize his hand was actually paralyzed. He also thought he would return to the front after a few days in the camp hospital. He asked his orderly to fetch a few things for him from his *cassetta*.

Each officer had a cassetta, a wooden box designed to fit on the back of a pack mule. Corti kept his clothing and a few personal items in it. Because he thought he would be returning to his unit, he only asked for socks, underwear, and his cigarettes. In his cassetta he also had a small Bible his mother had given to him when he had gone away to boarding school (at age twelve), and also some family photographs. As it turned out, Corti was evacuated to Rossosh and then to Kharkov. He never saw his cassetta or any of his personal belongings again.

The Julia Division battled on the southern front during the remaining days of December and the first few days of January 1943. Despite heavy losses, alpini of the Julia held their defensive lines. During the twenty-six days of almost uninterrupted attacks, casualties of the division amounted to approximately 3,500 men. Of these, 468 alpini died during battle. The number of wounded and frostbitten alpini amounted to approximately 3,000. Estimates indicated the Russians lost approximately 5,000 soldiers.[36]

ROSSOSH

It was important to get the wounded away quickly from combat zones. "Around eleven," Corti said, "the ambulance arrived, and we made our way to Rossosh, arriving there at night. Since I was able to sit up, I rode in the front of the ambulance. My friend Ettore was in the back. The Russians were bombing Rossosh as the ambulance arrived at the hospital, so I entered the building quickly. I saw Ettore removed from the ambulance, but I never saw him again and never found out what happened to him. Many months later, his father came to see me while I was in the hospital in Rome, recovering from surgery to my arm. It was a very painful visit. This poor old man wanted to know what had happened to his son; I told him all I knew. I told him that I hadn't seen Ettore dead."

In his diary, Corti described the hospital in Rossosh: "There are many wounded friends here. Corvino, wounded just before me is here with me. Costabile and others are here, more or less seriously wounded." The Russians bombed Rossosh throughout the night of December 28, yet Corti slept deeply, exhausted after so many days of practically no rest, little nourishment, and heavy fighting.

The following day all sick and wounded soldiers left on a train bound for Kharkov. The rail cars were actually freight cars fitted with two levels of bunks. Corti was in a lower bunk. Upon leaving Rossosh, the men received a little bread and cheese; nothing else was available. The only medicine the Medical Officer could give the soldiers was morphine. Whenever a soldier was suffering badly, the officer gave him an injection. Corti recalled he wasn't in any real pain, but now he realized his hand was paralyzed. The trip to Kharkov took two days. Corti slept most of the time, and never moved from his bunk.

The hospital in Kharkov was originally a Russian military tank school, now converted into a hospital for Italian soldiers. Soon after his arrival, Corti came down with a severe intestinal infection with dysentery, along with days of high fever. During this illness, he really thought he was going to die. The Medical Officer in the hospital had no medicine to relieve his symptoms, but Corti still had some sulfur drugs in his pack. The officer told him to take as much as he could tolerate and just hope it would make him feel better. The sulfur drugs seemed to improve his condition. Eventually he felt better, but had lost a great deal of weight and was very weak.

On January 8, 1943, Corti wrote, "I am still here in the hospital. I had seven days of very high fever. I am thin as a stick. My wound doesn't bother me. The radial is injured; I can't raise my hand and movement of my fingers is compromised. They are sending me to Italy because of this. I hope between electrical therapy, and/or an operation, I will be able to return to normalcy. It's not bad being in the hospital. Many soldiers from the infantry are here, almost all with frostbite. We have had many talks about our experiences…it seems the Russians broke through in many other places. The alpini are holding their lines, they are really marvelous because the conditions are more and more adverse."

On January 11, Corti wrote, "Kharkov…I am still here. We are waiting for a train to take us to Italy. I am starting to heal, but I am weak. We are not hearing exact news from the front. Last night a trainload of wounded arrived—a train similar to the one I took from Rossosh."

On January 19, he made the following entry in his diary: "We left Kharkov on the 16th. A big part of me stays with the alpini, with Marsan, with my friends, but it is also a joy to return to Italy and to see all of my dear ones again. My hand is still limp, and I don't have much hope it will ever be the same again. I am still reliving the memories of the past days."

On January 22, Corti arrived in Senigallia, north of Ancona on the Adriatic coast of Italy. When he entered the hospital, located in an old monastery, the pervasive, overpowering stench of the place overwhelmed him. Most of the soldiers hospitalized there were suffering from frostbite and subsequent gangrene. When bandages were removed from wounds treated on the front lines or in Kharkov, gangrene was rampant.

Corti spoke about one young soldier: "They took off the bandages wrapped around his hands. All of his fingers were black. They took off all ten fingers with a set of pliers! The soldier screamed and yelled, '*Mi, cosa faccio nella vita senza le dita, che ho solo lavorato con le mani?*' ('What am I going to do in life without my fingers, I only know how to work with my hands?') This excruciating scene, along with agonizing laments, was repeated many times over as other young men lost various gangrenous limbs."

Corti's sister Lucia was notified that her brother had returned from Russia, and was hospitalized in Senigallia. She immediately traveled there by train, arriving in the evening. She recalled she felt ill as she entered the hospital. The stench was formidable as she walked by large bins full of human limbs. It was an overwhelming experience, yet it was also a joyous occasion for her to see her brother again and to know he was safe. She shared the latest family news with him. Of course, she wanted to have news of her husband, but her brother could give her none. He hadn't seen Marsan during his time on the Don.

Once he was feeling stronger, he took a trip to Udine, where many troop trains returning from Russia arrived, to see if he could find any information about Marsan from officials in the various military offices located there. He said there was a total lack of organization, and nobody could tell him anything. He remained in Udine for a few days, talking to soldiers who had returned from Russia, but he couldn't find any alpini.

In Senigallia, the doctors realized they couldn't treat Corti's arm properly without a further diagnosis. Sent to Ancona, a neurologist told him he would need surgery. On February 13, he transferred to the Centro Mutilati Hospital in Rome, and from there to the Surgical Clinic of the University of Rome. On February 24, Corti wrote, "On February 15, I was operated on by Professor Paulucci, and by now the wound is almost closed. Here in Rome I saw Papà and Marco." He was able to see his father and younger brother, because his father, taken to Rome for a small operation, was recuperating from surgery when Corti arrived. Corti said, "Once my father was able to travel, the police escorted him back to Sala Consilina to resume his exile in southern Italy."

On April 4 he wrote, "I am having physiotherapy. My hand is not moving. I am not all right."

Chapter 8

ENCIRCLEMENT OF THE ALPINE CORPS

EARLY JANUARY 1943

Divisional commanders and officers of the Alpine Corps received little "official" news of the overall progress of the war while on the Don front. German liaison officers attached to the headquarters of each division provided their main sources of information. They could monitor radiograms transmitted from various German units operating in the region. It was only in this manner that commanders of the Alpine Corps heard about the encirclement of German troops in Stalingrad, the fall of the Romanian Third Army, the collapse and withdrawal of the Italian Eighth Army on their right flank, as well as assaults on the Hungarian Second Army to the north of their lines.[1]

Lieutenant Egisto Corradi of the Julia Division wrote about the lack of verifiable news: "We didn't know Stalingrad was now irreparably encircled and close to falling. We didn't know 7,000 survivors out of 35,000 or more of the Italian Thirty-Fifth Corps remained encircled in Cerkovo, and Italian divisions, other than the Ravenna and Cosseria, were swept away from the front. We knew nothing about any of this even up to January 15...."[2]

Between January 1 and 17, there was increased Soviet air surveillance and artillery fire across the Don, leading the alpini to believe it was only a matter of time before they would be attacked.[3]

Across the Don on January 9, Revelli and his men could see Russian trucks and armored vehicles heading south with headlights turned on.[4]

Toward January 10, alpini in the Vestone Battalion (Tridentina Division) began to hear ominous news. Two alpini in Sergeant Rigoni Stern's unit who had gone to the kitchens to draw rations, overheard several mule drivers say the Russians had encircled the Alpine Corps. Reports based on *radio scarpa* (the rumor mill) created an uneasy atmosphere of anxiety and tension among the men. Several alpini even asked their sergeant to tell them how many kilometers existed between their strongholds and Italy. Rigoni Stern was also feeling uneasy. He had noticed Russians across the river were cutting brush and undergrowth at night to "widen their field of fire." At night to the south, he could see flashes of light resembling "summer lightening." At other times, he could hear what sounded like rolling wheels across the river. Nevertheless, rations and mail arrived on schedule.[5]

One evening shortly after January 10, Lieutenant Moscioni, commander of the stronghold, told the sergeant he had received orders in the event the alpini should have to withdraw from the Don. There followed a careful examination of all automatic weapons. The alpini under his command turned their bunker into a virtual "workshop," dismembering machine guns, mortars, and the heavy machine gun, cleaning them, and "re-tempering the springs to adapt them more to the cold." Once tested, soldiers wrapped the "four machine guns, the heavy machine gun and the four 45mm mortars" in blankets and tent tarps to protect them from "the fine sand, which filtered into the dugout and penetrated everywhere."[6]

On the evening of January 15, units of the Tirano Battalion (Tridentina Division) received orders to "shunt all material to the rear, even weapons and stove emplacements, as if in a normal transfer. Mule drivers were sent back to their bases and [the battalion] went from one alarm to the next. Temperatures dropped below -40°." To the south, the alpini could hear thunderous firing from the Edolo Battalion of the Tridentina. Revelli writes, "From company headquarters a strange order arrived; every alpino had to build a sled with whatever materials he could find."[7]

General Reverberi, commander of the Tridentina Division writes, "On January 15, 16, and 17, enemy forces amounting to approximately two regiments supported by numerous batteries of mortars of all caliber, and katyushas, commenced attacking the zone between the Tridentina and Vicenza Division [now deployed in the zone the Julia had previously occupied before moving south].”[8]

Sergeant Rigoni Stern describes several attacks occurring on the lines held by the Vestone Battalion of the Tridentina. Before dawn, the Russians began firing mortars at various strongholds of the battalion. At dawn, the firing ceased as Russian soldiers began crossing the river to the left of Rigone Stern's stronghold where there was a small island in the middle of the now frozen river. They took cover on the island and subsequently ran toward the riverbank, close to the positions the alpini held. Mortar shells from the alpini hit that section of the riverbank and it seemed that this was the end of their attempt to gain ground.[9]

That same evening the Russians commenced firing with artillery and mortar rounds. This time, as they attacked they slid down in the snow to the riverbank and began running toward the alpini across the river shouting their battle cry, “Ura! Ura!” The alpini managed to fend them off, killing and wounding a good number. When a few Russians reached the barbed wire, the alpini threw the equivalent of a whole case of hand-grenades; they failed to explode.[10]

Shortly after, enemy forces began advancing once more. The alpini fired but Sergeant Rigoni Stern realized the Russians were gathering up their wounded. He shouted: “Don't shoot! They're gathering their wounded. Don't shoot!” Surprised the alpini had ceased firing, the Russians quickly gathered their wounded, placed them on sleds and dragged them back to their side of the river. They even removed their dead, except for the ones who had reached the barbed wire.[11]

Following this latest attack, Lieutenant Moscioni collapsed owing to days and nights of no sleep. He had been monitoring the situation intensely, constantly moving from one position to another, checking weapons and taking care of his men. Rigoni Stern writes, “He fell from sheer exhaustion, like a mule.” Moscioni told Rigoni Stern (once they returned to Italy), “It was like being turned into ice…I couldn't feel my legs any more. I couldn't feel anything. It was as if I'd only a head and very little of that. It was terrible.” Rigoni Stern took command of the stronghold until another lieutenant could arrive to replace Moscioni.[12]

The Russians began to attack once more, but this time with a different twist. The alpini could hear someone behind the soldiers, “shouting encouragement in Russian” [probably a political commissar]. The sergeant could make out a few words: “country, Russia, Stalin, workers.” The alpini held their fire as the Russians moved out of the woods and slid down to the riverbank. The moment they reached the bottom Stern ordered the alpini to fire, pinning them down. The same Russian voice began shouting again as Russians at the edge of the woods began to retreat back to their trenches, but then a new wave of soldiers appeared and without hesitation began running across the frozen river. It was broad daylight and few survived the barrage of firing from the alpini. A few Russians lay on the snow playing dead, then rose and dashed toward alpini strongholds. They never succeeded. The alpini lost several men during that attack.[13]

General Reverberi noted that the Russians attacked the Vestone Battalion seven times on January 15, leaving "800 dead enemy soldiers in front of their lines."[14]

Bianco Assunto, who served with the 1st Alpine Regiment of the Cuneense Division, recorded efforts on the part of General Battisti to press for an early withdrawal of the Alpine Corps from the Don. The source of Assunto's information comes from a meeting held in Cuneo, Italy after the war was over, between Giuseppe Lamberti, commander of the Monte Cervino Battalion, and Major Lequio, at which time Lequio shared the following information with Lamberti.

"General Battisti sent me away from the front at the end of December, having realized following the defeat of the Italian infantry divisions south of the Kalitva River that the Alpine Corps risked encirclement." Lequio also noted General Battisti tried to persuade General Nasci (commander of the Alpine Corps) and other superior officers to withdraw the Corps around January 10 (a week earlier than the actual date of the withdrawal, January 17) "because that way at least ninety percent [of the alpini] could be saved."[15]

Battisti could not convince General Nasci. In a last chance effort, Battisti sent Major Lequio to Italy by private plane in an attempt to persuade Prince Umberto of Piedmont to exert his influence on the military authorities in Rome. This effort failed as well.[16]

It is interesting to note that General Battisti makes no mention of these events in his final report, written when he returned from Russia.

Although a withdrawal of Italian troops from the Don was probable by the end of December, and a certainty by January 1943, "nothing was done to organize it except for the pathetic suggestion to the troops to throw together [with whatever means] some little sleds to transport materiel." Trucks and mules needed for transport of the troops should have transferred in a timely manner from rear zones to the front. Planning to distribute much needed supplies of warm clothing and provisions from warehouses stuffed with food and winter clothing did not occur. There was no careful preparation for a withdrawal route with planned stops and planned distributions from centers located in rear zones.[17]

During this period of rapid escalation of fighting, historian Giorgio Rochat characterizes the leadership of generals Gariboldi and Nasci as "disastrous." There was a complete "collapse of professionalism and attention to the troops that has never been sufficiently underlined, and it was the myth of the alpini that covered up the failure of their commands."[18]

On January 10, 1943, orders from central headquarters of German Army Group B arrived, directing the Alpine Corps and the Second Hungarian Army to "hold the lines on the Don up to the last man and the last bullet. No withdrawal from the front was permissible...without orders from the [German] command." Although these orders were clear-cut, General Battisti and his officers remained greatly concerned. Obviously enemy forces could attack the Alpine Corps frontally, but now a possible attack could come from the rear as well. On January 14, Battisti received a call from the headquarters of the Alpine Corps instructing him to prepare for a move of his entire division to another zone. Written orders to this effect would follow shortly.[19]

Lieutenant Egisto Corradi recalled that the alpini didn't realize the Hungarians deployed to the north of the Alpine Corps were withdrawing from their lines, even though German Army Group B had expressly forbidden a withdrawal. The Hungarians began withdrawing January 16, assuming sole responsibility for their action, following another negative response from the Germans stating that orders from Hitler were not up for discussion. In actuality, even before their official decision to withdraw occurred, various Hungarian formations had pulled back twenty-four hours earlier. Hungarian units directly deployed to the north of the Tridentina Division failed to notify headquarters of the Tridentina of their intentions. "The confused and disorderly Hungarian withdrawal quickly became a chaotic rout. In the following days, Soviet mobile forces would attack the alpine divisions as they marched west by taking full advantage of the dissolution of the Hungarian sector."[20]

OPERATION "OSTROGOZHSK-ROSSOSH"

As early as December 20, 1942, the Soviets were mapping plans for their third offensive. The goal was to encircle and destroy the Hungarian, and remaining Italian and German forces on the Don front, and liberate the major railroad lines Liski-Valuiki, and Liski-Kantemirovka, in order to advance toward Kharkov and the Donets Basin.

Operation "Ostrogozhsk-Rossosh" consisted of two main and four secondary attacks. The two main attacks included strikes in the north against the Hungarian Second Army, followed by an advance south toward Alekseevka. From the south, strikes southwest of Kantemirovka, followed by a north and northwest advance toward Alekseevka, would achieve a pincer-like encirclement behind the lines of the Alpine Corps and the Hungarians. Of the four secondary attacks, two were to occur within the pincer formation while two were to take place outside of it.[21]

On January 13/14, the Russians attacked the Hungarian Second Army, to the north of the Alpine Corps, penetrating deep into zones behind their lines. On January 14, the Russians attacked and destroyed units on the German lines held by the XXIV Panzer Corps in and around Mitrofanovka. Russian tanks quickly pushed through those lines, and that same evening they struck the headquarters of the German XXIV Panzer Corps where the commander, General Wendel, lost his life in the ensuing battle.[22]

On January 15, masses of Soviet tanks continued to attack the weakened Hungarian positions in the north, as well as residual units of the XXIV Panzer Corps to the south and southwest of the Alpine Corps. They decimated the German 27th Panzer Division, and the 387th Infantry Division suffered significant losses. The Russians managed to open a large breach in the area held by the Germans and were now able to push north, toward Rossosh, site of the headquarters of the Alpine Corps. In Rossosh, alpini of the Monte Cervino Battalion engaged in a desperate battle against attacking Soviet armored units. All available military personnel in the area, including those with no combat experience, fought in this battle. Approximately twenty Russian tanks roamed the streets of Rossosh, demolishing warehouses, storehouses, and any truck in sight. Using any available means—mines, incendiary bottles,

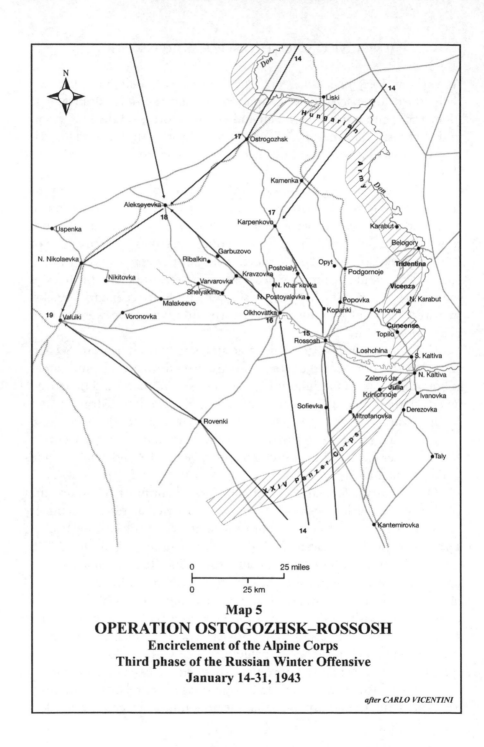

Map 5

OPERATION OSTOGOZHSK–ROSSOSH
Encirclement of the Alpine Corps
Third phase of the Russian Winter Offensive
January 14-31, 1943

after CARLO VICENTINI

and hand grenades—alpini of the Monte Cervino and auxiliary personnel managed to put five tanks out of commission. German ground-attack aircraft took out another seven or eight. The remaining tanks moved into Italian rear guard zones. That same afternoon, the headquarters of the Alpine Corps transferred from Rossosh to Podgornoje. Military hospitals were evacuated, as well as personnel from various auxiliary services. By noon of January 16, the Russians had occupied Rossosh.[23]

On the morning of January 16, a Russian plane dropped leaflets near the lines where the Julia Division was still fighting. On one side of a very small leaflet of yellow paper (written in Italian) it read, "Italian soldiers! You are surrounded." On the other side, written in Italian at the top and Russian at the bottom it read, "*Lasciapassare*" (pass or permit); "To all officers and soldiers who surrender we guarantee life, good treatment and your return to your homeland as soon as the war is over." The leaflet was signed, "Command of the Red Army of the Don."[24]

A second leaflet, written in Italian on light blue paper with more text, guaranteed the same rights to prisoners as that written on the yellow paper. In addition, the text advised Italian soldiers to "agree with your trusted companions to act together so you can avoid surveillance by [your] officers and their spies." It also advised soldiers to distance themselves from their commanders during a withdrawal, to fake a limp, and remain hidden in an izba until Russian soldiers arrived. "During a Russian attack, raise your hands. If there is a traitor in your midst, tie him up or better yet, kill him. Don't in any case take off your uniform. The international directive requests this. For Russians the rules of war are sacred. Every pass is valid for as many who surrender. If you don't have a pass, learn to shout these words loudly, '*Russ sdaius!*' ('I surrender')."[25]

On January 15, the ARMIR command requested permission from German Army Group B to withdraw the Alpine Corps along with the Hungarian Second Army, which was already withdrawing at that point. Hitler refused to allow the Alpine Corps to withdraw, but he permitted some troops of the German XXIV Panzer Corps to withdraw north of the Kalitva River.[26]

General Karl Eibl, who had assumed command of the XXIV Panzer Corps, ordered all remaining German troops operating with the Julia Division to withdraw. Vicentini writes, "The design of the German com-

mand was evident, namely to forge ahead of the Julia Division in the by
now inevitable withdrawal, leaving the Julia Division to form their rearguard, and at the same time having a clear road ahead in order to move
rapidly ahead of the Italians. This action weakened the already gravely
tested Julia, but most of all it left its flank, south of Krinichoje, completely exposed."[27]

As German troops to the south and southwest of the Julia Division
began to withdraw, alpini of the Julia had to quickly extend and
rearrange their defensive positions. ARMIR headquarters informed the
command of German Army Group B that it was imperative to authorize
the withdrawal of the Julia Division, as well as the other alpine divisions
still positioned on the Don, so as to prevent their encirclement.[28]

Despite tight German control of the Alpine Corps, General Nasci
and his officers had actually mapped out a plan for a possible withdrawal. It included a specific itinerary the divisions were to follow once
a retreat commenced. On January 15, General Battisti received written
orders for the withdrawal of the Alpine Corps from the Don. These
orders opened with the following statement: "Unfavorable events in
other parts of the front constrain the Alpine Corps to withdraw in order
to prevent encirclement." The three Alpine divisions (including the
Vicenza Division, incorporated into the Alpine Corps since November
20), the German XXIV Panzer Corps, and all troops and service units
posted in the Rossosh zone were to move toward the "alignment
Valuiki–Rovenki as quickly and efficiently as possible." Furthermore,
the orders stated that once the troops so deployed, a new defensive line
would be drawn, fortified by German troops arriving in that zone.[29]

The orders included specific routes for the divisions to follow.
However, as General Battisti notes, operational orders for the withdrawal were developed during the night of January 15, before columns
of Russian tanks and troops had reached and occupied Rossosh, and
two days before the Russians captured the strongpoints of the proposed
line of defense: Valuiki–Rovenki.[30]

In actuality, the overall situation on the ground had changed radi-
cally even before the withdrawal was to begin. In order to realize necessary deviations and to change course from the original plans for the
withdrawal, there should have been close and constant communication
between the Alpine divisions and their corps headquarters, as well as
communication with the superior commands, namely the Germans. In

fact, in the case of the Cuneense Division, communication between that division and the headquarters of the Alpine Corps ceased on the morning of January 15 (on January 20 a very brief radio connection was reestablished for only a short period).[31]

Already on January 15, General Nasci had ordered alpine units on the front lines to transport heavy equipment from supply depots and camp hospitals to Popovka and Podgornoje. Soldiers in charge of horses and mules located behind the lines received orders to move the animals to the front in order to transport these heavy loads. Some units failed to reach the front with quadrupeds because of Russian attacks. Consequently many alpine units, especially those of the 2nd Regiment of the Cuneense Division, began their withdrawal with approximately twenty mules per company. This of course had grave consequences for the mobility and survival of men in those units.[32]

The following order, received by General Nasci at 0600 on January 17, clearly demonstrates the control the Germans had over the destiny of the Alpine Corps: "TO LEAVE THE DON LINE WITHOUT ORDERS FROM ARMY [Group B] IS ABSOLUTELY FORBIDDEN. I WILL MAKE YOU PERSONALLY RESPONSIBLE TO EXECUTE THIS [ORDER]."[33]

Although enemy forces had encircled the Alpine Corps, General Nasci reported that the Corps was still in good shape, even though it remained under strict control by the Germans.[34]

At 1000 of the same day, Nasci received orders from ARMIR headquarters to withdraw from the Don, and to maintain close contact with the Hungarian Second Army deployed to the north. The General was also informed that Russian tanks had reached Postoialyj, which confirmed the fact that the Corps was completely encircled. In addition, German Army Group B placed the XXIV Panzer Corps under Nasci's command. It was now equipped with only four tanks, two self-propelled guns, and scant artillery including a battery of rocket launchers. Nasci noted that the 385th and 387th divisions of the Panzer Corps were "reduced to shreds," and their fighting ability could be considered "negligible."[35]

At 1100, General Nasci received another message from the headquarters of the ARMIR, authorizing the withdrawal of the Alpine Corps from the Don. The message ended with the following: "God be with you." The message also stated that the withdrawing Alpine Corps should maintain close contact with the Hungarian Second Army. Of course, that was impossible. By now, Russian forces had overrun the Hungarians and already there were reports of disorganized units of Hungarians near Opyt, northwest of Podgornoje. That same day, General Nasci received news that the Russians had occupied Postoialyj and Karpenkovo. The encirclement of the Alpine Corps was now complete.[36]

PART II

LA RITIRATA: WITHDRAWAL OF THE ALPINE CORPS FROM THE DON

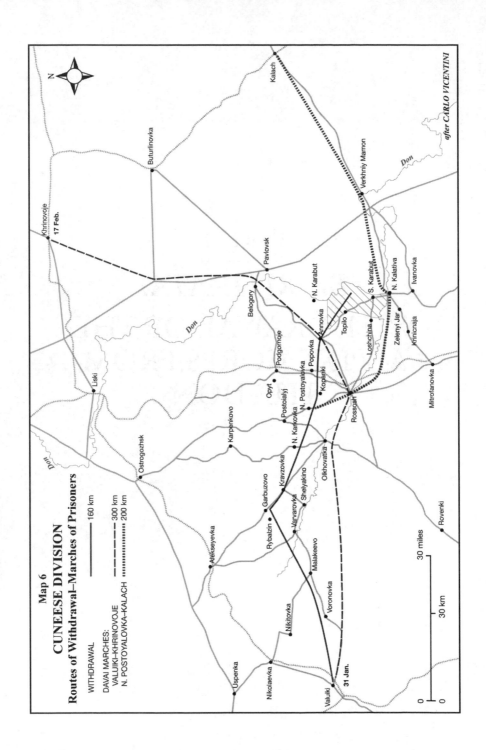

Map 6
CUNEESE DIVISION
Routes of Withdrawal–Marches of Prisoners

WITHDRAWAL
DAVAI MARCHES:
VALUJKI–KHRINOVOJE
N. POSTOYALOVKA–KALACH

160 km
300 km
200 km

after CARLO VICENTINI

Chapter 9

RETREAT DURING THE HEIGHT OF WINTER

THE JULIA DIVISION WITHDRAWS FROM THE SOUTHERN FRONT

On January 16, with Soviet forces now behind them on and on both flanks, commanders of the Julia Division received orders to withdraw from the southern front and march to Popovka.[1]

While meeting with his officers January 17, Captain Reitani briefly outlined the situation on the ground and described the route the division was to follow. Reitani told his officers the Russians occupied Rossosh, therefore the Julia Division was at risk of becoming completely encircled, cut off from the other alpine divisions. The distance to be covered was approximately seventy to eighty kilometers, mostly away from roads; the prospect of encountering enemy forces was a given. Reitani instructed his officers to talk to their men and explain the seriousness of the situation. Each alpino was to receive two pieces of hard tack and a small can of meat. The captain concluded his remarks by instructing his officers to count the number of men, mules, and sleds and to keep a watchful eye.[2]

About 180 able-bodied men of the 26th Battery prepared to march toward Popovka. Only 80 of the 170 mules of the battery had survived. As rations were distributed, Captain Reitani told his men that this was to be a forced march. He also told them to "treasure" the rations received, since they represented the last distribution of food until "this crisis is resolved."[3]

111

Battle-weary men of the Julia began marching north. They walked for thirty-two hours straight, dragging their wounded and frostbitten comrades with them, loaded on sleds. As they marched, snow swirled about them, driven by unrelenting winds. Their feet lost all feeling, their hunger raged, yet they forced themselves to keep walking, even though half-paralyzed from temperatures hovering around -40°. Bedeschi recalled that it was easy to hallucinate after hours of marching, often up to their knees in snow. Fatigue, exhaustion, lack of nourishment, and the bitter cold caused the mind to wander. In those dark hours, the men became detached from one another, entering a private world of suffering and anguish verging on half-crazed hallucinations. Blankets thrown over the men's shoulders and heads became rigid with ice; as dawn broke, each found it difficult to recognize companions.[4]

Corradi describes the effects of cold temperatures upon anyone walking for hours in such circumstances. "After several hours a crust of ice formed on the lower half of faces, from the nose down; and also often on the eyebrows. Long beards became blocks of ice. The only way to liberate oneself from this mask of ice was to enter a warm izba for a few moments. Icicles also formed on faces but only when there was a certain degree of humidity."[5]

Once they arrived in Popovka on January 18, the alpini found shelter for their exhausted mules and only then entered warm izbas. When they removed the overcoats they had not taken off in over a month, the frozen coats remained upright on the floor. The men defrosted their frozen pieces of hard tack, and canned meat, drank fresh well water out of pails passed from one to the other, finally quenching their thirst after a month spent in their frigid outposts sucking on snow. For the first time in over a month, they enjoyed the warmth of a fire, and then they slept.[6]

THE CUNEENSE DIVISION WITHDRAWS TO POPOVKA

On January 16, Lieutenant Colonel B [Bellani][7] of the Cuneense Division gave the following orders: "Tomorrow...unless counter-ordered...we will abandon the lines, withdraw to Annovka. All must proceed in absolute silence. The enemy must absolutely not become aware of what we are doing...."[8]

Lieutenant Gino Beraudi,[9] adjutant to Major Guaraldi of the 2nd Alpine Regiment, was shocked to hear the colonel's words while standing in his regimental headquarters: "Withdraw! Leave our lines...and choose the frozen steppe, facing troops drunk with victory and rich with tanks.... Going where?" He knew the alpini had no second line of resistance. He also knew at least 4000 kilometers lay between the Don and Italy! These thoughts raced through his mind for only a split second. He realized he couldn't even begin to grapple with unknown possibilities; all he could do was to report to his major and perform his immediate duties.[10]

At 1630, the Cuneense Division began to withdraw from their lines. Rucksacks were loaded with ammunition, hand-grenades, and a few personal possessions. Alpini of the division began the withdrawal in two columns and proceeded to march in a normal manner for the first few hours. They remained stopped for long periods, as units of the German XXIV Panzer Corps took to the same road, crowding it with their numerous vehicles and sleds. Units of the Julia Division, withdrawing from the south, also merged onto that road, as did disorganized infantry and Romanian units, as well as Russian civilians. Abandoned sleds, vehicles out of fuel, and all sorts of discarded equipment littered and clogged the road.[11]

Alpini of the Cuneense, especially those of the 2nd Regiment, forced to stop for hours in the snow and wind, had no prospect of shelter. Each company had one ambulance sled and soon these overflowed with soldiers suffering from frostbite. Mules loaded with heavy packs began to tire after being forced to stand for long periods. Drivers unloaded packs, then reloaded them once the column began to march once more, causing drivers to suffer additional fatigue. In the case of the Saluzzo Battalion, it took eighteen hours to cover twenty-three kilometers.[12]

In *The History of the Alpine Troops* (Faldella, 1972), an inexplicable fact is recorded, which had long-range repercussions. On January 16, the day before the withdrawal began, "One officer per company, along with a couple of alpine guides per platoon, was sent slightly west of Annovka, to reconnoiter positions on which a new defensive line was to be built."[13]

Several units of the Cuneense Division, especially those of the 2nd Regiment, began the withdrawal believing they were either going to move their lines to a position in the rear, or were actually going to build a new defensive line between Staraya Kalitva and Rossosh. Owing to this "misunderstanding" and believing the march would be a short one, when equipment in those particular units was loaded on mules or given to alpini to carry in their packs, both were overloaded. Items that would serve on a new defensive line took precedence; tools, blankets, and stoves, whereas supplies of food and ammunition were considered less important for this particular mission. As a result, overburdened men and mules in those withdrawing units quickly became exhausted. When the 2nd Alpine Regiment reached Annovka in the late morning of January 18, the troops had to stop, not only to rest but also to adjust and repack the mules' burdens—abandoning much of the now useless equipment.[14]

When troops of the division stopped in Minaj, each platoon chose an izba where the men rested and ate a small can of meat, wondering if this meal was both their first and last since all provisions of food had been sent ahead by truck to Popovka.[15]

At the beginning of the second day of the withdrawal, already the column began to lose a sense of order. More and more survivors of the Julia Division followed alpini of the Cuneense Division, as did groups of German soldiers. A few alpini lay frozen to death, abandoned on the snow along the sides of the route. The living continued to trudge forward throughout the night, hoping to reach Popovka, where they believed they could break out of the Russian encirclement.[16]

At dawn on the third day, the column arrived in Popovka. There the remains of the provisions sent ahead lay scattered in the snow among abandoned trucks. Beraudi saw huge wheels of parmesan cheese that had rolled off a truck onto the road. He tried to cut off a piece, but it was impossible because it was frozen. Instead, he picked up a five-kilo can of meat, but threw it away soon after, since it was too heavy to carry.[17]

THE TRIDENTINA DIVISION WITHDRAWS TO PODGORNOJE

On January 17, Sergeant Major Rigoni Stern (Vestone Battalion) received the news that the alpini of the Tridentina Division were to withdraw from their lines. Each section of every company was to leave their stronghold one at a time. He began to make preparations: "I changed into clean underclothes and left the dirty lice-ridden ones on the straw [covered floor]. I tried to put on as many clothes as I could wear without hampering my movements. The remaining two pairs of socks and jersey I threw into the pack together with some first aid kit, reserve rations, a tin of anti-freezing grease, and a blanket. I filled the rest of the pack with ammunition, mostly hand-grenades."[18]

Rigone Stern ordered his men to wear as much clothing as possible without impeding their ability to move, to fill their packs with whatever they thought was necessary, and to load up with ammunition and as many hand-grenades as possible. "No one must go on his own," he said to his men. "We must all stick together the whole time. Remember that, always stick together."[19]

At that moment, the sergeant was in command of his platoon's strongpoint since the former commander, Lieutenant Moscioni, had left due to exhaustion. The alpini looked to their sergeant for direction as they waited anxiously for exact news. He couldn't give them specific information as to when they were to leave or where they were going. He gave orders to various section commanders and told them the alpini needed to "load up like mules; we don't know what's ahead of us." He also told them to keep their men close to them and to have the men remove the spoons from their mess tins, because the withdrawal from the lines had to occur in absolute silence.[20]

To the north of the Vestone Battalion, two-thirds of the 46th Company of the Tirano Battalion began to withdraw from Belogory in small groups. A third of each battalion remained on the front lines to keep the stoves burning in the abandoned bunkers, and to fire shots across the river to mask the withdrawal. On January 18, Lieutenant Revelli and remaining alpini of the 46th Company left Belogory with orders to march to Morozovka and Podgornoje, where the whole of the Tridentina Division was to reunite.[21]

Chaplain Don Gnocchi describes the moments the Tridentina Division left the front lines. "In silence, broken by rumbling sounds of distant cannons, and echoes of battles flaring up all along the front, a black river of armed men, and sleds, trucks, and mules descended slowly on the trails from the Don lines...." As the alpini abandoned their lines, "questions and silent, impotent rage" beset them; none of them could have imagined withdrawing or becoming encircled.[22]

Fortunately, it was a dark night. It was very cold as squads left their lines one by one. Soon the wind rose, making it difficult to hold on to blankets covering heads and shoulders. Sergeant Rigoni Stern wondered if the noise of the wind had sufficiently masked the withdrawal of the

Vestone Battalion from their positions. He knew the alpini were supposed to reach a village to the rear of the front lines where there were
warehouses and headquarters. He writes, "But we didn't know any
names of places in the rear. The telephonists, the typists, and the other
base troops knew all the names. We didn't even know the name of the
village where our strongpoint had been.... All we knew was that the
river in front of our strongpoint was the Don, and that we were any
number [of kilometers], a thousand to ten thousand, from home. And
where east and west were. Nothing more."[23]

As the sergeant marched through the night, his breath froze on his
beard and moustache and with the snow blown by the wind, formed icicles, which he pulled up with his tongue and sucked.[24]

As units of the Tridentina began arriving in Podgornoje, they
encountered a chaotic scene. It seemed as though the whole village was
on fire. Buildings, warehouses, and supply depots burned, ammunition
dumps exploded. Hundreds of soldiers milled around searching for their
respective units, while columns of men, mules, vehicles, and sleds were
either arriving or moving out. It was a scene of sheer bedlam.[25]

THE JULIA AND CUNEENSE DIVISIONS REACH POPOVKA

Popovka was also teeming with alpini, a few German units, units of the
Vicenza Division, and soldiers from various service units. Hundreds of
leaderless troops from infantry units also milled around in this crowd.
There were many wounded, as well as soldiers suffering from frostbite.
As these thousands of men in poor circumstances attempted to find shelter in various izbas, cohesion of units broke down as did discipline and
control. All intact izbas were overflowing with soldiers, forcing the alpini of the Cuneense to spend that night out of doors.[26]

General Battisti and officers of the Cuneense and Julia divisions
wanted to get their respective units in order. Yet Battisti also wanted the
alpini to have a period of rest after their long hours of marching. As the
men rested, Battisti, along with other commanders, mapped out an itinerary with a specific timetable for the departure of each alpine unit from
Popovka. He changed the original orders of General Nasci because the
Russians now occupied the roads leading from Rossosh to Rovenki.
According to the revised orders, the alpini were to proceed to Valuiki;
the Julia Division scheduled to leave first, followed by German units.

Units of the Cuneense were to leave at 2200.[27]

While his men rested, Captain Reitani met with officers of other alpine units who brought him up to date on the current situation. When he returned to his battery, he gave his officers disheartening news. He explained that enemy forces had broken through the Hungarian front to the north of the Tridentina Division. Since January 15, the Russians had easily moved down from the north, joining their other forces moving up from the south: "Russian troops are consolidating around the Alpine Corps with the obvious intention of suffocating it in a vise without a means for us to exit."[28]

The captain noted that the entire Alpine Corps was now completely encircled and isolated. He continued, detailing troop strength. The Vicenza Division, with 12,000 men, had little offensive capability; the Cuneense and Tridentina divisions each had about 16,000 men. Although they had been attacked, the latter two divisions were still capable of fighting, whereas obviously, as they well knew, the Julia Division was not in the best of shape, since it had just finished a month of strenuous fighting in the south. Men and mules of the Julia were exhausted, and the division had few weapons, little ammunition, few sleds, and consisted of only 12,000.[29]

The current plan, Reitani continued, called for the alpini to break through the Russian encirclement in order to reach Axis forces that had left the front lines before the corps' withdrawal from the Don had begun. Reitani noted that more than 110,000 soldiers were now a part of the withdrawal. He explained: in addition to the divisions of the alpini, 5,000 Italians from Central Command and Services, 2,000 in a special battalion, a few from cavalry batteries, and about 5,000 soldiers from two infantry divisions would be following the alpini. Furthermore, 7,000 Germans with a variety of materiel but little ammunition, 7,000 Romanians, and 30,000 unarmed Hungarians would also be following the alpini. The only troops still capable of fighting were those of the Alpine Corps, a few of the Italian infantry units, and approximately half of the Germans. The rest would simply follow, "passively, weighing down and delaying the withdrawing columns."[30]

Although commanders of the alpine units in Popovka possessed no accurate information about the exact location of Axis lines to the west, or precise information about where they might encounter Russian resistance, it was decided that the three alpine divisions, as well as the

Vicenza Division, would march west, parallel to one another, separated by several kilometers. Captain Reitani continued to brief the alpini of the 26th Battery: "We only know that in twenty-four hours, we need to be west of Novaya Postoyalovka, a village approximately ten kilometers from here where it seems forces of the Axis rear-guard are waiting for us. If we don't join them within twenty-four hours they will be forced to withdraw completely and we will be left on our own...."[31]

Orders given to the alpini were as follows: to only carry their own weapons and ammunition, to destroy and burn everything else, including their rucksacks and mess tins; there were no more provisions. Extra ammunition and the few remaining large weapons were to be loaded on sleds.

As men began burning all the things ordered destroyed, they could see numerous fires in the distance, signifying that other units were doing the same. Bedeschi writes, "More than one hundred thousand men tragically deprived themselves of every possession in the attempt to save only one: their life. One hundred thousand mess tins, empty of food and full of ice, studded the snow marking the destiny of the combatants imprisoned within the encirclement near the Don."[32]

THE BATTLE OF NOVAYA POSTOYALOVKA

The 8th Regiment and units of the Conegliano Group of the Julia Division left Popovka around nine on the morning of January 19 to march toward Novaya Postoyalovka. Russian troops hidden in and around the village attacked the alpini at the outskirts. Colonel Cimolino ordered alpini of the Gemona Battalion and Conegliano Group to break through the Russian defenses: "This was the beginning of the bloody, desperate battle of Novaya Postoyalovka, lasting more or less uninterrupted for more than thirty hours."[33]

The Gemona Battalion, supported by nine howitzers of the Conegliano, attempted to enter the village, crossing an expanse of flat, exposed terrain lacking any sort of cover. They succeeded to take a portion of the village but were soon repulsed. The Tolmezzo Battalion moved into the fray, but when it reached the first houses, superior forces of Russians along with seven tanks attacked. The Cividale Battalion then attempted to advance to the village, but failed as enemy forces resisted.[34]

Throughout that day, the three battalions of the 8th Julia Regiment continued to attempt to drive the Russians out of the village, but each time the alpini were able to gain some ground, mobile Russian forces drove them back. At a certain moment, the Russians counterattacked, reaching the lines held by the Conegliano Group. The advancing tanks proceeded to charge forward, destroying cannons and running over wounded alpini lying in the snow. From several captured Russians, the alpini learned that more than 3,000 Russian infantry troops, supported by tanks, were in the village, along with numerous cannons and mortars, and more troops were arriving from Rossosh.[35]

As night fell the battle subsided. Hundreds of alpini lay out on the snow. Alpini removed the wounded from the battlefield, yet medical officers could do little to alleviate their suffering. Much needed medical supplies had been destroyed.[36]

The alpini regrouped that evening: "The exhausted and demoralized survivors and wounded spent that night stretched out in the snow with bodies of their fallen as their only protective shield."[37]

The Cuneense Division had also left Popovka in two groups on January 19. Colonel Manfredi, commander of the 1st Alpine Regiment of that division, marched northwest toward Novaya Postoyalovka, arriving that night in the small village of Soloviev (slightly south of Novaya Postoyalovka) where the commander of the 8th Alpine Regiment, Colonel Cimolino had his headquarters. There, medical officers and chaplains were tending to hundreds who were wounded during the battle that day.[38]

That evening the colonels determined that the Ceva Battalion of the Cuneense Division, commanded by Lieutenant Colonel Avenanti, along with the remaining alpini of the 8th Regiment of the Julia Division (reduced by now to little more than companies), as well as units of the Conegliano Group, should attempt another assault on Novaya Postoyalovka early the next morning.[39]

At 0330 on the morning of January 20, the Ceva Battalion moved toward the village hoping to reach the Russian defense line in a surprise assault. The response of the Russians was violent. With infantry troops and seventeen tanks, the Russians counterattacked, assailing the alpini who had almost reached the outskirts of the village. The Ceva Battalion suffered heavy losses and was forced back to its point of departure.[40]

While the battle was in progress, General Battisti and General

Ricagno arrived at the scene. Both generals and their chiefs of staff decided to attack Novaya Postoyalovka once again with two battalions of the 1st Cuneense Regiment, with support of the Modovì Group, remnants of the 8th Julia Regiment, the Conegliano units, and remnants of the Ceva Battalion.[41]

Units of alpini spread out across the snow and advanced forward rapidly at dawn, but Russian forces, protected by izbas, began firing on them as soon as they began entering the village. As the alpini sought to break through the fortified barrier, the Russians counterattacked violently with infantry troops and numerous tanks. Some tanks cut across alpine units, advancing quickly, firing their machine guns as they charged forward toward those locations where large groups of soldiers clustered, causing men in their path to throw themselves down in the snow. A few alpini courageously raced toward several tanks, determined to destroy them. They clambered up the sides and hurled hand-grenades down the turrets. Other tanks advanced, running over the men, crushing them beneath their tracks, while others maneuvered in a crisscross fashion, crushing the living and the dead, destroying many of the alpine cannons. Russian infantry troops followed the tanks and finished off the massacre, killing any alpino who was still alive.[42]

At a certain moment, a tank headed straight toward Lieutenant Corradi, who was close to a group of alpini firing a mountain cannon. The tank ran over the cannon, crushing it, and kept going. Then it turned around and headed straight toward Corradi. He quickly rolled into a small ditch and crouched within. The tank advanced and proceeded to move right over the ditch. Corradi who by now was on his back could read a few words written in English on a piece of metal on the underside of the tank: "This vehicle must be filled...." He writes, "That's all I read! It was an American Sherman tank. Maybe it was out of order, or hit. It stopped about thirty paces beyond. We were on top of it immediately and we beat savagely on the metal with our guns."

We yelled, "Come out!"

"*Niet*," they responded.

"We were like drunks, full of pride and rage."

The alpini set fire to stacks of straw they placed around the tank, causing the men within to emerge quickly.[43]

Lieutenant Corradi recalled a moment when there was a lull in the battle. He and several officers had withdrawn into an izba. Cannon and mortar fire had ceased, but soon the men could see Russian soldiers running past the open windows of the izba firing their automatic weapons. Corradi writes, "I felt the bitter painful end was near." As he turned to face his fellow officers, to his horror he saw one of them place a submachine gun under his chin. The officer's face was purple from the cold since all windows of the isba were open.

Corradi shouted: "Don't do that Sir!"

The officer replied, "It's over!"

As Corradi took the weapon away from the officer, the izba shook under several bursts of gunfire, causing plaster from the roof to fall. Suddenly a captain of the alpini ran out the door of the izba shouting.

"They're running away." He continued to shout the same phrase repeatedly. Several hundred alpini who had been in surrounding izbas came out yelling and shooting, chasing after the Russians.[44]

Bedeschi describes this desperate final assault as Colonel Verdotti hollered, "All those who are alive, attack! '*Savoia*!' "[45]

The men surged forward shouting their battle cry as they followed their commander into the fray. "A desperate throng hurled itself toward the enemy...pushed by the frenzy of wanting to either outrun death, or embrace it. Behind the first ones, they rose from the snow and thrust themselves forward in an incredible jumble of machine-gunners without weapons, quartermasters, and telephonists, non-commissioned officers, medical corpsmen, and drivers, doctors, mule drivers, artillerymen, and alpini who had used their last bullet."[46]

Corradi writes, "We flew...we were filled with a strange euphoria, maybe it was the fear we had just experienced that now gave way to courage."[47] Even wounded and frostbitten soldiers lying on sleds were shooting, and wounded men in first aid stations grabbed whatever weapon they could find: "bayonets, hand-grenades, sticks, pocket knives, and rifles used as clubs. They resembled a frightening apparition of lunatics, leaving only the dead and dying behind them. They fell upon their adversary, hurling themselves with impetuous fury; impotent to do otherwise, they rolled in the snow in mortal combat...."[48]

As it grew dark, the battle petered out, and the Russians moved back to their entrenched positions in the village. The survivors of this ferocious battle returned to the area where they had left their sleds. They carried their wounded and counted the dead, scattered over the snow among five immobilized Russian tanks. "We prevented them from killing us all, they said, still gasping for breath—but when they come back, it will be the end."[49]

General Battisti repeatedly attempted to contact the command of the Alpine Corps (withdrawing with the Tridentina Division) with no success; but at 0800, he was able to establish radio contact for a short period that morning. He explained that the alpini of the Julia and Cuneense had to break through the Russian barricades in Novaya Postoyalovka before more enemy forces could completely encircle the divisions and prevent them from moving west, but he needed self-propelled guns and tanks to accomplish this feat. He knew that the German XXIV Panzer Corps was withdrawing with the Tridentina Division, and asked for additional armaments as well as tanks from the Germans. Battisti was told the Tridentina Division was engaged in heavy fighting, along with the Germans in the zone of Postoialyj, about twenty kilometers north of Novaya Postoyalovka, and that German tanks and assault guns could only be sent to the Cuneense if the Tridentina and Germans managed to break through the Russian blockade in that zone. That radio connection ended at 0930. It was the only radio contact the Cuneense Division had with any of the other withdrawing alpine forces throughout the entire withdrawal.[50]

Following this message, General Battisti waited for several hours for reinforcements from the Tridentina Division and Germans, but soon realized that the Tridentina probably was still engaged in Postoialyj. He also realized that before it got dark the Russians could attack forcefully once more to prevent the alpini from breaking out from the zone of Novaya Postoyalovka–Kholkhoz Kopanki. At 1400, he ordered the commander of the 2nd Alpine Regiment to launch an attack on two villages further north of Novaya Postoyalovka with the Saluzzo and Borgo San Dalmazzo battalions, which had arrived from Popovka that same morning. Battisti ordered the Dronero Battalion to remain in place outside of Novaya Postoyalovka.[51]

Following a short but exhausting march in heavy snow, enemy forces attacked the two Cuneense battalions violently on their flanks. Both battalions sustained heavy losses. Soon infantry attacked again along with tanks and heavy mortars, causing almost a total destruction of both. The few alpini who returned consisted of the battalion commanders, a few officers, and approximately sixty alpini from each battalion. Dead and mortally wounded alpini amounted to 1,500.[52]

In the face of imminent annihilation, Medical Officer Lieutenant Italo Serri of the Julia Division attempted to care for the wounded with inadequate medical supplies, hoping his bare hands could continue to function in the frigid air. Serri observed a strange phenomenon as he worked. When he performed amputations of limbs, wounded men didn't experience pain. He soon realized sub-zero temperatures caused nerves to be numbed and stopped massive bleeding of wounds. This factor proved to be a blessing in disguise, saving many lives.[53]

Losses for all units of the 8th Julia Regiment and Conegliano Group were also frightfully high. Survivors attempted to bury the dead, but it was impossible in the frozen ground. The alpini knew another Russian attack would wipe out what remained of the battalions. They also realized that the twenty-four-hour deadline had expired and Axis forces had probably already withdrawn from the zone west of Postoialyj. Commanders of the surviving units sent out an order to place all remaining sleds in a circle. All troops were ordered to entrench themselves within the circle, to fight to the finish.[54]

Later, Captain Reitani spoke to his Medical Officer, Serri, saying the losses of soldiers, weapons, and the scarcity of ammunition called for a change of plans. Instead of remaining encircled by sleds, once it was dark they would resume their march as if they were moving left, but in fact they would make a verge toward the right, and seek to cross a number of deep gullies where they hoped the Russians would have weak surveillance. The captain noted that the group only had twelve remaining sleds and three cannons. Serri was to choose men who were unable to walk and to load them on the remaining sleds.[55]

The column moved out an hour later, protected by the dark. A few men remained behind for a while, to fire shots in order to give the Russians the impression that resistance was continuing. Meanwhile, the column pushed forward in knee-deep snow, first marching east, then north, then toward the west, heading toward the Russian lines, a few kilometers from the village of Novaya Postoyalovka. After a tortuous march, they arrived at the Rossosh-Voronezh road. They believed it was the outer limit of the encirclement and were filled with hope, even though they realized they were now isolated out on the steppe, with no idea of the location of other alpine units. By the light of the moon, a Russian surveillance plane spotted the marching men and bombed the column, hitting some men and mules. The march continued until early morning, when the men spotted Russian tanks in the distance. Luckily, they were able to hide in a nearby forest. The temperature rose slightly, but it began to snow. Mules were able to munch on shrubs in the forest, but the men had nothing; they had not eaten since January 17, four days earlier.[56]

That afternoon the column moved out of the woods and pushed on past Novokhar'kovka. On January 22, remnants of the Julia's 8th Regiment and Conegliano Group reached Novogeorgievsk, where they stopped to rest. As they were preparing to leave at midmorning, Russian forces attacked the village with mobile infantry and tanks. Colonel Cimolino, commander of the 8th Regiment, negotiated surrender in order to avoid massive casualties. By January 22, the 8th Regiment of the Julia Division ceased to exist as a fighting force.[57]

A few men did manage to escape capture, including remnants of the 26th Battery of the Conegliano Group. These alpini eventually managed to reach the withdrawing column of the Tridentina Division.[58]

As night fell on the evening of January 20, General Battisti concluded that his division could not break through the Russian lines in Novaya Postoyalovka. He also decided to disengage, pull back, and go around the area held by the Russians, taking advantage of the dark and the fact that Russian attacks had subsided that evening. The Dronero Battalion, placed at the head of the column, was to open up a new route in deep snow, taking advantage of small gullies. They moved northwest in the direction of Postoialyj, hoping to reach the Tridentina Division, and hoping that the Tridentina had managed to break through the enemy encirclement in that zone.[59] "Orders were given to abandon all heavy loads and—a painful necessity—also the wounded who could not walk and who could not be loaded on the few available sleds, to tighten up the ranks and to maintain absolute silence."[60]

By now, the Dronero Battalion was the only intact battalion of the 2nd Alpine Regiment. General Battisti remained at the head of the column throughout the remainder of the withdrawal. Beraudi observes, "He's on horseback with some of the officers from General Headquarters. He converses placidly with them and with Guaraldi [commander of the Dronero Battalion], as if they were out on an excursion. His calm is more encouraging than a heroic speech."[61]

In a final summary of the battle of Novaya Postoyalovka, given in *The History of the Alpine Troops*, Faldella notes, "For the few survivors, that tremendous battle is remembered as a useless sacrifice." Yet, by fighting Russian troops in Novaya Postoyalovka, the Cuneense and the Julia divisions did prevent those troops from moving north to attack the Tridentina Division, engaged in battles in the zones of Postoialyj, Opyt, and Skororyb the same day. "If the Tridentina Division succeeded in winning that battle, and [overcome] successive Russian resistance, and escape from encirclement carrying in its wake thousands of survivors of its sister divisions, the credit also goes to the Julia and Cuneense Divisions. In Novaya Postoyalovka, with the high cost of their blood, they wrote one of the most heroic pages of legendary deeds of the alpini."[62]

While the battle of Novaya Postoyalovka was in progress, after having fended off several attacks in Popovka by Russian units arriving from Rossosh, the 9th Regiment of the Julia Division began to march toward the village of Kopanki, southeast of Novaya Postoyalovka, arriving there at dawn on January 20. Enemy forces with tanks occupied Kopanki. Throughout the day, the Vicenza, Aquila and Val Cismon battalions attempted to dislodge the Russians in a series of attacks but it wasn't until evening that they succeeded. "The losses were enormous: seven officers and dozens of alpini lost their lives in these battles."[63]

There were no means to transport the dozens of wounded. Colonel Lavizzari, commander of the 9th Regiment, and Captain Stanislao Valenti, commander of the Val Cismon Battalion, made the decision to gather the wounded and place them in three izbas under the care of a medical officer. Two chaplains, along with Don Brevi wanted to remain with the wounded, but Lavizzari believed the Russians would show more mercy toward a medical officer rather than three priests. Several medical offers drew straws to determine which one would remain. Lieutenant Fabbrini of the 65th Company of the Val Cismon drew the deciding straw.[64]

It was at this point that distressing orders arrived from the command of the Julia: "Abandon everything, cannons, heavy weapons, mules, sleds, and rucksacks. Fill your pockets with provisions and with your rifles attempt to pass through the net of the Russian encirclement."[65]

The remainder of the regiment marched toward Samoylenkov, arriving there the evening of January 20. The commander of the Julia Division, General Ricagno, joined the troops there, ordering the 9th

Regiment to proceed with him toward a village north west of Samoylenkov. During the afternoon, General Ricagno and his chief-of-staff proceeded toward Novokhar'kovka ahead of units of the Julia in order to permit them to rest for a few hours in several barns of a kholkhoz. Russian troops soon surrounded the barns with tanks and began to demolish the wooden structures.[66]

Several years after the war was over, Lieutenant Egisto Corradi had the opportunity to obtain an account of this event in a meeting with Don Brevi, chaplain of the Val Cismon Battalion.

"The barn where the Val Cismon was entrenched," the chaplain said, "was literally pierced by bursts of gun fire, parts of the roof and walls were flying off in pieces…. The barn had become a real charnel house. There were perhaps two-hundred dead and four-hundred wounded." Don Brevi continued: "Captain Valenti was hit by sub-machine gun fire, fired by a gigantic Soviet partisan…before dying Valenti shot the partisan with his pistol as he lay on the floor immersed in his own blood." It was then that the command ordered the troops to surrender, "but alpini continued to fire for an hour before obeying the order."[67] With hopes of saving the few survivors, the alpini eventually surrendered.[68]

Colonel Lavizzari and commanders of the Val Piave and Udine Groups (3rd Artillery Regiment), and the Vicenza Battalion were captured. Although the new commander of the Aquila Battalion, Captain Sallustio, managed to distance himself from the surrender, the Russians captured him the following day. Vicentini writes, "The 9th Alpine Regiment ceased to exist and concluded its glorious epic begun December 17 on the front of Zelenyj-Jar."[69] The 35th Battery of the Val Piave Group and approximately 200 alpini of the Aquila Battalion were able to avoid capture because they had taken the wrong road when leaving Samoylenkov and had headed toward Postoialyj.[70]

Meanwhile, at the same time the 9th Regiment of the Julia Division was being destroyed, the commander of the division, General Ricagno, and Colonel Moro of the Julia's 3rd Artillery Regiment, had reached Novokhar'kovka where they met General Battisti with survivors of the Cuneense Division and those of the 8th Regiment of the Julia Division.[71]

Once the Cuneense Division began marching again, going north, "one could only count 7,000 men (5,000 of the division and 2,000 from service units of the Alpine Corps)." On January 23 remnants of the Julia Divisional Command, General Ricagno, officers, and alpini joined the column of the Cuneense Division and followed its route and destiny. This small group of 1,000 was all that remained of the Julia except, as noted, for the few survivors of the 8th Regiment and Conegliano Group who had reached the withdrawing forces of the Tridentina Division.[72]

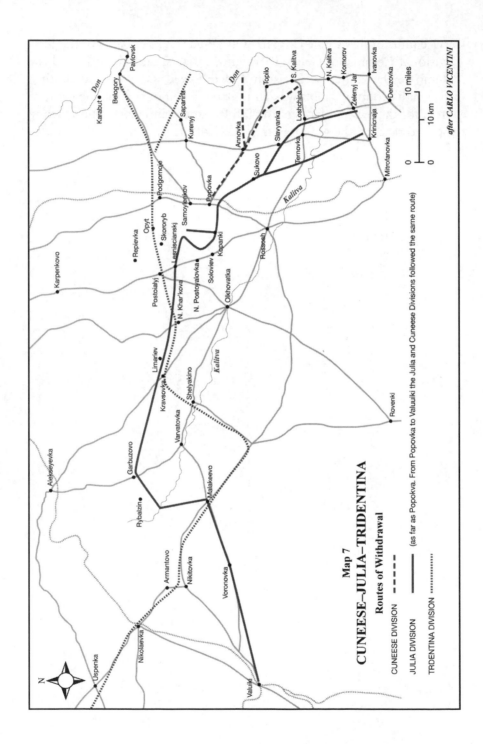

Map 7

CUNEESE–JULIA–TRIDENTINA

Routes of Withdrawal

CUNEESE DIVISION   - - - - -

JULIA DIVISION   ——————   (as far as Popokva. From Popovka to Valuuiki the Julia and Cuneese Divisions followed the same route)

TRIDENTINA DIVISION   ···········

Chapter 10

THE CUNEENSE AND JULIA CONTINUE TO WITHDRAW

During the evening of January 21, the command of the ARMIR was able to establish radio communications with German XXIV Panzer Corps, marching with the Tridentina Division, transmitting orders to change the direction of the withdrawal: "The encircled columns were to point toward Nikolaevka, not Valuiki, because that zone was now occupied by the enemy. But this important warning could only be given to the Tridentina; nobody could communicate with the Julia, Cuneense, and Vicenza divisions. . . ." Those divisions continued to follow previous orders to march toward Valuiki.[1]

FROM NOVAYA POSTOYALOVKA TO NOVOKHAR'KOVKA

Upon leaving the zone of Novaya Postoyalovka, survivors of the Cuneense and Julia divisions marched northwest in two columns throughout the night of January 20. At 1500 on January 21, the divisions arrived in Postoialyj where the Tridentina Division had fought the day before. Although the troops were exhausted, General Battisti decided not to stop. He pressed the alpini to continue marching. At 2000, the head of the column arrived in the village of Alexsandrovka, west of Postoialyj, where there was a small German garrison. The end of the column arrived four hours later.[2]

In order to give his troops time to rest and reorganize, General Battisti had planned to wait until late morning of January 22 before continuing to march west. Frequent Russian reconnaissance planes appeared during daylight hours, and it seemed advisable to seek suitable places for shelter once it was dark. Eager to reach the Tridentina Division, Battisti urged his troops to start marching at dawn on January 22, despite their level of exhaustion, hunger, and the frigid temperatures, and even though so many were wounded or suffering from frostbite. Mustering the troops and organizing the columns of men was particularly difficult that morning. Yet Russian partisan activity induced the disorganized, leaderless groups to abandon houses where they had sheltered and quickly join the departing columns. The alpini arrived in Novokhar'kovka during the evening of January 22, where they met up with the tail end of the column of the Vicenza Division. The Vicenza moved on to Kravzovka that evening.[3]

FROM NOVOKHAR'KOVKA TO NOVODMITRIEVKA AND RYBALZIN

At dawn January 23, following a quiet night, the troops marched toward the village of Shelyakino, passing through the village of Kravzovka. During this phase of the march, a contingent of German troops interspersed in the alpini columns with their large sleds. Around 1400 three Russian tanks suddenly appeared and attacked the head of the column, causing losses among a unit of pack animals and their drivers. Fortunately, a German mortar disabled one tank; the other two withdrew back toward the village of Kravzovka. Hand-grenades buried in the snow by units who had previously traversed the same route wounded a number of alpini during the march from Novokhar'kovka to Kravzovka.[4]

Following these events, the columns reorganized and marched until twilight of January 23, reaching a series of villages in the zone of Kravzovka-Lymarev where the Vicenza Division had been resting since morning. The Vicenza Division was planning to leave at 2000 to head toward Shelyakino. Troops of the Cuneense and Julia continued to march until they reached Novodmitrievka, which was occupied by the Russians. The Dronero Battalion, accompanied by the 4th Battalion of Engineers, quickly took the village over. The men stopped in the village to rest for a few hours.[5]

Around 2200, alpini heard sounds of intense shelling coming from the valley of Shelyakino, and believed the sounds of battle possibly came from the Tridentina Division. During the afternoon of that same day, following the attack of the three Russian tanks, the Chief-of-Staff of the Alpine Corps, General Martinat (who traveled by car), had met with General Pascolini, commander of the Vicenza Division, and told him the Tridentina was ahead by a day's worth of marching. General Martinat also stated that the Tridentina was in desperate straits and needed support from the other alpine units in order to break through the encirclement.[6]

Following a meeting held later between General Pascolini and General Battisti in Novodmitrievka, when Pascolini shared the information received from General Martinat, Battisti prepared written orders for the remaining officers of his division, urging them to pull their troops together and push forward with all their strength. He claimed that their only means of salvation was to move ahead with great speed and endure long marches. Battisti believed it was necessary to stay away from the roads and to avoid inhabited areas, because the division was no longer capable of engaging in new offensive action. Of course, these orders meant the withdrawing forces would have to march in deep snow, cross numerous steep gullies, and make their way through several forests, confronting constant danger posed by roaming Russian partisan bands. Battisti planned to continue marching west at dawn on January 24 in two columns (the 1st Regiment would march to the right), circumventing Shelyakino from the north by several kilometers, by crossing the valley of the Kalitva River approximately halfway between Shelyakino and Varvarovka (most likely heavily fortified with enemy forces), or alternatively possibly marching further north of Varvarovka.[7]

General Battisti gathered his remaining officers together shortly before midnight to ask them if they wanted to proceed marching as a united group under his command, or if they preferred to divide themselves into smaller groups to attempt to escape from the Russian encirclement. All officers said that they wanted to continue the withdrawal as a united group under his command, except for Colonel Scrimin, Commander of the 2nd Alpine Regiment, Lieutenant Colonel Bellani (Vice-Commander of the 2nd Alpine Regiment), and Lieutenant Colonel Vertone, of the Divisional Command. These officers told Battisti they wanted to attempt to break out of the encirclement on their own.[8]

The officers needed an interpreter. Knowing Marsan could speak some Russian, they asked him to go with them. Marsan recalled this episode: "This was absolutely incredible! They actually asked me to go with them! Of course, I said, 'No thank you, I don't want to go.' I didn't want to abandon my men. The very fact that these officers, our very own commanders, would abandon our regiment was a terrible blow for all of us; it was shocking! After I refused to leave with them, they found a corporal, an interpreter for the division, who agreed to go with them. Early the next morning, the three officers left on a sled, pulled by a horse."

When Marsan was asked if he and his men perceived the action of these three officers as an outright act of desertion he said, "Of course we did!"

He then drew an analogy: "When a ship is in trouble, the captain is the last one to abandon the ship, and in some cases goes down with the vessel. This action by these officers was really sad. Colonel Scrimin, aged fifty-seven, was the oldest of the three. Vertone was a frail man. Scrimin had probably requested to go to the Russian front in order to gain another promotion in rank. Vertone had difficulty walking, and perhaps that was a compelling reason for him to make the decision he made. On the other hand, Bellani was a man of good character, in good physical shape. He was a courageous man. We were very surprised he made the choice to leave."

When asked if an inquiry or investigation took place with regard to this incident, Marsan said, "No, no inquiry was initiated because these officers said they had received permission from General Battisti to leave. Battisti never denied this. But we believed General Battisti would never have allowed his officers to desert their men."

In his own report, Battisti states that the three officers received permission to leave. One can only assume Battisti is referring to "permission" he himself granted.[9]

Major Guaraldi assumed command of the 2nd Regiment after Colonel Scrimin and the others left. Beraudi claims that the officers realized small groups could probably escape from the encirclement, because the Russians mainly attacked large groups of withdrawing forces and tended to ignore small, disorganized ones. He writes the following with regard to the Scrimin incident: "Guaraldi knows well, and General Battisti even more so, if they could choose two or three hundred men who are still well and determined, and if they could abandon the rest of the column, it would be easy to exit from the enemy encirclement. But the temptation, even such an idea, that a commander could abandon his own men, never ever entered their minds...."

As the three officers prepared to leave, Colonel Scrimin's adjutant, Major Bina, recounted "at the moment of leaving, B. [Lieutenant Colonel Bellani] excused himself by saying: 'I have a son and I haven't the heart to think I might not see him again,' forgetting that Major Bina had two sons waiting for him in Milan."[10]

The three officers, who had hoped to escape from the Russian encirclement on their own, were captured very soon after they left and sent to Khrinovoje, considered by many to have been the worst prisoner of war camp in all of Russia. All three eventually died in that camp.

Moments before leaving the column, Bellani spoke to Major Bina and Lieutenant Marsan, advising them to burn the regimental flag. Marsan said, "We realized we would be meeting up with the Russians and fighting them very soon. Burning the flag was a typical event, since you must never abandon your flag, and it's no use to wait until the last moment to do this."

That same evening, Marsan and Major Bina found shelter in a small izba. The next morning they found four eggs hidden in a chest. Marsan recalled that moment: "This was a miracle, for days on end we had had nothing to eat!"

The following morning, as the march was due to start again, a good deal of disorder ensued as the hundreds of men prepared to depart. Marsan explained: "You have to understand, whenever there was a rest stop, men in the column would spread out to look for something to eat and for a sheltered place to sleep. When it became time to resume the march, of course everybody wanted to be first in line, since Russian partisans would often attack the ends of the column. That morning there was a great deal of disorder and confusion. Major Bina and I essentially became traffic cops. It was a Sunday morning; I shall never forget that day. With pistol in hand, I was basically directing traffic, attempting to create some order, directing the disorganized men into the marching column."

On January 24 the march resumed, with the troops maintaining a distance of eight to nine kilometers from the bottom of the Kalitva Valley. The advance was cross-country in deep snow, through wooded areas and steep gullies causing enormous fatigue among the men. Once more, the column frequently became a target for Russian partisans.[11]

At a certain point, a German light plane landed close to the marching column. A German officer approached Battisti saying he had orders to take the general out of the encirclement. Battisti refused, stating he wanted to remain with his alpini. Battisti sent two wounded men to fly out of the area in his place.[12]

When reading about this event, one cannot help but wonder why the Germans aboard the plane didn't give the commanders of the Cuneense and Julia divisions the important message (transmitted January 21 to General Nasci), to change the direction of the withdrawal from Valuiki to Nikolaevka.

At a certain point, General Battisti and a group of alpini of the Dronero Battalion, including Lieutenant Beraudi, distanced themselves for a short time from the column and approached a small, unnamed village wondering if Russian soldiers were hiding within the izbas. When soldiers knocked on the door of one of them, several women appeared. Although frightened, they offered a bowl of milk to the general. When questioned, the women said they knew nothing about the whereabouts of any Russian soldiers. The alpini cautiously continued to move further on into the village until they reached a large square where they saw an abandoned Russian tank. Stretched out on the snow were three Hungarian officers without boots or socks, shot through the head.

Beraudi writes, "One lay on his side, the others faced down, but their faces were turned slightly to the side as if they had attempted to not lose sight of the sky until the very last moment. The color of their feet and hands was rosy, like those of men who are alive. Their uniforms were bright and vivid, in contrast to so much whiteness." Beraudi noted, when temperatures fall many degrees below zero, "bodies lying in the snow assume a placid and decorative appearance, resembling wax figures. Freezing prevents decomposition, features remain rigid, neutral coloring assumes a degree of vivacity in contrast to the huge white sheet of snow."[13]

Throughout these days of withdrawal, each day claimed its share of soldiers who could no longer follow the advancing columns. Exhausted men sank into the snow at the sides of the route and quickly froze, resembling those "wax figures" Beraudi described.

As the alpini continued to walk for hours across the snowy plains, exhaustion and hunger lessened their resistance to the fierce, freezing temperatures and bitter, biting winds. Delirium often set in; some men began to hallucinate as the freezing process (hypothermia) took hold, causing a complete breakdown of physical and mental processes. Many alpini lost their lives because they could no longer walk owing to wounds or varying degrees of exposure. There was no way to transport them. Whenever possible, placed in an izba and made as comfortable as possible, they were told that a Red Cross truck would soon come to fetch them. "This," Marsan noted, "of course, was not true." We knew they would continue to freeze and soon die in the sub-zero temperatures."

The instinct for survival and self-preservation held sway over moral considerations as the soldiers continued to push on. The horror was that they had no other choice. Lieutenant Beraudi describes his own agony as a fellow alpino, Bottallo (a dispatch rider), fell wounded during an attack. As Beraudi leaned down close to him Bottallo said, "Lieutenant, don't leave me here."

"Can you walk?"

"No, I can't stand up."

"All right; now I will go down [the hill] and return with a sled."

Beraudi knew there was no sled for Bottallo. He also knew he wouldn't return. "It seems to me I'm assassinating him with my own hands."[14]

Lieutenant Carlo Vicentini recalled how he and others of the Monte Cervino Battalion abandoned a wounded alpino: "He couldn't be moved, and even if he could have been moved, we had no means with which to transport him. The wounded man understood, for him it was finished, but with the reluctance and dignity so typical of mountain dwellers, he didn't want to cause us to pity him." He didn't give his comrades messages for his family in Italy, "rather it was all resolved with an unconvincing 'See you'." Vicentini writes, "At that moment we felt we were contemptible. Of course we had left many of our alpini unburied in the streets of Rossosh...but to abandon a man who is conscious and defenseless required a degree of cynicism to which we were not accustomed."[15]

Marsan noted that as the days went by the column of soldiers passed more and more frozen men sitting or lying in the snow. Discarded weapons and personal belongings littered the route the alpini followed. It was only by chance that Marsan and his friends were able to obtain some nourishment during those long days and nights. On one occasion, they found a chicken in an izba. It took little time to boil it and share it with a dozen comrades. Another time they found a beehive and ate the honeycombs (including the wax and dead bees).

One night when Lieutenants Marsan, Greci, and Beccaria were able to sleep in an izba, a Russian peasant gave Marsan a boiled potato. Marsan writes, "It was during the withdrawal that we discovered the genuine humanity of Russian peasants, ready to share their humble izbas and what little food they had. Then, as well as much later, they accommodated us not as aggressors, but as victims of a common catastrophe."[16]

Marsan recalled that at times during the withdrawal, soldiers could sleep for a few hours inside an izba, warm and relatively safe. The men crowded inside, often sleeping sitting or standing up, or lying down practically on top of one another, taking up every inch of available space. Other times they rested lying on the snow, sometimes with a layer of straw beneath them. Temperatures ranged between -30° and -47°. The danger of freezing to death was ever-present and often soldiers who found no shelter would simply continue walking back and forth, or jump up and down in place to keep their circulation going. Thus, they were able to survive the cold, yet lost much-needed rest.

Marsan describes the loss of his orderly, Ottavio: "At a certain point Ottavio simply stopped walking; he sat down in the snow and wouldn't move. I told him to get up, and I told him that if he stayed where he was, he would die. There was no response. I slapped his face; I yelled at him, I told him to get up, to get moving, to save himself. There was no response; he was immobile, like a statue. I tried so hard to save him, but he simply didn't respond to any of my attempts. My friends and I put Ottavio on a sled and took him to an izba where there were at least twenty other soldiers lying on the floor, also suffering from various degrees of exposure. We knew the men were beyond suffering, and would die very quickly in that state."

Once Marsan returned to Italy, he met Ottavio's mother. She told him she had had ten children. Ottavio was her eighth child (in Italian, *ottavo* is eighth). Her other children were also named in numerical order: *Primo, Secondo, Terzo, Quarto, Quinto, Sesto, Settimo, Nono, Decimo*. Marsan recalled that when he spoke to Ottavio's mother he told her, "The person who should have received the medal awarded to me when I returned from Russia should have been your son." Along with the "Silver Medal of Valor," Marsan received an annual monetary benefit. At the meeting with Ottavio's mother, he promised her he would forward that monetary benefit to her from then on. She was very grateful for this gift, which she received until she died.

At 1800 on January 24, following a three-hour stop in a small, unnamed village, the two columns of alpini headed south in order to cross the valley of the Kalitva River, avoiding inhabited areas and thus a chance of running into enemy forces or partisans. Crossing the valley was supposed to occur approximately halfway between Shelyakino and Varvarovka, or slightly upstream from Varvarovka. The column of the Cuneense Divisional Command and 2nd Regiment reached a tributary of the Kalitva River near Garbuzovo before dawn on January 25, and continued marching to Rybalzin, arriving early in the morning.[17]

The column of the 1st Cuneense Regiment arrived in Garbuzovo at 0800 on the morning of January 25. The commander intended to depart immediately for Rybalzin, but the alpini spread out in the village looking for food and shelter. All of a sudden, heavy enemy mortar and cannon fire erupted around the disbursed alpini. Two Russian tanks with infantry assaulted the end of the column. Casualties were significant. Enemy forces demolished several sleds loaded with wounded and frostbitten alpini.[18]

Despite these tragic losses, what remained of the column moved out of Garbuzovo, threatened by partisans attacking the flanks of the by now thinned-out column. By noon, the exhausted and famished alpini of the 1st Cuneense Regiment reached Rybalzin. General Battisti decided to remain in the village until the evening of January 25.[19]

Marsan recalled the long days and nights of marching during the withdrawal: "It was during the withdrawal that friendships were welded, born from the solidarity between us as we confronted the terrible physical and moral trials of those days."[20] During those long marches, Lieutenants Marsan, Carlo Greci, and Mario Beccaria often walked arm in arm, especially during the night marches. Marsan elaborated: "Those night marches were like being in the middle of an ongoing, living nightmare. Holding on to each other was very important; in fact, it was essential. We hadn't had anything to eat for days, we walked for hours, and it was dangerous because there were hundreds of soldiers. It was a real mess. It was chaotic. A mass of moving soldiers was all around us, soldiers from many different units. The real danger was you could reach a point when you could easily fall asleep while you were walking, or standing in the column of men, or you could fall. At night, it was pitch black, and you couldn't see anything. In a sense, you felt you were completely alone. If you fell asleep while walking, or standing, you might wake up surrounded by men you didn't know, or you might wander off from the column. This happened. By holding on to each other, we prevented this possibility."

Beraudi recalls one night following a march of twenty-six hours straight without food or rest. He dropped down in the snow at the side of the route, utterly exhausted. A mule followed by a cursing mule driver stumbled over him in the darkness. Beraudi jumped up quickly, realizing he could have easily frozen to death. He writes, "[I could have been] transformed into one of those placid, rosy cadavers we leave behind more frequently. Then, finding myself in the midst of so many unknown men and accepting the fact I would have to struggle for a long time to reach the front of the column, I fully recognized how desperate our situation really was, and I quite regretted having been awakened."[21]

On January 25, the ninth day of the withdrawal, several German soldiers told Beraudi and other officers that the Russians were already in Kharkov, 150 kilometers ahead of them. Beraudi writes, "Why one proceeds now, nobody knows; nobody poses that question." He notes indifference substituted for the optimism experienced during the first days, "in the rage of battle and the ferocious anger of the successive ones." Too many died, and those who had survived, who continued to fight and march, did so only out of "habit," having passed the limits of "any normal resistance."[22]

Beraudi hadn't unlaced his boots once during the days of the withdrawal. He writes, "We are not men anymore, yet we speak to each other as if we were men, about things that have nothing to do with the war or with Russia.... If I had opened up the shell encompassing me, even for a moment, I might have become a man of a million needs and would have died immediately, or, I would never have moved from an izba, the same way that hundreds die every day, or are abandoned.[23]

At a certain point, a small group of alpini including Beraudi reached a small, deserted, out-of-the-way village. Within one of the izbas a "biblical figure of a man with a huge white beard and his wife served the uninvited soldiers" who entered their home. Some of the men removed honeycombs from beehives belonging to the daughter of the Russian couple, causing her to cry and whimper, fearing her bees would die. Beraudi writes, "I chew honey and wax with ancestral pleasure, like in the days of cavemen. The daughter looks at me disapprovingly through her tears." Attempting to console his daughter the old man said, "*Vojnà, vojnà* " ("[It's] the war; [it's] the war"). Beraudi noted that the old man probably wanted to say much more about war, including the fact it could be even worse, yet he hesitated to do so in the presence of the soldiers. He might have said, "If you irritate these men, you will become aware they are no longer men, but are foul, torpid, beasts, and, my poor spinster daughter, if they don't kill your father and mother and don't turn you into the wife of ten or one hundred, it's only because their bestiality is drowsing.... But, if you excite and irritate them with your constant crying, they will create an apocalypse...."[24]

Upon leaving the izba, Beraudi bowed in front of an icon and made the sign of the cross. The old man and his wife shed a tear, but seemed pleased by his gesture, whereas the young girl resumed her crying. Beraudi writes, "One can understand that pagans kill bees; but Christians!"[25]

Chapter 11

DISASTER ON THE STEPPE

FROM RYBALZIN TO MALAKEEVO

At twilight January 25, remnants of the alpini of the Cuneense and Julia divisions prepared to march on. Then a violent storm erupted with tremendous winds and snowfall. In one hour, alpini at the head of the column could only march forward a mere two hundred meters. Many suffered from frostbite on their feet and faces as the storm battered them. The column returned to the village of Rybalzin to wait out the storm, but many alpini failed to reach shelter. Their frozen bodies were discovered the following morning.[1]

At dawn on January 26 the storm petered out, and the alpini resumed their march in one column, determined to reach Valuiki. A German plane flew above the column; no messages or signals alerted the alpini to change direction. This one instance of air surveillance was the only such occurrence during the whole of the withdrawal of the Cuneense and Julia divisions.[2]

As the column began to descend a slope heading toward a village situated at the bottom of the Kalitva Valley, heavy mortar and machine-gun fire erupted. The alpini positioned their few remaining machine guns and responded to the Russian fire. Battisti writes, "In order to shoot, one had to light a fire by placing straw under each gun (every weapon was equipped with a tent tarp filled with straw to be lit in order to warm the machine gun at the moment of use)." The Dronero Battalion, the only battalion still in somewhat fair shape, was able to

140

close in on the enemy with the use of bayonets, causing the Russians to withdraw. Many dead and wounded alpini scattered on the snow paid the high price for this victory.[3]

The alpini continued to march until nightfall without encountering further action. Another attack occurred as they reached villages on the approaches to Malakeevo. The division separated into two groups and followed separate routes (eight kilometers apart) until 0100 on January 27, when the columns stopped to rest. At dawn, both groups resumed marching, but they were unable to sight each other or communicate until 1000, when a low-flying Russian plane flying low over the columns alternated between the two, bombing and strafing, causing casualties. Following this incident, the two columns of the division joined up together.[4]

That afternoon the column skirted the village of Voronovka because of intense mortar fire. At twilight, General Battisti ordered the alpini to stop in order to reorganize the column before proceeding to the valley of the Valui River, where he planned to cross the Valuiki–Nikolaevka railroad tracks, away from any inhabited areas, which according to information given by several civilians were occupied by enemy forces.[5]

As the march began, large squads of Cossacks sporting machine guns loaded on sleds attacked the head of the column. Once more, the Dronero Battalion managed to counterattack and was able to force the enemy to withdraw.[6]

Once the march continued, more attacks of enemy mortar fire resumed. Shrapnel from a mortar round hit Beraudi. The impact threw him several meters, where he fell on his knees into the snow. He was able to rise realizing he had been hit in the leg, yet he couldn't determine exactly where his wound was. Major Guaraldi immediately placed Beraudi on a passing horse after he ordered the rider to dismount. Beraudi rode for a while, aware, despite the pain he was feeling, that he had to keep moving his feet while on horseback to avoid the onset of frostbite. At a certain point another alpino, hit in the knee, could no longer walk. Beraudi got off the horse to let the other soldier mount. Beraudi continued on foot, limping badly. Again, enemy forces attacked. Beraudi writes, "I decided for me the war is finished. I want a corner in which I can lie down and sleep or die: (either one) it's the same thing."[7]

Once more, a fellow soldier found a horse for him; however, the horse soon collapsed, probably from fatigue and hunger. The alpino then picked Beraudi up and dragged him for a while, then walked beside him as Beraudi limped on. Finally they reached a village and Beraudi found an izba full of soldiers. He entered and sat down on the floor, hoping the others would soon leave. After several hours, the order to leave came. Many soldiers begged him to go with them. He refused and threw himself down on a couch. He was exhausted and the wound in his thigh was becoming unbearably painful. He took off his boots and discovered his socks didn't exist anymore. Around his ankles, he saw bloody grooves caused by his frozen boots. He felt his war was finished, and his life was finished.[8]

The march continued throughout the night, continuously harassed by mortar fire. At dawn, in an unexplainable move, the Dronero Battalion at the head of the column turned south. General Battisti sent several officers on horseback to redirect the Dronero west. Major Beraedi managed to reach the head of the column where a German officer, who was among the Italian officers in the lead, was urging the Dronero to move rapidly. Both the German and Italian officers refused to listen to Major Beraedi who implored them to alter their direction.[9]

As these soldiers reached an inhabited area, they raced toward houses in the village; once inside they didn't want to budge. Exhaustion, more than fear of capture, spurred them. Those unable to find shelter stopped in the middle of fields dotted with haystacks, setting fires to warm themselves. Every effort to redirect them to link up with the main column failed.[10]

At first light, groups of Russian partisans attacked, surprising those alpini asleep in houses in the villages where they had sought refuge. Alpini who were able to extricate themselves took up the march west, attempting to join the column to the north of them headed by General Battisti and officers of the Cuneense divisional command. Enemy aircraft began strafing the column to the south, and soon artillery erupted. A squad of Cossacks arriving from the north galloped along the bottom of the valley toward the column. One alpino, not realizing who the Cossacks were, hollered: "Here come the Hungarians." Others repeated his words and the news spread through the column like wildfire causing many to run toward the enemy. As the Cossacks encircled them, a few soldiers who hadn't followed the others attempted in vain to reach the column headed by Battisti.[11]

General Battisti continued to march toward a village a few kilometers distant from Valuiki, when enemy cavalry troops attacked the column once more. Following a short battle in which their ammunition was exhausted, the tortuous withdrawal ended. All surviving alpini of the Cuneense and Julia divisions, as well as soldiers from the various leaderless groups that had joined the column during the withdrawal, all who had fought so valiantly along the route with every means possible in an attempt to break out of the encirclement, were captured in and around the outskirts of Valuiki between January 27 and 28. Approximately 4,000 exhausted, famished men, many of whom were wounded or suffered from frostbite, were now prisoners of war.[12]

Marsan described these last moments: "We had seen the Russians already waiting at a distance on horseback, yet the three of us, Greci, Beccaria, and myself, decided to attempt to escape by spending a night in a windmill not far off on the left side of the route. Soon after we turned away from the main column, I stepped on something soft. Looking down I saw a small white bag half hidden in the snow near my foot. I picked it up; it was half-full of sugar! There was enough for each of us to have a handful of 'good omen.' However, a little farther on, as we were directing our attention to the right in order to follow the movement of the column, we heard, coming from our left, *'ruki vverch'* ('hands up'). To our surprise, there were three or four Russians on skis, wearing white suits that had made them hardly visible from afar. They immediately asked us for our watches. I had pushed my watch up on my forearm so they couldn't see it, so only the other two had to give up their watches. This, then, was the end of our struggle for freedom and the beginning of an obscure future."

In his report written after he returned from Russia from a prisoner of war camp in 1950, General Battisti briefly summarized events of the withdrawal of the Cuneense Division. He claims that the alpini of the division had walked for approximately 250 kilometers in twelve days and eleven nights, walking an average of sixteen hours every twenty-four hours for the most part away from established roads, therefore in deep snow.

During the withdrawal from the Don River lines, the alpini fought in approximately twenty battles with Russian soldiers and partisans. The additional enemies (hunger, freezing temperatures, fatigue, exhaustion, exposure, and frostbite) added to the losses the division suffered.

More than two thirds of the alpini of the Cuneense who were present when the withdrawal began were lost. The general claims that the number of deaths caused by the elements probably amounted to half of all losses occurring in battle.[13]

Chapter 12

WITHDRAWAL OF THE TRIDENTINA DIVISION

THE TRIDENTINA WITHDRAWS FROM PODGORNOJE

On the evening of January 18, battalions of the Tridentina Division were in the process of assembling in Podgornoje following their disengagement from the front lines on the Don. General Nasci, commander of the entire Alpine Corps, along with service units of the corps joined the Tridentina Division in Podgornoje.[1]

The commander of the Tridentina, General Reverberi, planned to move out of Podgornoje in two columns in a westerly direction. The 5th Regiment would proceed on the left (including the Val Camonica Group), and the 6th Regiment on the right (with the Vicenza and Bergamo Groups, as well as the section of divisional services).[2]

Podgornoje had been an important logistical base for the Alpine Corps. Now, dense smoke covered the town. Italian warehouses, ammunition dumps, and supply depots had been set on fire. As flames lit the sky and ammunition dumps exploded, Lieutenant Nuto Revelli (Tirano Battalion, 5th Alpine Regiment) and alpini in his company joined the chaotic crowds of soldiers leaving Podgornoje on January 19: "We merge on to the road leading to the main street and insert ourselves into the mob. Trucks, carts, sleds, and mule trains clog the columns, Italians and Germans yell, push, curse, stop, and run. Like stones in a flooded river, we roll, bumping into each other. We cross over columns, we cut off others, and others cross over and cut through our column. We hardly move, or else we run...it's continuous confusion."[3]

SKORORYB

Once the troops of the 5th Alpine Regiment reached the summit of a steep rise leading away from Podgornoje, they proceeded to follow orders moving toward Opyt, but a counter-order redirected them to advance toward Skororyb. As they approached, they realized the Tirano Battalion was already engaged in battle with enemy forces. Once alpini of the Edolo Battalion reached the outskirts of Skororyb, they removed the heavy weapons from their sleds along with cases of ammunition and carried them forward on their backs. As they advanced, they could hear the sounds of a furious battle ahead. A few riflemen who had gone ahead were now returning, sporting a variety of wounds; "some were holding a hand over their bleeding chest or stomach, others holding a lifeless arm or supporting a fellow alpino who was staggering or limping."[4]

As alpini advanced closer to the village, enemy forces began firing automatic weapons from izbas resembling "veritable fortresses." Alpini advanced in a zigzag manner, dropping in the snow, firing their antiquated rifles. There was no time to set up machine guns. Andrea Rico Fedriga, an alpino in the Edolo Battalion, wrote, "Now, an unexpected surprise: to our right two big [Russian] tanks appear." As the tanks advanced toward the alpini, Fedriga heard someone yell, "Help, help, they are killing all my alpini." Fedriga realized the voice belonged to one of the commanders who, realizing the danger the tanks posed, called for help. "[Help] from whom?" Fedriga wondered.[5]

Yet, at that very moment, from the left, a German tank appeared. Alpini half buried in the snow observed as the tanks advanced toward each other. The German tank was much smaller than the two Russian ones. As Fedriga watched them assume their positions, as if preparing for a duel, he recalled the biblical story of David and Goliath. He wrote, "I watch the German tank. I see the turret moving...I look at one of the Russian tanks. The first one is completing the same maneuver, but the German tank is faster and fires." Bull's eye, it was a direct centered hit! A mixture of smoke and flames rose from the Russian tank as it moved slightly and then stopped. "Now the German tank is stopped as if studying the movements of the second [Russian] tank. It had moved in order to get around the front of the first one, maneuvering its turret, aiming it against its enemy, but it's too slow; again, the German tank fires first and hits its target in the center. Smoke and fire also envelop the second monster...." Alpini witnessing this scene tried not to think about the Russian soldiers facing a hideous death within the burning tanks. Fedriga wrote, "One couldn't allow oneself to think such natural human thoughts. In war, one has to kill to avoid being killed, to kill with an almost savage joy, because the death of the other means life for one's self. Damn the war, and damn him who makes us fight."[6]

The battle subsided for a moment but then resumed, more furious than before. Alpini continued their advance, reaching a point approximately one hundred to one hundred and fifty meters from the village. At that moment, Fedriga heard orders passed verbally from alpino to alpino: "Insert bayonets, prepare for hand to hand fighting; move when you hear Savoia." Hearing the signal, alpini hollered their battle cry, "a terrifying scream," as they rose from the snow and advanced. Confronted by an "overwhelming avalanche" of men moving toward the village, the Russians stopped firing and began running away. As alpini advanced into the village, they could see enemy soldiers jumping out of windows, running out of doors, seemingly vanishing between izbas under a now darkening sky.[7]

Alpini began a search of village streets and izbas. Fedriga and a few men of his squad approached the entrance of an underground cellar. Two alpini stood at the sides of the entrance, while Fedriga and a few others stood a few paces away from the entrance with rifles at the ready. Those standing by the side of the entrance threw a couple of handgrenades into the cellar opening. Fortunately, the grenades didn't explode, but someone within was hit because the soldiers could hear a muffled cry.

Women and children emerged from the cellar gazing at the alpini with frightened faces. The alpini asked, "*Nema partisan?*" ("No partisans?") "*Nema, nema,*" they responded. Fedriga wrote, "We smile at them and reach out to stroke the children; they also smile, understanding they need not fear us." At that moment, shots directed at the alpini and civilians came from the right. All dropped in the snow, with the alpini protecting the civilians with their bodies.[8]

Following this event, Fedriga and his men took up combing the village once more. Fedriga walked slowly among the izbas, passing many dead soldiers scattered on the snow. As he reached a crossroad, he saw an izba on fire to the right, surrounded by people warming themselves.

An individual approached slowly. He couldn't distinguish the identity but he was certain the person wasn't an alpino.

"Who goes there?" he shouted.

There was no response.

"Halt right there!

The person continued to approach. Fedriga realized he should probably shoot, "but something within me told me not to." A corporal, attracted by Fedriga's shouts, reached him and told him to fire as he raised his own rifle and took aim. Fedriga pushed the corporal's rifle downwards: "Wait a moment, that person isn't a man."

The corporal responded, "Whoever it is, you mustn't wait until he shoots first, and anyway how can you distinguish whether or not it's a man or a woman, we all look alike bundled up the way we are."

In order to calm the corporal down, Fedriga told him he was keeping the person in his sights and if anything suspicious occurred he would shoot, but he didn't want to kill an innocent person.[9]

As the unknown individual advanced, Fedriga could hear a woman's cries. He approached. As he lowered her hands covering her face, he saw the tear stained countenance of a young girl. When asked why she was crying, she explained that the Germans had set her house on fire. Fedriga took her arm and walked toward her burning izba where he saw two elderly people kneeling before it, crying. Surrounding the izba, Germans and Italians were happily warming themselves. Fedriga writes, "Similar scenes would occur more than once in every village we would pass through. I immediately distanced myself, pained and disgusted by the scene just witnessed, which made me think of my old parents [and how they would react] if such an event should also occur to them."[10]

Alpini in Fedriga's squad received orders to remain at the entrance to the village while the remaining alpini of the Edolo Battalion advanced into the center. The squad remained until relieved by alpini who hadn't participated in the battle. By now Fedriga and his companions were freezing, and began to search for an izba where they could spend the night. They discovered most were already full, but soon they saw one where there was no light. As they approached the door, none of them wanted to be the first to enter; they were concerned partisans might be lingering within. Fedriga moved toward the front door, "Not to be a hero, not because I was more courageous than the others, but because I was freezing and I was in a hurry to get warm." He unlocked the safety on his rifle, held a hand-grenade in his hand and kicked the door open. Inside, the only light came from a candle placed under a sacred icon. An elderly woman sitting in a chair had her head on a table. She seemed to be asleep. As the alpini entered, she raised her head.

"*Nema partisan?*" Fedriga asked.

"*Nema partisan, italianskie choroshio*" ("No partisans, Italians are good"), she said.

Fedriga placed his hand gently on the woman's back and said, "*Russkie choroshio*" ("Russians are good").[11]

Using gestures, Fedriga attempted to make the woman understand that his alpini wanted to dry off, warm themselves, and sleep, even on the floor if necessary. Smiling, the woman took the alpini into another very warm room where to their surprise there were three pretty young girls. The girls smiled and treated the alpini with kindness, even though the men's appearance was that of rough, uncouth peasants. For a short while, Fedriga noted, he and his men forgot where they were and what they had experienced only a short time before; they almost felt happy.[12]

Just as the men were beginning to relax, an alpino arrived with orders to assemble in the village square. Thanking the Russians who appeared to be sorry to see them leave, and warmly shaking their hands, the alpini departed from the welcoming izba. After standing in the square for half an hour, they received orders to find shelter once more; departure for the battalion was scheduled for very early the following morning. Fedriga and his men found shelter in another izba and promptly fell asleep. He believes it was wise to have moved from the earlier friendly accommodations. Although so pleasant, the men wouldn't have taken a moment away from the pretty girls to get a decent, much needed rest.[13]

POSTOIALYJ, REPIEVKA AND OPYT

During this same period, the 6th Alpine Regiment had left Podgornoje heading toward Postoialyj via Repievka. Enemy forces occupied Postoialyj; nevertheless the Verona Battalion attacked, and its efforts were successful at the beginning. For a variety of reasons, the remaining battalions of the 6th Regiment were not available to support the Verona at a critical point when Russian troops, reinforced by tanks, were in a position to gain the upper hand. The Verona was forced to withdraw to Repievka, "but it was able to contain—despite a high price paid in losses—the pressure of the enemy." The Val Chiese Battalion moved on to Repievka to support the Verona, while the remainder of the 6th Regiment arrived in Opyt (to the southeast) as did the command groups of the Tridentina Division, the Alpine Corps, and the XXIV Panzer Corps, as well as a number of alpini from the Julia Division and one thousand leaderless, disorganized Hungarian troops. A Hungarian colonel who was among these troops, informed officers of the Tridentina that his division, ordered to withdraw to the right of the Tridentina, had been "broken apart in several [groups] and remnants of that division were attempting to escape from the enemy vise."[14]

During the early hours of January 19, another thousand or so Hungarian troops arrived in Opyt. Several thousand German troops (remnants of the XXIV Panzer Corps), now under the command of Austrian General Eibl, also arrived in Opyt with their many sleds. Four German assault guns, a battery of rocket launchers, and a battery of artillery (with five cannons of medium caliber) under the command of Major Fischer arrived with the Germans, who were now placed under the command of the Tridentina.[15]

General Reverberi summed up the situation on January 19: "Although in part the situation was becoming clearer, unfortunately it appeared very serious." The general described the overall predicament, claiming the original plan for the withdrawal from the Don had called for the Germans to withdraw to the left of the Alpine Corps. Now the German army consisted mainly of remnants spilling on to the Tridentina. The Second Hungarian Army, directed to withdraw to the right of the Alpine Corps, was in rapid retreat, leaving the right wing of the Tridentina exposed. Finally, Reverberi noted, "Russian units of imprecise but certainly considerable strength are to the front of our division."[16]

General Nasci ordered units of the Tridentina Division to remain in their positions in Opyt and Repievka on January 19, because another attack on the zone of Postoialyj was to occur the following day. Several factors led to the decision to remain in Opyt, the first being that there was now no doubt of the encirclement of the Tridentina. Second, the masses of fugitive soldiers, most of whom were allies, were creating a huge obstacle which would impede the advance of the alpini. It was decided to attempt to organize these hordes of disorganized soldiers flooding Opyt, and to reinforce the defense of the town in order to protect that gathering area once units of the Tridentina moved out the following day to attack Postoialyj.[17]

Remaining units of the 6th Regiment, except for the 54th Company of the Vestone Battalion, were sent toward Repievka to prepare for the attack on Postoialyj the following day. German units were also sent to Repievka to support the 6th Regiment. In Opyt, commanders planned to organize Hungarian soldiers into battalions, and to gather all other impediments such as sleds and mule pack units, in order to insert them into the columns in an organized manner.[18]

Plans for the attack on Postoialyj called for the 6th Alpine Regiment to capture the town and move immediately on to Novokhar'kovka. The 5th Regiment was also to take part in the strike, moving around to the left.[19]

Lieutenant Bruno Zavagli had left Rossosh with drivers and trucks from his transport section as the Russians attacked the city on January 15. His unit had followed alpini and soldiers attached to service units formerly deployed in Rossosh as they withdrew north, arriving in Opyt during the evening of January 19. The command group of the Alpine Corps had set up temporary headquarters in a large green wooden building. Zavagli reported to headquarters where an unnamed general gave him orders to salvage fuel from all trucks in the village. The general explained that the trucks would no longer be of use; from here on all fuel would be used for the few German tanks and armored vehicles. Two *carabinieri* (military police) assigned to Zavagli were to assist him on this mission.[20]

Zavaglia writes, "This was a difficult moment. It means we are to abandon all means of transport.... We won't proceed on a comfortable withdrawal by truck; the present situation begins to reveal the reality of our circumstances." As he passed from truck to truck draining every drop of fuel, drivers cursed and cast angry glances at him. "It's as if I am taking away their last drop of blood." Once Zavagli drained the fuel from a truck, he fired shots into the radiator.[21]

At 0200 on January 20, Russian forces attacked the zone of Opyt from the north. Alpini of the 54th Company of the Vestone Battalion and the 45th Battery managed to push enemy forces back, but now it was clear that the right flank of the division was completely exposed.[22]

At dawn, a second attack on Opyt began with intense mortar, artillery, and automatic weapon fire. Russian forces had obviously made use of the dark to move their forces around the zone, attempting an encirclement. All available units fought valiantly, knowing that if the Russians succeeded they could capture the command group of the Alpine Corps, and could cut the Tridentina in two by inserting themselves between the division's 5th and 6th Regiments. The battle continued, but the alpini failed to gain the upper hand until the 2nd Battalion of Engineers moved into the fray, managing to stop the Russian advance, yet losing sixty percent of their men in the process. Their bravery permitted the command group of the Alpine Corps as well as reorganized columns of Hungarians and other fragmented units to begin to move out of the Opyt zone.[23]

Meanwhile the 6th Regiment, supported by the Bergamo and Vicenza Groups and German units, was doing battle in Postoialyj with the support of the 5th Regiment and the Val Camonica Group.

Lieutenant Colonel Chierici, commander of the Val Chiese Battalion, recalled the battle of Postoialyj. He noted that Major Bongiovanni, commander of the Verona Battalion, who was ordered to take Postoialyj by General Reverberi, fell right into "a Russian trap." He writes, "Those who fight the Russians must keep three factors in mind: First, the skill with which the Russians camouflage their field operations. Second, their capacity, perhaps insuperable, to set a trap, namely the ability to remain in a place for days on end without giving signs of their presence, or to remain for hours lying on the snow so they cannot be seen, even from a short distance, especially at night. Third, if attacked frontally they don't give up, even when threatened by death."[24]

Major Bongiovanni, erroneously led to believe there were no large numbers of Russian troops in Postoialyj other than those sighted at a distance to the north of the village in a large kholkhoz, walked right into the deadly trap. As alpini of the Verona Battalion entered Postoialyj, enemy forces attacked them violently; every izba in the village housed "nests" of armed Russians who had remained hidden from all surveillance. [25]

Following several hours of a raging, bloody battle, including hand-to-hand combat, the alpini managed to occupy the town, capturing numerous prisoners. General Reverberi writes, "Around 1300 of this day, charged with events that for some hours created an almost desperate situation, the first enemy encirclement was broken, frustrating the Russian attempt to break the Tridentina. The unshakable tenacity of all…and firm willingness to push through enemy lines at any cost, triumphed." Reverberi noted that the many acts of "heroism" during this battle "reconfirmed and exceeded the traditional virtues of mountain troops," especially since alpini fought against overwhelming enemy forces supported by numerous tanks.[26]

For those who survived, viewing the battlefield the following day presented a "ghastly spectacle." Hundreds of alpini run over by tanks lay literally flattened on the snow, while dozens more, surprised by the enemy as they had advanced, lay scattered throughout the village.[27]

During this period, the commander of the Alpine Corps, General Nasci, attempted to contact the Julia, Cuneense, and Vicenza divisions by radio with new orders. He believed that if the alpine divisions united to march together, preceded by a strong advance unit, they would be in a better position to break through Russian lines. Unable to make radio contact with the other alpine divisions, Nasci sent his Chief of Staff, General Martinat, on a mission to deliver these new orders in person.

As noted earlier, General Martinat could only reach the mobile command post of General Pascolini (commander of the Vicenza Division) and convey to him Nasci's orders. He also explained that Nasci wanted all divisions to march together toward Valuiki, following the same route instead of the three separate routes assigned to the divisions while still on the Don. As it turned out, General Pascolini was only able to give General Nasci's message to the Cuneense Division two days later. Owing to a complete lack of accurate information, due primarily to poor reconnaissance, General Nasci could not have known that the VII Cossack Cavalry had already occupied Valuiki on January 19.[28]

In Postoialyj, General Nasci formed an "advance unit" which included the command groups of the Alpine Corps (with General Nasci) and the XXIV Panzer Corps (with General Eibl), two battalions of the 6th Alpine Regiment, and several batteries of artillery (alpini and German). The advance unit was under the command of General Reverberi. The remaining units of the Tridentina Division (three battalions of the 5th Regiment and one battalion of the 6th Regiment, the Verona, as well as remaining alpine artillery groups of the division, were placed under the command of Colonel Adami. Since General Reverberi was in command of the advance unit, Colonel Adami took command of the Tridentina Division.[29]

NOVOKHAR'KOVKA, LYMAREV, KRAVZOVKA, AND SHELYAKINO

The advance unit of the Tridentina left Postoialyj on January 20, marching southwest toward Novokhar'kovka, arriving there at 1700 to find the village occupied. Enemy forces consisting of two battalions supported by tanks, artillery, and mortars fought valiantly, but were soon forced to give ground. Alpini managed to put a number of tanks out of commission, and Russian forces withdrew as alpini moved into the village and prepared for the inevitable counterattack.[30]

Meanwhile, remaining units of the Tridentina followed in the path of the advance unit, fighting off ambushes by partisans who were able to hide in a number of wooded areas. The Verona Battalion, protecting the right flank of the column, fought off a Russian unit attempting to assault that flank of the division. Following this battle the Verona assumed a rearguard position. General Reverberi noted that by the night of January 21, alpini had "overwhelmed and broken" the second barrier the enemy had created to block the advance of the Tridentina Division.[31]

While stopped in Novokhar'kovka, General Nasci gave orders to proceed to Lymarev and Shelyakino on the night of January 21. By now, it was clear that the enemy would continue to obstruct the advance of the alpini by making use of their numerous motorized units, which they could rapidly enlarge as needed. It was also clear that the alpini needed to move ahead rapidly in order to prevent enemy forces from reorganizing. By marching primarily at night, and avoiding major roads and inhabited areas as much as possible, they could avoid attacks by enemy aircraft and large formations of tanks, and could possibly present the enemy with a degree of uncertainty as to their exact location. In addition, it was important to prevent fragmented Italian and allied groups from continuing to flow into the columns of the division, interspersing themselves and preventing cohesion among fighting groups of alpini. Finally, during rest stops it was important to take advantage of inhabited areas in order to offer refuge to the fighting men who were beginning to suffer the consequences of the extreme rigors of freezing temperatures. All the aforementioned realizations were "simple concepts yet difficult to actualize," noted General Reverberi. All required "ability and iron will on the part of commanders of all ranks in order to prevent any weakness that could compromise the desired result, which was to escape from capture and total destruction."[32]

As the advance unit under the command of General Reverberi marched ahead to Kravzovka it was suddenly caught in a barrage of heavy Russian artillery fire. After a successful counterattack, the alpini rapidly took over the village.[33] Since most of the izbas in Kravzovka quickly filled up with soldiers, General Reverberi and his advance unit prepared to leave the village to march ahead to Shelyakino in order to find shelter for the night. As Reverberi prepared to leave he received orders to remain in Kravzovka, because General Nasci desired to remain in the village overnight. A storm was brewing and the temperature continued to drop; cases of frostbite were multiplying. General Reverberi was unable to convince Nasci he needed to move on to find overnight shelter for his men. Nasci refused to allow the advance unit to leave the village: "That rest stop is still remembered as a nightmare by the survivors; around noon a snowstorm began and the temperature dropped to - 40°. Only a few units were able to find shelter in izbas." Those who remained outside in the storm lit fires close to the izbas causing several of them to catch fire, burning the men inside. The storm raged throughout the night as hundreds of men wandered around the village, desperately seeking warmth and food.[34]

That same evening, Colonel Adami and the remaining units of the Tridentina arrived at this scene of confusion and desperation. Their march from Novokhar'kovka had been a terrible ordeal. It had been sheer torture to walk in the storm's very strong winds. General Reverberi ordered Colonel Adami to continue marching on to seek shelter for his men in Lymarev, a short distance from Kravzovka. Once Colonel Adami arrived in that small village, he found the izbas occupied for the most part by throngs of disorganized units; thus, many alpini spent that terrible night outside in the cold.[35]

Chaplain Don Gnocchi was among those seeking shelter in Lymarev. He entered a semi-destroyed school where dozens of wounded and frostbitten soldiers lay on the earthen floor. At one point two soldiers entered, supporting a German general wounded in the foot by a hand grenade. In the flickering light from matches, the officer was operated on with a pocketknife, yet his life couldn't be saved; he died soon after, bleeding to death.[36]

As the wind rose outside and the temperature dropped, soldiers desperate to find shelter began to press against the doors of the school where alpini guarded the wounded and frostbitten gathered within. The weight of the men, "literally intoxicated by the cold, broke through the fragile line of the sentinels and men spilled into the schoolrooms, stepping on the wounded and dying men on the floor. It was a tangle of bodies, screams, curses, and pleas in the shadows of that hopeless hovel." Don Gnocchi managed to reach a sidewall of a room, "to allow that gush of madmen to pass by." Scratching those closest to him in the face, he managed to leave the schoolhouse. He writes, "Once outside I let myself walk along the wall, dazed by terror, speechless and impotent."[37]

Owing to the impossibility of obtaining more fuel, it was necessary to abandon the few remaining trucks carrying ammunition and provisions of food. As grave as this decision was, all remaining fuel was to be used to pull the heavy artillery. As the withdrawal had continued, increasing needs for transport of the wounded, frostbitten, and sick became necessary. Now, sleds used for that purpose were to be used to transport provisions of food and ammunition. This decision was "a hard but unavoidable necessity," and created serious consequences. Following these orders, General Reverberi writes, "One saw the most generous examples of camaraderie: alpini who carried the load of their more tired companions; alpini who carried stretchers with the wounded and sick; alpini who substituted themselves for quadrupeds pulling sleds.... Everything humanly possible was devised and carried out by soldiers of the Tridentina...so that the majority of our Italian and allied companions could enjoy victory upon reaching our [final] destination."[38]

On January 21, the Command Group of the ARMIR was able to transmit a radio message to the Germans withdrawing with the Tridentina Division: "The withdrawing columns were to aim for Nikolaevka, because Valuiki was solidly occupied by the enemy." Tragically, only the Tridentina Division received this vitally important message to change the route of the withdrawal, since no one was able to reach the other divisions by radio.[39]

As noted in Chapter 9, between January 21 and 23, a few units of the Julia, Cuneense, and Vicenza divisions had succeeded in reaching the column of withdrawing forces led by the Tridentina Division. Bedeschi was among them and describes what he and his men of the Julia Division witnessed as they joined the thousands following the Tridentina: "Almost 100,000 men struggled in a procession perhaps 30 kilometers long, an enormous body of human strength already undermined by hunger, by the cold, by battles, by exhaustion. Every unit dragged the wounded, frostbitten, and heavy weapons...." Along with the Italians, there were Germans, Romanians, and Hungarians. "There were some who had cannons, a little ammunition, and no food; others had a truck, a half-empty drum of fuel, and a little bread; some had a rifle, a handful of bullets for each man, and nothing more; some were only hungry.... The huge column advanced, abandoning its waste on the snow: broken sleds, cannons out of use, broken rifles, and vehicles with empty tanks...."[40]

From January 22 to 25, the withdrawing forces of the Tridentina continued to make progress, successfully battling Russian forces in the villages of Shelyakino and Malakeevo. The column passed through numerous villages whose names were unknown by most alpini. Villages were mainly distinguished one from the other based on whether they were occupied by partisans or Soviet soldiers, whether they were still inhabited by civilians, or by some specific geographical distinction.[41]

Vittorio Trentini of the Julia Division recalls entering an izba in an unnamed village with a number of fellow soldiers. The exhausted men were seeking a few hours of warmth and rest. Trentini had lost his gloves and suffered indescribable, piercing pain in his hands. The Russian woman living in the izba gazed at his purple hands. Silently, without speaking, she removed a sheepskin serving as a rug and left the room, returning shortly with two sheepskin mitts she had cut and sewn. "Lovingly she urged me to try them on, smiling once she was certain they fit well. I have kept those mitts; they saved my hands...I shall always remember that dear mother whom I hugged with intense emotion...I shall always remember her with infinite gratitude.[42]

During the withdrawal, Lieutenant Giorgio Gaza, commander of the 253rd Company of the Val Chiese Battalion, recalled an unusual moment during a snowstorm in which he offered to help Ugo Bodei, an alpino in his company who had exposed his private part while urinating, attempting to shield it from the wind with his hand. "I was passing by. I saw him, and immediately realized the grave risk he was taking (it was -40°) therefore I immediately intervened. He was standing. On my knees in front of him, I rapidly removed my gloves, 'treated' him in the manner needed, placing the 'part' in question back where it was warm, and buttoned his pants; an operation he couldn't have managed anymore, having hands paralyzed by the cold."

After thirty-five years, this experience was revisited as Gaza, Bodei, and Bodei's son met in a restaurant in Rezzato, Brescia. All agreed Gaza had performed a first rate "rescue operation" which prevented possible mutilation, not only "painful, but also humiliating."[43]

Casualties continued to mount as the thousands marched on. Sometimes Russian tanks fired on the column; sometimes katyusha rockets exploded in their midst. From time to time, Russian planes strafed the columns, causing bedlam, killing and wounding hundreds. Occasionally Russian tanks simply ran over sections of the column, crushing the living and those who had already died. Russian troops or partisans would suddenly appear, attack the columns at different points, and then disappear rapidly. This hit-and-run method, effective and deadly, caused panic and confusion. It was often difficult for men in the columns to defend themselves since so many were unarmed. Those who had weapons often lacked ammunition. In the confusion of the marching thousands, armed units also became scattered and disorganized. Armed units often fought in separate locations along the route, which now stretched for kilometers.

At times up to ten different columns of men marched parallel to one another. Revelli writes, "The march continues among shouts and shoves; at times one runs so as not to be cut out of one's column. It's a cursed march, it only takes a moment to lose contact with one's unit, because soon a mass of leaderless soldiers or other columns insert themselves and create chaos. Then, for the cut off company or part of a battalion, nothing can be done until the next rest stop is reached."[44]

Combat units were sorely tried and hampered by chaotic, disorganized throngs of soldiers (Italians and allies), who interfered with organizational and operative procedures of intact alpine units, especially when those units were preparing for specific operations. Armed roadblocks were set up several times during those days to stop such soldiers from interspersing themselves among combat units.[45]

Lieutenant Guido Vettorazzo describes the tens of thousands of soldiers following the Tridentina Division. "These are not people who refuse to fight...they don't participate because they have lost their ties to their own units. They are no longer organized, they are a confused, heterogeneous mass, comprising drivers without vehicles, artillerymen without cannons, medical and support personnel, soldiers in special services, mule drivers without mules, troops without commanders; most don't even have a rifle. They are not all Italians." It was impossible to command and organize these thousands while the columns were marching, and the possibility of stopping for that purpose didn't exist. [46]

Lieutenant Zavagli refers to "the usefulness" of the thousands of soldiers following the alpini of the Tridentina. Referring to the Italians, he writes, "For the most part they are without weapons, without organized leadership.... They form the 'rear' of the column.... They are the soldiers of corps and services; soldiers of destroyed units...." Zavagli claims they were often viewed with scorn or as a burden, yet many times they represented a "wall of cannon fodder" protecting the backs of the combatants. Their dead also lined the long route of the withdrawal. Among those who were still alive, some "gathered the wounded from any unit or corps, dragged them forward as long as they could and stopped only if the wounded died, or if they themselves froze...." Soldiers who lost their weapon in a surprise attack "made themselves useful in some other manner." These were not isolated events. "All soldiers remaining on the steppe between the Don and Kharkov indiscriminately made an incommensurable contribution, saving those fortunate men who [eventually] emerged alive from the withdrawal...."[47]

As the march continued, at a certain point Revelli and his men could see a low-lying crest ahead. Rumor had it German lines were just beyond. Revelli writes, "It's always the same: when a crest or small valley appears, one has hope. For hundreds of kilometers [one hopes]. Even the most desperate men hope: with their gangrenous feet, with their eyes closed from frostbite, with bullets and shrapnel in their legs and sides, they move on, bent over in two with their arms hanging down loosely, dragging themselves on the snow, falling and then getting up, moving on because they have hopes for German lines ahead."[48]

The thousands following the Tridentina across the steppes continued to suffer from the polar temperatures, exacerbated by frigid winds. Fatigue, exhaustion, thirst, and ravenous hunger tormented them and claimed more victims. Mules pulled sleds loaded with the wounded, who lay under blankets rigid with ice and covered with snow. Each man marched enveloped in his own shell of agony. Those who could no longer resist let their bodies sink into the snow, where they instantly fell asleep, soon to die of exposure.[49]

By now, many had cut strips off their blankets and wound them around their shoes, or their naked feet when shoes fell apart. Walking with strips around feet or shoes was even more exhausting, yet if their feet froze, they knew they would be unable to walk. They knew they would die abandoned along the route. Frozen limbs became gangrenous. Toes and fingers lost their flesh; entire digits even fell off. Numerous mules pulling the few sleds carrying the wounded could no longer resist and simply dropped in the snow. Famished soldiers immediately stripped their carcasses of flesh.[50]

Bedeschi describes what happened when, at a certain point, soldiers spotted a village. Men lurched, ran, pushed, and shoved, desperate to find shelter. Sleds overturned in the rush, and out-of-control mules and horses trampled men as the screaming throngs raced toward the izbas. Those already inside barricaded the doors. Germans fired their rifles, bayoneting and killing men who were pushing and shoving to gain entrance. It was as if this chaotic mass had lost all contact with its humanity; there was no pity, no shame, and no sympathy. Those forced to remain outside that night succumbed to the bitter cold and violent snowstorm, slowly freezing to death. Others, crazed by the intense cold, set fire to some of the izbas, burning to death many who were sleeping within.[51]

Early on the morning of January 25, several German planes circled above the withdrawing forces dropping food and ammunition supplies by parachute in large dark cylinders. It would have been necessary to receive many more airdrops of food to alleviate the hunger of the thousands on the ground. In this case, provisions of food were only for the Germans. Zavagli writes, "This discrimination of providing for the Germans and not us created immediate furious brawls around the fallen cylinders. Before Germans could reach the provisions, a good part of them disappeared in the pockets of soldiers closest to the containers.... When Germans arrived with their weapons at the ready, they recovered what remained. There were shots; there were some dead around the cylinders...."[52]

The appearance of German airplanes fueled a number of rumors among soldiers marching close to Zavagli: "The Germans" would soon send troops to break through the Russian encirclement and join the Tridentina; "The Germans" would send reinforcements by air; "The Germans" would manage to protect the columns from the sky. Zavagli wondered what illusions his companions were under when they said "the Germans." If the Germans wanted to help the Italians, Zavagli writes, "they wouldn't have left us alone on the Don, without instructions or news, as they began withdrawing two days ahead of us. If the Germans had wanted to help us, they could have let us know what they were doing. Instead they left us on the Don so we could engage the Russians, who would inevitably encircle us, while they could withdraw with a minimum of trouble."[53]

At this point, Zavagli recalled an episode, one he could scarcely believe upon hearing it for the first time. The event occurred when Russian troops had arrived in Kantemirovka after having broken through Italian infantry lines in December 1942. Apparently, Zavagli writes, "The Germans were the first to stop resisting and to flee with every vehicle, even stealing some Italian trucks. When Italian soldiers begged for a place from those already fleeing, and if they tried to climb on a truck, the good allies sneered at them, and hit their hands with the butts of their rifles until they let go. The same thing happens in this damned column when someone holds on to a German sled."[54]

Zavagli tackles "the myth of German heroism." In general, he admits, the Italians had a certain amount of admiration for German soldiers, especially for their discipline, their ability in the use of weaponry, and their seeming ease of understanding basic warfare. Referring to "the myth," Zavagli offers his own opinion of the German soldier who was also capable of "unimaginable cruelty fueled by unlimited egoism and unnecessary ferocity.... His egoism trampled enemies and friends indifferently, without mercy, often thoughtlessly. During the withdrawal, after our initial admiration of these [German] groups mixed up with us in a common tragedy, we could observe unlimited wickedness and egoism, causing them to carry out operations which could only be justified by fear, bordering on madness."[55]

Following the airdrop of German supplies, soldiers from Zavagli's transport unit divided the few items they had scrounged from the dropped canisters. They shared pieces of chocolate, a few crackers, and six small bags of sugar among twenty men. Zavagli comments on the solidarity remaining among his men, despite their ravenous hunger and physical deprivations, which profoundly affected the physical as well as moral state of all. He recalls how fearful brawls broke out among soldiers as they fought over a piece of mule meat or a mess tin of water. In the case of his own small unit, he writes, "Following the very small number of calories we consumed [from the German supplies], we took up the march once more. The psychological effect was equal to a lavish meal."[56]

NIKITOVKA

On January 25, as the advance unit reached Nikitovka, Russian partisans hidden in izbas of the village opened fire. The alpini were able to quickly subdue the partisans and take over the village. Several men perished, others sustained serious wounds during the assault. General Reverberi ordered Colonel Adami to remain in Nikitovka and lodge his units in izbas. The advance unit was to move on and seek shelter in other small villages situated along the road leading to Nikolaevka. It was getting dark as the advance unit left Nikitovka. As it reached the last izbas of the village, an Italian infantry soldier (name unknown) came running toward the column from the opposite direction. As he ran, he shouted to the alpini to stop. Colonel Chierici walked toward the soldier who told the colonel he had just escaped from the Russians in Nikolaevka. He explained he had been a prisoner of the Russians for forty days. He was a driver and had transported mortars and anti-tank guns for the Russians.

"I know all the defenses the Russians have prepared in that village.... I know where the Russians are positioned...there is much more artillery; there are two regiments of infantry with many machine guns...."

The soldier warned the colonel not to attempt to move toward Nikolaevka in the dark: "If you continue to go ahead, you will arrive in the dark, and you will surely be destroyed while you descend to the railroad tracks at the bottom of the valley."[57]

Upon hearing this news, General Reverberi decided to wait until the next morning to attack the Russian barricade in Nikolaevka. The alpini settled in for the night in the villages of Tereshkov and Arnautovo. Reverberi met with commanding officers of the division to plan the attack for the following day.[58]

THE BATTLES OF ARNAUTOVO

In the middle of the night, Russians attacked the alpini sheltering in the village of Arnautovo with large numbers of troops and tremendous firepower. A bloody battle raged, often digressing into hand-to-hand combat. Alpini used their few cannons and machine-guns as hordes of Russians advanced, surrounding the village. The first attack was repelled, leaving many Russians and alpini dead and wounded. The Russians attacked a second time and once more, the alpini drove them back. Each time forced back, the Russians responded with violent concentrations of artillery. The battle was now in its fifth hour. As supplies of ammunition dwindled, alpini fought hand to hand, determined to protect the defensive line between Arnautovo and Nikitovka, where other units of the Tridentina were at rest along with the command of the Alpine Corps. The alpini held their lines in the freezing temperatures, hoping for reinforcements, as mortars and artillery fire rained down upon them. Reinforcements came, but too late, to save the many lives lost in that first bloody battle in Arnautovo. At a certain point, the Russians stopped their assault. It was not clear as to why; dawn was approaching and it became very quiet, yet the atmosphere remained ominous.[59]

Meanwhile, the Tirano Battalion, on its way toward Arnautovo, became the target of the Russian assault. This second battle of Arnautovo quickly escalated and raged intensely. Finally, after fierce combat, alpini were able to drive the Russians back, but the price paid in lives in Arnautovo was high. The many wounded included Captain Grandi, commander of the Tirano Battalion. Only 150 alpini of the Tirano Battalion were still in any kind of shape to continue fighting.[60]

THE LEGENDARY BATTLE OF NIKOLAEVKA

While the battle of Arnautovo was still underway, the advance group of the Tridentina Division in Tereshkov was preparing to attack the Russian defensive barriers in Nikolaevka. Three German armored vehicles, two greatly reduced alpine battalions, and a third alpine battalion with a reasonable level of fighting ability left the village. These units moved forward on a vast, snow-covered incline lacking any kind of vegetation leading down to the town below. Violent enemy fire hit the alpini as they rapidly descended. Their advance wasn't stalled, but many were wounded, and casualties mounted during this initial offensive. Once they reached the railroad tracks, alpini spread out, moving into the town. At first, it seemed as though their maneuvers were leading to a favorable outcome, but soon the Russians launched a violent counter-attack.[61]

The bloody battle of Nikolaevka continued with an ongoing series of attacks and counterattacks, as well as hand-to-hand fighting. Part of a company of alpini reached the church and was able to capture a complete antitank battery. Another unit attacked an antitank barricade frontally and succeeded in breaking through, putting the cannons out of commission, but almost all taking part in that frontal assault were killed. Only two alpini of the group remained alive.[62]

At one point, when the bitter battle de-escalated, alpini took advantage of this time to regroup and reorganize their fractured fighting units. The group of alpini who had reached the church, and the group reaching the railroad station, remained stuck in those positions with no more ammunition. As Russians advanced toward the church, alpini drove them back with hand- grenades, bayonets, kicks, and rifles wielded as clubs.[63]

Meanwhile, the battle-weary survivors of the battles of Arnautovo began to make their way toward Nikolaevka. As they began to descend the long sloping incline to join the on-going battle, the Russians hit them with enormous firepower. In addition, a squadron of Russian planes circled the area and began bombing and strafing the throngs of men in the columns who were waiting for the alpini to break through Russian lines.[64]

Lieutenant Giorgio Gaza, commanding the 253rd Company of the Val Chiese Battalion, led his men down the incline: "Swirling snow, pieces of ice, and shrapnel fly in all directions. It's impossible to make sense out of anything in the indescribable din and crush, among screams of the wounded and the agony of [our] extreme fatigue (only two hours earlier we had fought in the very difficult night battle in Arnautovo)."[65]

Gaza was hit violently in his back and thrown several meters. He couldn't move his legs. Thinking this was the end for him, he decided he wasn't going to die there without trying to fire his last rounds at the enemy. While attempting to grab his rifle he discovered his arm was broken. Although he felt no pain, he could see blood trickling from his sleeve. About one hundred meters in front of him, on the bank of the railroad tracks, a Russian machinegun pointed directly at him and dissuaded him from moving. He remained completely exposed, surrounded by firing weapons of friend and foe. Miraculously, alpini of his company managed to reach him. "I'm not alone," he writes, "My alpini won't abandon me, and even though they think I might be dead...they advance in that hell to see if I need them, if I can be saved. And they do save me, but two of them fall, shot dead by that machine-gun that doesn't stop firing."[66]

At a certain point during the late afternoon, a German light plane landed near the spot where General Reverberi and Colonel Heidekamper were conversing along with other officers. Colonel Heidekamper had assumed command of the German XXIV Panzer Corps after General Eibl had been killed in action on the 21st. The German colonel boarded the plane and spent several hours conducting reconnaissance, attempting to discern points where Axis forces stood a chance of breaking through the Soviet encirclement. Once the colonel returned, "the crew aboard the plane, either following orders or upon their own initiative, invited Heidekamper and Reverberi to board the plane and leave the battlefield." Both officers declined the offer.[67]

The day was ending and soon it would be dark, yet the battle continued. General Reverberi realized that not only the the alpini, but also the mass of unarmed soldiers, the wounded, sick, and frostbitten following the division couldn't survive that night out of doors. It was imperative to get through the Russian barricade and occupy the village at all costs. This meant every able-bodied man with a rifle or hand grenade had to join in the battle.

As the general moved toward the town, reaching the area near the station, he climbed on top of a German tracked vehicle parked there, ordering it to move. With a bold gesture of his arm pointing west he hollered: "*Avanti Tridentina, avanti*" ("Move forward Tridentina, move forward")." "That shout, and the accompanying gesture were perhaps seen by few in the area, but those close by repeated it to those further away. As fast as lightning, behind the general standing erect on top of the German armored vehicle, an avalanche of shouting, uncontainable men, armed and disarmed, supported by the strength of their desperation, precipitated down the snowy slope blackened by blasts of enemy shells and the bodies of those who had fallen...." The well-armed

Russians possessed a far greater number of troops, "Yet when they saw this advancing, unwavering mass of men determined to break through their barricade at all costs or be annihilated, they began to give ground and then turned in precipitous and disorderly flight, abandoning hundreds of their wounded and dead, entire batteries of artillery, and a huge amount of materiel of every type."[68]

Alpino Pasquale Corti recalls those dramatic moments: "I remember the evening of January 26, 1943 as if it were yesterday. It was almost nightfall as a [German] light plane arrived to take General Reverberi to safety. He refused to board the plane…. Few men would have had the strength to do what he did: to give up a secure path to safety. The general refused to distance himself from that hell and continued to guide his division in battle. I saw that scene with my own eyes and listened to his words, which infused courage among us to move ahead and not give up." To this day Pasquale Corti wonders how Reverberi managed to survive, exposed as he was to enemy fire.[69]

Sergeant Major Mosè Candeago of the 17th Battery, Udine Group, writes, "Nobody was saved from fighting, thousands died, and when a man fell, simply because he slipped on ice, he was crushed by the [advancing] hordes…a mass of men of all races…. Finally, once the battle was won, the dead weren't counted any more."[70]

The wounded were gathered. Medical officers did what they could, though they had virtually no medical equipment.[71] That night the alpini remained in Nikolaevka, sheltered from the winds yet suffering from the cold in semi-destroyed, windowless izbas, where ice covered the walls.[72]

General Reverberi reported forty officers killed in Nikolaevka. It is difficult to know how many Italian troops lost their lives during that bloody battle. Russian sources claim that the bodies of approximately 11,000 men of all nationalities lay in and around Nikolaevka, once the spring thaw commenced.[73]

As Revelli recalled the bloody battles of Arnautovo and Nikolaevka, he expressed his anguish over the fate of so many alpini of the Tirano Battalion: "So many died…." Exposed, without cover, "we moved ahead…without knowing where the enemy was, without knowing if there were ten or one thousand Russians…. Alpini of the Tirano, mowed down by automatic weapons, by tanks, by artillery, with our weapons that didn't fire, with our hand-grenades that didn't explode.

Sinking in snow up to our knees, the alpini fell and no one was there to lift them up."[74]

Major Maccagno of the Tirano Battalion also recalled a moment during those frightful hours of battle: "We were under fire.... To my left there was a German officer in a camouflaged uniform...about thirty meters from me. With a harsh voice, he shouted: *'Avanti. E` il momento di andar avanti. Che cosa fanno quegli uomini la` distesi? Devono andare avanti.'* ('Move forward. It's time to move forward. What are those men who are laying down doing? They have to move forward.') I turned my head to the right; there were dozens of alpini half hidden in the snow. I shouted: *'Sono tutti morti. Sie sind alle kaputt'* ('They're all dead. They're all kaputt'). The German stood at attention and saluted."[75]

Sergeant Mario Rigoni Stern of the Vestone Battalion recalled a surreal moment during the last hours of the battle of Nikolaevka. At a certain point, during a lull in fighting, he entered an izba to look for something to eat; to his horror, he faced fully armed Russian soldiers sitting around a table eating from a common bowl. He stopped in his tracks petrified. There were women and children in the izba as well. One of the women offered him a plate full of milk and some kind of meal: "I take a step forward, sling my rifle over my shoulder and eat. Time doesn't seem to exist anymore. The Russian soldiers look at me. The women look at me. The children look at me. No one breathes a word. The only sound is of the spoon on my plate; and each of my mouthfuls. *'Spaziba'* ['thank you'], I say when I have finished. And the woman takes the empty bowl from my hands...." As he turned to leave, he noticed beehives at the entrance of the izba. With gestures, he asked for a honeycomb. The woman gave him one as he left.[76]

Years later, as he reflected upon this unusual incident, he claims this experience wasn't at all "strange, but [seemed perfectly] natural—with that naturalness there must have been between all men at one time." He elaborates: "After the first surprise, all my gestures were natural. I didn't feel any fear or any wish to defend myself or to offend them. It was very simple...." In that izba, "harmony, which wasn't just a truce," existed between all of those present. "It was something much more than respect which animals in the forest have for each other. Circumstances, just for once, had helped men to remain human...." Perhaps, he thought, all those who were in the izba during those moments would "remember how we behaved then. Particularly the children." Filled with hope, Rigoni Stern claims that if such an episode "happened once, it might happen again. It might happen again, I mean, with innumerable other men and become a habit, a way of life."[77]

Following the battle of Nikolaevka, Lieutenant Eraldo Sculati with the Udine Group gathered survivors of his unit together to set a time and place for them to regroup the following morning. He then entered an izba where he observed five men sitting around a table and two women busily cooking. It was fairly dark in the izba, and it was only as the Lieutenant advanced toward the table that he realized the seated men were Russian soldiers. Each had a pistol and a parabellum. Sculati's own rifle hung over his shoulder. The Russians turned toward him, smiling, pointing to a chair. He writes, "I sit down, and a woman brings me a large bowl of boiling soup, sour cabbage and potatoes.... Then vodka; the Russians stretch out on the floor near the stove and sleep. I do too. At dawn, they awaken me, and accompany me to the door smiling as they point to the west. I go to meet my men at the designated time and take up the march once more."[78]

Sergio Dalla Rosa, an alpino in the Val Cismon Battalion, and a few surviving alpini of his company who had fought together on the front the Julia Division had held for so many days during December and January, was among those following the Tridentina Division. During the withdrawal, these alpini attempted at all costs to remain united, helping one another to survive the terrible ordeals facing them. In Nikolaevka, Dalla Rosa suddenly became very ill. His friends managed to find a sled for him and tirelessly searched for a medical officer. Once found in an izba, a medical officer diagnosed Dalla Rosa's illness as bilateral bronchitis with pleurisy, but had nothing with which he could treat the alpino. Dalla Rosa writes, "In fact, that fine medical lieutenant, whose name I never knew...advised my companions to leave me in the izba and to continue on in order not to compromise their already precarious situation." Once the officer left the izba, Dalla Rosa's friends distanced themselves from their friend for a moment, huddling together to decide how they wanted to proceed. When they returned, Dalla Rosa heard a unanimous chorus—"*Un compagno non si abbandona*!" ("One doesn't abandon a companion!"). These alpini, "who by now were only supported by desperation, pulled me for hundreds of kilometers, struggling along the steppe with snow up to their knees, gripped by cold and hunger, while I was completely delirious...."

These alpini didn't release Della Rosa until they reached the village where Italian military ambulances were waiting for survivors of the withdrawal. Dalla Rossa writes, "This gesture by those men put their own existence at risk to save mine, during a period when human values seemed truly lost."[79]

During the long, cold days and nights of the withdrawal, soldiers ate and drank whatever was available, causing some to become sick or develop intestinal ailments. Lieutenant Gaza observed extraordinary solidarity among alpini taking care of one of their battalion commanders who was suffering from a case of "frequent uncontrollable explosive diarrhea." The commander couldn't stop to relieve himself, and walking in frozen pants that soon resembled "tubes of concrete" was torturous. Yet, he never went without an exchange of valenki or pants. Both officers and simple alpini in the commander's battalion provided an adequate supply of clothing and footwear, collecting it mostly from the dead. Whenever it was possible for the officer to enter an izba, his men helped him to undress quickly and dressed him in those scrounged items of clothing.[80]

The victory in Nikolaevka by no means signified "the end of suffering" for the withdrawing forces. "The encirclement of fire and ice opposing them was broken, but the march toward the west had to continue because the Soviets wouldn't release their grip on the withdrawing forces, and the risk of being trapped by them remained elevated."[81]

On January 27, the withdrawing forces began to move on from Nikolaevka. Of the three German armored vehicles, only one was operational. At the outskirts of the town, the Russians barricaded the road. Major Belotti ordered the German armored vehicle to move forward along with alpini, but the Germans refused, believing the Russian antitank gun up ahead was too dangerous. Several alpini skirted the road, walking in deep snow for about a kilometer, and then circled back to attack the Russians from behind. With a fortunate burst of a handgrenade, they hit the soldiers operating the antitank gun. A frontal assault quickly eliminated the remaining Russians.[82]

After this relatively short skirmish, the column moved forward, assuming that the Russians were most likely all around them. The column moved off the road into deep snow, which meant walking was even more exhausting. The threat of confronting more Russian defensive barriers caused the commanders of the alpini to push the men to their limit, to move ahead as fast as possible before the Russians could reinforce their ranks. Many men dropped by the wayside now, as exhaustion, hunger, and cold claimed their lives. Russian partisans attacked the flanks of the column, taking prisoners. Airplanes bombed and strafed, machine-gunning the columns.[83]

Alpino Pasquale Corti recalled the final days of the withdrawal: "The last days of the march were terrible.... Russian airplanes continued to strafe us firing their machine guns, but we didn't even throw ourselves down on the ground anymore. We proceeded in the middle of shots...We asked for death and envied those who remained stopped [at the side of the route] immobilized in the tranquility of an eternal sleep."[84]

The Russians had a tremendous advantage because they could move around the steppes quickly with their motorized vehicles, receiving continuous reinforcements of supplies and fuel. In one hour, they could maneuver over the same ground covered by the column in twenty hours of marching. Following each clash with Russian soldiers or partisans, fewer men took up the march once more.[85]

On this eleventh day of the withdrawal, Medical Officer Serri remembered the small can of meat and two pieces of hard tack he had eaten eleven days before. Speaking to Captain Reitani he said, "I can't understand how we've been able to endure until now with only a few bites of frozen turnips and rotten peelings. Look at the soldiers! They are miracles. We find ourselves in these terrible conditions, nevertheless they are walking."

The Captain asked Serri how long he believed the men could survive under these conditions of atrocious cold without food or restful sleep. Serri couldn't give him an answer. All he could say was he was surprised they had withstood as long as they had.[86]

Gunfire during an air attack that morning wounded several mules. Alpini in the vicinity literally jumped on them with their drawn bayonets and knives. As they rose, they placed large slabs of meat on their backs. Although pleasurable thoughts of roasted meat at the next rest stop spurred them on, after a short time it was impossible for them to carry the extra weight. They attempted to cut off a small piece but by now, the meat had frozen, so they dropped it in the snow.[87]

No evidence suggested anyone from their forces was searching for them. The soldiers felt abandoned, written off. Thousands of men "lacking every means of life had now walked for eleven days among battles and pain, in the glasslike, intense cold of the steppes." So many had died or were left abandoned along the route. Bedeschi writes, "Those who still had the strength carried evident signs of the effort: they seemed like a drunken throng, not like soldiers, more like macabre puppets perpetuating their madness, dragging those sleds dripping rot and urine of the wounded. Mules, reduced to skeletons covered with a coat of ice, contributed with their presence to the terrifying picture of a wandering, desperate insanity."[88]

One saw specters of men driven ahead by ferocious will. "They were bent, limping, hopping, and gravitating on improvised crutches, tormented by fever and lice. With red blisters between bandages yellow with pus, blue in the face or deathly pale, gasping for breath, and famished like stray wolves, they determined to keep pace with the column. They swore or prayed, emitting from their nostrils and split lips a single bloody dribble falling to accumulate and freeze on their beards and on their clothes.[89]

While some soldiers were able to continue the march, others could no longer put one foot in front of the other; they sat down to rest at the side of the column overcome by exhaustion. In such stressed conditions sitting down to rest was dangerous; the freezing process begins insidiously. Lieutenant Zavagli attempted to help some soldiers who had succumbed, but it was impossible to force them to get up and there was no room for them on the few sleds transporting the wounded. Although these men were slowly dying, "they had a kind word for those who continued to march: 'Have a good trip, don't stop [walking], they said. It is heartbreaking, but the laws of nature offer no choice. He who wants to survive can only continue to walk; to delay for too long could be fatal. It is awful when they cry and implore us not to abandon them, and we can do nothing."[90]

As mules dropped from hunger and the cold, sleds full of the wounded were abandoned. Those unfortunate soldiers screamed, "Don't abandon us, we are also Italians," as they grabbed on to their companions who were barely able to stand owing to their own fatigue. A wounded man implored Don Gnocchi, "Chaplain, Sir, shoot me for the love of God, but don't leave me here."[91]

Don Gnocchi writes, "There may be nothing more desperate and humiliating than not having the ability to offer help, having no bandages for a wounded man, no strength to extend a helping hand to a frostbitten man, dragging himself forward on all fours behind the column. No ability to give a drink to a dying man (the wells were often frozen), or a piece of bread to an exhausted man, but even more terrible was not even possessing the ability to empathize or to suffer...."[92]

Yet, at other times when a mule fell wounded or exhausted, Antonio Marino observed a "surreal example of human solidarity" as mule handlers hitched themselves to sleds, taking the place of the animals, while others pushed the sleds from behind, determined not to abandon their wounded comrades who begged them not to leave them on the steppe.[93]

After marching for more than forty kilometers in the deep snow, the withdrawing forces reached the villages surrounding Uspenka, where they stopped for the night. The following day, January 28, after five hours of sleep in abandoned izbas, the men scavenged for anything edible: sunflower seeds, turnips, even frozen garbage. The march resumed. "Fatigue, hunger, thirst, and intense cold, lack of sleep: these five elements existed in various ways in the body of every man, and already the first few kilometers of walking demanded desperate tenacity to proceed...."[94]

That afternoon a low-flying German plane dropped a message alerting the forces they were approaching German lines and needed to head north to Novi Oskol where there were German troops. As it turned out, Novi Oskol was now in Russian hands. Officers attempted to round up enough armed men to form an assault group. It was a futile effort. In the column of thousands, there were not enough armed men; even the Tridentina was out of ammunition. Soon another German plane indicated the way, and the column marched on to two small villages. In one, a few men found a cache of potatoes. The column continued, following a zigzag course to avoid Russian forces spotted by German planes.

Once again, a German plane made a food drop, and once more German troops ate without sharing their provisions: "Hooded German infantry men walked among the Italians chewing chocolate and smoked fatback." The Italians observed them: "A few couldn't resist their own desire; they winked, pointed to the food, and extended their hand. 'Nein' [the Germans] responded curtly; 'We can't,' or they said nothing and chewed, staring ahead with a blank expression as if they didn't understand. 'Strangle yourselves you carrion,' the disappointed men swore, as they brought snow up to their mouths."[95]

On January 29, the withdrawing forces reached a small village following a march of thirteen hours. There they rested in partially destroyed izbas with ice on the walls.[96]

The following morning as the men took up the march they noticed an armored vehicle in the distance. As they moved closer, they could see someone standing on its roof.

"It's the commander of the Alpine Corps, it's General Nasci," an alpino shouted.

As the men of the Tridentina passed by the general, who had been with a leading column in the withdrawal, he informed them they were now in a safe zone, occupied by Axis forces, but that these could also be attacked at any moment so it was important to be vigilant. As they walked by, a few alpini attempted to salute the general with their swollen hands. A wounded alpino lying on a sled yanked off a blanket covering him and began to yell hysterically, "We're out of the bag, *mama mia.*"

Others took up the cry shouting "*Viva L'Italia, Viva L'Italia*". Shouts of joy resonated all along the column.[97]

The troops moved into a fairly large inhabited village where citizens gazed aghast at the pitiful condition of the men: "Women ran to the kitchens and returned with bowls of milk they offered to soldiers, whose filthy beards drowned in the foam." The column broke up into smaller groups. Alpini took bowls of milk to the wounded remaining on sleds and returned to the izbas where Russian peasants offered them even more milk. As the men passed through the village, Russian peasants gave them bread, honey, and butter.[98]

"The story of rotten turnips is over," some said, as they devoured bread rolls given so generously by the locals.

Medical officer Serri cautioned the men not to eat too much. He warned them they could die of indigestion, "as he held a loaf of bread between his hands weighing about three kilos of which he had already consumed half. An alpino responded: 'Whatever God decides lieutenant! For fifteen days we've been living on nothing…rubbish not even fit for a pig…we'll all die with you, full of bread and milk.'"[99]

Now the men advanced rapidly, their spirits elevated. That afternoon they arrived in the village of Bol'shie Troizkoe and promptly found shelter in izbas. Officers reminded the men to remain vigilant; the road to the east was open and Russian forces could attack at any time. Women from the village assisted Serri as he re-bandaged wounded and frostbitten soldiers. The alpini remained in the village overnight. Generous Russian peasants offered boiled potatoes, milk and even a few pieces of chicken.[100]

RUDIMENTARY ASSISTANCE

Prior to January 17, various service units of the Alpine Corps in zones behind divisional lines had managed to cross the steppes safely, and converged near Kharkov. The Italian Eighth Army had transferred its headquarters to a village about thirty kilometers southeast of the city. Lieutenant Colonel Odasso, Operations Officer of the Alpine Corps, had the task of uniting and organizing those service units arriving in the area. Odasso established a receiving center for these men in the village of Lyubotyn, a few kilometers west of Kharkov.[101]

German Army Group B established its headquarters in the city. The Germans treated the Italians with disdain and were not at all interested, or willing, to provide any assistance to those arriving in the region: "It was awful to see how, in a foreign country and under the eyes of an enemy population, the Italian soldier was subjected to so many mortifications on the part of their allies."[102]

Many obstacles prevented the services for the soldiers from functioning smoothly. The main problem was lack of fuel for Italian military trucks. The Germans claimed all available fuel was required for their own operations in the region. Despite difficulties they encountered, officers of the Alpine Corps continued to organize soldiers in the Kharkov zone, but their main concern focused on the eventual arrival of the thousands of alpini who were still somewhere out on the steppes attempting to escape from an ever-tightening Russian encirclement.[103]

Lieutenant Colonel Odasso continued to prepare for the arrival of the withdrawing alpini. There had been little news of these men, although hopes rose when news arrived about the victorious battle of Nikolaevka. Assuming the alpini would arrive in the zone of Novi Oskol, personnel in the Lyubotyn center began to prepare vehicles and provisions to set up an advance base to assist the arriving troops in Belgorod. A convoy of Italian trucks loaded with medicine and food reached Belgorod on January 28. When news arrived that the withdrawing forces had deviated to Volchansk, because the Russians occupied Novi Oskol, the convoy returned to Kharkov and moved on to Volchansk.

Once in Volchansk, the soldiers were told that the withdrawing forces would be arriving further north in Shebekino, so the convoy moved again and set up a rudimentary receiving base in that village. From Shebekino, Lieutenant Colonel Odasso and a group of officers traveled east toward the zone of Bol'shie Troizkoe. It was there that they encountered the first column of the Tridentina Division, led by General Nasci and General Reverberi. Odasso informed the generals that they could now consider themselves to be in a relatively safe zone, and soon a convoy of trucks would arrive to bring them food and evacuate the wounded and most severe frostbitten victims to hospitals.[104]

Chapter 13

OUT OF THE ENCIRCLEMENT:
THE MARCH CONTINUES

On January 31, the alpini resumed their march. When units arrived in a small, out-of-the way village, peasants offered potatoes, milk, hot water, and rags for the cleaning of wounds. The villagers were amazed; they couldn't believe the men had walked all the way across the snow-covered steppes from the Don in the terrible cold.[1]

 Later the alpini took up the march once again. On the outskirts of Shebekino (southeast of Belgorod), they saw a convoy of trucks at a distance. As the trucks approached, an alpino shouted, "They're Italian!"

Thousands of voices echoed that phrase. Drivers and soldiers greeted each other with hugs, while some soldiers stroked the sides and tires of the trucks to be sure they were not dreaming. Alpini immediately carried the most severely wounded, sick and frostbitten soldiers to waiting trucks of the rescue convoy.[2]

Medical Officer Italo Serri assisted with the first evacuation: "The frozen and wounded of Ivanovka were leaving. Those [same alpini] who hadn't wanted to leave the front lines in Novaya Kalitva, the wounded of Novaya Postoyalovka, the bloody escapees of…Nikitovka, Nikolaevka, all those who had dragged wounds and open flesh, sowing tears, and cut off toes, feet green with gangrene; they left, taking hunger, lice, putrid rags, and the smell of death with them."

As Captain Reitani and Serri watched the retreating trucks, Serri asked the captain how many men from his battery remained: "Fourteen men, thirteen mules, a few empty rifles, a few handguns and the rags we have on our feet…."

176

The captain then recalled that his battery had originally consisted of 230 men, 160 mules, mountain cannons, weapons, ammunition, materiel, and had occupied an entire train when it departed for Russia in 1942.[3]

Later, in an izba, a Colonel Verdotti spoke to survivors of Reitani's battery. He told them that when the Julia Division was originally sent to Russia it consisted of approximately 20,000 men; the number of survivors of the division amounted to 2,300, including those just sent to the hospital. "For us", he said, "the withdrawal from the encirclement seemed to be a disaster...instead it was a tragedy without a name.... We aren't among those who were most unlucky.... The other divisions also arrived emptied."

The colonel continued and noted that the full catastrophe of the withdrawal was largely unknown by most alpini gathered in the izba. "You haven't yet any idea of what happened during the march. We saw what was happening around us, but often we weren't aware of what occurred kilometers away from us, in the night, in the snowstorms, in the villages during the rest stops. The column was dozens of kilometers long, often broken up; Russian units attacked the end of the column composed of those who were most confused and fatigued, and they isolated and captured them...."

The colonel explained that units were separated, contact between regiments was lost, and some took wrong roads. "We know those who died in battle, we saw those who fell, now frozen in the snow, [and] in all, they represent a minimal amount in contrast to the number who are absent. Generals, colonels, and many dozens of thousands of soldiers are missing, and complete units are prisoners. It's a tragedy that couldn't be more serious and painful, my sons."[4]

At the time it was estimated that approximately twenty-five thousand soldiers of the Alpine Corps escaped from the encirclement. Ten to twelve thousand were wounded, frostbitten, or sick and unable to walk, needing transport by truck. The rest were able to continue walking, even though they were exhausted and in pitiful shape. The logistics of the immediate situation were staggering. Other than the center in Lyubotyn, no other facility was prepared to receive the thousands of arriving men. Medicine and food were loaded onto trucks and transported to Schebekino. Convoys of trucks filled with wounded, frostbitten, and ill soldiers continued to shuttle between Schebekino and

Kharkov. On January 31, four thousand soldiers were transported to hospitals.[5]

Commanders decided to remain in Schebekino to give the men time to rest, and to wait for any late arrivals. A few stragglers did arrive during the first two days. Those who waited stood outside in the freezing cold as long as they could, with hopes to see more survivors. By the fourth day no more appeared.[6]

Lieutenant Zavagli arrived in Schebekino with the hundreds of Italian soldiers from various units who had followed the Tridentina Division throughout the withdrawal. As the alpini began to organize their units in Schebekino, Zavagli was somewhat unsure of what he should do at that moment surrounded by men he didn't know. As he walked toward a group of trucks, he noticed four parked behind others, bearing the insignia of his transport group. He realized that these trucks were from his unit that had left Rossosh the night before the withdrawal had begun.

"Several drivers stood in front of one truck, chit-chatting. I moved closer and asked if they had some hard tack and water. They looked at me as if I was a strange animal. Of course, between my beard and dark skin burned by the cold, I wasn't very presentable...but they had seen the other troops arrive and I wasn't the first example." One of the drivers went to search for some hard tack while the others continued to talk among themselves, casting furtive glances at Zavagli. A few minutes went by. Then, one of the drivers cautiously approached him.

"Lieutenant, is it really you?"

At that moment, Zavagli wasn't sure if the driver wanted him to say "yes" or "no." He responded, "Fellows, it's me."

Overjoyed, the men hugged him "like a brother." Zavagli recalled, "It was perhaps the most beautiful moment of my war."[7]

Several days later, an officer of the Alpine Corps sent Zavagli to a suburb outside of Kharkov to a unit of his transport group. By now, Zavagli was suffering from bronchitis and had a high fever. After a few days of bed rest, his condition began to improve, but there was no time to recover fully. Orders arrived for transport to prepare their trucks and await orders. There was no word as to their eventual destination.[8]

The Russians were advancing toward Kharkov. Axis trucks and troops clogged the roads in the city and periphery. Zavagli and his unit waited for orders, but none arrived. One evening the men could hear

Railroad station of Cuneo, July 1942. Alpini of the Cuneense Division leaving for the Russian front, whereas Fascist officer Antonio Bonino, wearing the light colored uniform, remains at home. *From the archives of the Istituto Storico della Resistanza e della Società Contemporanea in Provincia di Cuneo. Permission granted by Michele Calandri, director of the Istituto.*

The train carrying the 46th Company of the Tirano Battalion (Tridentina
Alpine Division) traveling toward the Russian front, July 1942.
From the archives of ISRSCPC, permission granted by M. Calandri.

General Emilio Battisti, commander of the Cuneense Alpine
Division, traveling toward Russia, July 1942.
From the archives of ISRSCPC, permission granted by M. Calandri.

This photo was taken during the withdrawal following a Russian mortar attack in the Opyt zone, January 21, 1943, as enemy forces attempted to encircle alpini of the Tridentina Division. *From the archives of ISRSCPC, permission granted by M. Calandri.*

Mule pack units reorganize as the alpini move on from Opyt to Postoialyj, January 21, 1943.
From the archives of ISRSCPC, permission granted by M. Calandri.

The thirty-kilometer-long column of over 100,000 withdrawing troops in the vicinity of Shelyakino.
From the archives of ISRSCPC, permission granted by M. Calandri.

A moment of rest during the withdrawal, January 1943. *From the archives of ISRSCPC, permission granted by M. Calandri.*

During the withdrawal, General Luigi Reverberi, commander of the Tridentina Alpine Division (center) conferring with Colonel Paolo Signorini (right), commander of the 6th Alpine Regiment of the division. *From the archives of ISRSCPC, permission granted by M. Calandri.*

The withdrawing column, shown here near Nikitovka, was soon to engage in the legendary battle of Nikolaevka, January 26, 1943. *From the archives of ISRSCPC, permission granted by M. Calandri.*

Gino Beraudi, 1938.
Permission granted by the Beraudi family.

Gino Beraudi
during his first
days in the
Alpine Corps,
1938.
*Permission
granted by the
Beraudi family.*

Left: Lieutenant Gino Beraudi. *Photo permission granted by the Beraudi family.*

Below: Captain Gino Beraudi (wearing glasses) and Major Guaraldi, commander of the Dronero Battalion, Cuneense Division in Russia. This picture was taken by a German journalist on the Don front in the fall of 1942 and was published in an Italo-German newspaper called ADLER. *Photo permission granted by the Beraudi family.*

Gino Beraudi in May 1946, upon his return from Russia after being held in a prisoner of war camp from January 1943 until October 1945. Upon release, he began his long homeward journey, arriving in Italy in mid November 1945. *Permission granted by the Beraudi family.*

Lieutenant Veniero Ajmone Marsan just before leaving for Russia with the Cuneense Division in July 1942. *Permission granted by the Ajmone Marsan family.*

Left: Veniero Ajmone Marsan upon his return from Russia, 1946.
Permission granted by the Ajmone Marsan family.

Below: Veniero Ajmone Marsan at age 85, in the mountains near the family summer home in Chiareggio, Italy.
Permission granted by the Ajmone Marsan family.

A group of Italian partisans in the Valle d'Aosta in the summer of 1944.
Nello Corti is the third from left wearing his alpino hat.
Photo courtesy of Nello Corti.

Nello Corti and his father Alfredo Corti in 1946. *Photo courtesy of Nello Corti.*

Ninety-two-year old Carlo Vicentini who served in Russia in the elite Monte Cervino Battalion. Carlo is wearing his original alpine hat that miraculously arrived in Italy in his cassetta (sent to Rome in December 1942), four years before he returned from a Russian prisoner of war camp in 1946. *Photo courtesy Carlo Vicentini.*

bombing in the distance. Zavagli and five or six officers sought shelter for the night in a stall. As the officers prepared to leave the following day, Zavagli told the commander of his group to leave him there, "on Russian soil." His fever had returned and he knew he couldn't survive another withdrawal like the one he had just completed: "It's better to be a prisoner, perhaps to be cared for, rather than free and dead after a couple of hours."

A medical lieutenant realized Zavagli needed medical help and sought to find a place for him in a military hospital, but there were long lines outside the hospitals; soldiers waiting for someone to die inside, releasing a place for them.[9]

The following day Kharkov was completely blocked; nobody could enter or leave the city. Zavagli remained alone in the freezing stall after his fellow officers left to join their transport units. After five long hours, the medical officer returned and told Zavagli to follow him. Soon they reached the Kharkov railroad station. The officer told Zavagli he had found a place for him on a hospital train. "Don't delude yourself," he said. "The last hospital train left the day before yesterday and none will depart unless the Germans arrive...."

The two officers made their way carefully, passing through the mined station, paying attention not to touch wires strung across various sections. It took some time to find the two rail cars designated as hospital cars. The medical officer attached a cardboard sign around Zavagli's neck, helped him climb into a compartment, and handed him a package containing cigarettes and hard tack.[10]

On the train, wounded and frostbitten alpini surrounded Zavagli. Most suffered from both. They were lying across seats of the crowded car, as well as in luggage racks above the seats. A sergeant major advised Zavagli to find a place for himself in a compartment at the end of the rail car where several medical officers were playing cards. He found a corner where he could stretch out. By now, his fever was raging. Throughout the night, there were heavy bombardments. At one point, the railcar lurched violently and those within thought a bomb had hit the car. The soldiers could hear loud German voices outside of the rail cars, shouting in the infernal racket of the on-going bombardment. The Germans were attempting to attach two more railcars and a locomotive to the two standing cars. Once they succeeded, the train began to move slowly.[11]

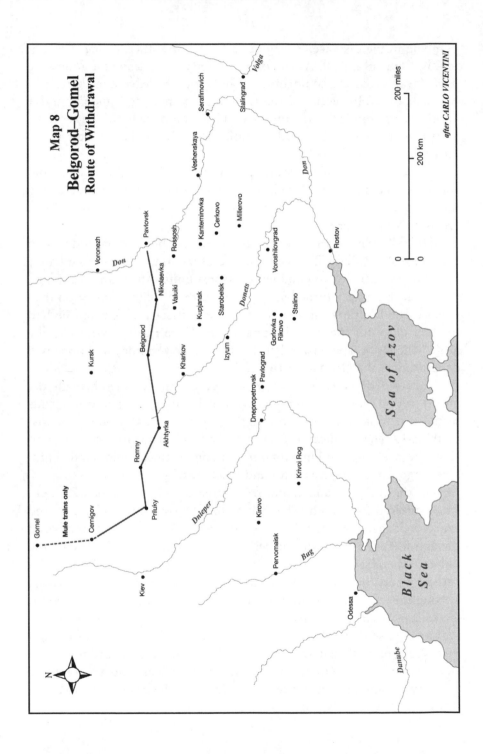

Map 8
Belgorod–Gomel
Route of Withdrawal

after CARLO VICENTINI

At dawn, the train stopped a few kilometers beyond Kharkov. "Two soldiers of the German *Feldgendarmerie* order us to unload the dead every time we stop. None of the medical [officers] moved, so I take two alpini who seem in better shape than the others. At the first stop, we remove four [dead]. The Germans make us sign a receipt! I dive back into my sleeping bag exhausted after this small exertion."[12]

As the train made its way across the snow-covered plains, soldiers received nothing to eat and no medical care. Realizing they were fortunate to have escaped from the city, the men expressed concerns about their comrades left in the hospitals in Kharkov. Zavagli writes, "Every half day a stop to unload the dead. The railcars become lighter; in three days there were nineteen bodies, and two feet, amputated from an alpino owing to gangrene.... Lice have found a refuge in my sleeping bag...the rail car is full of them.... I am afraid of typhus; but how can one avoid catching it?"[13]

Zavagli wondered if the so-called medical officers were really doctors. None of them paid attention to the wounded and they behaved in a very strange manner. Nevertheless, the soldiers were grateful to be traveling further and further away from the bombardments. Eventually the train arrived in the city of Brest-Litovsk: "A gray city, dirty; the streets were covered with yellowish mud." Germans ordered all soldiers to get off the train and stand in a line. The two rail cars attached to the cars holding the Italians were full of wounded Germans.[14]

"We marched for one kilometer to a large pavilion in which there was a tiny stove in the middle, half hidden behind the stomach of a German second lieutenant who didn't move aside for one moment and yelled orders from there: everyone must undress." Zavagli thought, "In this cold we'll all die!" Soldiers placed all their clothing and any other possession into a numbered bag. The men proceeded to the showers where four of them huddled under each showerhead. They received a tiny piece of soap resembling pumice stone. The water was cold for the most part, but every now and then, there was a burst of boiling hot water. Some men had black, green, or yellow gangrenous feet and couldn't walk; others helped them wash. Many resembled skeletons with wounds oozing pus. The men could smell chlorine and wondered if the water contained disinfectant.[15]

Once the men finished showering they were handed a tiny towel and were required to walk barefoot to another room where they dried off,

"moaning and cursing in low voices, out of fear of the fat German officer who, by the intensity of his voice makes himself understood since we
don't understand one word he says, or actually vomits." Each soldier
received his numbered sack with his clothing: "Not one pin was missing and since [our clothing] came directly from the autoclave, we now
are wearing dead lice." Following this episode, soldiers were given a
place to sleep on wooden beds with a bit of straw spread on top.[16]

Meanwhile, during those same days, following a period of rest for
alpini who had remained in Shebekino, the march continued. They were
ordered to march northwest to Belgorod, where another 3,000 wounded men were evacuated, and then on to Akhtyrka. General Reverberi led
the column of the Tridentina. Colonel Moro (commander of the 3rd
Artillery Regiment of the Julia Division) led the column of the Julia and
survivors of all other Italian units. The distance between Belgorod and
Akhtyrka was another 140 kilometers.[17] (Map 8)

Survivors of the Alpine Corps reunited in the zone of Akhtyrka,
assumed they were safe from the Russian advance; therefore, the plan
was to remain in the zone for two days. Units regrouped and services to
assist the alpini were organized.[18]

On February 10, Revelli wrote the following entry in his diary: "We
are falling apart, sick, more or less frostbitten, with non-stop diarrhea,
with horrendous visions of our Calvary.... It's necessary to stop for a
while to calm our nerves to look once more over our shoulder. Then, we
will try to forget everything forever, everything; everything, except one:
hatred for the Germans."[19]

By now, Revelli noted, the alpini had walked for six hundred kilometers across the steppe from the Don: "We dragged ourselves in deep
snow up to our knees, on the ice, and in snow that seemed like sand—
fighting, without sleep, without food, suffering from the terrible cold
and all the rest. We have arrived here. Now we have to walk further, we
don't know for how long...." As the men continued to advance, they
passed by railroad stations and trains, but could only "observe those
rail cars, because those are for the Germans...."[20]

Continuing with Revelli's diary entry, he writes, "Now we are just
a mass of disarmed men...we aren't good for anything, we are a burden
for those German dogs who have to maintain us. They don't care about
our wounded and frostbitten, we pull them on sleds in order not to lose
them. I'm still moving along, exhausted, my ankles are swollen, as big

as my calves; my fingers are broken and frostbitten, I can't feel them. I've had it."[21]

On February 11, 1943, one could count the survivors—21,000 alpini. Subtracting about 4500 men who came from Lyubotyn, and adding 11,000 wounded, frostbitten, and ill in hospitals, it seemed 27,000 came out of the encirclement along with 3,000 mules.[22]

On February 12, the march continued along routes the Germans prescribed: Akhtyrka-Priluki (270 kilometers), and Priluki-Nizhyn (120 kilometers). Some alpini were to travel by truck, the rest were to go on foot. Those on foot marched in six groups. Once in Nizhyn, all alpini transported by train or truck to Gomel, except for units of pack mules; they proceeded all the way to Gomel on foot, another 180 kilometers.[23]

When Revelli arrived in a small village after a fifteen-hour truck journey from Nizhyn, he recalled that the convoy had passed a "column of skeletons covered with colored rags." These unfortunate people were "barefoot, bent over under the weight of multicolored sacks.... It was a column of Hungarian Jews, deported to the Don to dig trenches for the Germans; now like us, they marched west, but without hope."[24]

On February 23, 1943, General Reverberi could say the withdrawal had ended: "We have finally reached safety.... My officers and alpini have been heroic, but so many are missing. Mine, in comparison to those of the other divisions who are for the most part prisoners...are dead or wounded. In only one day, that of [the battle of] Nikolaevka I lost forty officers...."[25]

On February 25, alpine commanders included the phrase "*ricordare e raccontare*" ("remember and tell the story") in an *ordine del giorno* (order of the day). Revelli believed it was too soon to remember "the saddest days of our existence...to hear again the screams and prayers of the abandoned wounded, and of the exhausted. It was too soon to remember again the dead run over and crushed by the crazed fleeing mass, and to see the columns waiting for the last rifle shot of the Tridentina Division in order to take up the flight again...."[26]

By the time of the final "Halt," survivors of the Julia Division had walked 1200 kilometers in seventy days! The Tridentina Division had walked 1000 kilometers. As the men stopped near a railway station, their feet, wrapped in rags, were able to walk on mud in which the first blades of grass were sprouting.[27]

Chapter 14

SURVIVORS OF THE WITHDRAWAL RETURN TO ITALY

On March 9, as they waited for trains to take them on their final trip back to Italy, remnants of the Tirano Battalion assembled for the reading of orders of the day from Mussolini and Army Headquarters. Major Zaccardo, commander of the battalion, recalled "the causes of the tragedy of the withdrawal." Revelli admired the officer's honesty, sincerity, and clarity.

"With the thousands of dead, frostbitten and dispersed soldiers, certain orders of the day are useless," Zaccardo said.

The major continued: "It's an insult to our dead to continue to speak of an alliance with the Germans; after the withdrawal, the Germans are our enemy, more so than in the war of 1915."

Revelli describes the words of the major as "moving and courageous," and claims Zaccardo "has wanted to speak out in this manner for a long time."[1]

Colonel Manaresi brought personal greetings from Mussolini to officers of the Tridentina during a meeting on March 10. Revelli reacted angrily to the Duce's words: "Scoundrel! Nobody believes your falsehoods anymore. You disgust us. That's what survivors think of this immense tragedy.... Your pompous, empty words are nothing more than a final insult to our dead. Tell your story to somebody who shares your opinion; those who participated in the withdrawal don't believe in rank anymore and say to you, '*Mai tardi...a farvi fuori!*' ('It's never too late...to boot you out!')"[2]

By the middle of March, alpini of the Julia Division were leaving

Russia by train in freight cars with straw on the floor. They were still famished. Once they reached Poland, German Social Services gave them vegetable soup, but this alone did not satisfy their intense hunger. In Brest-Litovsk, following delousing, they were loaded on an Italian troop train: "They returned unrecognizable, tattered, with tired feet covered with rags, with ragged clothing like beggars; they had hollow eye sockets and cheeks, pale, thin noses from which the white cartilage shone through."[3]

The men begged for food on the train traveling slowly toward Italy. All they received was broth and half a bread roll. "Don't you realize we are dying of hunger? Don't you realize we survived on rotten, frozen turnips? You have two rail cars laden with provisions, give us something to eat!"[4]

No words could adequately describe the emotional moments when trains carrying the remnants of the division reached the Italian frontier at the Brenner Pass. Alpini descended from the train to touch the ground with their feet still bound in rags. In tears, some knelt down to touch the Italian soil with their hands, while others bent down and kissed the earth.[5]

When told to return to the train, the stationmaster ordered the alpini to close all windows. An attendant locked all doors from the outside and said no one could get off the train or look out of the windows when the train passed through local stations.

Alpini reacted, shouting, "We're not animals! Open up! Open up!"

They lowered windows and attempted to open doors. "We're in Italy! We're the alpini! We're the alpini," they hollered.

The attendant replied, "The population must not see you; that's an order."

Unable and unwilling to comprehend or accept this response, the men beseeched the attendant: "We don't have the plague! We're the alpini returning from Russia."

The exasperated attendant hollered: "Don't you realize what you look like? Christ, don't you realize that you look disgusting?"[6]

Alpino Vincenzo Cucchietti of the Cuneense Division describes his arrival in Udine. "In Udine they unloaded us like animals. There are eight hundred of us, four hundred are sick and wounded. They gather us in the station square, where there is a cordon of carabinieri watching us. We resemble prisoners...."

The troops were loaded on hospital trains with seats covered with red velvet. Cucchietti writes, "We don't dare sit on them. The train is warm, the lice awake, they walk on our jackets, they appear like rows of mules." The following day when the troops arrived in Lavagna, "the population waits for us. Folks who cry, everybody cries, I do too. We are placed in a cotton mill used as a hospital, the beds have white sheets [and] we fill them with lice."[7]

When Lieutenant Zavagli arrived near the Italian frontier aboard a hospital train, he and the remaining alpini transferred to an Italian hospital train with sleeping berths. In Merano, all officers were ordered off the train. A marshal of the carabinieri approached and ordered Zavagli to get into a van: "I am angry and ask for an explanation. [The marshal] doesn't say a word.... I would have liked to have shaken and shoved him against the sides of the van had I had the strength...."

Once he arrived in front of a hospital, a doctor told him the population wasn't supposed to see the returning men. Zavagli writes, "As if the truth about our withdrawal could be hidden there behind the grating of a van...."[8]

Early on the morning of March 17, Lieutenant Revelli crossed the Italian frontier at Tarvisio and traveled down through one of the valleys where men had been recruited for the Julia Division. "In every station there's a small crowd of women dressed in black, already marked by mourning, imploring us for news. They show us photographs of their relative; they want to know the fate of the Julia Division. We only know the Julia almost vanished completely on the Russian front. We don't know what to say."[9]

Revelli describes what happened in Udine when the train stopped on a sidetrack approximately a hundred meters from the actual station: "We are isolated as if we had the plague. On the station platform, there's the usual crowd of family members and relatives, attempting to move toward us. A barrier of carabinieri prevents the crowd from reaching us. The excuse given is there is a fear of typhus. In reality they don't want us to have contact with the population."[10]

Revelli and his men remained quarantined in Udine. During this period of required isolation, they reconstructed events of the withdrawal to account for every man in their respective unit. Revelli's company originally consisted of eight officers and three hundred forty-six alpini. In Udine, only three officers and seventy alpini were present. Survivors gathered information about each missing man: "Who saw him for the last time, when and where.... For those who died, dates were recorded if they were known. The census-taking work continued, attempting to account for each alpino. It's like recomposing a magnificent mosaic on a map."[11]

On March 24, an officer from Rome arrived in Udine. Revelli recounts that he wasn't sure who this officer was, or what rank he had; however, he was *un pezzo grosso* (a bigwig). General Reverberi, commander of the Tridentina Division, began to recall the story of the withdrawal. The officer from Rome, along with the alpini, listened. When the General alluded to the heroics of the soldiers, the alpini spontaneously let Reverberi know they didn't agree with him.

Revelli writes, "No soldier in that hell would have known how to fight and die in order to open the road for a column of dispersed soldiers.... It won't be enough to construct a monument of words, of rhetoric, to soothe our dead. Those responsible for our adventure will need to face a firing squad. The buffoons [from Rome] will also need to face a firing squad."

Revelli recalled the horrors of the long march once the alpini had reached safety: "In Slobin we were still covered in rags; around our feet we still had pieces of blankets. We needed bandages, surgeons, pity. The wounded died bleeding to death; those who had frostbite lost their feet. Typhus was at the door. From Rome they send us a fool...."[12]

FINAL REFLECTIONS

In all narratives of the withdrawals from the Don, whether on the routes directed southward or westward, with Italian infantry troops or the alpini and the thousands who followed them, there came a point when "survival" meant moving forward at all costs at the mercy of unrestrained basic primitive instincts. Chaplain Don Gnocchi elaborates upon this theme, and captures feelings and sentiments expressed by countless men who later wrote descriptions of those tragic days. "During those fatal days I can say I finally saw man...unclothed, completely exposed, owing to violent events much larger than him.... I saw men vying for a piece of bread or meat with blows of bayonets. I saw hands of wounded and exhausted men who grabbed on to the sides of a sled, beaten by butts of rifles...."[13]

The chaplain describes instances when a soldier possessing a small piece of bread crouched like a dog in a remote corner to eat, fearing he might have to share. He also saw officers who held on to their personal cassetta, utilizing a much-needed sled for the wounded. On yet another sled, he even saw a hunting dog and a Russian woman wrapped in blankets, while wounded and frostbitten soldiers remained abandoned on the ground. "I saw one man shoot his companion in the head when he wouldn't give up a bit of space on the floor of an izba, and then coldly stretch himself out in that man's space to go to sleep.... Yet...I also gathered a rare flower of goodness, kindness and love—especially from the humble folk—and it is the sweet and miraculous memory of them that has the power to make the memory of that inhuman experience less dreadful."[14]

On March 26, Don Gnocchi said Mass and delivered a sermon to survivors of the Tridentina Division: "There are only a few of us in Udine, most didn't return. We also died during the withdrawal. We return to life improved!"

Upon hearing these words, Revelli writes, "...it seems as if I'm dreaming. It's a bit like when the withdrawal was over and I encountered mule drivers who had escaped from the encirclement: armed alpini, [they were] clean, [they were] men, not animals. Did the alpini still exist? Didn't all of them die during the withdrawal? Is there anyone among us who still knows how to speak of goodness? Can one really emerge improved from a beastly world?"[15]

"Our return from the Russian front is an important moment," writes Revelli. "It's a moment in which one relives the experiences just suffered. Feelings, rages, and contradictions explode. Each one of us has emerged from that endless tunnel, changed by the hell of the withdrawal. It's difficult for each of us to recognize our former identity."[16]

When the war was over, Egisto Corradi had the opportunity to meet Celestino Gherli in Milan. Gherli had been a brigadier of the carabinieri attached to the Julia Division. During their meeting, Gherli told Corradi he still recalled one specific incident during the withdrawal. He was with a group of about forty or fifty men who had distanced themselves from the larger column. As they entered a small village, they encountered a woman with two small children beside her who was screaming "fire" in Russian, as she pointed to her burning izba. A group of women surrounded the well in the middle of the road pulling up pails of water, which they were throwing against the flames. The alpini stopped and rushed to help. More pails were collected and alpini formed a line between the well and the izba, passing pails of water from man to man. It took about half an hour to extinguish the fire.[17]

After the war, Corradi also had an opportunity to speak to Cesare Brigenti, a captain in the Julia Division. It was Gherli who had saved Brigenti's life during the withdrawal. Brigenti had lost an arm and an eye during one of many battles. Gherli placed Brigenti on a small sled inside a sleeping bag, taking care of him and even taking the horse pulling the sled inside an izba during rest stops, fearing the horse might be slaughtered. As Corradi and Brigenti spoke, Brigenti also recalled the incident of the burning izba. "I don't speak about the war in Russia, but of this incident I sometimes do. It was the most wonderful thing we could do, one we could be proud of."[18]

In most narratives written by Italian soldiers who experienced the withdrawal, descriptions of the behavior of the Germans are similar. Witnesses characterized it as arrogant, overbearing, domineering, and ruthless toward non-Germans. For the most part, German troops were the only ones who had motorized vehicles during the withdrawal. As noted, some stole gasoline and even trucks from the Italians as they planned their own early withdrawal from the Don. They also managed to pull out of Postoialyj on January 15, even though General Nasci requested they remain to wait until the withdrawal of the Alpine Corps began (January 17). The Germans refused and moved out, leaving the alpini on the front lines to defend their rear as they proceeded on their own organized flight.

Lieutenant Eugenio Corti, Chief Patrol Officer of the 61st Artillery Battalion, Pasubio Infantry Division, writes about his impressions of Germans who withdrew from the Don along with his division in mid-December 1942. "...while on the one hand I abhorred the Germans for their inhumanity (which at times disqualified them, in my eyes, from membership in the human family), and for the really trivial haughtiness with which they demonstrated that they considered every other man as an inferior being—born to be exploited and expected to be grateful to his exploiters—I also thanked heaven they were with us there in the column...." Although Corti disliked them, he acknowledged, "As soldiers they have no equal. Whatever my human aversion to them as a man, it is only right that, as a soldier, I acknowledge this."[19]

Even in the midst of the tortuous withdrawal, Corti admired the military discipline of German troops, in contrast to the "endemic" disorganization that characterized the behavior of Italian troops.[20] He claims that one cannot expect men suddenly to become "orderly" just because they are in the military. "How," he asks, "can you expect people who are unused to being well-ordered in normal civilian life to become orderly, as if by the wave of a wand, simply because they find themselves in uniform?"[21]

After the war was over, Corti was able to reconstruct events of the withdrawal and realized that troops of the Pasubio and Torino infantry divisions probably would have had a better chance of breaking out of the encirclement sooner, and with fewer casualties, if they had done so on their own. "Apart from the vicissitudes of the alpini (who from the very start of their time in the [encirclement] proved superior to the Germans, so much so that the latter put themselves completely in their hands), if the Pasubio and the Torino had, like the Sforzesca [division], acted by themselves, I believe we would have gotten out earlier and with fewer casualties."[22]

When Egisto Corradi recalled the days of the withdrawal, he claims the word *raus* (from the German word *heraus*), still resonates within his ears. "Raus" (in this case meaning, "get out"), "was the scream of war in the encirclement. The Germans shouted that word using two rs, 'rraus,' to chase us out of stinky, warm izbas; we shouted it to chase them out. One began to shout 'raus' at twilight when fighting for a place in the izbas, or [when we] assaulted closed izbas from which the word 'raus' was hollered. The Germans shouted that word like savages, barking 'Raus! Raus!' "[23]

Revelli noted that he certainly came "to know" the Germans during the withdrawal: "Frenetic to save their own skin, capable of crushing our dead with their large sleds, our dead who also opened the road for them. Arrogant, convinced they could treat us as inferior...." Although the Germans did shoot from time to time, he claims they didn't sustain many losses. "On the other hand, the alpini fought like infantry every day against the Russian infantry, partisans, tanks, and everything else, sacrificing two thirds of an army."[24]

In 1946, General Gariboldi (commander of the Italian Eighth Army) wrote a report about the behavior of the Germans throughout the Russian campaign. The general claims that the Germans were surprised by the strength of the Russians, but that wasn't the singular element of their undoing.

"[Actually] what is worse, [the Germans] were betrayed by the inculcated, unshakable faith in the infallibility of their methods and invincibility of their troops. This faith blinded them to the reality they faced and pushed them to the irreparable. They found themselves in grave situations, without equipment, without supplies, among growing threats from every side...." As a result, they experienced "a bitter reawakening from cherished illusions...."

General Gariboldi emphasized that this may have explained a certain number of "things, a number of actions and a variety of arrangements, BUT NOT EVERYTHING." Their "bitter reawakening" from those "cherished illusions" cannot explain "the tenacity of not seeing the danger, of not admitting to being wrong, of not wanting to make painful, but necessary decisions...."

"Most of all," Gariboldi claims, "it doesn't explain and justifies even less the malice, injustice, the falseness with which they attempted to save themselves and their own prejudices and to judge the behavior of the Italians; it doesn't explain the inhuman cruelty with which German commanders and German troops acted against us."[25]

PART III
PRISONERS OF WAR

Chapter 15

CAPTURE AT VALUIKI

On January 27 and 28, 1943, the survivors of the Cuneense and Julia divisions in the zone around Valuiki were captured by Soviet forces.

Sheltered in an izba on the outskirts of Valuiki, Captain Gino Beraudi had fallen into a deep sleep believing his end was near. Marsan and several alpini already captured by the Russians came into the izba to wake him. They helped him put his boots on his bare feet, telling him the Russians were shooting soldiers who couldn't walk. Soon another alpino entered the izba, claiming the Russians were ordering everyone to come out immediately, threatening to blow up the izba.[1]

Beraudi describes the scene he witnessed as he went outside with his hands raised: "An armored car has its machine guns aimed at the door. A young lieutenant is at the side of the car.... Every ten meters there are a couple of Cossacks aiming their rifles at us; they form a corridor through which we inevitably have to pass. The first soldier stops me in a friendly manner. He isn't interested in my pistol, hanging by my side, but asks me for my watch. Receiving it he laughs happily, thanking me."[2]

The captured alpini soon lined up; in Beraudi's words, they resembled "a herd of defeated men," ordered to march between guards who frequently shot rounds in the air to intimidate them, and to remind them not to attempt to break out of ranks. Beraudi suddenly realized he still possessed his pistol. Knowing how dangerous this might be, he carefully pulled it out of his holster, disarmed it and threw it in the snow, unobserved by the guards.[3]

When the prisoners entered Valuiki following a two-hour march, they were required to walk by a crowd of jeering "enemy soldiers inebriated with joy and vodka." One Russian soldier offered a blanket to Beraudi. As the Captain reached for it the soldier pulled it away causing those who observed this gesture to laugh and cheer. Silent civilians lining the street watched the Italians march by.[4]

In the past, Beraudi had always imagined shooting himself before permitting the Russians to capture him! Yet, as he marched through the streets of Valuiki only two thoughts preoccupied him: "Will we get to wherever we are going soon? Will they give us something to eat?"[5]

Later he wondered what day it was. "It seems to us that it's January 28. I calculated that our withdrawal continued for twelve days. With the digression to the north and the successive withdrawal toward the southwest, we covered more than 300 kilometers. However, the date will remain a mystery. Many ascertain [including Marsan] we were captured January 27."[6]

Beraudi writes: "We, who are so accustomed to giving importance to a calendar, noting important events according to dates, will never ever know on what day we ceased being men, combatants, persons [but instead were] transformed into repulsive objects."[7]

Russian captors also paraded Vittorio Bellini of the Cuneense Division through the streets of Valuiki. Children yelled "Italianskie, fascisti, go to hell," spitting on the soldiers. A few civilians kicked the men as they passed by. When Russian women "took pity on us, seeing in what poor shape we were, they went to a well to get water to give us a drink, but the guards hit their pails with their rifle butts, and the pails fell back into the well."[8]

When Russian soldiers captured radio telegrapher Luigi Venturini, along with thirty-seven other officers of a command unit January 27, they were placed in line with numerous other captured alpini. Two Mongolian guards immediately began searching two soldiers at a time. Suddenly a shot rang out and one of two prisoners searched fell to the ground. Venturini writes, "I am devastated by terror." Another shot rang out, and another soldier fell to the ground. As Venturini came closer to the checkpoint he realized the Mongolian soldiers conducting the searches were drunk: "The scene is amazing; they make two people advance, they search in their coats and jackets, grabbing watches, rings, and all personal possessions, then they look at the nationality. If the soldier is German he is pierced with a bayonet, or shot point-blank; if he is Italian or Hungarian, his life is saved...."[9]

On January 22, Russian partisans had captured Captain Giuseppe Lamberti (commander of the Monte Cervino Ski Battalion) along with several German soldiers. Lamberti and alpini in his group possessed some German-made equipment. Forced to undress, "convinced we were Germans, the partisans put us against the wall to shoot us (after taking everything from us; ring, watch, compass). They were not joking." Lamberti and his men attempted to convince the Russians they were Italians, but the partisans didn't believe them.

"It's not possible that you Italians are here," they said.

Even though Lamberti's attendant could speak a smattering of Russian, he was unable to make the Russians understand that the Italians were not Germans. Fortunately, at this point, the partisans asked if any of the Italians could speak French. "Luckily there was a sergeant who spoke French well. They interrogated him for a long time, and from the information he gave, agreed to recognize us as Italians."

"The interpreter came to us and said, 'Move over there, apart from the Germans, it's going to be all right for you: You are saved.'"[10]

The partisans shot all the Germans, whereas Lamberti and his men were marched on foot all the way to Valuiki. He recalled, "Valuiki resembled an apocalypse. Everywhere were the dead, the wounded, the dying. The dead were undressed because everything was lacking, especially clothing. One froze in that temperature. I had frostbite on my left foot, and a wound in one arm.... They put us in a huge shed where we found the remnants of the Cuneense Division and the Julia...the scene was Dantesque, it was terrible."[11]

Although some soldiers were able to spend their first night of captivity in a variety of buildings in Valuiki, others had to spend the entire night outdoors because there was not enough room inside for the hundreds of prisoners. Those fortunate enough to be indoors were crowded to the point that some of them slept on top of each other. Vittorio Bellini was able to find a place inside a shed: "The following morning we found [those soldiers forced to stay outdoors] all dead. Also inside... many of our fellow soldiers were dead and already nude because someone had taken away their clothing. And this I can say because I saw it with my very own eyes."[12]

Beraudi describes what he witnessed that same morning: "The morning light illuminates tangled, bloody bodies, shocked faces, two-week-old beards." Nearby he noticed a soldier dressed in a white snow-suit. He surmised the man was German:

"How did you manage to get here? Are you German?"

The soldier responded with a pronounced German accent: "*Nein. Sono italiano.*" ("No, I am an Italian").

Amazed the German soldier had managed to infiltrate among the Italians, Beraudi recalled how Russians had shot German soldiers the day before: "Yesterday evening while our sad column marched toward Valuiki, I saw a Russian on horseback galloping toward us...he stopped in the middle of the road. With a fierce look, he asked if we were Germans as he removed his parabellum from his shoulder. Once informed we were Italians he lowered his weapon saying: "*Italianskie? Italianskie choroshio!*" ("Italians? Italians are good!") Then he left."[13]

While Beraudi remained in that room overflowing with soldiers, he heard his friend Captain Piazzoli was one of the alpini who froze to death during the night spent outside. He recalled he had met the captain's wife in the Corona Hotel in Cuneo, when she came to visit her husband at Christmas time: "That nice, sweet lady will now wait for him in vain. How many of our wives will wait in vain for us? Even if I can return after many years, will I find [mine] alive?" He imagined Italian newspapers would be reporting the news from the Russian front and realized his last letters to his wife most likely hadn't been delivered. He imagined his wife would anxiously wait, day after day, eventually receiving her own returned letters. "On the envelope the terrible words 'not deliverable' will be written." In the past, such words might have meant the recipient of the letter had changed their address: "But today they mean that your husband doesn't exist anymore; he is a pile of rot on the steppe; or he is in the hands of ferocious enemies, who by all accounts are mysterious and ruthless." Radio Moscow broadcasts "depressing propaganda discussions in Italian," frequently repeating, "From Russia one doesn't return!"[14]

On January 29, all officers were required to assemble in a courtyard of one of the buildings. From there they moved to a large stable with straw on the floor. Chaplain Don Oberto was able to exchange

Beraudi's flashlight for a few bars of chocolate from one of the guards. Another officer shared a small can of jam he had been saving. Beraudi, the chaplain, and four or five men divided these items equally among themselves. They had not eaten in three days.[15]

Three hundred officers and four thousand Italian soldiers were now in Russian hands in Valuiki. The Russians had very little food available for the prisoners. Beraudi recounts how they solved this problem. Since they didn't have enough food for all prisoners, they made the decision to only feed the officers: "Fraternity is over. Each person defends his own food. We are not at a point in time when the shiftier of us will be able to rob the bread ration from the person close by, thus condemning him to death. But we are getting close."[16]

Regular Russian soldiers no longer guarded the officers. Now guards were Russian partisans who entered the stable frequently, pilfering whatever personal possessions the officers still had on their person. The men soon realized they could fool the guards. For example, Beraudi and Marsan were both wearing well-made mountain boots, not the regular boots issued to the military. They knew the guards had been observing their boots, so they each exchanged one boot knowing the guards would not want a pair of mismatched boots.[17]

While Marsan was in the stable, he stretched out on the straw next to an older man, a captain by the name of Cappa. "He was a historian," Marsan said, "and had been teaching at the University of Geneva in Switzerland. Cappa had left Italy because he was an anti-Fascist, but when he heard the alpini were going to war, out of feelings of solidarity, he came back to Italy to join his companions."

Captain Cappa was the regimental historian of the 2nd Cuneense Regiment. During the withdrawal, he had had to keep a daily record of the course of events, taking many notes throughout the day. Marsan recalled, "In order to fulfill his duty, he removed his gloves whenever he wrote, exposing his hands to the sub-zero temperatures. Covered with blisters his hands had swollen. Cappa rode on horseback during most of the withdrawal, thus limiting circulation in his legs and feet. In Valuiki, as he dismounted from his horse, he stumbled over a hand grenade buried in the snow; it exploded, severely injuring his right leg and foot."

Marsan continued: "Although Captain Cappa had memorized many of the Psalms, he often asked me to read specific ones while we were in the stable. I read to him from the small Bible Lucia's mother had given to me before I left for Russia. As the days passed, Cappa's condition deteriorated, despite the care I gave him. Gangrene soon set in emitting an increasingly foul smell for all who lay next to him. Since the Russians were eager to obtain watches from their prisoners, I exchanged my watch with a Russian officer for a round loaf of bread I shared with Cappa.

"After several days, we were told that those men who could walk, or weren't sick or wounded, were to leave by train for better-equipped camps. As I prepared to leave, Captain Cappa, unable to walk, remained stretched out on the straw. He looked up at me, and said, 'Marsan, don't leave me!' I remained in Valuiki with the captain, an act I now believe may well have saved my life."

Hundreds of prisoners made their way to the station, loaded onto freight cars, locked on the outside by Russian guards. Almost immediately, German aircraft bombed the station killing hundreds of men unable to escape from the locked rail cars during the bombardment.[18]

Marsan recalled, "Those who did survive were now forced to march on foot toward Khrinovoje, a camp that would become known for some of the most atrocious conditions in all of the Russian prisoner of war camps, including cannibalism. Those additional kilometers, added to the many already covered, were disastrous. When I realize I would have had to walk 300 kilometers, on top of all the kilometers we had already walked during the withdrawal, *mi viene male* (I feel sick). Fortunately, I was spared! Maybe I would have survived that march, maybe not, but Cappa certainly saved me from that experience!"

Chapter 16

MARCHES OF THE DAVAI

"Davai...davai bystro!" ("Move, move, hurry up!") was the phrase the Russians used as they herded thousands of prisoners in long columns across the steppes. These marches became known as the "marches of the davai."

Vicentini elaborates: The phrase davai bystro "would obsess us for months, yelled—actually barked by guards escorting us. They repeated it with an exasperating rhythm, not only to speed up those who walked at the head of the column, but most of all to threaten those who were exhausted, or limping, on feet that were like marble, who dragged themselves forward at the end of the column." The Russians used this same phrase, during the long period spent in prison camps, "to accelerate our muster, the distribution of food, the cleaning of various areas, the shoveling of snow, the cutting of a tree, the digging of a pit, the hoeing of a row. Davai! The whole tragedy experienced by tens of thousands of Italian soldiers on Russian soil exists enclosed within that word."[1]

By the end of 1942 and beginning of 1943, the Russians had taken an estimated 70,000 Italian prisoners.[2] During this same period, the Soviets were committing thousands of men to maintain the momentum of their successful winter offensive. Even though the last of the encircled German troops in Stalingrad surrendered on February 2, 1943 (95,000 prisoners), the German Wehrmacht remained a fearful adversary on Russian soil.[3]

Most prisoners captured in combat zones represented a real impediment to ongoing Soviet military operations. It was necessary to move them away from battlegrounds quickly. The majority of Italian prisoners were in pitiful shape when captured, and many required immediate medical attention, even hospitalization. The Soviets were in no condition to offer any assistance or recovery; in fact, medical assistance for their own troops was rudimentary at best. No motorized vehicles or sleds were available to transport wounded, ill, or frostbitten prisoners since the Soviet Army was utilizing all such resources for its own needs. This was when the terrible davai marches began.

Guards escorting columns of prisoners on these forced marches were often young recruits, with the more seasoned soldiers on the front lines. These marches took many days, often covering the same routes soldiers had taken during their withdrawal. Those who died during the marches fell near their comrades who had lost their lives during the withdrawal, now covered with snow at the sides of the roads. Russian guards force-marched most Italian prisoners across the frozen Don to railroad centers. Once a train became available, prisoners were loaded and transported in locked freight cars to prisoner of war camps scattered throughout the country.[4]

On January 16, Lieutenant Carlo Vicentini and the remaining alpini of two companies of the Monte Cervino Battalion (commanded by Captain Lamberti) had left Rossosh after the Russians occupied the city. Although they had fought courageously in Rossosh, they were no match for the masses of Russian tanks and infantry entering the city. Vicentini and his fellow alpini walked almost continuously for three days and three nights, moving from Rossosh to Olkhovatka, Shelyakino, and then Varvarovka, hoping to escape before enemy forces completed their total encirclement of the Alpine Corps.

Vicentini recalled that the men needed to walk cross-country, away from roads and trails for the most part, since the Russians controlled the major routes leading north and west, primarily with tanks and strafing aircraft. The men were involved in several serious clashes, and soon realized the Russians were now not only controlling the major roads but were also making incursions into the small surrounding villages. In fact, Russians captured Captain Lamberti and several alpini of the battalion as they attempted to scout a safe passage across one of the major roads leading to Nikitovka.

It was at this point when ten alpini and Padre Leone (the battalion chaplain) followed Vicentini, setting out to attempt to reach Nikitovka on their own. Vicentini knew they had to move quickly, yet he also realized the men had to stop for at least six hours before being able to walk throughout that night. They were exhausted; it was now their fifth day of fighting and walking, with very few hours of rest. They stopped in a small village that appeared to be safe and promptly fell asleep in several izbas. Soon they were awakened by loud shouts of "ruki vverch" ("hands up"), as several partisans entered the izbas shooting into the air.

Vicentini recalled that moment: "It was January 19, 1943. I looked at my watch just before the Russians confiscated it; it was three o'clock in the afternoon. As the partisans lined us up and we began to march east in rows of four, I suddenly realized I still had four hand grenades in my pockets. The partisans had taken our weapons and our watches, but they had not searched us. It occurred to me I could use the hand grenades to attempt an escape. I soon realized, even though there were only four partisan guards and many more of us, the explosion of a grenade would probably also kill some of us and only one or two Russians. The remaining Russians would probably finish the rest of us off with their automatic weapons. I decided to let the grenades drop in the snow. Alpini pushed them further down in the snow as they followed behind me.

"Once we reached Nikitovka, the partisans led us into an abandoned school. It was warm in there. An old man inside one of the rooms lit a fire for us in a wood burning stove. He said, '*Italianskie choroshio*' ('Italians are good'). He told us the Russians would take good care of us, and would give us food and tobacco.

"A few hours later, a unit of soldiers from the Russian Army arrived. They were hostile and rough in contrast to the partisans. They shot in the air and at us, between our feet, and hit some of us with their fists as they continuously shouted 'Davai...davai bystro.' Soon they lined us up and forced us to march in rows of four abreast. There were about twenty German prisoners marching with us, held in the same school in a different room. That night, three Russians appeared on horseback. One of the men was an officer and could have been a political commissar:

"He asked, '*Nemzy est?*' ('Are there any Germans?').

"We said we were Italians.

"Then guards shoved four Germans out of the column. The Russian officer ordered all Italian officers to come forward. I stepped forward with our chaplain, an impressive-looking man with a large black beard. At first, the Russians thought he was a general, but he immediately told them he was a priest. The officer told us both to get in line with the Germans. He dismounted from his horse, pulled out his revolver, placed it on the chest of one of the Germans and shot him directly. He moved on to the remaining three Germans and shot them as well, in the same manner. The fourth German didn't die immediately so the officer shot him several more times.

"I remained immobilized, absolutely paralyzed as this was occurring. The Russian officer then stood in front of me and spoke to me, and I didn't hear a word he was saying, I was still completely stunned. He mounted his horse and took off. Padre Leone and I remained standing in the same place. As soon as the officer left, the guards pointed to us and said, 'You two take the boots off the Germans.'

"It was difficult to get their boots off, and I couldn't do it quickly enough to satisfy one of the guards. He kicked me in the rear and I landed on top of one of the dead Germans.

"Once we got the boots off, we began to march once more. I was a mess, a complete wreck, after this ghastly episode and became violently ill and vomited. As we marched on and I began to get my bearings back, I asked the chaplain, who could speak more Russian than I could, what the officer had said to us before he left. 'He said that we came to occupy and to destroy his country, but he believed the Italians were different from the Germans, yet we will have to stay here until we rebuild everything we destroyed.'"

Vicentini continued: "The next morning we arrived in a village; it was some kind of an operational center. The guards put us in a long line and began to search us. They took everything we had: wallets, pens, lighters, my pipe, my binoculars and compass. They didn't interrogate us though, they never asked for our name, rank, or the name of our unit. Two or three hours later, on January 22, we arrived at Varvarovka, where they put us in a church. Since our capture, we had received nothing to eat. While we were in the church we could hear the sounds of a raging battle nearby; the Russians may have been fighting a unit of Hungarians, but I am not sure about that. We stayed in the church for a whole day. The next day we walked all the way to Rossosh, where we stayed in the barracks of an Italian engineering unit. There were many other Italian prisoners in Rossosh, and we joined their group.

"Once we left Rossosh, there were three separate units of men forming the column. Each unit consisted of 400 men, marching four abreast. Just before we left Rossosh, the Russians searched us once more. Some of the prisoners were from the Julia Division. Just after Christmas, a few of them while fighting on the southern front had received valenki. The guards took those felt boots from the alpini, which meant those men had to wrap their feet in whatever they could find. Some used pieces of their greatcoat, or rags they tied around their feet with string."

The march began again but now Russian boys who couldn't have been older than fifteen or sixteen guarded the prisoners. They frequently shot off rounds in the air or just over the heads of the prisoners. The pace they set was probably normal for them "but fierce for that procession of starving men, exhausted by days and nights of walking, brutalized by the cold...."[5]

The column of prisoners was kilometers long, "selecting the strongest from the weakest. Those who were better equipped, from those who had little to protect themselves. Those hardened by the hazards of being on the front lines, of sleepless nights, work, fatigue, tours of guard duty in the frigid cold of more than thirty below, from those who were unprepared for the difficulties ahead because they had been in command centers, messes, and telephone centers." Alpini of the Tridentina and Cuneense were at the head of the column. They were in far better shape than alpini of the Julia Division who had just completed a month of fighting on the southern front. Guards became impatient with soldiers at the end of the column who could barely walk: "Threats and gunshots didn't make men who could barely stand up walk faster or make men move who had thrown themselves down in the snow, unable to move forward on their swollen feet. The guards resolved the problem without scruples...they eliminated them with a round of shots to the head."[6]

Vicentini and the chaplain moved to the end of their column in an attempt to help men in the rear move faster: "At the end of the column were dozens who dragged themselves forward with terror in their eyes. Every time a Russian killed somebody, desperation mounted their energy, it made them forget their pain, mined new strength, but for many, this was their last burst of energy, and after an hour, they were more exhausted than before. If they were not supported and helped physically, but most of all consoled and resuscitated, that was the end for them."[7]

As Padre Leone walked with the men, he made up stories to keep them moving. He told them the guards were planning to give them food at the next stop, that the sick and wounded would be picked up by trucks and driven to the camps: "As a good psychologist he didn't speak too much about God, he didn't suggest praying, he didn't assume any pitiful expression; quite the opposite. He spoke with firmness, with that frank gruffness that mountain dwellers understand...." The Padre realized these men "needed courage, not commiseration." Vicentini recalled those days as "a desperate battle." Nevertheless, he and the good Padre managed to prevent any more shootings that day, "also because we figured out a system to keep the slow-walking men from disengaging from the column; a group of us regulated our pace to that of the slowest moving men. The guards were furious, shouted, threatened, and shot in the air, but they couldn't shoot all of us."[8]

Vicentini recalled the moment the column crossed the frozen Don after passing through Novaya Kalitva: "We never imagined crossing over into this territory. We couldn't believe what we saw—barricades and lines of trenches for as far as the eye could see. Obviously, the Russians had been well organized before they came across the river to attack us. On our side, we only had one line of defense with no troops in the rear as reserves!

"We continued marching all that day, without a break. That night we found no shelter and stayed outdoors in the bitter cold. In the morning, we found about thirty soldiers lying on the snow who froze to death during that frigid night. The next day we marched again, all the way to Verkhniy Mamon. At night, when we stopped, we were able to find a spot where we could sleep—a dilapidated lean-to next to an izba. We found a frozen squash we were able to defrost, using some matches one alpino had been able to hold on to despite all the searches. We also found some cabbage immersed in brine in an underground storage barrel. An old lady who lived in the izba gave me a glass of hot tea."

Guards who escorted the column as it left Verkhniy Mamon were made up of elderly men who didn't shoot their guns as much, but who did shout "davai," almost continuously. As the men marched, they saw the remnants of the columns that had preceded them—frozen, nude bodies of soldiers lay at the sides of the road. The column proceeded day after day. Men who could no longer walk were either shot or simply left by the side of the road, where they eventually froze to death.

On the seventh morning of the march, prisoners received their first bite of food. Each group of ten men received a loaf of black bread they divided among themselves, using the handle of a spoon to cut equal portions, and then consumed in one gulp. "It was miserable, but it was the end of a relationship that had really frightened us. Up until now, they had done nothing else but eliminate the weakest and starved the rest, to weaken us over time. Maybe now that we were in their territory, never occupied by the Axis, there was some organization, and perhaps the Russians were now in a position to let us eat every day. At least that was our illusion."[9]

Finally, the column reached Kalach. Vicentini writes, "The marches were over. If I am not mistaken with my counting, that day was February 2. I had walked for eighteen days, four during the withdrawal and fourteen toward a new destiny. When I returned to Italy, I could look at a map of Russia, and discovered I had walked for about four hundred kilometers."[10]

Alarico Rocchi an infantryman in the Torino Division captured in Arbusovo in December 1942 also recalled the forced marches: "We marched for ten days. Whenever we passed a source of water, our guards would shoot anyone who attempted to get a drink. As it got dark, guards permitted us to get out of line to seek food and some kind of shelter. Local peasants gave us a place to sleep in their izbas and generously gave us a little food, even though they had so little for themselves. The Russian peasants are the best people on earth!"

During the marches Rocchi and his two friends, Attilo Schiavoni and Pietro Mazzulo, walked together. Rocchi was a strong robust man and helped his friends maintain the pace set by the guards, often holding Schiavoni's hand or carrying him on his back to an izba when searching for food and shelter:

"I was like a mule," he said, as he spoke about caring for his friend Schiavoni. When Schiavoni returned to Italy, December 8, 1945, he claimed Rocchi had saved his life during those terrible exhausting days.

While marching, Mazzulo repeatedly asked Rocchi the same question: "How do you think our families will feel when they hear we have been captured?"

Rocchi said he always responded in the same manner: "You need to take care of yourself. Here! Believe me our families are much better off where they are!"

Occasionally a soldier was able to escape during the marches. Such was the case for Vittorio Bellini, an alpino in the Cuneense Division, captured in Valuiki on January 27. When the Germans bombed the Valuiki railroad station, he was in a locked freight car with other alpini. Once released, he was force-marched with other survivors toward prisoner of war Camp Khrinovoje.

When interviewed by Massimo Sani, Bellini said, "These were eleven terrible days. Those who could not resist died. When I realized that I couldn't continue marching, I escaped (it was all the same to me if I died from a shot while trying to escape or if I died from exhaustion). When we arrived in the vicinity of an inhabited area where there was a small bridge, I threw myself over the balustrade and didn't move."[11]

Fortunately, the guards didn't notice. Bellini remained under the bridge as the column continued. Once he assumed he was safe he walked toward a nearby village. An old man offered to take him into his house and gave him a couple of cooked potatoes, a little milk, and a place to sleep. The following day the old man told Bellini he had to leave: "Go. If you don't go they will kill me."[12]

Bellini followed a path from the old man's house and soon found himself in front of a "beautiful door with a bell hanging next to it." He rang the bell but nobody responded. Since the door was open, he simply entered, crossed a courtyard and walked into the house. A woman inside was washing the floor.

Staring at him she said, "*Italianskie*? Prisoner of war?"

Then she said, "Lice?" Bellini nodded.

The woman left for a moment and returned with her husband, "a really imposing looking man...."

He questioned Bellini: "Italian prisoner of war? Officer?"

Bellini replied, "No, soldier."

The man's name was Kimij Ivan Zakarovic, a schoolteacher.[13]

In a more extensive interview with Nuto Revelli in 1965, Bellini said the villagers called the schoolteacher Uccicili. He lived with his wife, his daughter Katia, and Katia's son Slavo, a boy of nine or ten.[14]

Uccicili's wife brought a large tin basin into the kitchen for Bellini to bathe. She also gave him a towel, soap, and civilian clothes belonging to Katia's husband, a tank captain fighting at the front near Kharkov.[15]

From then on, Uccicili's family treated Bellini as a member of their family. He received plenty of food and a room of his own. He cleaned the house and took care of a cow and nine sheep: "The family treats me like a son. I have a very dear memory of them. One day I would like to return to them to thank them for all they did for me, because I owe my life to them."[16]

In the evenings, Uccicili spent time with Bellini, teaching him simple phrases and "useful" words in Russian; he also taught Bellini facts about Italian geography, pointing to various Italian cities on a large map of Europe, describing their characteristics.

"He points to my city Cuneo and says: 'Cuneo is a cold city in a cold zone.' He speaks about Torino, 'City of fashion.' He speaks of 'Artistic Florence,' of Rome, where there is the 'Great Father—the pope.' He speaks about Naples...and moves his hands as if playing a mandolin: 'There they sing well, they sing *sole mio, sole mio*.' He points to Sicily: 'Beautiful sun....' "[17]

The teacher was kind and affectionate. The villagers also liked Bellini, frequently inviting him to share meals with them. Uccicili never spoke about politics but now and then, he would comment: "It's all right to kill Mussolini just once; Hitler needs to be killed twice. Killing Stalin three times is not enough."

"He doesn't hate the Italians because he says we are also victims of the war."[18]

Two other Italian soldiers were also sheltered in the village: "One hundred meters from our house, Lieutenant Luigi Finardi from Pavia, son of a stationmaster, a brave and loyal friend, is the guest of a woman, the mother of four children. Corporal Major Sora Eugenio of the 5th Alpine [Regiment], Morbegno Battalion, lives in another house."[19]

At the end of April, Russian authorities ordered the three alpini escorted to to a prisoner of war camp: "A Russian guard arrives at the teacher's house and the scene of leaving this family, my second family, is atrocious. "I cry, and the teacher says, 'Viktor, a soldier must not cry'."

Bellini remained with the women and Slavo. "Slavo wants the guards to leave at all costs and says, 'Viktor is not leaving. Understood?'"[20]

Although the guards were reluctant to take Bellini and the others away, they knew they had to follow orders. As Bellini prepared to leave, Uccicili's wife and daughter gave him a cloth sack containing "eight kilos of dry bread, lard, a small package of sugar and other provisions. They added scissors, a needle, thread, letter-writing paper, and a pen."

At the last moment, the daughter gave him a pair of woolen gloves, saying, "Viktor, take these and don't forget us."

Bellini and the other two Italian soldiers left accompanied by the Russian guard.[21]

Chapter 17

PRISONER OF WAR TRANSPORTS

DEPARTURE FROM VALUIKI

Toward the end of February 1943 a train became available to transport Italian prisoners remaining in Valuiki to a prisoner of war camp. The train in question had arrived in Valuiki full of Russian soldiers destined for the front. Alpini almost welcomed news of an imminent departure since by now what little food available was almost gone. For days, the men had received very little nourishment; sometimes all they received were two spoonfuls of beans.[1]

Beraudi recalls it was only as he staggered to the train station that he became aware of how weak and ill he had become. Stronger men helped the weaker ones. For the wounded and the very ill, there were a few sleds. As prisoners passed by houses on the outskirts of the town, women and children stood and watched them with expressions of "pity." A few bold ones gave soldiers a little bread, or a boiled potato. If the guards witnessed this, they shoved or kicked those civilians.[2]

In the station stood a long train made up of freight cars, each one intended to hold forty men. As Beraudi stepped up into one of the cars he heard loud noises outside. A group of civilians had assaulted several individuals who were carrying sacks full of bread loaves to the train to dispense to the prisoners during their long journey. A few individuals grabbed some of the bread before Russian guards came running toward the scuffle. Ten other individuals immediately assaulted one man who was able to retrieve a full loaf of bread. A fierce fight ensued. Using their teeth and fingernails, the civilians fought and then fell to the ground. Once they stood up again, bruised and bloody, each held a fistful of bread. Beraudi saw the man who only minutes before had held the full loaf. Now he too stood there with only a fistful, crying desperately. This sobering event caused the alpini to realize that conditions for the Russian population were just as harsh as those they themselves had to endure.[3]

Beraudi, Beccaria, Greci, Marsan, and Captain Cappa were in a freight car with thirty-five other alpini. Most had to sit on the freezing floor; there were only a few plank benches. No railcar had sanitary facilities, nor was there any medical assistance for the wounded and sick or those suffering from frostbite; they moaned and sometimes screamed whenever the train lurched. Soldiers who could help attempted to ease their suffering. Marsan continued to care for Captain Cappa.[4]

Covered with lice, the men were on edge, irritable, suffering from hunger and the savage cold. During the first three days, they only received one distribution of bread. Beraudi, Marsan, and Greci tried to divert their thoughts from their hunger by telling each other stories. Beraudi, an accomplished attorney in civilian life, told Marsan and Greci about famous legal cases, sometimes making up various versions. He also spoke about his experiences as a youth and about books he had read. Many hours passed in this manner.[5]

The men received no water during the first two days of the journey. On the third day the train stopped at a station and guards opened the door of the car. They permitted Marsan and two other alpini to get off the train to obtain water for the rest of the men in their car. All they had was a five-liter bucket, which was to serve the forty men. Once they returned, several of the stronger and more vigorous soldiers threw themselves on the bucket of water, causing almost all of it to spill. Fortunately, the Russians agreed to allow the men to fill it again. This time, six alpini, including Beraudi, surrounded the bucket. Using a small, discarded meat can, they doled out the precious liquid, first to those who were ill or wounded, then to the rest. They refused water to any man whose clothing was wet. Those complained and fussed, and some said their clothing was wet because they were only close to the scuffle. A half-liter of water remained in the bucket. Soldiers who had so far received no water believed they should get what remained.

Captain Chiaramello said the remaining water could serve to dissolve disinfectant tablets for the wounded, while others said to divide it equally among all the men. Beraudi, who had assumed a leadership role in this instance, agreed, but claimed the only fair way to decide the issue was to vote for one of those options. He also reminded the men to remember they were soldiers. The men voted in favor of using the water for the ill and wounded.

Beraudi writes, "Dear Chiaramello, who is so strong, handsome and athletic; he is humiliated by being physically disabled. We amputated several of his toes with a rusty razorblade. However, the more serious sorrow is a moral one. He left his girlfriend in Italy. He feels remorse because he didn't marry her before he left. Moreover, he says, with tears in his eyes, 'I love her...I vow to marry her as soon as I return.' "[6]

When Marsan had left the train to obtain water for the men in his rail car, he came across a gathering of Russian peasant women who were offering boiled potatoes in exchange for clothing of any sort. He patiently explained he had nothing to offer. One of the women handed him a large potato as a gift: "I jumped for joy and gratitude as I brought that potato back to the train."

Beraudi writes about what happened next: "I am sitting on the floor and Marsan is standing next to me, when all of a sudden I feel his hand placed over my mouth. I open my mouth and half a boiled potato disappears between my lips. You don't know, my dear Veniero, the value of the gift you gave me! Closing my lips, I kissed the hand as if it had been my mother's, and silent tears slipped down my cheeks." Recalling how Marsan gave him precious nourishment, Beraudi understood that his friend had also given him the gift of hope and a degree of "certainty that our degradation is temporary and extraordinary.... Moreover, you gave me, who knows why, also certainty of my return.... From that day forward, every time I vacillated and hungered for mercy and for hope, the memory of your gesture satiated my hunger."[7]

The journey continued, seemingly endless. Marsan recalled that the train passed by many stations; sometimes it just stopped for hours in the countryside. "The men remained locked up inside like animals."[8] Sometimes guards would open the doors. "When this occurred," Marsan said, "guards permitted some of us to fetch water or fill a bucket with snow. Now and then, we exchanged a few words with civilians, and sometimes we could exchange one of our few remaining possessions with an eager civilian." Even their filthy, lice-filled shirts got them a piece of bread from a civilian who obviously possessed so little himself.[9] "From time to time," Marsan noted, "guards removed dead soldiers from the railcars. Periodically they would open the doors and yell, 'skolko kaputt?' ('How many dead?'). When guards gave us permission, alpini carried the dead men to the rail car directly behind the locomotive."

As the journey continued, Captain Cappa's condition deteriorated to the point that he became delirious. At one point in his delirium, he told Marsan he knew an American, a member of the U.S. Embassy in Moscow. He said he wanted Marsan's help to write a letter in English to the American, to tell him where they were, and to say they needed his help. Captain Cappa died soon after dictating that imaginary letter.

Beraudi writes, "Captain Cappa is dead... he died delirious, like an abandoned animal. For days, his gangrene made the rail car stink. Now dead, he traveled with us, occupying a precious space, and he kept on stinking needlessly."[10]

The Russian guards had not opened the rail car door for some time, so the men made an "audacious" decision to remove Cappa's body. One alpino, held firmly by the legs by others, dangled out of the small ventilation window high up in the corner of the freight car. From that position, he was able to remove the iron bar blocking the door. As the train rolled into a dark station, several men, including Marsan, opened the door cautiously, and took the captain's body off the train and laid it on the snow. A sentinel saw what was happening. Soon the commander of the guards, along with several of his men, came running with rifles at the ready. The commander shouted to his men to grab ten soldiers and to shoot them, but once he saw the captain's body lying on the snow he realized what was occurring and became reasonable and calmed down. He allowed Marsan and several others to carry Captain Cappa's body to the rail car behind the locomotive.[11]

In death, Cappa had helped his comrades. The guards permitted several alpini to get water at the station after they removed Cappa's body. Beraudi writes, "Thirst is worse than hunger." He recounts that when guards failed to bring water, or when civilians at the stations didn't fill their water bucket full of snow (dangled out of the small window of the rail car), men would suck on the iron bolts of the rail car, where icicles had formed. The little bread the men received from time to time was very hard, difficult to chew; without water, it was almost impossible to swallow.[12]

Grato Bongiovanni was loaded onto a train in Valuiki along with 1,200 other Italian prisoners. His freight car held sixty men. Only twenty-six survived the trip to the Akbulak camp in Kazakhstan, arriving there on March 21. Bongiovanni describes the anonymity of soldiers who died along the way: "One night the guards enter our rail car, they remove the dead who traveled with us for twelve days. They take out fourteen from my rail car. Goodbye companions! Italians, poor souls, nobody knows your names, you are forgotten by the whole world."[13]

On March 1, 1943, Captain Lamberti also left Valuiki bound for Camp Akbulak. He and hundreds of others arrived at that destination after nineteen days in atrocious, unimaginable conditions. In an interview with Massimo Sani, Lamberti said, "It was a most tragic period for us. Throughout our entire trip in freight cars we never had any assistance medical or otherwise (then again the Russians didn't have any for themselves, either)." The soldiers received hard bread and smoked herring, causing tremendous thirst.

Lamberti continued, "We traveled with large numbers of dead soldiers, because all of them were wounded and gangrene had set in. The memories of those scenes still horrify me today, and I can't even begin to think about certain events because they were so horrific. Hands, noses, feet, ears that became black shreds, popped off, broke off the body, with the minimum of vibration of the train." When guards removed dead soldiers they threw them over the escarpment. "Dead without a name they [eventually] will be called dispersed." When Russian soldiers opened up the doors of the freight cars and asked if there were any dead men, "we would be quiet in order to receive more rations of food. And then there was the obsession with lice, which multiplied infinitely, and we could do nothing about that."[14]

MORE PRISONER OF WAR TRANSPORTS

Over 400 prisoner of war camps were located throughout the Soviet Union. The Russians transported the thousands of Italian prisoners to the camps on rail journeys sometimes lasting for more than twenty days. All prisoners, locked up in freight cars, received much the same inhumane treatment as those who had left Valuiki.

William Craig interviewed Felice Bracci, an officer who served with the 3rd Bersaglieri Regiment deployed southeast of the Alpine Corps, captured December 21, 1942, and Cristoforo Capone, a medical officer with the Torino Division, captured in December in Abrusovka, also known as the "Valley of Death."[15]

Following a forced march across the steppes, and then crammed in a freight car along with thirty-five other Italian soldiers, "Bracci and his men were barely alive. Twenty-four slept in shifts on the ice-covered floor, where they curled up in embraces to draw heat from each other." Some soldiers told each other stories about experiences of the past or "future dreams" in an effort to pass the time. One officer was convinced the Russians would keep the train moving until all of the soldiers died. "It seemed that way. Just once a day, guards pulled the door open to give them a hunk of black bread and a bucket of water. While the thirstiest howled for more than their share, Bracci and his friends watched a soldier whittle the frozen bread into equal portions. The men never took their eyes off the knife as it shaved and jabbed the rock-like meal."[16]

On yet another train, Doctor Cristoforo Capone traveled north toward the camps with other Italian prisoners. He also recounts that the men in his freight car clutched each other to attempt to get some warmth, and how, deprived of adequate water, he would "lick the icicled walls to quench his raging thirst."[17]

While infantryman Rocchi and his friends remained locked in freight cars following the long forced march across the steppes, they received scant amounts of hard dry bread from time to time and very little water during their long journey to Kazakhstan. They also licked icicles on the bolts of the freight car doors and resorted to drinking their own urine to quench their thirst.

Vicentini and others who had survived the tortuous marches across the Don waited for two days and nights in a stall approximately one kilometer away from the Kalach railroad station. When it was time to leave, Vicentini was pushed into a freight car along with ninety-nine other prisoners. The crowded conditions reminded him of an Italian city bus during peak commute hours. All had to stand, it was impossible to move. Then, the Russians shoved in ten more prisoners, but the following day they removed thirty. Those who remained found they could sit down if they sat in a position similar to that of sitting on a sled. For the first two days, no food was forthcoming. Thirst tormented the prisoners more than hunger, and those who could, attempted to lick the condensation on bolts on the sides of the car. Vicentini spent the next thirteen days in that locked freight car until it reached Camp Michurinsk.[18]

Chapter 18

PRISONER OF WAR CAMPS— THE FIRST MONTHS

Once captured soldiers survived the horrific marches and train transports, they imagined that a prisoner of war camp would at least offer a place to sleep protected from the cold, food on a regular basis, and facilities for bathing. However, "a tremendous tragic reality awaited them."[1] The ten- to fifteen-day train journeys brought many Italian prisoners to the province of Voronezh, approximately 200 kilometers north of what had once been the ARMIR front. It was there they entered the camps of Khrinovoje, Tambov, and Michurinsk, considered as temporary "sorting or internment camps," where prisoners would remain for a short period before being forwarded elsewhere in the Soviet Union.

KHRINOVOJE

The camp in Khrinovoje had once been the site of a barracks for the Cossack Cavalry but now it was in shambles. Guards herded prisoners from their rail cars into decrepit stables without doors or intact windows; twenty-seven men occupied each stall designed to hold only one horse. It was almost impossible for them to stretch out to sleep on the icy floors.[2]

Of the 27,000 soldiers who died in this camp, approximately 20,000 were Italians. Chaplain Guido Turla writes, "In Khrinovoje one doesn't live like men, one dies like animals. We eagerly wait for a mess tin of nourishment. Disgusting bread is handed out occasionally, every two or three days, 100 grams a head…." The chaplain recalled the occasional soup distributed to the men contained potato peelings and a few grains of millet. As guards arrived with containers of soup, they threatened to beat prisoners in order to keep the hungry horde from trampling them.[3]

Desperation led hungry soldiers to the unimaginable: They "retrieved excrement from huge latrine ditches and with bare hands picked out undigested corn and millet, which they washed and ate." German prisoners swiftly improved the process: setting up an assembly line of sieve-like tin cups, they strained the feces through them and trapped so much grain they started a black market in it."[4]

Chaplain Carlo Caneva writes, "Sadly it was hunger that made this camp famous; hunger so desperate that it reduced soldiers to a level of madness, and in that state of madness to cannibalism."[5]

When Vittorio Bellini arrived in Khrinovoje in the spring, he and a squad of Italians had the gruesome job of burying hundreds of dead soldiers thrown into a large pit during the winter months. Soldiers pulled corpses out of the pit and dragged them to trenches that became a mass gravesite. Bellini was horrified as he observed a few soldiers extracting gold teeth from corpses. He questioned those men: "How is it possible for you to find the courage to to do such a thing?"

When Bellini moved bodies of soldiers, he used his hands, "because I respected them, they were our dead brothers without a name; but others simply kicked them or threw them into the trenches. This work continued for three months."[6]

MICHURINSK

As prisoners disembarked from trains near camp Michurinsk, Russian guards had a difficult time lining them up to begin counting them. One or two prisoners fainted, falling in the snow, causing the guards to begin the count all over again. Once this process finally concluded, the men were marched through a wooded area for several kilometers until they reached three small izbas. Officers, separated from the soldiers, entered an izba one by one where a Russian registered them according to nationality, rank and unit. Guards searched the prisoners and then marched groups of thirty to a clearing in the woods where it looked like there were numerous tents jutting out of the snow; they were under-ground refuges. Assigned to bunker 21, Lieutenant Carlo Vicentini and others descended the steps of the bunker and found themselves in a dark, completely empty space; "the frozen ground of the floor was the bed the new camp offered."[7]

There were approximately forty such bunkers in the camp. Officers occupied the six adjacent bunkers to bunker 21, while the troops occu-pied the remaining ones. Many of these soldiers were alpini, but the largest numbers were Hungarians. Upon inspection of the grounds sur-rounding the bunkers, the officers discovered there were no lavatories, there was no water, and there was no kitchen—"the camp offered absolutely nothing that could give us hope for an existence less animal-like from those experienced up to that point." The one consolation was a regular distribution of bread which one member of each bunker retrieved from the same izba where soldiers had registered. Every ten prisoners received one loaf of poorly baked black bread.[8]

Hungarian prisoners began building a barracks for a kitchen. A few days later, believed to be February 20 or 21, prisoners received their first hot food, the first in over a month in the middle of a Russian winter. Prisoners had few receptacles to hold their food. Among thirty men in Vicentini's bunker, there were four mess tins, ten tin cans of varied sizes, and eleven spoons. As prisoners stood in line to receive their small portion of soup, some used their alpine hat or a gas mask as a recepta-cle. Those among Vicentini's group who had mess tins placed them-selves at the head of the line, ate their soup quickly and then passed their mess tin to an alpino with none. One could hardly call the liquid poured into receptacles soup; it consisted of boiled barley (with husks) and water.[9]

The combination of half-cooked bread and poorly digestible soup caused a multitude of cases of dysentery added to the sheer hunger. Numerous soldiers who had managed to stay alive until this point died. Within Vicentini's bunker two or three were slowly dying, they had no strength to get up, refused to eat, and died within three days. Vicentini and others took their bodies outside of their bunker. Captain Payer, the eldest in the group, ordered the officers to salute their fallen comrades as one alpino quietly hummed a mournful tune. The officers removed a greatcoat from one of the dead officers to create a sort of curtain to close the opening of their bunker and placed the fur lining over others who were sick. The following morning officers discovered the corpses stripped of all remaining clothing.[10]

By now, although trenches existed serving as latrines, the camp resembled a disgusting "dung heap." Soldiers suffering from dysentery couldn't reach latrines in time and simply relieved themselves immediately outside of the bunker, if they could make it that far. Unburied bodies surrounding bunkers increased in number. Five more officers died in bunker 21. Officers could tell if a man had actually expired when they saw lice on his body congregate on the surface of his clothing preparing to move on to a live body.[11]

As the days wore on, relationships between the men cooled and solidarity between them waned. Lack of proper nourishment hardly supported men who were living in circumstances almost equal to being out of doors in sub-zero temperatures. As their strength diminished, they attempted to resist and survive. "Every form of generosity toward others was a diminution of their own possibility for salvation; selfishness had the upper hand....This degradation didn't occur with the same intensity or same manifestations for everyone; officers were less vulnerable to this moral meltdown but they too fought for their lives with little empathy [for others].[12]

Fights between Hungarian and Italian soldiers and officers occurred as men went to fetch the ration of bread allotted to their bunker. Soon the Italians formed squads to retrieve their rations in order to fend off these vicious attacks. Russian guards didn't intervene on behalf of either side. The same was true for distributions of soup. Soldiers and officers received their soup according to nationality. Hungarians were in charge of the kitchen and their co-nationals received the better portions. At times, the Italians only received hot water.[13]

As the number of dead increased, Russians ordered prisoners to dig new trenches which filled with hundreds of corpses. Huge fires burned to defrost the frozen ground before digging could begin. Soldiers took turns digging and nurturing the fires around the clock for many days and nights. An elderly Russian guard would often sit with the Italians as they huddled close to the fires waiting for their turn in the trenches. He wanted to know about life in capitalist countries. When alpini told him about their experiences in Italy, he couldn't believe what they said.

Vicentini cites one of these conversations between the guard and a few alpini:

"Is it true that you can buy whatever you want? Even a pair of shoes?"

An alpino responded, "Even a car, even a house, even a rifle."

Surprised, the guard said, "That's not possible; the government allows a person who's not a soldier to own a rifle?"

"Many Italians own a hunting rifle."

Puzzled the Russian said, "But not peasants and laborers."

"Of course they do," replied another alpino.

"Well then," the Russian asked, "why don't they revolt against their bosses?"[14]

Soldiers continued to die as this work progressed slowly. Only fifteen officers remained in bunker 21. At a certain point a long line of prisoners dragging themselves forward arrived in the camp. Vicentini writes, "Many of us ran toward them to see who they were. Almost all were Italians, completely exhausted; beneath their hats we saw skulls instead of faces, they didn't walk, they rocked to and fro resembling drunks, and as they emerged from the station it was obvious that their desperation alone kept them walking." Vicentini observed the newly arrived soldiers, hoping to see a friend or a colleague, and rejoiced when he heard someone call his name. "I couldn't recognize who the scarecrow was as he approached me, and when he told me his name I kept looking at him incredulously: he was a radio telegrapher from my squad, falling to pieces, unrecognizable. He told me the chaplain and five others of the Monte Cervino [Battalion] were also arriving."

Joy at finding survivors of his battalion soon disappeared, replaced by the harrowing news the newcomers gave him. He realized these men had little chance of survival based on the little the camp could provide. These soldiers had also left Kalach a few days after Vicentini, locked in freight cars for almost a month before reaching the camp. Vicentini had spent thirteen days aboard the train whereas these men had remained in a train for twenty-five. Many of the Monte Cervino had died during the journey. Padre Leone had survived the journey, but when Vicentini encountered him he saw a man who "had given up...something had broken inside of him...he died a few days later while I was working."[15]

Assigned to the death squad, Vicentini dragged dead soldiers scattered around the camp to a common pit. He soon stopped this gruesome task after he had attached a belt to the ankle of a corpse and to his horror observed the buttocks of the body were missing, completely cut off. There had been rumors of cannibalism but he hadn't believed them up to this point. Now he realized they were true. Unfortunately, many more soldiers witnessed such mutilation of dead soldiers.[16]

At the end of March, Russian guards ordered remaining officers to prepare for a transfer to another camp. At the rail station prisoners had the opportunity to take showers in a special rail car set up for that purpose while their clothing was disinfected. Vicentini noted that this should have been a marvelous occasion: "For seventy days I hadn't removed my shoes, hadn't undressed, and I wore the same underclothing I had on in Rossosh on January 14.... For seventy days I had slept on the ground, on church floors, in semi-destroyed izbas, in empty warehouses, under lean-tos, out of doors in village squares, in stables full of manure, in freight cars and underground pits." He was disappointed. The shower water was tepid, there was no soap, and the returned clothing was still damp. Unfortunately, some officers, already infected with typhus, including Vicentini, carried the disease with them to Camp Oranki.[17]

TAMBOV

It was estimated that of the "60,000 Italians captured during combat or the withdrawal, approximately 15,000 were wounded, sick, frostbitten and in precarious condition." Gambetti writes: "...considering the long marches across the Don to railroad centers, scant nutrition, rigid climatic conditions, and long train journeys, I calculated approximately only 40,000 were able to reach the prisoner of war camps and Soviet hospitals." By the time those destined for Tambov arrived in Rada, most were in pitiful physical shape. "In those days they weren't soldiers or men. They were just beings, desperately trying to survive."[18]

Alpino Alfonso Di Michele, of the Aquila Battalion, captured on the front lines near Ivanovka December 23, 1942, and force-marched east across the Don, arrived at the gates of Camp Tambov January 11, 1943, following a ten-day journey locked in a freight car crammed with captured Italians.

In his diary, he writes it would have been fitting to place a sign at the entrance of the camp that read, "Welcome to Hell." Below those words, he would have added a phrase borrowed from Dante's *Inferno*: "All hope abandon ye who enter in."[19]

Camp Tambov, known as number 188, was located in Rada, on the outskirts of Tambov, 459 kilometers southeast of Moscow. Originally designed as a temporary reception/internment center, it had a rudimentary level of organization. Prisoners were supposed to remain there for short periods, until authorities could forward them to one of many labor camps. Reduced to a minimum, the number of Russian soldiers present served mostly as guards around the perimeter of the camp. Prisoners who could speak Russian (for the most part Romanians and Hungarians), were selected from the camp population to carry out day-to-day management of internal camp services, namely supervision of barracks housing the prisoners, management of the kitchens, warehouses, storage centers, bathing barracks, and the rudimentary infirmary.[20]

In Camp Tambov, there were approximately eighty semi-underground bunkers of various dimensions ranging from approximately thirty to one hundred and ten square meters. Entering or leaving the bunkers required taking careful steps on a steep chute placed at the entrance of each. Within the bunkers, large two-tiered scaffolding made out of rough, uneven tree trunks served as sleeping quarters for the men. There were no sanitation facilities, and there was no running water. Bunkers had dirt floors, often covered with water from melting snow, especially when the wood-burning stove within the bunker was in use.[21]

Unprepared and overextended, the Russians faced feeding these thousands of captured soldiers. At that time, the frightful scarcity of food in the camps mirrored the scarcity experienced by most of the civilian population throughout the Soviet Union.[22] The daily ration for prisoners during the first weeks of confinement in Tambov "consisted of six-hundred grams of bread which was fifty percent water, and two soups with a few fish bones and leaves of cabbage at the bottom."[23] Romanians, who often took larger portions of the meager rations, handled distribution of food in the camp: "A day didn't go by without a fight.... Like animals without restraint, we went after them with shoves, punches, kicks, and bites for a portion of [that] dishwater [soup]. By now, human dignity had vanished...."[24]

During those first weeks, "one actually spoke about some prisoners who were feeding themselves with human flesh. Some of our companions had seen corpses missing certain body parts...."[25]

Under these atrocious conditions, Gambetti writes, "He who wants to live doesn't think of anything or anyone. He only thinks of himself. How he can survive until tomorrow. He only thinks of the means of eating something more, to warm himself better, to cause the lice to be less annoying, to make his wooden mattress less hard. Within himself, as he becomes more like an animal, he destroys every form of respect, every feeling, every human weakness...."[26]

An epidemic of dysentery began during the month of January. Barracks resembled hospitals; there was no medicine. Filthy conditions, poor quality of rations, and the inability to isolate the sick exacerbated the situation. Numbers of dead increased from consumption, intestinal ailments, pneumonia and scurvy, as well as from surgical "interventions, meaning amputations of limbs in an advanced gangrenous state with the use of knives, saws, and rusty scissors."[27]

At the beginning of March, trainloads of alpini captured in Valuiki arrived, as did German prisoners captured in Stalingrad. Gambetti writes, "One fourth of the railcars are full of corpses." Many survivors of those tortuous train journeys had typhus. Although separated from the rest of the prison population, the disease spread throughout the camp like wildfire. "There was no cure."[28]

When Marsan, Beraudi, and approximately 300 other alpini arrived in Rada after their thirteen-day rail journey, they walked as best they could for several kilometers from the train station to the camp. At the entrance, Russian guards took all personal possessions from them during a meticulous search, but didn't ask for their name, military rank, or unit.

Once inside the gates, guards escorted Marsan and the others to the barracks. Within their designated barracks, Marsan, Beraudi, Beccaria, and Greci climbed up to the second level of scaffolding and staked out a space for themselves. It was there they made a solemn pact, the alliance of the *frisa*. Marsan explained: "Frisa is a word in Piedmontese dialect. Translated, it means crumb. We vowed to share each crumb or extra bit of food equally with each other. We also promised each other reciprocal help, solidarity, and mutual support."

Beraudi writes, "We had just settled in when a Russian soldier ordered us to line up outside. He explained that we needed to choose a leader for our barracks who could speak Russian. Lieutenant Caruso, who could perhaps pronounce twelve words in Russian, which strangely resembled Neapolitan [dialect], volunteered immediately. Eventually, he will take Marsan on as an interpreter who will earn a little more food which he will share with us."[29]

Soon after their arrival, all prisoners proceeded to the bathing barracks. Marsan recalled the long, drawn out bathing ritual: "The bathing area was in a large barracks divided into two sections, a dressing space and a bathing area. In the dressing area, we removed all of our clothing, folded all our things and tied them up like a package, which we then gave to an attendant, usually a Hungarian prisoner. Once our lice-infected packages of clothing were set inside a large oven for sterilization by intense heat, we proceeded into the bathing area, where some wooden benches lined the wall. We received a wooden basin with two or three liters of water in it and a tiny bit of soap. When we had washed ourselves as best we could, we returned to the dressing area, where we waited for our package of clothing. We were completely nude, except for our shoes, and forced to wait in the cold for a very long time. Sometimes it would take hours! When the packages of clothing were ready, the attendants just threw them on to the dressing room floor. Sometimes various pieces of our clothing were missing, especially those items still in fair condition."

Apart from primitive housing, absence of drinking water and latrines, minimal medical assistance, draconian bathing rituals, and the lack of general cleanliness, the most serious deprivation facing the prisoners, which also had the most far-reaching effect, continued to be the lack of food. That winter the prisoners were barely alive, teetering on the edge of starvation, tortured by hunger. Like the few surviving earlier arrivals in the camp, they received little nourishment. Generally, their daily ration consisted of a piece of bread in the morning, and at noon a ladle of hot water with a few grains of millet floating in an indescribable liquid. Every day a few prisoners from each bunker had the responsibility of obtaining the daily ration of bread for their entire group. Scuffles and even fistfights occurred as these men tried to defend their "precious cargo" from assaults by stronger, aggressive prisoners.[30]

Bunkers soon filled with sick and dying soldiers. Life for the prisoners was "atrocious" both in and outside of the bunkers. Beraudi writes, "He who has the strength, staggering on infirm legs, goes outside for at least an hour each day and has the double advantage of oxygenating the blood and escaping from the nightmare.... Except for the narrow paths, the snow is covered everywhere with excrement. Skeletons of men wrapped in rags wander in this atrocious city. I have deep compassion for them. Then I realize I am like them...."[31]

Some prisoners just gave up and slowly died, their nude corpses thrown in mass graves. All clothing removed from the dead soldiers was stored in warehouses: "These warehouses overflow with clothing, uniforms, and boots.... Bloody shirts, worn-out jackets, shoes that survived the painful marches will serve for the living; but [those in charge] will get the best of these. The leftover rags will be for us, when those we are wearing fall to pieces, unless, in the meantime, we ourselves decide to enrich the warehouse."[32]

At a certain point, Russian guards escorted Marsan and his three friends to another part of Camp Tambov called Little Tambov. Ordered to work on the "death gang," Marsan transported nude bodies of soldiers stacked on sleds to large pits inside the forest. He recalls how women villagers pulled up their aprons to cover their eyes as he and his companions passed by on the road leading to the pits, which would become mass graves for thousands of unknown soldiers of many nationalities.

The physical condition of the men deteriorated steadily, not only from lack of proper nutrition but also from an epidemic of typhus as well as chronic dysentery and cases of diphtheria. Greci, Beraudi, and then Marsan and Beccaria developed typhus. Despite repeated sterilization of their clothing, prisoners continued to be plagued with lice. Even when they were ill with high fevers and chills, they were still required to undress completely and wait for long periods in bathing barracks in freezing temperatures until their packages of clothing arrived from the ovens.

During the late spring, while the typhus epidemic still raged within the camp, Beraudi recovered slowly. From time to time, he went outside of the barracks in order to enjoy the marvel of the new season. He noticed a few prisoners were eating clumps of new grass they had pulled out of the soil. One day, he observed an alpino on all fours who was searching, "with the expertise of a peasant," for edible grasses. The man was completely absorbed in this task, driven by hunger to be sure, but that wasn't the only motive: "In that grass he senses his countryside, all his memories, and all his hopes. As he proceeds, he moves close to the barbed wire which is severely prohibited." At a distance of about thirty meters, a Russian guard, rifle at the ready, slowly moved toward the alpino still on the ground. Beraudi writes, "We shout to our companion to turn back; but he doesn't hear and doesn't see. All he sees are his fields; all he hears is the voice of his past. Now the guard is only five or six meters in front of him. The guard permits himself the luxury of aiming and firing and he kills; he kills those soft thoughts, those gentle images."[33]

Alarmed prisoners, camp officials and a woman camp doctor came running to the field. Bending over the alpino and using her foot, the doctor rolled the man over on his back. Before she turned to leave, she pronounced her diagnosis: "Kaputt."[34]

When Marsan became so ill with typhus, he wondered if he could still survive. He recalled how he would say to himself, "God, you accepted that Lucia and I married; now you aren't going to break up all of this. We only had fifteen days together, you can't end it now!" Marsan and Beraudi did survive, yet it was a time of great sorrow for them because so many of their compatriots did not, among them Greci and Beccaria.

In Camp Tambov, there was no medical assistance except for bismuth pills for dysentery, distributed by a kindly Russian woman doctor. An Italian soldier claiming to be a medical officer joined the Italian group in the camp. Recognized by the Russian camp authorities as a medical doctor, he had privileges including a real bed with sheets. It was later discovered he was merely a corporal (a member of one of the Fascist military units taking part in the war), dressed in a medical uniform taken from a dead medical officer he came across during the withdrawal. His name was Rampinelli. Even though he only "played" the part of a doctor, he was always kind to the sick soldiers. Marsan recalled that he offered encouragement and gentle words, and attempted to make them as comfortable as possible.

CAMP 160, SUZDAL

In Camp Suzdal, northeast of Moscow, conditions were much the same for Lieutenant Bracci and Medical Officer Cristoforo Capone. Housed in barracks with no windows, they vainly hoped to receive an increase in their food rations. In this camp, men died at alarming rates, mainly from starvation.[35]

While in Suzdal, Capone devised a macabre way for his compatriots to receive more food. The soldiers barely existed in freezing cold rooms in squads of fifteen men. Each morning, Russian guards brought daily food rations to each room. The guards counted the men and left rations for the number of men present. Instead of removing the dead, Capone "propped bodies upright in their chairs." He and his compatriots pretended to have conversations with the corpses when guards entered. The Russian guards would count the men and leave fifteen portions of rations. Dr. Capone could keep the corpses for weeks because the freezing temperatures in the rooms kept the bodies from decomposing. Once men in his room began to feel stronger because of more nourishment, he established a form of "lend-lease" with other groups of prisoners, carrying frozen corpses to other rooms requiring more rations.[36]

Bracci and Capone also observed bodies with missing limbs or organs: "The Russians shot every cannibal they caught, but faced with the task of hunting down so many man-eaters they had to enlist the aid of 'anti-cannibalism teams,' drawn from the ranks of captive officers." Armed with crowbars these teams roamed the camp, "looking for telltale flickers of flame from small fires where the predators were preparing their meals."[37]

Russian authorities were concerned about the great number of deaths among Italian prisoners during the first three months of their captivity. Marsan noted that Stalin had proudly announced the number of captured Italians amounted to 80,000. News claiming that the number of survivors had fallen below 20,000 resulted in transfers of prisoners to better camps in regions with a milder climate, or camps with some medical facilities.

Beraudi writes, "We are slightly more than 400 men. It's being said...in this small camp [Little Tambov], capable of holding about

2,000 persons, 12,000 men entered successively in stages, to replace those who had died. The amount may be exaggerated, but actually, it can't be too far from the truth. The 300 men who entered the camp with me have almost all died."[38]

CAMP 74, ORANKI

Camp 74, equipped as a rudimentary hospital camp, was located 400 kilometers east of Moscow. Vicentini, suffering from typhus, remembers little of his arrival in the camp in late March.

Sick prisoners housed in wooden barracks were squeezed tightly in two rows on two levels of rough wooden scaffolding. Weakened men lying on the upper level had to climb down to reach a large barrel that served as a toilet. When possible, they filled lower vacated spots to avoid the strenuous climb to the upper level. Each pair of sick soldiers lay on a thin straw mattress sharing one blanket. Vicentini writes, "During that period the barracks resembled a Dantesque circle...a concert of laments, whimpering, hysteria, and loud, raving delirium." The one blanket for every two soldiers was small; one morning Vicentini woke and discovered he had been holding on to a dead companion throughout the night. Every day claimed its dead, and civilians living close to the camp also contracted the disease as well.[39]

At the end of April, a doctor began to care for the Italians. He was a medical officer of the Cuneense Division. He took temperatures and gave each soldier a drink of "violet water," a mixture of water and drops of iodine.

Vicentini describes a typical breakfast in the barracks. Twenty wooden bowls sitting on the one table in the barracks were filled with a mixture of various cereals such as oats or barley or grain (not ground). Once the first twenty prisoners finished eating, the same refilled bowls passed on to the next group of twenty. "No one questioned the fact the bowls and wooden spoons weren't washed between servings, or if the prisoner who had licked his spoon clean had bronchitis or dysentery." This same process continued for servings of tea, except there were only ten glasses.[40]

Once recovered, the few who survived the typhus epidemic transferred from the so-called hospital, which was no more than a rudimentary infirmary, to another part of the camp wearing wooden sandals, cotton shorts and shirts. Romanian prisoners greeted them. One of them spoke perfect Italian. He told the newcomers they would receive a set of clothing: "We will dress you correctly; here there's enough clothing to outfit a whole regiment because all the Italians who wore these clothes have died."[41]

As the days wore on, soldiers began to gain some strength. Vicentini writes: "The distributions of what we referred to as 'dishwater' were the most important moments of the day. Eating occupied our minds, and it never abandoned us, it was the object of our dreams and the subject of our conversations. It also offered a distraction, interrupting the monotony of our existence...."[42]

Breakfast consisted of tea and bread, at midday soup, and in the evening, the prisoners received what resembled *risotto* (a rice dish) made of millet. Waiting for meals was painful, caused by agonizing hunger pangs. Complaints followed the scarcity of portions received, as well as inevitable arguments among prisoners on edge. Discussions about special meals eaten in the past, the art of cooking pasta, favorite foods and wines filled the hours between distributions of rations. Prisoners spoke about the exquisite meals they would eat once they returned to Italy. These discussions failed to assuage their hunger and only added to their suffering.[43]

Vicentini remained in Oranki until November 1943, when he transferred to Camp Suzdal.

In the late spring, transfers from Camp Tambov and other internment camps continued. Soldiers and officers of all nationalities moved to camps with rudimentary hospital facilities located throughout the Soviet Union. In the middle of May 1943, Beraudi and others transferred from Tambov to a camp near Chelyabinsk, Siberia, whereas Marsan and about twenty Italian officers and numerous soldiers transferred to Borovoje in Kazakhstan.

By May, Marsan's weight had dropped to fifty-two kilos; normally, he weighed seventy-five. He recalled he would never forget walking from Camp Tambov to the train station in Rada, a distance of several kilometers: "I was very thin. I had no strength and could not walk by myself. Two fellow prisoners held me up, one on each side. Walking to that train was one of the worst efforts of my life. It was terrible! When we finally arrived, a stout, very aggressive Russian woman shouted at us, directing us to the standing freight cars. In a disdainful manner, this woman called us '*bourgeois*,' because we were officers. She used crude, rude language as she harshly shouted her orders: 'That's your car! That's your car!'"

Marsan spent a week on that train locked in a freight car along with other Italian officers and soldiers. Giuseppe DeMaria, an alpino of the Dronero Battalion, recalled that the soldiers received rations every day, and discipline meted out by Russian guards was reasonable in contrast to the terrible journey in the past from Valuiki to Tambov. None of the soldiers died on this trip.[44]

BOROVOJE

Marsan recalls that the train crossed the Volga River on a huge bridge. All the ice had melted by then, and the river was immense; it took more than half an hour to cross. The train crossed the Ural Mountains and finally arrived in Borovoje, southeast of Omsk, in Kazakhstan. Personnel of a western Russian medical clinic occupied the camp. Nurses and one doctor had transferred to Borovoje from a clinic situated close to the Polish frontier.

When Marsan and his comrades got off the train, he said they were first led to a place where they took hot showers. "You can't imagine how wonderful it felt to have hot water! It was *fantastico*!" The officers enjoyed their showers even though they were embarrassed as young girls came and washed their backs for them. After showering, prisoners received bath towels and walked across the little village to the clinic with them wrapped around their waists. Nurses directed the prisoners to small rooms in which there were four beds with sheets. Marsan recalled, "It was heavenly to once more have sheets on our beds!"

Every morning the prisoners were required to go outside to do a few exercises. A young nurse directed this activity. "You can't imagine the effort it took to do these exercises. We were so thin; we had no muscles. We were bald because all our hair had fallen out when we had been so ill with typhus. The young nurse teased us. She told us she didn't think our wives would want us looking the way we did. We were very embarrassed. The food wasn't very substantial, yet it was better than what we ate in Camp Tambov, and we were fed regularly. We had the impression the staff of the clinic kept a part of our rations. At night, we could detect the savory smell of baking bread. Of course, one must realize, members of the staff were hungry, too. They had just come from a war zone."

Marsan continued: "A few of us still had typhus or other diseases. At a certain point, there was a request for the donation of blood to help one of our officers. He was a young man who, like me, had married shortly before his departure from Italy for Russia. I remember seeing him saying goodbye to his wife when I was in the station in Cuneo, leaving for Russia. The doctor of our clinic asked us if any of us would be willing to donate blood for the young officer. The doctor also said whoever was willing to donate blood would receive a special diet afterward. I volunteered. Unfortunately, the young officer died a month later. My special diet consisted of a cup of broth with a few bits of bread for just a few days."

While in Borovoje, authorities asked Marsan to be an interpreter in a very unusual case. Rampinelli, the "fake" doctor in Tambov was now also housed in Borovoje, and the Russian police were interrogating him. Marsan recalled what transpired during that interrogation: "The police asked Rampinelli if he was a doctor. His answer was 'yes.' Then the police asked him if he could tell them how a doctor can ascertain if a woman is pregnant. I translated this question and Rampinelli told me to explain when he had graduated from medical school as a doctor, he was the owner of three large clinics in northern Italy. One was on Lake Garda, the second on Lake Maggiore, and the third on Lake Como. He went on to say he had chosen to be the administrator of the three clinics and could not answer any of these types of medical questions. I translated this, and it seemed the Russians were convinced he was a doctor. Soon after this episode, Rampinelli disappeared. I never found out what happened to him. I was never able to discover a clue as to his fate.

"As the weeks passed we were regaining our strength. In Kazakhstan, the immense steppe looked like a sea of grass. Now and then, we saw camels going by. I would often sit outside looking, with the help of the sun, in the direction of Italy. When we heard the news Mussolini had been deposed [July 25, 1943], we all sincerely believed we would be going home soon. Actually, we would have to wait for another three years!"

LABOR CAMPS

Not all prisoners ended up in camps considered "sorting camps"; instead they were sent directly to labor camps located in Mordovia (600 kilometers southeast of Moscow), camps in the regions of Perm and Sverdlovsk (1800 kilometers east of Moscow), and camps in Kazakhstan near the borders of China and Afghanistan.[45]

Within these camps, prisoners experienced the same horrific loss of life as those in the so-called sorting camps, but in addition, the longer journeys to such camps meant that those who were still alive once they reached these camps were in desperate straits.[46]

Once prisoners from sorting camps began to arrive in the labor camps, they brought the germs of typhus with them. Unprepared for an epidemic of typhus, prisoners were generally not isolated, causing a massive loss of life among the already weakened prison populations.[47]

Most troops of alpine and infantry divisions separated from their officers spent the remainder of their imprisonment in labor camps. Overall conditions in labor camps varied, as did conditions in any one camp, depending on location, time of year, and the type of work required. Authorities frequently transferred soldiers from camp to camp depending on their changing needs for labor. Most labor camps had rudimentary infirmaries, but medical supplies were wanting.

Once soldiers arrived in labor camps, medical evaluations made by doctors and Russian officials determined their assignment to one of three or four "categories" based on their physical ability to work. Each category received specific daily amounts of rations.

In a labor camp in Karaganda, Kazakhstan for example, authorities divided prisoners into three categories. "Category 1 included the strongest men receiving rations of water, cabbage and potatoes." Category 2 consisted of those considered "mediocre," able to carry out clean-up work within the camp. Their rations were the same as those for category 1, but the quantity increased. Category 3 included all who were either sick or too weak to work. This group received "a sort of meatball made of a variety of grains, as well as bread and ricotta." Periodically a doctor and nurse reevaluated the physical condition of all prisoners, reassigning them to a different category if their physical condition improved or deteriorated.[48]

All soldiers were obligated to work. The system imposed in all labor camps required a prescribed amount of completed daily work, (a quota or standard) for all prisoners depending on the job, as well as the arbitrary whims of those in charge. If a soldier reached a specified quota, he earned supplementary rations; in other words, "the more you produced the more you ate." The most common type of work outside of the camps was construction, cutting wood, agricultural work in the kolkhoz, picking cotton, making bricks, clearing roads, and occasionally mining. Within the camps, some prisoners engaged in activities they had pursued as civilians, as bakers, carpenters, masons, cobblers, tailors, and electricians. Frequently personnel of the camps made use of these skills for their own personal needs, as did the civilian population living outside the camps.[49]

Once the typhus epidemic waned, soldiers in labor camps were plagued with dysentery, colitis, and various bronchial ailments as well as scabies. In some camps, particularly those in Kazakhstan, troops became victims of malaria. Although rations were distributed on a regular basis, malnutrition was constantly a given in all labor camps.

In most camps, ongoing political indoctrination occurred. Political commissars flanked by Italian exiles operated in the camps intent on indoctrinating prisoners with communist ideology. Di Michele, held in POW labor camp 29 in Kazakhstan, notes that attempts to "brainwash" prisoners was generally unsuccessful, primarily because most troops came from backgrounds unfamiliar with political activism. Attempts by political commissars to develop political activists among Italian troops yielded few recruits. The most obvious reason was the reality of their situation as prisoners, their deteriorated physical health, as well as worries and concerns for their families in Italy with whom there was no communication. Their indifference to political activity also stemmed from the fact that most were peasant farmers or agricultural workers with minimal education; in fact, some were illiterate.[50]

A few soldiers did adhere to the Communist line, but Di Michele maintains most of these did so for opportunistic reasons, hoping to obtain better treatment, more food and possibly a quick return to Italy. The few who joined the Communist Party took on the role to recruit others within the prisoner community. [51]

Russians treated prisoners refusing to participate in political activity with a certain degree of distrust and suspicion. In some cases, they suspected prisoners of being subversive or members of the Fascist Party. Such prisoners were subject to frequent long interrogations, which Di Michele characterized as "psychological torture and brain washing" within a "regime of "inquisition."[52]

The Russians repeated the same mantra: "You came to Russia, sent by that outlaw Mussolini to invade a peaceful people, therefore now you [have to] pay for the damage you caused, and pay back the costs for your upkeep. Here we all work, not like you lazy bums in Italy, where one [man] works and others stand around and watch."[53]

Guards frequently entered the barracks to interrogate prisoners at night. At other times, they entered to search the barracks and forced the men to remain outside until they finished going through all of their clothing and few personal belongings, "pretending to look for weapons, notes and who knows what else." Di Michele writes, "These [events] were only performances. What kind of a plot could we, a mass of desperate, destitute beings, organize [while] abandoned in that miserable camp almost at the border of China, thousands and thousands of miles from Italy?" This form of harassment, Di Michele maintains, was a strategy of the Russians to engender an atmosphere of tension and suspicion among the prisoners themselves.[54]

There were a few spies among the prison population, and it wasn't clear if these men had bartered their eventual release in exchange for providing information about other prisoners to the Russians, or if they were actually functioning as a part of the internal Soviet structure. Prisoners became isolated from each other as tensions and suspicions rose among them. It got to the point that nobody really knew who among the prisoners they could trust. Di Michele writes, "Perhaps only one thing remained intact; it was this, the dignity of not betraying one's homeland.... In that moment, to adhere to the Soviet propaganda meant going over to the enemy and betraying Italy."[55]

Toward the end of his imprisonment, Di Michele contracted malaria. He weighed 35 kilos on the day he boarded a train homeward bound in the fall of 1945.[56]

Chapter 19

CAMPS SUZDAL AND KRASNOGORSK

During the the last months of 1943, most Italian officers transferred to Camp 160, on the grounds of the medieval monastery of Suzdal, 300 kilometers northeast of Moscow and about 45 from the city of Vladimir. Authorities transferred a number of Italian medical officers to hospital and labor camps scattered throughout the Soviet Union not only to care for their compatriots, but also for prisoners of other nationalities.

SUZDAL, CAMP 160

Camp 160 was reserved for officers of multiple nationalities—Hungarians, Romanians, and Germans, a few Spaniards and Finns, and about 700 Italian officers. Marsan recalled that after so many months of living on the very edge of survival, he, along with other fortunate officers, could say, "We're still alive!" He writes, "The tormenting occurrences that for months had annulled any thought not directed at survival were behind us, even though we could not placate the sorrow for the deaths of many dear friends."[1]

Officers were not obligated to work, but they were responsible for some internal camp chores. Occasionally camp authorities required officers to participate in the clearing of snow from roads, transportation of wood, and harvesting potatoes threatened by freezing. For non-compliance in such instances, threats of a reduction of rations or heating in their bunkers occurred.[2]

Lieutenants Marsan, Beraudi, and Vicentini arrived in Camp Suzdal in the late fall of 1943. Fearing another outbreak of typhus, the Russians segregated newly arriving officers from the rest of the camp population for a time, placing them in a series of what were once cells occupied by monastery monks. Vicentini and eleven of his comrades were housed in a small cell containing three-tiered scaffolding with sacks of straw serving as mattresses.[3]

Soon after the Allies announced that the Italian government had signed an armistice (September 8, 1943), ending Italy's alliance with the Germans, Colonel Novikov assembled the Italian officers and saluted them as allies. Marsan recalled Novikov's words: "We have received news the Italians have signed an armistice with the Allies; we can't consider you as enemies any longer." Marsan said, "We were convinced we would be going home, but of course, that was not to be. Shortly after that, at least a dozen of us signed a letter we wrote to the commander of the camp, asking him to permit us to go and fight the Germans. We never received an answer to our letter." When asked why the Russians would not permit the Italians to go home at that point, Marsan said, "Oh no, they never considered that as an option. They considered us *bourgeoisie*! It wasn't a matter of war and peace. It was also a matter of ideology!"

Nevertheless, rumors spread among the officers concerning their repatriation. One officer maintained that since Italy had signed an armistice making Italy a cobelligerent with the Allies, they would surely be sent home soon.

Another officer responded to this comment: "Cobelligerents? Don't make me laugh. Who would risk placing a rifle in the hands of Italians knowing within six months they might become turncoats once more? We Italians made a shitty impression."

The first officer replied. "The one who made a shitty impression was Mussolini with his cardboard army, his eight million bayonets; [in this day and age] one doesn't make war with bayonets, but we, and all those who paid with their lives did...." [4]

As newly arrived officers housed in their small cramped cells waited to join the larger prison population, such baiting discussions filled long hours for the men who had nothing to occupy them, and ranged from stabs at political subjects to the best way to cook potatoes. The ringing of a bell, signaling the prisoners to line up for meals or assemble for roll call were the only interruptions of these endless, often "monotonous exchanges."[5]

Every day all officers were required to assemble outside. A Russian officer greeted them in a loud booming voice: "Greetings, Italian officers!"

Following roll call of those present, the assembly dragged on while the Russians checked officers who were sick, and then took the roll call of prisoners of other nationalities. This same long procedure took place even when it was snowing and temperatures registered well below zero.[6]

Once the Russians permitted quarantined officers to join the larger population of the camp, the men began to piece together fragmented information about the number of missing officers and soldiers of the ARMIR. Originally there were approximately 6,000 officers in the ARMIR, and 700 were now present in Suzdal. Three captured Italian generals (Ricagno, Pascolini and Battisti) and ten German generals remained in Suzdal for a short time, kept in isolated quarters away from the rest of the prisoners.

A few officers continued to believe there were other camps holding Italian officers, but in fact, there were none. There began attempts to reconstruct events of the withdrawal to account for the missing. Chaplains listed names of those confirmed dead by survivors on tiny scraps of paper; these amounted to approximately one thousand. The officers knew absolutely nothing about the fate of captured troops. [7]

During winter months there was little daylight; the sun rose around ten in the morning and disappeared around two in the afternoon. Temperatures were frigid. Officers confined in their rooms during this period filled the hours with discussions about events of the campaign, sometimes degenerating into arguments, focusing primarily on the lack of proper equipment and weapons, and poor performance by Italian superior officers.

One officer remarked, "It's not worth searching for tactical or strategic justifications.... What happened was the result of wanting to go to war unprepared, while at the same time stubbornly underestimating the strength of the adversaries.... Don't you understand, the chiefs of staff and career officers were happy [to be sent to Russia] because in that way opportunities to receive promotions and medals multiplied.

They didn't give a damn if their assets weren't efficient or prepared....[8]

According to Marsan, the overall treatment of prisoners improved in Suzdal. Although rations were not abundant, prisoners were no longer desperately hungry. On Sundays the Russians permitted a priest to say Mass, and a Seventh Day Adventist remained excused from working on Saturdays. Officers received permission to use a library with a selection of books in Italian. Ninety percent consisted of translated writings and speeches by Stalin and Lenin. The men longed for Italian literature, and together they recalled all poetry and segments of literature they had committed to memory while attending school. They wrote the memorized pieces on smooth wooden tablets (the prisoners had no paper) and formed an anthology, a treasure, which became a great source of comfort for them.[9]

To fill the long hours, some officers played card games. Others organized to offer lessons in a variety of subjects: English, Spanish, law, military history, anatomy, and biology. Some prisoners passed the time by making objects out of wood, bone, or aluminum from scraps they picked up around the camp, while others took up knitting much-needed wool socks using miscellaneous strands of wool taken from used garments. A few officers took up mending uniforms. As time wore on, items made by soldiers were in demand from civilians outside of the camp, especially rings and small medals made of bone, combs made of horn, and wooden boxes.[10]

Every evening, following a recording of the Russian national anthem, officers heard a news bulletin given in Russian. Reports included news of continued Soviet advances, the destruction of German units, numbers of captured Germans, names of liberated cities, and amounts of captured booty. Each news update concluded with the same pronouncement: "Death to the Fascist invaders," which the Italians perceived as a personal affront since they were no longer allies of the Germans. Younger German officers in the camp also took offense. They maintained Fascism was a distortion of Nazism: "They were amazed or disbelieved us when we told them that Hitler took lessons from Mussolini and Mussolini took power ten years before their Führer."[11]

A translation of news bulletins appeared every morning on a wallboard along with translations from various Russian newspapers giving news about the war on other fronts. The Russians emphasized that they were achieving one victory after another and that the Anglo-Americans were facing tremendous difficulties attempting to break through the Gustav Line in Italy and moving forward from Anzio.[12]

The major difference between prisoner of war camps in the Soviet Union and those in other countries was Soviet political organization within their camps. "Soviet authorities were immediately concerned with the political re-education of prisoners. Already in the first months of 1943, a newspaper was printed for all nationalities, while a political commissar operated in every camp accompanied by an immigrant of the same nationality as the prisoners...."[13]

The Italian newspaper called *L'Alba,* published weekly in Moscow by a group of Italian exiles, was the prisoners' primary source of news. From it, they gained some idea of what was going on politically in Italy. Marsan claims the news, weighted heavily with praise for the Soviets, was, over time, perceived with distrust and eventual indifference.[14] On the other hand, *L'Alba* "represented the only connection with the world still in flames."[15] Newspapers for German and Romanian officers were also printed; Hungarian and the few Finnish prisoners didn't receive a regular newspaper.[16]

The Soviets initiated a program of political propaganda and indoctrination in Suzdal as they did in labor camps. An anti-Fascist club formed in Suzdal under the direction of a political commissar, who was an Italian exile. A few prisoners joined. The main activity of the club was to create a wallboard newspaper with anti-Fascist points of view. These wallboard newspapers expressed the many differing anti-Fascist beliefs among officers. There was no preference given to the few Communist ideas presented. Most anti-Fascist rhetoric focused on criticism of the alliance of the Fascists with Nazi Germany, as well as the denunciation of the miserable military preparation of the Italians sent to Russia.[17]

Approximately twenty officers joined the anti-Fascist club openly. Within the group, there were those who had opposed Fascism while still in Italy. Among younger officers, whose allegiance to the Duce waned following their experiences in Russia, there was a certain degree of confusion and disorientation with regard to political ideas, but these officers didn't lean toward Communism. In good faith, they believed they could discuss matters concerning politics in an open give-and-take manner with the Russians, yet soon realized there was only one valid rule: "It wasn't enough to be an anti-Fascist, they had to be Communists." You were either with the Communists, or against the Communists. There was no trusted middle ground.[18]

Still another group of anti-Fascists was formed of those who possessed little knowledge of Communism but who enthusiastically accepted the ideas of "class war, dictatorship by the proletariat, and the historical antithesis and contradictions of capitalism. They accepted these ideas impetuously and with the ardor of neophytes." Officers within the camp referred to this group as the "enlightened"—one member had written an article in which "he thanked the Russians for having opened his eyes and illuminated his mind."[19]

Some anti-Fascists consisted of those who joined mainly to receive certain favors—a little more food, better sleeping arrangements, or to exact a "pardon" for having been an officer in Mussolini's militia in Italy [which hunted Communists]. These officers were dangerous; they were opportunists and lacked scruples, and could easily be manipulated by the Russians. They were spies and informers and were "disposed to declare in writing whatever the Russians wanted them to say; [for example], the Italians had brought lice and typhus from Italy, the Italians had burned certain villages in the Ukraine, Italian soldiers at the front ate worse food than the food eaten by the prisoners. Such declarations were published [in the L'Alba newspaper] to bad mouth the Italian Army, even though the Russians knew they were false, but as masters of propaganda they were pleased that the Italians dirtied themselves."[20]

Officers loyal to the Fascists even continued to use the Roman salute. Some higher-ranking officers with potential future military careers reminded lower-ranking officers that they had taken an oath of loyalty to the monarchy and their country. Moreover, they maintained officers should remain apart from any opinion or unauthorized act, especially in foreign or enemy territory. A few even thought the Germans could still win the war. Some even believed the deposing of Mussolini July 25, 1943, the Allied invasion of Sicily, and the armistice with the Allies amounted to fabrications of Russian propaganda.[21]

Marsan noted that Fascists were isolated, as were those who supported the Communist line. Simple anti-Fascists were in a difficult position, considered pro-Communist by their Fascist comrades, and pitied by Russian authorities, who believed Communism was the only true anti-Fascism.[22]

An Italian political commissar gave lectures to the prisoners focusing on the achievements of Soviet workers and listing the disastrous results of Fascism. According to Vicentini, the commissar seemed to enjoy telling the officers about the battles between the Allies and the Germans in Italy, and the hardships experienced by Italian civilians as the war dragged on. At intervals, the commander of the camp or someone dispatched from Moscow would give "official" lectures in Russian (later translated into Italian). Participation in all lectures was obligatory. At the end of each lecture, Russians invited officers to air their opinions in what they called "a liberal assembly." The few responses came from anti-Fascist groups.[23]

Although these lectures were boring they were somewhat harmless in comparison to another method which was far more underhanded as well as dangerous—that of interrogations. The Russians called them "conversations" even though many of them lasted all night. All prisoner responses were recorded in writing. The NKVD (Russian political police) conducted these so-called conversations with an Italian commissar acting as interpreter.[24]

From time to time Paulo Robotti, brother in law of Togliatti (acting head of the Communist Party in Italy), arrived in the camp. A number of officers underwent questioning and probing as to their political ideas. During those days, there was a good deal of anxiety and fear owing to the fact that following Robotti's visits, several officers were transferred from Suzdal because they were thought to hinder the activities of Russian propaganda. Officers never knew who would be required to face an interrogation.[25]

Now and then mysterious people arrived in Suzdal as the NKVD attempted to make contact with a few selected Italian officers. These unknown Russians approached a number of prisoners and questioned them.

"In my case," Marsan said, "the Russians took me to a small camp where conditions for officers of various nationalities were exceptional (good food, Russian war films shown in the evening, and even a rapid excursion to Moscow). At a certain point, they invited me to a meeting with two Russian civilians; one spoke perfect Italian. After offering me cigarettes and chocolates and some small talk, they asked who the Fascists were in the camp. I told them there were no Fascists. Then they presented a map of Turin and asked me to point out the location of the FIAT factory. Half the world knew where the factory was, so I had no qualms about pointing to the correct location on the map. When I returned to Suzdal, I discovered the Russians had approached other prisoners in a similar manner. It was evident they were attempting to create possible future secret support in Italy."

In Beraudi's case, a Russian soldier approached him in Suzdal and whispered in his ear, "They are calling you from headquarters." Beraudi followed the soldier and met two men dressed in civilian clothes, who greeted him cordially. The younger one, Max Karpovic, spoke Italian, and the older one, who seemed to be of a higher rank, spoke French. They talked about this and that and attempted to discover Beraudi's political persuasion as far as international events were concerned. Beraudi spoke in generalities, and the two men seemed pleased with the "clarity of his ideas." At a certain point, Karpovic asked Beraudi if he wanted to write a letter "to his dear ones in Italy." He explained; a man was soon to be sent to join the partisans in the region of Romagna (Italy). He would carry Beraudi's letter by hand. Beraudi writes, "The idea makes me smile. I know, full well…the postcards will never arrive. I also realize that to refuse the offer is impossible." In addition, the men asked Beraudi to write a letter to one of his "dear political friends."[26]

Beraudi began to write a letter to his wife. At that point Karpovic said, "We must be sure that our emissary will not be betrayed. In your letter, insert a certain fact known only to you and your wife so she won't doubt the letter has been written spontaneously; add the fact the messenger is the person who saved your life, to be sure your wife won't denounce him."[27]

Of course, Beraudi began to worry, but it was impossible not to proceed. He finished his letter to his wife and then wrote one to the honorable Cino Macrelli (a politician friend). The two Russians told Beraudi not to discuss their conversation with anyone. At first Beraudi worried about this encounter, but after several weeks passed and nothing happened he forgot all about it.[28] Little did he realize that this was just the beginning of a long, drawn-out process of recruitment to enlist him as a Russian agent operating in Italy.

When Vicentini was subject to interrogations, the Russians asked him to give names and addresses of his family and friends, names of schools he attended, and detailed accounts of any trips he may have taken. At other times, the subject of the interrogations focused on his military training, his experiences in Russia, and the names of villages he either passed through or remained in for some time. Interrogators questioned him if soldiers in his unit had requisitioned civilian homes or livestock, or forced Russian civilians to work for them. He writes: "I realized this was a minefield and I was very careful responding...I had nothing on my conscience...but one couldn't really trust the Russians; it was evident they were searching for war criminals and realizing they couldn't find any they hoped to fabricate them."[29]

Vicentini notes that the Russians did terrorize one officer by telling him a girl in a village his unit had occupied had been raped. They threatened to have him confronted by those villagers. The officer in question was one who didn't fall for their propaganda and the accusations brought against him appeared to be a form of "blackmail." Vicentini adds, it wouldn't have been difficult to find a woman who would accuse a soldier. Fortunately, nothing came of this incident, "but it poisoned the life of that poor man until he arrived in Italy."[30]

Vicentini also notes that, as far as forcing Russian women to work for the Italians, women came to the Italians on their own, volunteering to work to avoid deportation to Germany. They cooked, cleaned, and did laundry for various units of Italian soldiers.[31]

Officers remained prisoners but eventually they received permission to work outside of the camp in the countryside. "According to international law," Marsan noted, "officers are not required to work when imprisoned, but we volunteered. A few German officers volunteered as well, but when the local peasants saw how physically run down these Germans were, they tried to help them and began to fraternize with them. When the Russians noticed this, they immediately cancelled permission for Germans to work outside the camp. The Russians didn't want Germans to mingle or fraternize with the local peasants, because they were the enemy, but we were allowed to work in the countryside."

Marsan's wish to work came from a desire to be free from a life increasingly closed within a narrowing horizon defined by the bitterness of political divisions among the prisoners. Most of all, he wanted the opportunity to have some contact with the Russian civilian population after his short-lived experiences during the days of the withdrawal.[32]

He described working in the fields near the camp, cutting corn stalks in the snow: "We carried the corn stalks back to the camp on sleds. Later on, we pulled potatoes out of the ground. There were about a dozen of us doing this work, guarded by one Russian soldier. He really didn't pay any attention to us. As we worked in the fields, we learned more about the famous black soil of Russia. It's a kind of greasy, almost plastic-like soil. In October, it was almost frozen. I can't begin to tell you how cold it felt. We had to dig to find the potatoes, then pull them out and clean them off before we put them in a sack. The black soil just stuck to our hands, and they would start to ache terribly, to the point we finally protested. We complained and said we couldn't continue this work, because our hands were aching from the cold. The Russians told us the next day we would work pulling up carrots in another field. That suited us since you only have to pull the carrots out of the ground, and you don't get that cold soil all over your hands. But what surprised us was that the next day, in the field where we had worked digging up potatoes, now there were Russian women doing what we had been doing, and this in a sense really shocked us."

CAMP 27, KRASNOGORSK

On March 12, 1944, authorities transferred Beraudi and twelve other officers to Camp 27, in Krasnogorsk, a small village twenty-seven miles from Moscow. Beraudi had no idea why this transfer occurred, but soon he realized the camp resembled a "breeding ground," where every person was studied and catalogued. "Most of my companions endured the usual mysterious interrogations."[33]

One day while walking around the camp, a German prisoner told Beraudi to present himself in the guardroom near the entrance, but warned him that he should not be seen going there. When he reached the guardroom, a Russian captain saluted him, offered his hand, and asked him if he would like to take a little walk outside the camp. The two men went to the village of Krasnogorsk and entered a building Beraudi assumed was the seat of Soviet operations. Max Karpovic was in an office waiting to see him. Karpovic asked Beraudi how he was feeling. Beraudi replied that he was feeling fine, but Karpovic interrupted him: "No, no, you have to be sick; in a few days, when I will order you to do so, you must complain of strong pains in your abdomen and your kidneys; you must complain all night, twist and turn, and call your colleague Doctor Manna. He speaks Russian well and will surely accompany you for a medical visit in the morning. It is quite probable the woman doctor on call will not assume that you are sick."

Karpovic continued to give Beraudi instructions. He was to insist on an examination by Major Spaski, director of camp sanitary services. Karpovic told Beraudi the major was well aware of a plan to transfer Beraudi to Moscow, but in order to make the plan work Beraudi would require a diagnosis of having kidney stones, necessitating a "radioscopic" exam in a hospital in Moscow. Once Beraudi transferred to Moscow, Karpovic explained he could have "a nice vacation." He would show him around the city and introduce him to the "achievements of the regime."[34]

Although Beraudi gave the impression of being pleased, he was worried, knowing the Russians wanted something from him but he was unsure what it might be. At the same time, he realized he probably wouldn't want to do it. He also worried he might be blamed if the messenger carrying his letters to Italy was caught. "If I officially leave as a sick person who may have to undergo surgery, it will be easy to assume the surgery went badly and make me disappear forever inside the walls of the Lubianka [prison in Moscow] or in a common pit. If that should happen at least my family needs to know the truth."

Beraudi spoke to his companion Marchi and told him everything that had transpired, swearing him to secrecy. Without telling Marchi, he also confided in his friend Figliuoli: "Figliuoli thinks they will take me [to Moscow] to indoctrinate me. We agree I will observe everything that will give me proof, or at least the suspicion, that some other colleague, among those who have disappeared, has been manipulated by the Russian secret police the way they are working on me; and Figliuoli will watch the movements of our other companions in the camp to see if they are transferred singly."[35]

Many days went by, yet nothing happened. On May 1, the Soviet workers' holiday, there was a celebration in the camp. One prisoner from each nationality was to make a speech on a large stage erected for this purpose. Beraudi was to represent the Italian contingent. He spoke briefly and explained the origins of the celebration of workers. He said he hoped Italy would regain her freedom: "Thanks to the military effort our combatants and the partisans are expending, and the heroic sacrifice our allies are making for us, in the future we shall also be able to celebrate the first of May in Italy in fraternity."

Beraudi believed he had given a reasonably good speech, since he notes his words "came from the heart." Russian officials called him in to headquarters and reprimanded him for not singling out the Soviet Union since, in their opinion, "it merited the larger portion of gratitude by the Italians since it was exerting the most effort [in the war]."[36]

Beraudi wondered if his imprudent speech was a fatal mistake, but was soon relieved when once again, guards took him to see Max Karpovic, who told him he now was ill with colic of the kidneys. Without following the previous instructions of tossing and turning and screaming throughout the night, Beraudi went to see Manna, the Italian doctor, the next morning. He didn't want to see the Russian woman doctor, who in his opinion was "young carrion" who "sadistically longed to humiliate and torment the prisoners." He didn't believe he could fool her, but he did tell Manna he had gone to see the woman doctor and she had declared that he was all right, and now he wanted Manna to take him to see Major Spaski, the director of sanitary services, whose office was in the medical barracks.[37]

Once in the medical facility, a German orderly refused to announce him, but Beraudi insisted. The orderly permitted him to enter Spaski's office where Beraudi complained about his imaginary colic and told Spaski the woman doctor had turned him down. Spaski began to examine Beraudi when the woman doctor arrived. Beraudi writes, "I began to sweat. Spaski asks her if she examined me, and while I could hardly breathe, she looked at me attentively and answered '*da, da*' ('yes, yes'). Evidently she had observed so many of us with such little attention she thought she had actually seen me." Beraudi recalls what happened next: "I really felt like laughing because Spaski, in a pedantic mode, is explaining to his colleague how she made a mistake, how my symptoms are pronounced and definite. She opens her eyes wide in surprise, observing her superior, who is wasting his time and energy over such vile matter. Nevertheless, things in Russia proceed in a peculiar manner;

now the woman doctor, who made a mistake because of me, observes me with great respect." Spaski gave Beraudi the required documents permitting a transfer to a hospital in Moscow. As required, Beraudi took his documents to a German doctor who gave orders to have Beraudi's head shaved. Beraudi refused; nevertheless, orders for his transfer to Moscow arrived: "I am accompanied by Karpovic, who gives me a civilian coat to cover my gray-green rags."[38]

MOSCOW

Karpovic and Beraudi drove to Moscow. At the first stop in the city, Beraudi received a complete set of civilian clothing, as well as a toothbrush, pocket comb, and safety razor, all of which "appeared like manifestations of super luxury after a year and a half spent in prison."[39]

Karpovic then took Beraudi to a rather modern-looking apartment house, and introduced him to Liuscia, who was an owner of the one of the apartments. Beraudi offered his hand to Liuscia, a tall, rather voluptuous young woman and introduced himself as "Beraudi." He immediately realized he had made a mistake by using his real name. Karpovic had instructed him to use the name Alfredo Cangiani while in Moscow.[40]

Liuscia couldn't speak a word of Italian, and Beraudi soon realized the little Russian he could speak was like an "Esperanto of the camp," understood only by the prisoners because their broken Russian pertained primarily to a few essentials such as food, work, and threats. At that point, he began to use gestures and touch: "I touch Liuscia's hair: 'Hair'—and she gives me the Russian word. Then I touch her forehead, her face, and her nose. I stop my finger a centimeter from her smiling lips—'Mouth.' Then I move close and say 'Kiss' and follow with a kiss. She pulls away, threatening me with one finger. How beautiful this is! No, I don't desire her. Even though I have not touched a woman for almost two years, I don't desire her young, soft body. I only desire her company...."[41]

Beraudi was required to remain in the apartment for three days while Max consigned his passport to the police. Every Russian citizen had to have a passport and was required to present it every three months for authorizations permitting the holder to leave the city for even one day or to take a trip outside of the city for 100 kilometers. A photographer came to the house and took photos of Beraudi with and without his glasses. He realized the Russians would more than likely forward the photographs to the archives of the Russian secret police. The Russians also took Beraudi's fingerprints.[42]

In Beraudi's passport, his address was listed as "Gorki Street, number 10," but this wasn't the address of Liuscia's apartment. Beraudi was concerned about this fact, but Karpovic explained that nobody should be able to trace Beraudi's whereabouts, including the police. He told Beraudi that only the secret police and Karpovic were aware of who Beraudi was and where he was living.[43]

In the days that followed, Karpovic accompanied Beraudi on walks, to movies, twice to the Bolshoi Theater, and to a soccer game. Beraudi only had the equivalent of four dollars in his pocket. He was completely free, but he did realize that Liuscia was watching his movements. She would interrogate him "in a sweet manner" now that they were on friendly terms. Sometimes she would refer to his activities while speaking on the phone to someone unknown to him. One day when he was about to go out on his own, Liuscia asked him where he was going. Giving her a military salute, he responded: "Commander, I'm going for a walk."

Liuscia responded. "Why are you saying that?"

Beraudi answered: "My dear, it's just a joke."

Beraudi writes, "Liuscia probes my feelings and opens up with her own confidences in order to provoke my confessions. She is twenty-three, and her husband is a colonel in the infantry on the front. She is Lithuanian, a convinced Communist, but despises the Russians. Her husband is a Ukrainian."[44]

Two other Russian families lived in Liuscia's apartment, which consisted of four rooms, a tiny kitchen, and a bathroom. One was a family of four and the other of five. Liuscia forbade Beraudi to have any contact with these people. Yet, whenever she left the apartment, curiosity got the best of the women who shared it. They came to visit Beraudi, and observed and disapproved of the meals Liuscia prepared for him. He pretended not to understand, even though the women spoke using simple Russian words he understood.[45]

As the days went by, Karpovic spent time with Beraudi. One day while the two were out walking, he asked Beraudi how his language lessons with Liuscia were progressing. Beraudi said they were making very little progress.

"But Captain, don't be so reserved. We put you in the home of a young woman so you might have possibilities. After all, she is a young wife with a husband who is far away. In addition, so you won't incur any danger, Liuscia is three months pregnant."

Disgusted by this revelation, Beraudi writes, "Nausea rose in my throat.... It seems the police make use of the body and soul of everyone. A man is fighting at the front for the grand cause while, for the welfare of the State his wife is prostituted. Liuscia, that little tart, so intelligent and nice, she knew how to deceive me so well! How will I be able to continue to smile at her?"[46]

Fully realizing he was being manipulated, and fearful of the "trap" being woven around him, Beraudi responded forcefully:

"For us, pregnant women are sacred."

Karpovic replied. "Don't be such a juvenile! Don't you realize we've been fair with you? If we had wanted a weapon to blackmail you, we wouldn't have placed you with a pregnant woman. Just think what a weapon it would have been for us if you had—or thought you had—a son in the USSR. You wouldn't have been able to tell your wife without destroying your family, and you would have trembled for the welfare of your child."

Fear gripped Beraudi. He responded cautiously and carefully, pretending to take this episode in stride. He asked Karpovic to change the subject and remarked that in Italy "a man doesn't speak about favors [he] can receive from a woman." Yet, he was alarmed and shocked and repulsed by Liuscia. Nevertheless, he maintained a "friendly demeanor" during encounters with Karpovic. Two months had gone by and he felt more and more ill at ease, sleeping poorly. He felt he was in an increasingly "enormous trap."[47]

Several days later Karpovic brought a friend to the apartment. Nothing unusual occurred. As Karpovic was leaving, he mentioned he would be bringing another friend, a general, to the apartment after dinner. Now it seemed, Beraudi thought, the time had come when the Russians were going to ask him to do something for them. He wondered if the Russians would ask him to do something "atrocious" in Russia or maybe in Italy. If asked to carry out some kind of activity in Italy, Beraudi decided he would accept, "and once I'm home I certainly will know how to disengage." Yet, if asked to carry out an activity in Russia, that would be an altogether different matter.[48]

When the general arrived, he spoke to Beraudi in Russian, and Karpovic translated. Beraudi listened attentively as the general outlined his vision of the future of Soviet relationships with capitalist countries after the end of the war:

"America, with the help of England, will dominate your world and will attempt to suffocate the USSR. I've been told that you believe in the possibility of friendship and collaboration between Italy and the USSR. You are correct; but you will soon see that all of the traditional forces of Italian capitalism will want subservience to America."

The general knew Beraudi was a Republican and told him when he returned to Italy he should register with that party in Italy and become politically active: "We will see that you are elected as a deputy. It isn't excluded that we can make you become an under-secretary."

Although the general told Beraudi he could accept or refuse, he asked Beraudi to remain in contact with the Russians to let them know the names of men who were opposed to Communist policies in Italy. The general also said Beraudi would need to forward "interesting documents relative to political tactics of your party" to the Russians.[49]

Throughout the general's speech, Beraudi listened attentively. He writes, "I am full of joy: well now, they are asking me to do something later, something they must know I won't do when I am out of their hands. A quick, precipitous acceptance, however, will appear suspect. Therefore, I pretend to think it over and put forward several exceptions...."

Once the general left the apartment, Karpovic asked Beraudi to sign a pledge of absolute obedience to the NKVD. He reiterated the fact that Beraudi's *nom de guerre* was Alfredo. Max also asked him to choose various conventional phrases their representatives could use when contacting him in Italy and to point out a safe place in Rimini (his hometown) where he could meet a Russian agent. Once Max left, Beraudi felt that he was "liberated from the nightmare." He now believed he would surely return to Italy.[50]

One day at the end of June, Beraudi was dozing on the couch in the apartment when he felt a hand on his shoulder. It was "a very serious Karpovic." As he spoke, he moved a small pistol from one trouser pocket to another in such a manner Beraudi would obviously notice.

"I am sorry but you have to return to the camp. Your absence cannot go on without arousing suspicion."

Beraudi tried to hide his happiness. He realized a return to the camp would offer "the best evasion," because he would then be able to hide his true feelings about the whole affair.

Karpovic appeared pleased when Beraudi told him he was prepared to return to the camp. He didn't see Liuscia before he left. He felt she probably would be happy to end their relationship, but she would also be sorry to give up the benefits she most certainly received while taking care of him. While driving back to the camp, Karpovic told Beraudi he would have to be very careful about what he shared with his fellow prisoners. He should say he was treated well; he should say he hadn't needed an operation because the radioscopic exams proved he didn't have kidney stones, and he should describe the different sights he saw in Moscow. Karpovic warned him not to make any involuntary mistakes; if he did, a Russian prison would await him. Soon the car in which the men were riding stopped out in the countryside in the middle of nowhere. In a nearby hut, Beraudi found a package containing his old prison rags. He writes, "I only notice now how filthy and smelly my prisoner's clothes are, but in my conscience I feel I smell even more."[51]

Figliuoli and Caruso, a lieutenant in the carabinieri, were the only Italians remaining in Camp 27 in Krasnogorsk. Beraudi told Figliuoli everything about his experiences in Moscow, and Figliuoli told Beraudi some of his fellow prisoners had also undergone similar experiences.

Soon Figliuoli transferred back to Suzdal. After Beraudi and Caruso insisted, they also transferred to Suzdal in August. In Suzdal, political divisions among the prisoners had become more pronounced, causing tensions to arise among the men. Beraudi writes, "Here one cannot live, one suffocates."[52]

OCTOBER 1944

In October, Paolo Robotti arrived in Suzdal to recruit students to attend an anti-Fascist school in Camp 40 in Krasnogorsk. A few officers asked

Robotti if the school was one that solely espoused Marxism, or if there would also be space for democratic anti-Fascist points of view.

"We believe," Robotti, said, "correct anti-Fascism is only that of Marxism, and we address our lessons in that manner. Nevertheless, there is room for anti-Fascists. Each one of you will be able to have room for debate."[53]

Marsan, Beraudi, Bizzocchi, Marabotto, and Ferretti (a Communist) were among a dozen prisoners who decided to attend the school. They were interested to learn more about political matters. Some teachers in the school were Russian, others were exiled Italians. The Italians gave a fairly objective view of Fascist Italy, whereas the Russians stuck to the doctrines of Stalinist materialism.[54]

During the first few days in the new camp, the officers stayed in a dormitory. By now it was very cold. The dormitory had a wood burning stove but no wood. The men discovered a broken table used as a pallet underneath a bunk and chopped it into firewood. Smoke from the stovepipe caused a certain Lieutenant Smirnov to come running to the dormitory. He was furious and ordered the officers into a meeting room.

"You are saboteurs. You are destroying the fruit of hard work of the Soviet people. You have burned at least twenty-seven square meters of tables."

He continued to rant and rave for half an hour. Then, according to normal Soviet procedure, when he finished speaking he asked: "Isn't there someone here who has something to say?"

Beraudi responded: "We burned a broken table because we believed it was useless. In any case we have only been here for three hours and it's absurd to accuse us of having destroyed twenty-seven square meters of a pallet in such a short time...."

Smirnov pointed his finger at Beraudi shouting, "You are a Fascist! You are a Fascist!" "[55]

CHRISTMAS 1944

The Christmas season was fast approaching. Although officers had received permission to celebrate Mass on Sundays in Suzdal, it would have been impossible to celebrate a Christmas Mass in camp 40. The Italians were informed in the nearby Camp 27, Zone 2, that a German

Catholic chaplain was planning to hold a Mass. Marsan immediately requested permission to attend and was told to find out if any other prisoners wanted to attend. Out of sixty-eight Italians, more than forty wanted to attend.[56]

Guards summoned all officers to a meeting on December 24. Colonel Porfionov, the commander of the school, began to address the prisoners in Russian in a violent and threatening tone. Foschi translated. The colonel spoke about various religious belief systems, noting they were "ridiculous superstitions" believed in by "poor, ignorant people" and used by "those who are not ignorant to impose fear and resignation among people."

When he continued, the colonel made it clear one could not "keep one's rear on the seat of superstition and at the same time on the seat of Marxism." If a person attempts to do so, he will crash to the ground and won't get up again.

Following this tirade, the colonel asked if anyone had anything to say. Beraudi responded, but lacked the courage to express his true feelings. What he had wanted to say was that he and his comrades came to the school believing they wouldn't be "obligated to sit on the seat of Marxism," and that he was "sitting securely on the seat of Christian idealism," and "our Christian truth is supported by the word, whereas their Marxist truth required an army of police and spies."

Instead, he said, "We are Italian soldiers and officers. You have spoken well as a Russian officer and as a Marxist."

Foschi translated Beraudi's words and the colonel made a "sharp and threatening gesture." Then he responded: "You recognize the fact that I have spoken well; therefore the meeting is over." Without waiting for the officers to come to attention, the colonel left. Beraudi writes, "Marsan smiles at me with his indulgent and serene eyes."[57]

On December 31, another meeting took place at the foot of a tree decorated for Christmas with colored lights. Colonel Porfionov announced the expulsion from the school of two Germans, one Hungarian, and two Italians, Marsan and Ceccarrelli, "traitors to the people's cause."[58]

Several days before the announcement of the expulsions, Beraudi had attempted to prevent such an outcome by speaking to the head of the school, an Italian captain. The captain responded to Beraudi's pleas:

"You know it seems to me that the colonel is right. Marsan couldn't have limited himself to simply asking if someone wanted to attend Mass, he must have engaged in propaganda. Otherwise, how can you explain that almost all of the Italians said yes?"

Beraudi realized he couldn't reason with the captain, so he went to see Robotti. He told Robotti it would be a grave injustice to punish Marsan because Marsan's motives were not malicious. "Marsan is transparent, and everyone can see what sort of a man he is. If he should be expelled from the school, I'm afraid several others will also be persuaded to give it up."

Despite Beraudi's attempts to persuade Robotti to see his point of view, Robotti didn't think he would be able to convince Colonel Porfionov to change his mind.[59]

Marsan transferred to the third zone of Camp 27 in Krasnogorsk. Prisoners attending the school also went there every ten days to bathe, so Beraudi could see him for a few hours. There were many Italian soldiers in Camp 27. Because Marsan could speak a number of languages, the commander of the camp shared several Russian newspapers with him, as well as one English-language newspaper printed in Moscow. Marsan "comforted" the Italian soldiers by translating various articles of interest to them. One day he translated a speech given by Roosevelt in which the President stated men should have faith in God. The inevitable spies told the Russian authorities, and they in turn accused Marsan of propagating religious propaganda. From then on, he was no longer permitted to have any contact with Italian soldiers.[60]

SUZDAL

Meanwhile, officers who had remained in Suzdal during this period were in dire need of decent winter clothing. The rags they were wearing offered little protection from the cold, and a few soldiers were showing signs of frostbite. Lieutenant Vicentini and others were aware the Russians were keeping clothing removed from dead soldiers in the bell tower of the monastery. It seemed impossible to get into the tower because the only entrance was through a locked wooden door. By chance, a few officers discovered an opening to the tower at ground level, closed with brickwork in a state of deterioration. Every day a few men removed bricks and then replaced them temporarily, covering up any sign of their work with snow piled close to the tower. Eventually officers managed to reach the stash of winter clothing. They found all sorts of woolen sweaters, socks, and gloves but left valenki and fur-lined German boots because they knew Russian guards would know where they came from.[61]

Soon after, one of the Italian officers in Vicentini's barracks questioned him. "Can you tell me why all you alpini are thieves?"

An irritated Vicentini responded, telling the officer he had framed his question poorly: "You want to know why the alpini seem to manage in all circumstances."

The officer replied, "Well, if you want to put it that way, but you [alpini] are light fingered."

At this point Vicentini pointed out that even though there were two alpini in their barracks, nothing was ever stolen from any of the officers living there.

"Well," the officer responded, "I never would even think of robbing the bell tower or the orchard, and even if I did think about it, I wouldn't know how to begin."

"Exactly. You wouldn't do it because you don't know how."

The officer then posed another question: "Why is it that you alpini can figure things out and then carry your plans out so successfully?"

Vicentini patiently explained that mountain folk, with whatever modest means they may have, are required to tackle large and small problems presented by their challenging environment. Therefore, from a very early age, an alpino has learned to meet challenges using his imagination and tenacity: "That's why, even in war, where there are plenty of difficulties and restraints, he always manages, sometimes by robbery as you refer to it, but mostly with shrewdness."[62]

As their conversation continued, Vicentini shared several examples of useful equipment alpini obtained by means of bartering. In one case, the Monte Cervino Battalion managed to obtain four mobile German kitchens towed by trucks (no other unit in the ARMIR possessed mobile kitchens). The kitchens remained turned on even while moving from one place to another, which meant the alpini could have a hot meal soon after arriving at their destination.

In another case, alpini obtained German telephones and telephone wire, far more efficient than those issued by the Italian Army. During the summer, for a few cans of meat and some sugar, alpini were able to obtain a few Ukrainian carts allowing them to remove their heavy rucksacks by placing them in the carts. Once winter arrived, again by means of bartering, alpini substituted the carts with sleds. The Italian military never considered sending sleds to Russia despite the experiences of the CSIR forces during the preceding year: "Maybe they deluded themselves that the campaign would be finished before the snow fell."

In conclusion, Vicentini noted that the alpini knew how to tackle obstacles proactively: "They found ways to correct deficiencies which the organization couldn't, or didn't want or know how to eliminate."[63]

CAMP 27, KRASNOGORSK

Classes for the group of Italian officers attending the anti-Fascist school in Krasnogorsk ended in the spring of 1945. Of the seventy Italian officers in the group, only ten requested to sign up with the Communist Party, whereas in the past, a higher percentage of attendees had joined.

Most officers returned to Camp Suzdal, whereas Beraudi, Bizzocchi, and a few soldiers remained in Camp 27. Another group of recruits arrived to attend a new series of classes.[64]

To fill the endless hours, Beraudi cut trees in the forest on occasion, and sometimes worked in a vegetable garden by the river. At a certain point, all Italians in the camp were engaged in a two-day camp cleanup. They were under the impression that perhaps a general was to arrive for a visit. On the third day, almost all Italians as well as service personnel were taken to the vegetable plot approximately two kilometers from the camp. They remained there until evening. Owing to their chronic hunger, especially for fresh produce, the men stuffed themselves with ripe cucumbers and onions, ignoring protests from the guards. Upon returning to the camp that evening, the few "enlightened" members who had remained in the camp to give a good impression to an Italian trade union group made up of various political parties told the officers the visitors had never arrived—all was for naught. Evidently, the Russians had been concerned Beraudi and others who had completed the previous anti-Fascist school course of study might speak to the expected visitors.[65]

At a certain point, rations for Beraudi and Bizzocchi diminished. They suspected this was due to their lack of cooperation during their stint in the school. The men complained. The Russians told them they had earned the right to smaller portions of food because they were only completing the camp chores required of all officers.

One day soon after, when they had completed their usual camp chores, Beraudi and Bizzocchi received orders to spread hay out on the fields. They protested to no avail, and with rakes on their backs walked to the fields grumbling, accompanied by a young Russian lieutenant. The lieutenant attempted to strike up a conversation with the officers. They ignored him. He then attempted to provoke them.

"You don't feel like working, do you?" The officers continued to ignore him.

"Don't be upset. Just give a few whacks with your rake and then we'll stretch out in the sun."

The officers began to work feverishly while the Russian officer begged them to stop. At a certain point, Bizzocchi remembered he had a few rubles in his pocket. He noticed a peasant house close by and told the guard he wanted to buy milk and eggs from the peasants living there.

"But you can't do that," the Russian responded. "It's forbidden for you to have any contact with civilians."

The officers continued their work and once again ignored the lieutenant. After a while, he approached them: "Let's do this—give me the rubles and I will go and do the shopping for you."

He gave the officers his hat and his belt holding his pistol and left with their mess tins and soon returned. He had stuffed his shirt with eggs and walked carefully so as not to spill any of the milk from the mess tins. Beraudi writes, "At this point our hearts melted and we offered him some of our treasures."[66]

Beraudi wondered if his behavior in the anti-Fascist school would affect his relationship with his so-called Moscow friends. He had only heard from them once while attending classes. Summoned to headquarters of the camp following a day of chopping wood, he had met a Russian captain and a young woman. The woman could speak Italian well and told him his Moscow friends wanted to know how he was and would like to receive a note from him. His hands were sore and stiff from the day's work in the freezing temperature; it was difficult to grasp a pen and his hand trembled as he attempted to write. Nevertheless, he managed to write a cordial note, and the captain took it with him as he left. The young woman then moved closer to Beraudi, rubbing her breast against his sleeve as she asked for information about specific colleagues. He refused to cooperate, determined not to become an informer.

When Beraudi saw his friend Garombo in the third zone of the camp, Garombo told him he had undergone an interrogation in which Russians questioned him about Beraudi's activities in Italy, his behavior toward soldiers serving under him, and his treatment of Russian civilians; all the while, a young woman had provocatively rubbed her breast on his sleeve. Following this interrogation, the Russians had dismissed Garombo and denied his request to attend the anti-Fascist school.[67]

When Marsan prepared to transfer back to Camp Suzdal before Easter, he had asked Beraudi if he wanted to receive Communion before he left. Beraudi writes, "I would have considered anyone who asked me such a thing as either crazy or a provocateur, but not Marsan. He made many miracles, beautiful miracles: humble, communal ones, very difficult ones. With one word, he restored faith to those who were desperate; with a smile, he gave serenity and certainty to those who felt destroyed. I simply said 'Yes.'"

Marsan told Beraudi that one of their chaplains was in the second zone of the camp, and when he said Mass, he consecrated some bread made of wheat. Marsan had wrapped some of the bread, cut in tiny pieces, in a piece of white fabric. Marsan told Beraudi he would divide the fabric and pieces of bread and give him half.

"You can distribute them to those who want to receive Communion. Burn those that remain...all the soldiers have to do is confess to themselves, and make [an act of] contrition."

Beraudi writes, "That bread gave me absolute security. Without fear and in great secrecy, I distributed the sacred pieces to other students, excluding those who declared themselves atheists. While the sun shone and the wind caressed the first flowers in one corner of the camp, I gave myself Communion. After that in every difficult moment, that white rag wrapped in paper, close to my heart, gave me strength."[68]

KRUTIEZ

Once Marsan returned to Suzdal, he began to work in several nearby villages. He became acquainted with local civilians (mostly women, children, and old people) and soon discovered that they, too, were victims, living in extremely harsh circumstances, almost comparable to those of the prisoners. He wrote, "Collaborating with the locals in our work created authentic bonds, founded upon common human values of sacrifice and of hope. I remember the mothers and brides, deprived for years of any news of their family members who were off fighting the war; this was a torment understood by those, like us, who from the time of our capture waited in vain for news from home."[69]

"Of the work done by me with some of my fellow prisoners outside of the prison camp, I want to remember the relationships with the inhabitants of the village where we lent our help, owing to the absence of the men who had been called to arms."

An elderly peasant woman whose last name was Kutusova lived in the village. Every week Marsan exchanged his daily bread ration (250 grams) with her for a quarter liter of milk: "For he who is really hungry—we had experimented—bread is the food most longed for, the one that 'fills' the stomach, even though for only a short time." Marsan told Kutusova about his marriage to his wife Lucia a few days before leaving Italy for Russia.

"She always said to me when we met: 'I am sure in this moment your bride is thinking of you.' How can I ever forget those words?"[70]

Marsan asked Kutusova if she had a Bible. "She told me to lift the cover of the kneading trough next to the wall; it was full, to the brim, of fine grain. Then she told me to look at the bottom where I would find her Bible." When asked why she kept it there, and who would ever attempt to look for it, she replied, "As long as they use the church as a storage place for tractors and other agricultural machines, I will keep the Bible hidden."

Marsan noted that Kutusova "hadn't forgotten the days of expulsion of the *kulaki* (small proprietors of land) during the process of agrarian collectivization initiated by Stalin in the 1930s. And Stalin was still alive."[71]

Marsan worked northwest of Suzdal, cutting down trees in a huge forest. The wood was required for railroad ties: "We worked in the forest every day," he said. "It was heavy work, but not at all unpleasant. In the morning, we felled the trees with an axe and a two-man saw, and cut all the branches off. Then we rolled the trunks up a ramp on to a truck, and drove back to a sawmill sitting on top of the wood. The driver of the truck was a woman who treated us with great disdain. I never could understand why.

"When we arrived at the sawmill, we unloaded the wood and rolled the logs up a ramp where they were then sawed in a very primitive sawmill with a special mechanical saw, powered by steam produced by a huge furnace run by a young girl. She was always completely black, covered with coal dust from the coal used to heat the furnace. According to Russian law, if it was -30°, we could go into the furnace room for thirty minutes every hour to warm up. If it was -20°, we could stay in the furnace room for twenty minutes every hour; if it was -10°, we could remain for ten minutes every hour, and so on. This was the general rule for the Russians, including prisoners of war. Generally the temperature ranged between -20° and -25°."

Every fifteen days, Veniero traveled back to Suzdal to get provisions for the squad of Italians working in Krutiez. Depending on the season, he made the trip on a sled or cart pulled by a horse, along with a Russian who had just recently returned from serving in the army. The trip back to Suzdal took about ten hours.

Marsan conversed as best he could with the veteran. One day, he told Marsan about his own experiences in the war as he had crossed Austria and then a part of Germany; he couldn't understand why the Germans decided to wage war on Russia.

"During our advance," he said, "I entered many of their homes. They had everything one could desire, absolutely everything, in comparison to our miserable houses!"[72]

One day while returning to Suzdal the driver asked Marsan why he and the Italian soldiers came to fight against the Russians. "The question was an embarrassing one for me, but it was asked without any hostility, with only the evident desire to understand my reasons, and the humanity with which it was asked called for an honest answer. In short, I explained, when my division transferred to the Russian front, I did not want to evade that call.... Also, there was not the opportunity then, as there would have been only later, of the possibility of my remaining in Italy to participate in an active, organized underground opposition to the war and Mussolini's alliance with Hitler." Marsan explained that at that time Italy was a "police state." Had he joined the underground, "this would have meant confronting risks comparable to the war in Russia." The sled driver didn't respond; "his silence seemed to me to symbolize his understanding. In any case this discussion was not returned to."[73]

Marsan and his fellow officers lived and slept in a bunker on wooden beds while they were in Krutiez. They cooked their meals on a large wood-burning stove. The officers received adequate provisions. "One officer was a good cook, and meals were excellent in comparison to what they had been in the camp. Of course, the Russians realized we needed decent provisions in order to manage the heavy work in the forest."[74]

On Sundays, the officer who did the cooking would prepare a "sort of cake." A little boy observed as he poured some powdered sugar from a bag: "When we offered the child some sugar he looked at it suspiciously; he didn't know what it was. One of us showed the boy the sugar was something to eat. He tasted it and smiled, enjoying the spoonful of sweetness." Marsan noted that this episode was only one of many indicating the miserable conditions experienced by the people of the village. "We brought our flour to the bakery in the village for the making of our bread, and when we returned with our wagon full of round loaves, the villagers, who were present, spit on the ground (a typical gesture of anger by the Russian people). Evidently, they thought prisoners of war received better treatment than they did. We then decided to hide our loaves of bread by covering them with sacks."[75]

Although Camp Suzdal was a camp for officers, a few Italian soldiers were present, responsible for some camp services. Marsan writes, "At a certain point we noticed some of them looked rather well fed. We soon discovered the reason: a few of them were shoemakers, and somehow they managed to make a pair of women's shoes which were offered to the commander of the camp." Their success was immediate! Wives and daughters of the camp operators, as well as their friends residing in nearby towns wanted to have a pair of those beautiful high-heeled shoes. In exchange, "the clever shoemakers received double and triple rations."[76]

"Some soldiers were even more successful as experts of plastering and finished marble. About ten of them were engaged to decorate a government building in Moscow." Every morning they were transported to their workplace in the city. At a certain point, these soldiers asked Marsan to write a letter for them in Russian. They wanted permission to settle in the country. They explained: "Here in Russia, they appreciate our work very much. We eat well, we even get oranges from the Crimea…and some of us have also found a nice girl; we fear it won't be easy to find as much in Italy." Marsan did write a letter for them that was sent to Moscow. Not surprisingly, nothing came of it. Marsan elaborated: "It should be noted that Stalin was absolutely against permitting resettlement of citizens in the Soviet Union who came from capitalist countries."[77]

KRASNOGORSK, CAMP 27

During this same period, officials in Camp 27, Krasnogorsk continued to humiliate the remaining Italian officers. They designated Beraudi along with other prisoners as "camp street sweepers," required to sweep the whole camp. They carried the trash out of the camp on a cart. There were advantages to this work, because the prisoners could stay outside of the barbed wire and have a smoke. They also had the opportunity to make friends with children playing outside the camp. Beraudi made friends with a little girl named Marinella. He held her little hands and swung her around in the air, much to her delight. Whenever Marinella saw Beraudi, she ran to him and asked him to twirl her. He would only stop when his famished body caused him to become short of breath. Beraudi noticed one little boy who didn't participate in the games. He soon discovered the child was jealous of Marinella because she received so much attention. From that moment on, Beraudi made playing with the boy a priority.[78]

Being street sweepers had another advantage; a woodshed was close to the place where prisoners dumped the trash. Every time the prisoners emptied the trash they lined the bottom of the cart with cut wood, covered it with a bit of trash, and bartered it for bread with women who lived nearby. This humiliating work was actually somewhat agreeable, but one day as the men were on their way to dump the trash they ran into Major Terescenko. He smiled at the officers, and with a sarcastic tone said: "Gentlemen officers, do you like being street sweepers?"

Insulted by this remark, the next morning Beraudi appeared in front of the head of the school and told him that up to this point he had offered to work somewhat voluntarily, mainly to pass the time and to be useful. Now, since it seemed clear to him this kind of work was merely a means to humiliate the Italians, he refused to continue and referred to the Geneva Conventions, which stipulated that officers who were prisoners of war had the right not to work. That same morning, as the other four prisoners began to do their sweeping, Beraudi stretched out in the sun in a field.[79]

Soon an orderly arrived who told Beraudi that Colonel Porfionov wanted to see him. When Beraudi arrived, Foschi was there to translate the colonel's words. The colonel was in a rage. Beraudi writes, "With blazing, eyes he asks me if it is true that I refused to work and why. I answer yes and I explain why...." Pointing his finger on Beraudi's chest, the colonel hissed: "You are a Fascist."

Following this encounter Beraudi was put in a jail within the camp.[80]

After several days, the Russians held a "justice assembly" in which a few Italian officers and soldiers accused Beraudi of minor assumed infractions. In spite of this uproar, he was soon released. While other Italian prisoners worked, Beraudi did not, but one day he met the wife of the vice-commander of the camp, and she asked him if he would like to work for her. She explained that since this was harvest time, she needed someone who would supervise the storage of various vegetables being harvested—onions, carrots, and potatoes. She also told him he would have the key to the warehouse where the vegetables were to be stored.

He couldn't believe his good luck. For fifteen days, he continued this new job, but he was worried. By now it was August 1945, the war was over, but the Italians were still prisoners of war. What was going to happen to them? Would they soon go home? If so, when? What about the NKVD? His thoughts alternated between "black pessimism and modest optimism." At a certain point, a Russian officer approached him as he worked in the kitchen and asked him if he was Captain Beraudi: "...to my affirmative response, he pronounced the fateful phrase, the one I heard many times, the one that opens the threshold for a leap into the dark: *'Davaj, transport'* " ('Hurry, it's time to leave').[81]

Before leaving the camp, Beraudi met with the police lieutenant who was the camp's political commissar. He was the same man Beraudi had addressed when he said he was going to adhere to the rules of the Geneva Conventions. In the past, the two men had spoken French with the assistance of an interpreter, yet this time the lieutenant spoke fluent French.

"I must ask you a question.... Are you a friend or an enemy of the Soviet people?"

Beraudi responded: "I have already spoken about such matters many times. I can't tolerate the fact you doubt my sincerity. On the other hand, if you do doubt, what purpose would my response serve?"

The Lieutenant then accused Beraudi of being "bourgeois and impulsive," yet even though his bourgeois ideas weren't acceptable, he noted that Beraudi seemed to indicate a "liking toward the USSR."

The lieutenant informed Beraudi he would now transfer to the third zone of the camp "as punishment." Before leaving, the lieutenant assured Beraudi he would be returning to Italy before other prisoners. As he departed he said, "Your friends in Moscow greet you."[82]

Beraudi returned to the third zone. Marsan had been there, as well as Bizzocchi and other friends, but now Vadagnini was the only remaining Italian among German, Hungarian, and Romanian officers. There were about 100 Italian soldiers in the camp, separated from the officers by barbed wire. Beraudi could only exchange a few words with them. Now it was September, and soon winter would set in. The war was over, and Beraudi feared he would not return to Camp Suzdal. He writes, "I am in disgrace in the eyes of the bosses; I'm considered to be a Fascist by the enlightened; a Communist in the eyes of my colleagues. Wherever I go, it will be winter, not only in the sky but also in the faces of those who surround me. Only Marsan, only Bizzocchi, only Marabotto and a few others will be able to warm my heart. But they are far away."[83]

Several days later, Beraudi was summoned to appear before the political commissar of the camp who spoke to him in Italian: "Are you Captain Gino Beraudi? A letter has arrived from your wife."

As he stood there, Beraudi felt faint: "Where is it? Where is it? Give it to me!" Thoughts of his wife and home raced through his head as he recalled kisses and hugs, and wondered if his wife and parents were even still alive. He writes, "There is only a letter from Tinin. What does it say? Does it reveal tears, desperation, or a dear certainty, a secure hope?"

Like a splash of cold water, the commissar said he didn't have the letter. It was in Moscow! He then added that the letter came from Rome. Beraudi deduced his family must be dispersed if they were in Rome.

The commissar said, "Yes, from *Via Gambalunga* number 31."

Beraudi realized the Russian couldn't pronounce Rimini and had substituted the word *Rim*, which in Russian is Rome. Via Gambalunga was his address in Rimini. He was elated! The commissar told him he would receive his letter in a few days on his way home via Moscow.

"I pull myself together," Beraudi writes. "I don't want him to see my emotions on my face. The delusion of not having the letter is so powerful, even the news of my imminent return doesn't console me. I leave, walking rigidly. I drag myself as far as the toilet and vomit...."[84]

The days passed and nothing changed. Then one morning the soldiers heard "grand news! The Italians were to leave the camp. Beraudi and Vadagnini ran to the area where the Italians were gathering. A Russian officer slowly called out names one by one. Beraudi writes, "The roll call is finished, and Vadagnini and I are excluded. We return to the barracks without speaking. The next morning our soldiers leave, singing, and who knows how, they even created a sparkling Italian flag. It's clear—I think—the friends in Moscow are trying to cause me to fall to pieces. I am destined to remain here and they are driving me toward insanity."[85]

Ten days later, Beraudi decided to speak to the political commissar. When he asked why he hadn't been among the Italians who had left the camp and he asked for his wife's letter, the commissar responded: "*Ne ponimaju*" ("I don't understand").

Beraudi writes, "I begin to tremble. Did I make a mistake? Isn't this the same man I spoke to a few weeks ago? It can't be him. He spoke Italian. This one must be his brother, or a double.... I attempt, with a trembling voice to repeat my requests in French. He listens. I press on.

I speak for a long time.

He repeats '*Je regrette.*'"[86]

By now, Beraudi was confused, frustrated and demoralized. As he left this encounter, he felt a "crushing weight on his shoulders." Somehow he recovered the strength and determination "to return to being hard and strong." He vowed that this form of mental torture would not drive him crazy. He writes, "For five years, I have been in this war: in the trenches, in prison. It's a miserable life, but it's a life. The spirit remains, no matter what the experience may be."[87]

CERNIZ

An "Auxiliary Agricultural Sector" was located in the village of Cerniz, about thirty kilometers from Suzdal. Because few local workers were available in the area, a request went out for some of the prisoners in Suzdal to come and work there. Thirty to forty Italian officers, including Marsan, were sent to the village.[88]

While Marsan was in Cerniz, a woman (whose name he cannot remember) did the laundry for the Italian prisoners. Marsan recalled, "We couldn't pay her because we didn't have any money. In exchange for her work, we gave her food because she had so little to eat. Since I spoke some Russian, I was the one who went to see her and bring our laundry. The woman was required to live outside of the village, because she had children but had never been married. She had two daughters living at home and a son who was away at war. She hadn't heard from him for a long time. Although forbidden to live in the village, she milked the villagers' cows. This worked out well for her, because it allowed her to come home with one or two bottles of milk for her daughters.

"One day I had a fever for a few days, and just imagine, she sent a bottle of milk to me with her daughter, Valentina. Over time, I became acquainted with Valentina. One time I reworded a famous Russian song for her. I told her when I go home to Italy I will take you if you want to go. She was very happy. She in turn changed the words of a familiar Russian rhyme into the following: 'Dear Mother, I'm not yours any longer, I am going to Italy, not for a month, but forever.' When I returned to Italy, I brought back the name Valentina and gave it to our first daughter."

During the summer of 1945, the Italian officers mowed the fields of clover with mowing machines, and threshed and piled up hay in fields around the village of Cerniz. When the men returned to the village from their work, they would often gather in the local garage. This was a time when they would converse with each other and the local villagers. Sometimes the men appeared happy, other times they were sad, especially when they gazed at tattered photographs of their families they pulled out of their pockets to share with the Russians. In their conversations, the officers frequently condemned Hitler and Mussolini for sending them to fight in Russia.[89]

While Marsan was in Cerniz, he became acquainted with two residents of the village— Antropov, the local blacksmith, and Novikov, a veteran. The three men spent many hours together and developed a close friendship. Antropov owned an extensive collection of books he had obtained from a teacher in Suzdal in 1943 in exchange for bread. Both Marsan and Novikov borrowed books from his library, which held books in other languages as well as Russian. Antropov and Novikov were impressed by Marsan's ability not only to speak Russian, but also to read it. Marsan often acted as interpreter for other Italian officers who came to the blacksmith's shop for repairs of the farm machinery they used in the fields.[90]

Griscia was the name of the guard who watched over the Italian officers while they worked in the fields or spent time in the village. He was a Cossack, a very large, tall man who treated the Italians respectfully.

When authorities in the prison camp discovered Marsan and other officers were reading books they obtained from Antropov's library, members of the NKVD came to Cerniz and confiscated the library, with the exception of those books still out on loan. Griscia's superiors gave him a severe warning after summoning him back to Suzdal.

"What am I supposed to do," Griscia asked, "Beat them if they read books?"

The Italian officers continued to spend time with Novikov and Antropov, and they continued to share long conversations. The authorities frequently reprimanded Griscia for allowing so much fraternization among the Italians and villagers.[91]

"After the war was over," writes Novikov, "our radios, confiscated in 1941, were returned to us." Novikov's friend Vasin attempted to fix the radio with no success. One day an Italian prisoner examined Novikov's radio. After detaching the antenna and cleaning the metal insulating wire, the radio functioned.

"You are a clever young man," Vasin said.

Pointing to the radio, the Italian said, "Marconi."

Novikov said, "No, Popov."

"No, Marconi! Marconi!"

Novikov writes, "The prisoner couldn't speak Russian well, but these words didn't require translating...."[92]

One night when the temperature reached -30°, Novikov, on his way to visit a friend nearby, fell in a heap of snow: "I don't know how long I remained unconscious, but fortunately my Italian friends who were returning from work saw me and took me, numbed with cold, back to my home. If they hadn't found me I would have frozen to death. That's how the Italians saved my life. Again, I thank them. The day after, Marsan and Griscia came to see how I was doing."[93]

Novikov suffered from a paralysis of his left hand and a partial paralysis of one leg from wounds he suffered during the war. Marsan asked him if he had been on the front lines, and Novikov shared his experiences of the war with him. Novikov recalled how Marsan, still so young, could respond with compassion. Marsan had told him, "Hope is the best cure."[94]

Another time, the blacksmith Antropov spoke to Marsan about his illness, a then incurable facial lupus.

"I wish to heaven, Leonid Alexandrovic, you could be with us in Italy on the shore of the beach, in the rays of the sun."

Antropov replied, "That, Marsan, is a beautiful idea, but for now it is unobtainable."

Marsan told his friend his blisters would soon disappear if he could spend time on an Italian beach.

"Marsan, for all of you, the war is finished, while I will have to fight for a long time with my illness."

Marsan acknowledged that the war was over in Italy, "but we, Leonid Alexandrovic, still have to succeed to survive."

Antropov noted that Marsan had managed to survive and would soon see his family, "while I must place my hope in science; maybe they will be able to discover a cure after the end of the war."[95]

Italian officers built their own kitchen in Cerniz. The half-starved children of the village gathered around it, as Rivorelli, the officer in charge, prepared meals. He would look at their little hungry faces and give them minestrone and cascia. Through an interpreter, he said, "There is nothing more distressing than the eyes of a famished child."[96]

Conditions in the village were harsh. There was very little food, and residents had almost no bread. By now, the Italians received abundant rations from the camp in Suzdal, as well as from the agricultural sector. However, they did not receive any milk from the prison camp. The officers exchanged bread for milk and tobacco with the villagers. Novikov claims that their good will, along with their bartering, saved the local residents from starvation during the harsh winter of 1945–46.[97]

PART IV

IL RITORNO:
RETURNING HOME

Chapter 20

THE HOMEWARD JOURNEY

OCTOBER 17, 1945

It began to snow in October. Beraudi remained housed in the third zone of Camp 27, but now he had no responsibilities, and the lack of any activity made the hours seem even longer. Things changed suddenly when a Slovene prisoner came to his barracks one evening to escort him to the guard barracks and then to the first zone of the camp. When Beraudi questioned his transfer, the Slovene said he had to accompany Beraudi to the hospital because he was ill.

As a supposedly sick man, Beraudi entered the hospital where he remained for four days. A German doctor prohibited him from smoking, but he found ways to circumvent those orders. One morning the doctor caught Beraudi smoking and threatened to discharge him from the hospital. Evidently the Russian woman doctor (the one Beraudi had previously called a "carrion") heard the doctor's threat and made sure Beraudi received his clothes and marching orders. The German doctor met him on his way out of the hospital and was very upset he was leaving.

Beraudi really didn't know what he should do at this point, because he had no place to sleep and had nothing to eat, but soon he heard someone calling him, and subsequently a guard escorted him out of the camp. He saw a truck with its motor running and lights on parked just outside of the camp entrance. A Russian officer was giving orders to three German soldiers who stood by the truck, evidently preparing to leave. When the officer approached him, he placed his hand on Beraudi's back and whispered in his ear: "Soon you will be going home!"

Beraudi writes, "I'm relieved the darkness hides the silent tears staining my face."

The officer then addressed the Germans, ordering them to move a box from the seat so Beraudi could sit down.

The truck stopped in the third zone of the camp. The guard led Beraudi to a barracks where about forty Germans were packing their rucksacks preparing to leave. He was able to see his friend Vadagnini briefly, and reassured him that once he was in Italy, he would write to his family to let them know he was all right. [1]

Eighty soldiers were loaded on a Red Cross railcar with no amenities and only enough room for the men to lie side by side. There were no other Italians. Beraudi was lying next to a gaunt Austrian from Innsbruck and six Dutch soldiers. There was no kitchen on the train and the men only received a piece of dry bread, raw peas, and potatoes. In order to cook the vegetables it was necessary to have enough time to gather wood for a fire and to find water when the train stopped at a station.

Instead of permitting Beraudi to cook his food over their fire, the Germans extinguished their coals with their feet once they finished cooking their vegetables. Beraudi felt he really couldn't blame them, because a few days earlier the Austrian soldier had told him he was one of the last German soldiers to leave Rimini in October of the previous year. Beraudi's home was in Rimini and when the Austrian said the city was completely destroyed, Beraudi objected: "Not all of it.... Try to remember. At least one house was still standing."

The soldier replied sadistically, "*Nein, nein, alles kaputt.*"

The following night, "because he had invaded my space by only one centimeter, I grasped his head and kept beating it against the side of the rail car until the others pulled him out of my hands."[2]

Several days later when Beraudi got off the train in Kaunas (Lithuania), he could hear Italians speaking inside freight cars in a train stopped on a parallel track. He banged on the doors of the railcars until one opened. When he entered, Brero, an alpino with whom Beraudi had served in Albania, recognized him. Immediately he received a mess tin full of cold soup. The alpini told Beraudi their train had a kitchen and the Italians were in charge of it, therefore they had plenty to eat. They asked him to stay with them. But he decided, "I prefer not to intervene with destiny."[3]

As it turned out Beraudi's train and the one carrying the Italians arrived in the various stations about the same time. Beraudi received frequent hot meals from his companions. He describes one incident: "Cenni gives me a full, piping hot mess tin, and standing before me at attention, he says: "Captain, here is breakfast, Sir."

The Germans in Beraudi's railcar observed this event with obvious envy and admiration.[4]

Once in Poland Beraudi assumed the role of beggar. Whenever the locomotive was changed, he wandered out into the countryside asking for alms at farmhouse doors. For his own security, he only asked "old mothers" for food and always received bread and milk. He also always mentioned he was an Italian, because he was afraid the women might think he was a German.

One day he approached a young woman. As she hesitated for a moment and he imagined she wondered if he really was Italian, he said, "I don't look like most Italians with dark, curly hair who always sing."

"What does it really matter whether you're an Italian or a German? You are somebody who suffers, and you are in need. God doesn't tell us to only help our friends, he tells us also to help our enemies."

Beraudi noted that Polish peasants in particular felt extreme hatred toward the Russians, so much so it almost "caused them to forget the horrors of the German occupation."[5]

On the twenty-fifth day of his journey Beraudi arrived in Frankfurt. He describes the German countryside he passed through on his way to that city as "a pile of ruins." He also passed by many trains carrying Prussian citizens west: "Old people, children (there are no young men).... Those faces display no desperation or dismay, only an impressive coldness. Without raising their voices when their trains are next to ours, these refugees reprimand their soldiers because they lost the war and lost their country."[6]

He observed long trains traveling in the opposite direction taking Soviet ex-prisoners back to Russia. Every time he spoke to one of them, they asked about the treatment given to prisoners in Russian camps. He soon discovered they wanted to know about them because they were on their way to those camps for de-programming from exposure to

Western life. Trains carrying these soldiers were full of items sacked from German homes. Beraudi saw dozens of bicycles on top of every railcar, along with furniture, pillows, clothing, and even door handles.[7]

In Frankfurt soldiers separated according to nationality. Beraudi was the only Italian. The guard at the entrance to the prisoner holding camp refused to allow him to enter. No matter how hard Beraudi attempted to explain his situation, the guard would not permit him to enter the camp. He knew he would soon die of hunger because he saw dead German soldiers outside the barbed wire surrounding the camp. From others he heard that before authorities sent German soldiers out of the camp, they received two days' worth of rations and instructions to return to their homes. Few possibilities existed for a soldier to hitch a ride, catch a train, or find other means of transportation. Once a soldier consumed his rations, he was on his own.[8]

While Beraudi stood in front of the gates of the camp, he noticed a prisoner who looked Italian. The two men spoke, and after a rather heated discussion between the prisoner and the stubborn guard officer at the gate, the guard finally permitted Beraudi to enter. The Italian prisoner took him to a barracks for Italians. Inside he met several men who jumped to attention when he told them he was a captain in the Alpine Corps. The officers were surprised. They told him no Italian officers had returned from Russia to this camp. They added his name to a list of Italian prisoners, but didn't add his rank because they felt it could be dangerous if the Russians discovered an Italian officer was in the camp.[9]

Beraudi received clean clothing, a comfortable cot, and plenty of food. After two days, he was on his way back to Italy. The train made a long detour around the city of Berlin. As he observed the mountains of rubble, he realized he might well be returning to a destroyed city himself. After three years without news, he didn't know if his family even existed anymore.

The train proceeded slowly. Once it reached the last station of the Russian zone, the Italians transferred to another train composed of a variety of different types of Italian railcars. After a short time, the train stopped and several Russians came aboard. They looked at each soldier and asked if he was Italian, and then left. Beraudi noted that not all on the train were Italians. There were two or three refugees in each railcar, the so-called "stateless of tomorrow": Poles, a few Germans, Lithuanians, Estonians, and Latvians. When the train stopped at an out-of-the way station, American soldiers put boxes of canned meat and large boxes of hard tack in each railcar.

During the morning the train passed through the Tyrolese region, Austria. Soldiers were doused with disinfectant in Mittenberg. There, Beraudi also received a pair of white, lightweight cloth shoes, three sizes too big to replace his shoes, which no longer had any soles. He also received chocolate and sandwiches. He writes, "Finally I experience a shiver of emotion. I give the sacred rag of cloth containing the clandestine consecrated bread to a priest."[10]

That same evening the train arrived at the Brenner Pass. Beraudi had imagined returning to Italy throughout the days of the withdrawal and his years as a prisoner. He had imagined kissing the ground at the frontier, even exchanging an item of clothing for fruit and wine, "as if I could re-baptize myself Italian with the fruit and wine."[11] In fact, he did none of these things.

Once he reached Trento, he felt ashamed of the way he looked. In the train station in Pescatina, many relatives had waited for the train to ask soldiers for information about their missing relatives. Beraudi attempted to offer answers to their "agonized questions about the fate of so many loved ones who had disappeared." He writes, "A few months later, I began to understand how family members placed more faith in pitiful lies rather than harrowing truths."[12]

Upon arrival in Pescatina, military authorities interrogated the returning men. "Among those who interrogated us, I knew how to pick my man. I realized the lieutenant of the Alpine Corps Artillery questioning me was interested in things other than those who had died." Beraudi asked the lieutenant if he believed the local commander of the military police could be trusted "with confidential information." The lieutenant reassured him, requested his address and told him not to take any action until someone could be sent to talk to him further. "In that manner," Beraudi writes, "I relieved myself of my Moscow adventure."[13]

At two in the morning the train arrived in the Bologna railroad station, now a mound of rubble. Soldiers were directed to a barracks, but Beraudi didn't join them. Instead, he began walking through the city: "I am 100 kilometers from home and I don't feel anything."[14] He didn't even attempt try to find a means of transportation to speed his homecoming.

The following morning Beraudi left his pack in the barracks and refused to stand in line with other soldiers who were receiving new clothes. A few soldiers loaned him some money. He began walking around the city once more, and then decided to visit his friend Pugliesi who was also an attorney and came from Rimini. He writes, "I will finally find out what fate my family has endured. Halfway up the stairs I stop, stunned. In a minute, I will know. At the same time, I feel nothing; absolutely nothing. Am I a criminal or just a wreck?"[15]

Beraudi told Pugliesi who he was, "otherwise he wouldn't have recognized me." Pugliesi told Beraudi that his wife, children, and parents were well; his father-in-law had died, but his mother-in-law was still alive. Pugliesi didn't know if Beraudi's family was in Rimini or in Morciano where they had gone as refugees. He also said he didn't know if the family home was still standing.[16]

When Beraudi finally arrived in Rimini he walked toward his house and ran into Monti, a lawyer friend, who offered to go ahead to let his family know he was on his way. Beraudi saw that his house was still standing.

He passed through the front gate, noticing the kitchen door was open. He writes, "I look in the kitchen...Monti has climbed the stairs. I hear him say (to whom?)..."

"*Signora*, there is good news about Gino...."

"Is he on his way?"

"He is here."

"Already in Italy?"

"Here."

"I hear a scream, her scream and that of the children. I run up the stairs and halfway up I am kneeling within a tangle of bodies fastened to me, bathed by their tears...."

It seemed as if five years were canceled in an instant, "as if everything has only been one big nightmare."[17]

REPATRIATION OF TROOPS OF THE ARMIR

Between August 1945 and March 1946, soldiers of the ARMIR imprisoned in Soviet labor camps began returning to Italy in irregular numbers. Officers remained in Russia because the Italian Communist Party (under the leadership of Palmiro Togliatti) wanted them to remain out of Italy until after the elections of June 2, 1946. On June 2, in the first free elections in over twenty years, Italians were to decide by referendum between the monarchy and a republic, and to vote for representatives to the Constituent Assembly.[18]

Marsan explained: "When returning troops had reached Italy, there were anti-Communist demonstrations against the Italian Communist Party among the returning men. Soldiers had written *abbasso comunismo* (down with Communism) on their railcars when crowds greeted them waving flags of the Italian Communists. Fights between returning prisoners and Communist Party members ensued. Soldiers returning from Russian prisoner of war camps had had their fill of the Communist system and the majority wanted no part of this new unknown Communist surge in Italy, which had occurred after the war of liberation in Italy had ended."

Generally the Russians handed Italian soldiers to the Allies once they reached Austria or Germany. From either country, their journey on to Italy progressed in a "chaotic manner." Some managed to return by train either alone or in small groups, and others by makeshift means. After a period of quarantine in Pescatina (Verona), or for the sick a stay in a hospital in Merano, Bologna, or on the Adriatic coast, they finally made it back to their homes.[19]

In interviews with numerous alpini who returned from Russian labor camps, Nuto Revelli noted that their memories were "anything but serene. Following their long journey across a Europe devastated by war, and their arrival in Tarvisio or at the Brenner Pass, they felt as if they were foreigners in their own homeland, since the 'centers of reception' were unprepared to take care of them. All were undernourished, sick, and fragile, requiring immediate medical assistance. They had one common wish, that of quickly shedding the formalities of military bureaucracy and hurrying home."[20]

Events of the Russian campaign, and the fact that thousands of soldiers were still missing soon became fodder for exploitation by Italian political parties. When, for example, 150 sick prisoners of war returned to Italy in August 1945, provincial newspapers reported reconstructed stories of the withdrawal from the Don and the difficult conditions experienced in prisoner of war camps in Russia, based on information given by the veterans. On the other hand, Communist-leaning newspapers accused those who spoke negatively about conditions in Russian camps as being members of the Fascist Party. Political controversy over-shadowed one of the problems, specifically a "human one." Instead of helping these ex-prisoners reintegrate into civil society and gain their medical certification for deserved war pensions, there were patriotic speeches, and veteran needs were lost in the flurry of rhetoric.[21]

On the home front, the population welcomed the returning soldiers, but their welcome was "marked by two diametrically opposite posi-tions." Soldiers were greeted with a degree of "understanding and affec-tion" on the one hand, yet met with "coolness and hostility" on the other. Some veterans spoke out about their treatment by the Russians, and about how those who had not returned were treated. Still others claimed, "Russia was not at all 'the paradise of the worker,' and this did not agree with the large part of the Italians in those days."[22]

Giuseppe Viale described his return from Russia in March 1946. As the train stopped in stations, in every town crowds of people, begging for information met it, holding up photographs, "so many pho-tographs.... So many screams, everybody screams.... We can't even rec-ognize those who are still alive in those photographs." Alpini within the trains felt bewildered by the onslaught of voices from the crowds asking for news of the missing alpini.

In Udine, the police had to push back the crowds so that Viale and others could leave the station to transfer by truck to a hospital, where "each of us finally had a bed."

The following day, Viale and his fellow alpini went out for a walk in the town. Viale recalled that people crowded around them. "Folks are always arguing around us; some speak in favor of Russia and some speak against Russia. We melt away [in the crowd]. One night the Americans intervene to pull apart the quarreling people around us." Several days later Viale managed to travel to his home in Borgo San Dalmazzo. At once relatives came to his home to ask for information about missing alpini. Viale had no information to give to them.

"I was a peasant when I left for the war," he said. "Now I have returned home—I'm still a peasant, but now I've grown old. I have lost my youth and my health forever."[23]

Following two years of hospitalizations, Viale received a small mil-itary pension, which the authorities cancelled soon after. As Viale spoke to Revelli, he said, "It's sad to return from the war.... I wound up with no strength, no health, with nothing. Luckily, my family helped me; during the first years [at home], I was in no condition to work and I could have gone begging. In any case, I would have been in desperate straits. I hope never to see war again. *Basta con la guerra* (Enough already, no more war)."[24]

Guido Castellano also spoke to Revelli recalling his return to Italy: "[In Italy] the population is divided in [various] political currents. In Milan, Communist activists take us to a place close to the station and order a fairly decent dinner. Then they begin their propaganda: 'Tell us you were treated well [in Russia]' they say to us. Chaos erupted. We respond: 'How dare you tell us to say such things?' And then we almost come to blows."[25]

Infantryman Alaricho Rocchi recalled his return to Rome. The train stopped at a station on the outskirts of the city, in December 1945: "When we left for Russia, May 26, 1941, a military band played; we were offered coffee and treats and there were crowds surrounding the train wishing us well. When we came home, there was nothing! There was no official welcome! Crowds of people in the station were screaming names of military units and names of soldiers, holding up photographs, begging us for information!"

Rocchi and other returning soldiers were loaded on trucks transporting them to the main Rome railroad station in the center of the city. Some soldiers escorting the truckloads began to sing a well-known Communist song.

"If you have to sing," Rocchi said, "For God's sake sing something else!"

The singing soldiers ignored him. An angered Rocchi told the men to stop, threatening them.

"If you don't shut up I'll personally throw you off this truck!"

Rocchi spent the next two days wandering around Rome, completely disorientated. He searched for the Saint Peter's railroad station (a small local station in Rome) where he knew could catch a train to his hometown of Anguillara, but he couldn't remember where it was located. Eventually, by chance, he saw the dome of Saint Peter's basilica in the distance. Realizing the station was close by, he asked for directions from a passerby.

Once he arrived in the Anguillara station, he ran into an old family friend who told him he had recently had a drink with his father. "It was then," Rocchi recalled, "I found out my father was still alive."

When asked to describe his arrival at his home, Rocchi said, "I walked to my house and stood in the garden under a window, calling my mother."

He stopped speaking and his eyes filled with tears. He couldn't find words to describe his overwhelming reunion with his mother, still so vividly etched in his memory.

REPATRIATION OF ITALIAN OFFICERS

Most Italian officers returned to Italy in July and August of 1946. General Battisti, commander of the Cuneense Division, General Ricagno, commander of the Julia Division, and General Pascolini, commander of the Vicenza Division, all captured in Valuiki January 27, 1943, were repatriated during the summer of 1950. A few Italian officers accused of war crimes by the Soviets repatriated in 1954.[26]

Italian officers held in Suzdal and the few held in other camps left the USSR in April and May of 1946. A few officers received mail before leaving. Marsan received six Red Cross postcards, and he recalled that wonderful moment: "This was the first mail I received since leaving the Don front in January 1943! Five cards were from my wife Lucia and one was from my mother, all dated from the fall of 1945. There was no news about my father."

Before leaving Suzdal, Russian guards searched all the officers once more. Vicentini writes: The joy and belief that everything soon would be over made us forget the last vexations by the Russians, who searched us before we left and took almost everything from us: writings, diaries, drawings, and portraits. With their usual inscrutable criteria, they allowed some officers to keep their notes and took away any [recent] correspondence; they permitted others to keep an album of drawings…and from still others they only took a pipe." Vicentini only possessed a haversack, a mess cup, and a pair of socks. "In my pocket I had a small toothbrush, and my one [recently received] letter, a few pieces of paper with notes, and 100 rubles they gave us as pay for three years of work."[27]

Officers left the camp by train. Marsan recalled how different this journey was in comparison to his previous journey, going to the camps: "We traveled in freight cars, but this time we could open the doors when we stopped in railroad stations along the way. When people in the stations realized we were Italians, they greeted us warmly and shouted: '*Italianskie choroshio*' ('Italians are good'). It was incredible and so uplifting to hear this over and over! Many times the Russians would speak to us about our music, especially operas by Verdi. Sometimes they would ask us to sing for them. There definitely was a human connection between us. We knew Russian peasants had saved so many Italian soldiers during the withdrawal and the marches of the *davai*."

After ten days the officers arrived at the outskirts of Odessa, and proceeded to walk to reach their housing in the countryside. After two hours of walking, the column of five-hundred officers had slowed down and lengthened.

Some officers at the end of the column were tired, others were limping: "An impatient Russian soldier who didn't know what he could say or do to close the ranks, pushed tired and limping men at the end of the line. Maybe he was accustomed to creating order and obedience among prisoners with shouts and threats with his rifle.... His threats didn't scare us; by now we were on the road home and the Russians wouldn't dare use force...."

Finally, the frustrated Russian became so impatient with the slow-moving men at the end of the line that he began kicking them. At this point, an officer who was having a difficult time keeping up with the others simply sat down by the side of the road, and turned to the guard and said: "Hurry up, shoot me!"

"The soldier hesitated for a moment but then, offering a rosary of curses, began to walk once more and left him there."[28]

Eventually the officers reached a huge building on a hill. Marsan recalled the building was completely empty; it didn't even have a chair in it. "We slept on the wooden floor. The building was a holiday resort for Russian workers in the past, stuffed with beds and so forth, but at that time it wasn't being used anymore.

"When I arrived in Odessa," Marsan said, "I was wearing a pair of blue Italian Air Force pants and a military jacket of another color. Some local peasants came to see us and offered us food. They wanted to exchange food for our clothing, and I was able to exchange my jacket for a blue cotton jacket, like the one a mechanic might wear."

After six days, Russian guards told the officers to gather their things and get in a line because they were to leave. They believed they were going to board a ship and sail to Italy. Instead, the guards led them to a dilapidated factory where iron gates closed behind them. A Russian guard holding a machine gun stood in the guard tower looking down on the Italians. Vicentini writes, "We were in a camp once more." This time, housed in a large building, the men slept on wooden benches lining the sides of the rooms. After a week they moved to another building close to the beach. Accommodated in clean rooms, they slept on the floor, but they received pasta for lunch and were able to swim in the sea.[29]

"While we were in Odessa," Marsan recalled, "we were free to roam around the city, but we had to return to our quarters by a certain hour every evening. Only one soldier was in charge of all of us. He realized we wanted to return to Italy; therefore, he was convinced we wouldn't try anything foolish, so there were no problems. We were well treated. We had enough to eat and went to the beach every day. When we went swimming, we were amazed to see the Russians swimming in the nude.

"There was a tram we could take into the center of town where there was an opera house. One night we decided to go to the opera. We had very little money, yet—and this is typical of the Communists—it cost almost nothing to see an opera at that time. We sat in a box and stayed until the end of the first act. We knew it would get to be too late if we remained for the whole performance. The opera was by one of the minor composers and we enjoyed it immensely. Next to our box were some young people, including a girl my age. She asked us where we came from and we told her we worked on a ship that had come to Odessa from Italy. Then I asked her what she did. She pulled out a medal from her bag and showed it to me. She said, 'This is what I earned when I was in the rearguard during the war.' She was very proud of that medal. It could be said half of the Russian victory was due to the women of Russia; they were wonderful!"

Other officers also ventured into the city. Vicentini and a few of his friends took a tram into the center of the city and were amazed nobody seemed to notice them or question their presence. The men went to the harbor to see if there were any Italian ships anchored there. Nobody could give them any kind of information. At a kiosk, the men were able to buy some wine. Vicentini writes, "While the lady who sold the wine filled our miniscule glasses with the amount permitted, I felt it necessary to tell my companions that this was a solemn moment: it was the first wine we were drinking after four years of abstinence. We drank it on our knees in front of the amused lady of the kiosk and passers-by."[30]

Captain Giuseppe Lamberti (commander of the Monte Cervino Battalion) began his homeward journey leaving Moscow on June 8, 1946. An elderly man leaning on a walking stick approached Lamberti and a few fellow officers standing on the platform of the Moscow train station.

"Who are you?"

"We are Italian prisoners."

The Russian then asked where the men were going.

"We are going home."

At that point, the old man said, "Well, this time things went well for you—but should you ever [decide to] come back again, it would be better [for me] to immediately break your head!"

Lamberti recalled how the old man "raised his walking stick in the air as if he wanted to strike us on the head. He was right."[31]

Lamberti writes, "Within this expression everything of the Russian soul and understanding exists, which discerns the difference between Italy and Fascism, and between the Italians and the Germans; that same Russian soul revealed its benevolence during the tremendous days of the withdrawal; that same Russian soul understood we too were the victims of a colossal adventure."[32]

The officers left Moscow by train, eventually arriving in Odessa where they joined the larger group from Camp Suzdal.[33]

On June 2, officers protested their long wait in Odessa and the promises kept and broken with regard to their return to Italy. Chaplain Guido Turla claimed the Russians, "always liars," blamed the Italian government for not providing a ship for the ex-prisoners of war: "We realize the wait in Odessa is a part of a pre-established plan, based on political calculations; we must not be in Italy for the elections; our presence would be deleterious for Communist propaganda."[34]

Turla continued: "It seems phases of our repatriation are conditioned by directions given by radio from Rome by Palmiro Togliatti [leader of the Italian Communist Party] connected to his brother-in-law Paulo Robotti." In fact, Robotti had arrived in Odessa accompanied by members of the Russian press and radio, with the job of cutting phonograph records for propaganda purposes. Only a few officers cooperated. Recorded propaganda messages were similar. On one phonograph record titled, "We go to the city," groups of officers "reduced to rags" speak into the microphone for a recording, "saying they are going to visit the artistic beauty of the city of Odessa and to amuse themselves with women." Another recording titled "To the sea" was made in which a member of Radio Moscow, using water from the Black Sea, made sound effects indicating the officers were bathing in the sea.[35]

The officers continued to wait for news about their departure for Italy, still believing they would be returning by ship. One day guards told them to line up quickly. They began to march, thinking they would be going to the harbor. Instead, their destination was the Odessa railroad station. They were loaded on freight cars, surrounded by Russian guards. After they received their rations, guards locked the doors of the railcars. Vicentini writes, "Within us, there were no feelings of surprise, delusion, or anger, we were simply stunned; certain blows don't cause pain, they cause you to feel [as if you are] losing your mind."[36]

By the next evening, the train had almost reached Poland, 600 kilometers from the Black Sea! The officers were dismayed. In the morning, Russian guards permitted them to get off the train to swim in a river and once the train began to move again, doors of the freight cars remained open, permitting the men to dangle their legs over the side.[37]

Once the officers reached the plains of Transylvania, they remained for several days in Szeged, Hungary. Officers in need of clothing received what they needed. Vicentini writes, "I took advantage of this offer because the jacket and pants I had been wearing since I left the camp...were no longer recognizable as an Italian gray-green uniform.... Their color was un-definable.... We were given a brand new uniform made of light blue cloth; it was the uniform of the Italian Air Force!" By now the officers were convinced the Russians had sent them to Odessa in order to fatten them up a bit, also to replace their pallid color with a tan. Once they received the new uniforms, they actually believed they were on their way home.[38]

Soon after, Vicentini bartered his new uniform for eggs, white bread, and large salami, as well as a pair of worn pants and a shirt, which were more ragged than the ones he had exchanged. He writes, "Apart from the fact that I wouldn't have known what to do with an air force uniform once in Italy, a sense of revenge motivated me: why should I arrive at home dressed in new clothing when up until the very last days the Russians had left me dressed like a ragamuffin?"[39]

The officers traveled through Hungary on to Austria. They also observed trains returning to Russia, loaded with Soviet troops locked in freight cars, guarded by armed Russian soldiers. These troops were former prisoners of war held by the Germans, liberated by their fellow citizens, yet destined for punishment in their homeland for having fallen prisoner. "Their return to their homeland was quite different from ours, since having been captured was considered to be a crime by the Russians and was judged and punished [by the authorities]."[40]

In Wiener Neustadt, Austria, the Italians saw trains loaded with machinery, various parts from industrial factories, bicycles, cars, and furniture: "On a flatbed car there was even a piano, and on top of it, a desk, arm chair, and some boxes. The usual guard with a rifle guarded those rail cars taking the spoils of war back to Russia."[41]

Once the officers arrived in Sankt Valentin, Austria, the Russians placed them in a camp that included people of all nationalities. When the Italians asked the Russians why they were being detained instead of sent on to Italy, the Russians responded with reasons that changed every day: "There were no trains; the Americans wouldn't accept us in their zone; our diplomatic representative in Vienna didn't make any plan [for Italian prisoners]", and so forth.[42]

In Sankt Valentin, Marsan met ten Italian civilians, nine men and one woman. He recalled their sad story: "These Italians had been imprisoned in a Nazi concentration camp. After their liberation, they married Russians they had befriended while they were together in the Nazi camp. Once the couples settled in Italy, the Soviet ambassador in Rome offered them a free trip to Russia, so the Russians could visit and introduce their Italian spouses to their respective families. The couples accepted this offer and began their journey. Once they reached Sankt Valentin, the Russians stopped them and immediately separated the couples. The Russians were imprisoned whereas the Italians were offered a free trip back to Italy. Of course, they objected to this treatment, but to no avail. They soon realized their marriages were finished. The Russians told the Italians they would receive death certificates for their spouses. These poor people returned to Italy with us on our train. You can imagine in what kind of an emotional state they were! They hadn't even been permitted to see their spouses before our train left Austria."

After more than a week in Sankt Valentin, the Italian officers were loaded onto locked freight cars under guards who "barked threats and prevented us from even looking out of the small ventilation windows." That same evening the train stopped in Vienna. When the doors opened, Russian soldiers were on the platform, along with two British officers and several civilians who spoke Italian. The civilians were representatives of the Italian Embassy in Vienna and the Red Cross. The officers were reassured that soon they would be on their way to Italy: "Finally we had a reliable source, and bombarded these people with questions about how things were going in Italy, but there was no time to speak about details; another train arrived on the opposite side of the platform, and we were locked up once more."[43]

It turned out the reason the Italian ambassador and Red Cross representatives greeted the officers in Vienna was because two Italian officers had escaped from the camp in Sankt Valentin, and had made their way to the Italian Embassy in Vienna. The authorities in Vienna were not aware Italian prisoners were in Sankt Valentin, only 150 kilometers away; they were still waiting for them at the Hungarian frontier! In order to obtain the release of the Italians from Sankt Valentin it was first necessary to appeal to the Inter-Allied Commission.[44]

Vicentini writes, "All that happened during our trip convinced us the Russians were looking for every excuse not to let us go. The accumulated and by now uncontrollable anxiety to see the end of our odyssey after three months of travel, made spasmodic by the series of ups and downs, of liberty and segregation, broken promises and nurtured hopes, which were immediately dashed, convinced us of this fact."[45]

Recalling those difficult and frustrating days, Vicentini noted there were many factors at play during this first period of Russian occupation of Germany. The Russians were primarily interested "in sacking the invaded territory, to find archives and documents, to discover criminals, to sequester scientists, and to argue with the Allies for futile bureaucratic and prestige reasons." Vicentini continues: "At the same time, they were busy putting their own soldiers in quarantine, guilty of having discovered that in capitalist counties, even though destroyed and starving, one lived better than in the country of socialism." Dealing with 500 Italian officers awaiting repatriation wasn't a top priority for the Russians at that moment in time. If one Russian commander failed to resolve the problem, he probably merely passed it on to another.

"Probably the Russians had no intention of keeping us, but owing to their own disorganization they were unable to get rid of us."[46]

The officers remained in locked freight cars as the train sped through the night after leaving Vienna. They were tense as they listened to voices outside of the cars whenever the train stopped. They could hear Germans and the commands of Russian guards. The next morning when the doors of the railcars opened, the officers could see a wooded area. They had arrived at the Austrian-Italian border. Greeted by an Italian commission, they got off the train. At this point, some officers received mail. Vicentini received a letter signed by his father, brother, and fiancée, but not by his mother. "This was a terrible shock. I realized I wouldn't find her at home, and she wouldn't be able to see me return after having waited and wished for this day for all those years. That veiled communication took away all my pleasure of reentering my homeland, as well as my desire to arrive at home."[47]

JULY 10, 1946

Marsan recalled the moment when the train carrying Italian officers arrived in Tarvisio at about five in the morning July 10, 1946: "It was a very moving moment for all of us as we crossed the frontier and entered Italy. It was like a dream come true, we were in heaven, but I was concerned because I hadn't had any news of my father in the postcards I received just before leaving Camp Suzdal.

"On our way to Milan we stopped in all the stations. At each one, crowds of people were holding up pictures of their sons, fathers, or husbands, shouting out names, asking us if we had seen them, or if we had any information about them. These were wrenching scenes, repeated over and over, in every station." When asked if he recognized any of the men in the photographs he saw, or names shouted across the sea of faces, Marsan said he didn't at the time.

Vicentini describes the arrival in Udine: "The platform was a carpet of faces, of searching eyes. As soon as the noises of the wheels and brakes of the locomotive ceased, a clamor rose up from that sea of people—it wasn't an applause of welcome, it was an anguished cry. Surnames, names of units and battalions were called out, looked for, invoked; hundreds of hands held pictures of smiling young twenty-year-olds, proud under the brims of their alpine hats." It was impossible to remember those faces; officers could only remember "faces destroyed by fatigue and suffering, eyes full of desperation or hallucinating from hunger." There were few within the crowd who could hug their loved one again, "for all the others, only tenacious, illusory hope remained." The emotional scene in Udine left few men with dry eyes.[48]

As Vicentini boarded the train once more, he noticed someone had used chalk to write *NOI SOLI VIVI* (WE ALONE ARE ALIVE) on the side of the railcar. He writes, "In the presence of those people, I felt ashamed of our impudent good fortune as well as my own."[49]

In Verona, a portion of the train continued on to Milan and Turin, while the remainder of the train headed to Rome. Marsan traveled to Milan. When he spoke about his arrival, he said, "What was fantastic was the Milan station! We arrived there around midnight. It's a huge station and the crowd that night was immense. You can't imagine the number of people!

"When we got off the train, it was impossible to move. The noise around us was deafening. At last, as I made my way slowly through the crowd, I saw Lucia in the distance. A man and a woman were helping her make her way through the crowd. My mother was behind her, also being helped, but I didn't see my father. When I didn't see him, I feared the worst. Later I found out he was ill and had remained at home. I was so relieved."

As Marsan recalled those moments in the Milan station as he slowly made his way toward Lucia, a gentle faraway look came over his face, and tears glistened in his eyes: "It was a moment...."

He stopped speaking for a while as his thoughts went back in time to that moment of almost unbearable joy. When he resumed the conversation, he said, "She was moving toward me, and I toward her, slowly, through the crowd, and then we were together once more, it was such a climax, an incredible moment tinged by my worry about my father, but complete once I knew he was alive."

In Verona, Vicentini had remained on the portion of the train directed to Rome. In Bologna, railway workers erased the writing on the sides of the rail cars, but somebody rewrote the same words: NOI SOLI VIVI. Vicentini writes, "Italians needed to know the truth!" It took another twenty-four hours to reach Rome, sometimes moving at a snail's pace over temporary bridges, evading collapsed tunnels, and waiting for other trains when only one track was available. In Rome, a quiet crowd was waiting at the train station: "There were no uniforms, there weren't any flags…. The government, military authorities, the Commune, in other words, official Italy, pretended not to know the prisoners from Russia had returned. Their presence was probably an embarrassment."[50]

Vicentini found his father and brother waiting for him on the platform. Just behind them, he saw his fiancée holding his mother's arm: "We threw ourselves against one another in a tight, almost hysterical, suffocating, liberating hug. At that moment she could never have imagined, and didn't know, that by neglecting to sign the letter I received in Tarvisio, the last hours of my journey home and the moment I had waited for and dreamed about for 1300 nights had been poisoned."[51]

Captain Lamberti describes his homecoming in Cuneo: "At home, my wife who had thought I was dead for two years, checked me from top to bottom to see if I had a wooden leg or an artificial arm. She couldn't convince herself I was still in one piece. On the outside, I was in one piece, but not inside. It's difficult to explain how I felt. The tragedy we experienced remains within us; everything we suffered, and many times even hoped for, remains imprinted within us, indelible."[52]

While the Italian officers were in Hungary, Soviet authorities, in collusion with representatives of the Italian Communist Party, had prevented fifty officers from leaving with the others. In essence, they were hostages. The Italian Communist Party was still concerned "how public opinion would react to stories the officers would tell with regard to what happened in the prison camps." They remembered how soldiers had reacted "with brawls and beatings of 'friends' who had come to greet them with red flags and old-fashioned [Communist] slogans they had had to put up with for years [in the camps]." The fifty officers were repatriated a month later, "when it was clear that testimony by the officers would not have caused excessive trouble."[53]

The Soviets flaunted the return of the officers as an "act of generosity," which meant no civilian or high-ranking military officers greeted the returning officers. The Italian government also refused to authorize the publication of a message, written secretly and signed by 526 out of the 552 returning officers in Austria on July 7, 1946, addressed to the Italian people. In their text, the officers remembered their fellow soldiers who died in Russian prisoner of war camps "from hunger, the cold, epidemics, and inhuman treatment." They requested prompt liberty for all

Italians still held by the Russians. The officers greeted the new Italian government and new Republic and declared themselves to be solidly behind "the moral and material reconstruction and renewal of Italy." They also greeted their families "with whom, for a long time, the sacred right to correspond was denied." The last portion of their message addressed Bolshevism:

> Witness to what we saw and suffered, no matter what our political tendency may be, we repeat to every Italian: BOLSHEVISM stripped of its demagogic rhetoric means a regime of police and terror, it means dictatorship; it is synonymous with external national enslavement and internal tyranny by one party on the nation, the family, and the individual. *VIVA L'ITALIA DEMOCRATICA, LIBERA, ED INDEPENDENTE!* (Long-live free and independent democratic Italy!)[54]

Italians only became aware of this message two years later "when it was published by the *Unione Nazionale Italiana Reduci Di Russia* (National Association of Italian Veterans of Russia) in a single issue called '*RUSSIA*' in April 1948."[55]

A detailed history of issues coloring the Italian political landscape during the years following the end of the war is beyond the scope of this book. Suffice to say, once all survivors from Russian prison camps returned to Italy, "controversy and exploitation exploded in a most cruel manner" on the part of both right- and left-leaning political parties. The word "dispersed" was used indiscriminately for all soldiers of the ARMIR who had not returned from Russia, from whom there was no further news.

Dispersed was an ambiguous word. It created illusions and hopes among families of missing soldiers and, in a sense, would offer hope and all sorts of speculation and angry controversy in the future. Opposing political parties used the controversy depending on their ideological persuasions. For example, at a certain point a story circulated that the dispersed soldiers were almost all alive and were "being held in the USSR as forced labor to repair the damages of the war." For years, misinformation abounded, tormenting the hopes of families and relatives of soldiers who had not returned.[56]

During the 1960s, Revelli interviewed families of soldiers declared dispersed in World War II. In 1970, in *L'ultimo fronte, lettere di soldati caduti o dispersi nella seconda guerra mondiale* (The Last Front: Letters of Fallen or Dispersed Soldiers in the Second World War), he published letters soldiers had written to their families while on the Don front. He also gave voice to the plight of mothers, wives, sisters, and sons of those missing men. In very few cases, families eventually heard news from a veteran from the Russian campaign who could give them accurate information about the fate of their family member, but most families had to cope with a complete lack of closure, implied within the ambiguity of the pronouncement *"disperso sul fronte russo"* ("dispersed on the Russian front").

Claudio Isoardi, declared disbursed, served in the war in Greece and then Russia in the Monte Cervino Battalion. When his mother spoke to Revelli she said, "One day [Claudio's] Captain Lamberti came to see me. He said, 'Cry for all the dead, there are no more who are alive.'" Lamberti (who returned from Russia in 1946) told Claudio's mother he had seen her son in a Russian prison camp hospital, gravely ill.

When Claudio's mother spoke to Revelli she said, "Napoleon left all his men in Russia. Why [should we] also send our [men] there! Mussolini and Hitler believed they could conquer the whole world. Our young men should have revolted, they shouldn't have left [for Russia]."[57]

Sergeant Major Giuseppe Rovera, declared dispersed, served in Greece and then with the command group of the Alpine Corps in Russia. His wife told Revelli her husband came home for the last time on August 1, 1942. "He wasn't resigned; he was fairly desperate and wanted to hide his anguish. He left the next day at five...I still see him as he walked away, I still hear his last words 'I will return, I will return.'"

Rovera's wife and daughter Bruna continued to live with her parents in the countryside. She had no money. She was able to find temporary work as a janitor and eventually became a janitor full time. "I washed so many floors. I promised my husband to have Bruna study so she wouldn't repeat our experiences, and I kept that promise."

"I blame those who sent [our men] to die in Russia. Our war pension is a joke...."[58]

Medical Officer Rocco G.B. Carbone, declared disbursed, served in the Monte Cervino Battalion. His sister Angela told Revelli that every morning a small crowd waited for the arrival of the bus carrying mail to the village of Pirocca. "Toward the end of January [1943] the letters from Russia became rare... [Then] complete darkness until June 1946...."

In 1946 Angela's family received news of Carbone's death from their village priest. A veteran, Torlai Francesco of Castell'Azzara, Grosseto, who returned from a Russian prisoner of war camp, had written a letter to the village priest of Pirocca with the following information: "On the morning of January 16, 1943 the battle of Rossosh began. I was wounded...I dragged myself toward the [camp] hospital where I met Medical Officer Carbone...[Later] as I left the barracks I saw Lieutenant Carbone supported by two alpini: he was wounded in the abdomen. I joined them...he was weakened because of the loss of blood...we stopped in a Russian hut. The lieutenant was fully conscious, in fact he examined me briefly and assured me I would definitely heal. He spoke to me about his family and his fiancée. Since I had no shoes, he authorized me to wear his after his death. [On] the night of the 18th toward 2200, he died."[59]

Sergeant Major Giacomo Origlia, declared dispersed, served in the 2nd Alpine Regiment. His wife saw her husband for the last time August 2, 1942. He told her the troop train bound for Russia would pass through Centallo the following day. "At dawn I was [standing] by the railroad tracks with Augusta in my arms and holding [my son] Giuseppe's hand. At nine, the train passed by quickly. I returned toward home when Giuseppe said, 'Why did you cry? Were you afraid the train would hit you?'"

Origlia's wife told Revelli she and her sister-in-law took care of their land together. "We were two women alone with our husbands dispersed in Russia: there were six children, the oldest was five. I was expecting another child...."[60]

Origlia's son Ricardo was born in April 1943. When Ricardo spoke to Revelli, he said he frequently dreamt of his father's return. "I dreamed of a festive encounter, I dreamed of my mother's joy. Then I began to read books about the war in Russia, and I began to despair."

He continued: "As an orphan, what really offends me the most about the last war is the mass of commanders. My father had the right to an exemption [from the military], there were three brothers serving. My mother went to the Military Recruitment Office to take care of the paperwork for exemption and always encountered a cruel and pitiless bureaucracy. A few southern [Italian] employees behaved like murderers; they even teased her and said, 'So young one, are you afraid of becoming a widow?'"

"When I imagine the death of my father I can't find any words to define war. I would like to think my father fell in battle and didn't die on a train transport full of human wrecks. And I blame those who sent him to die...."[61]

Marshal Antonio Votero Prina, declared disbursed, served in the Greek conflict and then in the Dronero Battalion, Cuneense Division in Russia. His wife also encountered endless senseless bureaucracy when she went to the Military Recruitment Office to submit paperwork for her right to a military pension. A medical officer had confirmed the fact that her husband had died in a prisoner of war camp.

When she spoke to Revelli she said, "I encountered deaf stupid bureaucracy, I also encountered vulgar bureaucrats who offended me with phrases like this: 'Come with me one evening on the *Viale degli angeli* (Road of the Angels) and your paperwork will be taken care of immediately.' I ran away despairing, saying to myself a submachine gun was needed to eliminate those draft dodgers."

"So many became rich, so many thieves, said '*viva la guerra*' ('long live the war'). For us there was only suffering, disasters, and humiliations."[62]

Chapter 21

LE PERDITE— LOSSES OF THE ARMIR

In January 1943, when news of the withdrawal from the Don reached Italy, it signified the end of Italian military activity in Russia. In newspaper articles and on radio broadcasts, "the gravity of the event was minimized by the Fascist regime."[1]

In March 1943, when troops of the shattered ARMIR returned to Italy after the disastrous withdrawal from the Don, the Fascist government never clarified at any level what had happened in Russia, nor what had happened to the soldiers who hadn't returned. The real news came from those who were fortunate enough to have survived the withdrawal—they were the ones who brought home news of the "military disaster; propaganda gave way to the truth." After the fall of Mussolini's regime on July 25 1943, news about the fate of missing soldiers disappeared from national and provincial newspapers, "creating a real and present void of news, destined to persevere at least until the liberation [in 1945]."[2]

After the war ended, most books written about Italian participation in the Russian campaign recounted experiences of the alpini and "contributed to seal the conviction that the ARMIR and the Alpine Corps were the same." When discussing losses of Italian soldiers in Russia, it is important to remember these losses refer to *all* soldiers of the ARMIR. Even today, when people in Italy speak of the Russian campaign many still believe the alpini alone served along the Don front: "But we alpini were a minority: 60,000 out of a total of 227,000 men [of the ARMIR]."[3]

In later years, as president of the National Association of Veterans of Russia, Carlo Vicentini frequently spoke to groups about the Russian campaign. He observed that those who knew what had occurred to Italian troops in Russia knew there was the "tragedy of the ARMIR," concluding with the "disastrous withdrawal of the alpini, and the disappearance of thousands of men." Vicentini writes, "My immediate obligation was to state there were seven other divisions on the Russian front in addition to the alpini, and that all of them had had to withdraw and endure the same adverse environmental conditions as the alpini." Of the thousands who did not return, 35,000 were alpini: the other 50,000 were soldiers who came from all parts of Italy including Puglia, Calabria, and Sicily. Therefore, "the tragedy of the ARMIR wasn't only the 'tragedy of the alpini.'"[4]

Vicentini recalled an incident occurring at a ceremony held in the crypt of Cargnacco (near Udine) where remains of some Italian soldiers who served in Russia are buried. An undersecretary of the Italian government spoke, and at the end of his speech he shouted: "Long live the alpini." Men in the audience responded angrily, shouting: "Alpini weren't the only ones serving in Russia!"

How was it possible that so many thousands of men of the ARMIR did not return to Italy from Russia? What was their fate? How many were captured and held as prisoners of war? Of these, how many were still alive? Such haunting questions have begged for answers ever since the end of the war. Carlo Vicentini has been at the forefront of the attempt to find the answers. In numerous interviews, he generously shared the latest information as to known facts and, sadly, unknown facts about the thousands of missing men of the ARMIR.

The story begins in 1946, when the Historical Records Office of the Italian General Staff published the number of soldiers of the ARMIR who had not returned to Italy from the Russian campaign. These numbers came from calculations made in March 1943, as the withdrawal from the Don front ended. At that time, General Italo Gariboldi, commander of the Italian Eighth Army, reported 84,830 soldiers dispersed. The general came to this conclusion while still in Russia, by subtracting the number of missing men from those who were present in each unit at the end of the withdrawal. "The major defect of the published number was that only one number was used to indicate all who were absent; in other words, all those who had either died in combat, were captured, or had died during the withdrawal were lumped together in that one figure."[5]

A more systematic form of documentation took place during the 1970s, when an Italian census determined the names of soldiers who had not returned from Russia. Its result showed the total number of soldiers who had been missing in 1943 actually amounted to 95,000.

In 1945–46, the Soviets released almost all Italian prisoners of war. The total number of veterans who returned to Italy varies, according to several sources. Giusti claims 10,030 returned, whereas the National Union of Italian Veterans of Russia claims 10,087 returned. Vicentini uses the number 10,000 when discussing this number of soldiers. The small discrepancy in the exact figure arises from sources with differing dates.[6]

For purposes of this narrative, this author relies on figures given by Vicentini during several interviews in Frascati, Italy.

When attempting to discuss losses of the Italian Army in the Russian campaign, Vicentini begins by pointing to the number of documented names of soldiers of the ARMIR who actually returned to Italy in March of 1943. That figure amounted to 125,000.

Once the war ended, it was impossible to obtain accurate information about the exact number of Italian soldiers captured by the Russians, or the exact number held in Russian prisoner of war camps. No information was forthcoming from Russian authorities with regard to the number who were still alive or had died in prisoner of war camps. There was no accurate information indicating the number of soldiers lost during the withdrawal, marches of the davai, and on the train transports. Even more frustrating was the fact that nobody really knew how many Italian soldiers were on the Don front after December 12, 1942. All military records were destroyed before the withdrawal began. Generally, it is believed that approximately 220,000 Italian troops were deployed on the Don front on December 12, 1942.

Vicentini notes, "During the first few days of the withdrawal, commanders, subaltern officers, [and] quartermasters could observe and keep track of those who died in combat, but they didn't know the fate of others who didn't show up for roll call...." Following a battle or a night spent in scattered izbas in a village, units often lost their cohesion. Information collected by officers and quartermasters was lost if they were captured or killed. "Communication between frontline troops and rearguard troops ceased once the withdrawal began, as did "news of their fate."[7]

Marsan noted that during the withdrawal, when units dispersed, more than likely one wound up marching with soldiers from many different units: "Often we didn't know any of the men marching alongside of us." Vicentini stated that during marches of the davai, while being herded by Russian guards, you knew even fewer people: "When someone fell by the side of the column and died, nobody stopped—each man was on his own; survival depended on always moving forward."

During the withdrawal, historical diaries of units of the alpini were lost. During the German occupation of northern Italy, regimental warehouses were burned or sacked, and military documents and registration papers disappeared. Returning veterans who could have provided useful information to the authorities became dispersed during the chaos in Italy that erupted after the signing of the armistice with the Allies September 8, 1943.[8]

When survivors of the withdrawal returned to Italy in March 1943, some of them gave testimony to military authorities during the census-taking that occurred. Later, when survivors of prisoner of war labor camps returned in late 1945 and early 1946, they were the only sources of scant news about the fate of their comrades. The authorities didn't undertake a careful system of interviewing them. Vicentini did point out that the deaths of officers were noted and reported far more than those of soldiers, because officers were known by so many of the troops.[9]

THE SEARCH FOR ANSWERS BEGINS

Carlo Vicentini has spent many years leading the attempt to shed light on the fate of missing soldiers, and to provide exact information as to what happened to them. Answers to this heavy question remained completely elusive until 1991, at which time the archives of the former Soviet NKVD (in charge of the POW camps), were made accessible to the Italian government, yet total clarity has yet to be achieved.[10]

In 1991, a representative of the *Onorcaduti* (Commission to honor the war dead) was permitted to gain access to archives in Moscow, dealing with all prisoners captured by the Russians during World War II. In order to find records of Italian prisoners it was necessary to comb through a "monstrous" card file in which millions of handwritten index cards held records of prisoners of about twenty different nationalities. Hundreds of index cards referring to Italian prisoners were photographed or copied, and later transcribed by computer.[11]

In 1992, Italian authorities received 2,600 pages of computer printouts with the names of 64,000 Italian prisoners. "These names should have been accompanied by detailed information: the date and site of capture, the name of the camp where the individual was imprisoned, and for those who were deceased, the date and cause of death and the site of burial and number of the original file." Vicentini notes, "Slightly more than one third of the recorded names on the printouts provided this essential, detailed documentation. That third comprised the names of those men repatriated in 1945–46, as well as those who were part of the census-taking occurring after the outbreak of disease had abated (claiming so many lives during the first months of captivity)."[12]

Vicentini explains that this lack of detailed information owes to the fact that during the first period (December 1942–January/February 1943), especially in those camps where prisoners were assembled and sorted, then sent on to various camps according to a variety of criteria, "there was no immediate census-taking or registration of prisoners. There was only a daily count of the dead, and this information was both vague and often erroneous."[13] For example, in Marsan's case (captured January 27, 1942), he wasn't asked to give his name or rank until April 1943, while he was in Camp Little Tambov.

Italian authorities received printouts of lists of 25,000 Italians who died in specific prisoner of war camps. To further complicate matters, these lists were either incomplete, or when alphabetized, included only a portion of the alphabet, or only referred to specific periods of time, or contained names not included on the main computerized list. Criteria for recording information differed from camp to camp. Patronymic names were missing on the general printouts. Lists compiled from hospital camps gave the cause of death, but omitted this information on computerized lists.[14]

Vicentini transliterated and translated all information made available to Italian authorities. Members of two private associations, who for years had devoted their attention to the problem of determining the fate of the missing soldiers of the ARMIR, assisted in this research: The Italian National Union of Russian War Veterans (UNIRR; Vicentini is a member of this group), and the Alliance of Families of the Dispersed in the USSR.[15]

All information received was "quantified, classified, and analyzed." Whenever possible, families of identified deceased soldiers received official notification. "Based on a quantitative analysis, names found on the computerized list were classified as follows: Thirty-eight thousand names referred to prisoners who died in the camps. Twenty-two thousand names were those of prisoners repatriated. Two thousand names of prisoners had no indication as to having died or been repatriated, and twenty-five hundred names were listed twice, or were prisoners of other nationalities, entered on the general list erroneously, or were Italian civilians or Italians from the Alto Adige area [South Tyrol]."[16]

It was determined that, of the repatriated prisoners, only 10,500 belonged to the ARMIR; the others were Italian soldiers who had been interned in Nazi concentration camps after September 8, 1943, and were later taken into custody by the Russians. These internees (1,153 found on the general lists) survived the Nazi camps only to die in those of Stalin.[17]

From information gleaned from the various lists of prisoners examined, it was determined that Italians had been imprisoned in over 400 camps scattered all over the Soviet Union in two basic types: regular prisoner of war camps and hospital camps.[18]

When dates of deaths on the various computerized printouts were examined carefully, it became possible to ascertain the rate of mortality of 95 percent of the listed names. This scrutiny reveals, "Between January and June of 1943, more than 32,000 Italians died (85 percent of Italian prisoners who entered the camp and were part of a census). During the month of March, the number of deaths reached almost 10,000, which means in that month more than 300 soldiers had died each day."[19]

Indications of burial sites for just a few soldiers were noted on the printouts, and in a number of cases crude maps were available, indicating burial sites, cemeteries, and/or the location of plots.[20]

Vicentini points out that the "quantitative analysis" of the printouts required years of work as well as scrutiny, but attempting actually to determine "who" died in the camps was a big problem. Transliteration was not the issue; the difficulty lay in the fact "that in many cases the Russians wrote surnames of Italian soldiers phonetically, using Latin letters that resulted in completely foreign sounding names, impossible to pronounce and which often made no sense at all." Therefore, it was necessary to examine lists of Italian soldiers who had not returned to Italy to attempt to seek a remotely matching name. Only 23,000 names of Italian soldiers listed as deceased on the printouts have been accurately identified; 3,000 names remain in an "unsure" status.[21]

Vicentini claims that even though access to Russian archives has not completely resolved all questions about the fate of many missing soldiers of the ARMIR, based on what is known now, although imprecise, it's possible to reach certain conclusions. The number of documented names of soldiers who returned from Russia in March of 1943 amounted to 125,000, leaving 95,000 soldiers missing from a force estimated at a strength of 220,000 in December of 1942 (10,000 of these were repatriated in 1946, leaving the actual number of missing soldiers at 85,000). It is estimated that 25,000 soldiers died in combat or from exhaustion and/or environmental factors during the withdrawal.

The Red Army captured an estimated 70,000 soldiers of the ARMIR. Since 10,000 of these repatriated, that means 60,000 Italian soldiers died either in prisoner of war camps or on forced marches or train transports. Of the 60,000 prisoners who did not return, there is only documentation for 38,000 men who died in the camps. The authorities believe 22,000 men died during the marches of the davai and on train transports.[22]

Unfortunately, only 3,000 names of soldiers out of the 25,000 assumed lost during the withdrawal are known. Of the 22,000 men lost during the marches and train journeys, only about 1,000 names are known. It must be emphasized that these numbers are still considered to be estimates. The only definite number is of those men who did not return to Italy from Russia; that number is 95,000 (less the 10,000 repatriated in 1946).[23]

It is probable that the totals allocated at this time to deaths occurring during the withdrawal, the marches, and train journeys include a large number of soldiers who died in the camps prior to any census or registration of prisoners. At this point, that number has not been confirmed one way or another. For example, Giovanni Riba (19th Company, Dronero Battalion, Cuneense Division) said, "This is why one cannot know who died in Russia. They captured me on January 27, 1943. Yet, up until April 25–30, nobody ever asked me anything in Camp Tambov. The census begins only now; they want to know all the facts about everybody. Up until today, nobody ever knew who I was."[24]

Every Italian soldier was given one thin brass *piastrino* (dog tag) when joining the military. Each piastrino provided his military identity number as well as the year of the beginning of his military service, followed by his full name, his father's first name, his mother's maiden name, and his date and place of birth. Some soldiers kept their piastrino around their necks on a chain or string, while others had them sewn into their jackets. Many piastrini were lost during the withdrawal, and still more were exchanged for morsels of food during the agonizing marches of the davai and the tortuous train journeys to the camps. In some cases, soldiers attempted to take identity tags off the bodies of their dead comrades. Military chaplains attempted to keep lists of names of dead soldiers on scraps of paper, but the Russians confiscated all such records before the chaplains left the camps.

Adolfo Tosello, a captured alpino of the Cuneense Division, offers his testimony as to how he and his comrades tried to keep a record of soldiers who died. After enduring a long march in order to reach a railroad center, he was crammed inside a locked freight car along with seventy other soldiers. About one half died during the twenty-day journey ending in Camp Piniug, near Kirov: "After a while, one didn't pay any attention to those who died. Those who were surviving said, 'That one died' and we took him and put him on the pile of other dead, thrown to the side like so much garbage.... We tried to find out their names in some way, to save their identity tags; but then in the camp, the authorities searched us and took everything; therefore the names, written on a small paper, and also the identity tags disappeared."[25]

Vicentini noted that bodies of the dead were dumped in an empty barracks during the first months of captivity because it was impossible to dig communal pits in the frozen ground. None of the bodies of different nationalities had any sort of identification tags on them. When Marsan served on the death squad in Camp Tambov and was required to transport frozen nude bodies on sleds to communal pits, he recalls none of them had any type of identification on them.

Giovanni Riba was also required to transport bodies of prisoners who died in Tambov: "Naked, completely naked, the dead are taken to the woods on sleds. The enormous pits there could hold 3,000. Once dead, they undress you, you are naked and you lose any nationality: the dead mixed all together—Germans, Italians, Hungarians, and

Romanians. The ground is hard, frozen. We light a fire to warm the ground to be able to dig. I go many times to bury the dead. On Easter of 1943, I buried 170."[26]

Remaining Questions: Why were so many soldiers of the ARMIR captured? Why did so many prisoners die? Vicentini attempts to answer these questions. He notes that so much of the information about the campaign in Russia "attributes the tragedy of the ARMIR mainly to the withdrawal of the troops from the Don, combat, and the long marches in adverse climatic conditions with unsuitable clothing, hunger, and exhaustion. This explanation is true, but is only a partial explanation." As far as combat during the withdrawal, Vicentini states that it was only true for some of the withdrawing forces, but not for the whole of the ARMIR. The truth is, "Actually two or three days after leaving the Don, the ability of almost all units to fight was reduced to virtually zero."[27]

The following words of Vicentini shed further light on the tragic fate of so many Italians who went to Russia and never came home again. "The immediate abandonment of the artillery and motor vehicles owing to the lack of fuel, followed by the abandonment of the mortars, machine- guns, even the rifles, once the small supply of ammunition was exhausted, left our soldiers a *mani nude* (empty handed, defenseless), against a well-armed enemy, master of the land, the roads, and the inhabited centers." As the withdrawal continued, troop units "split-off," units became mixed up, creating "large groups of dispersed soldiers cut off from their own units and impatient with all forms of discipline. The absence of liaison determined there was an absence of command, and therefore disorientation and confusion...."

On the third day of the withdrawal, the Julia and Cuneense divisions were "finished" following the hard-fought battle of Novaya Postoyalovka, as far as their ability to fight was concerned. Thousands of soldiers of the Torino and Pasubio [infantry] divisions were killed in Arbuzovka (called the Valley of Death) and the 3rd Bersaglieri were literally annihilated in Meshkov. Enemy tanks and partisans then attacked survivors of these assaults as they attempted to escape to the west or the south. "Many died, but many more were taken prisoner.... The real tragedy of the ARMIR was that tens of thousands of soldiers could not fight and had to surrender."[28]

Brutally freezing temperatures, exhaustion, and lack of proper clothing resulted in the death of many during the withdrawal. "These same factors had an effect even more devastating for those who were captured…many more kilometers were added to those of the withdrawal during the marches of the davai…." Following these eight to ten days of atrocious cold suffered during the withdrawal, soldiers were exposed to another period of exposure, sometimes lasting for two weeks, "which became even more destructive because it was accompanied by the despondency of a long imprisonment." During the marches of the davai, soldiers rarely found a sheltered place to spend the night. "An overnight stay didn't mean sleeping, it meant drawing together like a flock of sheep to try not to freeze to death." A prisoner received little or nothing to eat for ten to twelve days until he arrived across the Don. "Finally, after having marched for so long and tramped on the snow, instead of finding refreshment and hospital trains, which were available to those who came out of the encirclement, prisoners were piled up in freezing freight cars, where they continued to suffer from the cold and hunger, and lived like animals for weeks."[29]

These continuous detrimental conditions affected all prisoners, however, for those who were less fit or unaccustomed to marching (having worked in the rear of the lines) the effects were devastating. When survivors of the marches and train transports arrived in the camps, "they certainly did not find conditions of life or nutrition allowing them to recuperate, instead being crammed into underground bunkers and given the equivalent of dishwater for food…. Then the typhus epidemic arrived, and for individuals in that condition, it was the definite coup de grace."[30]

"Malnutrition," Vicentini claims, was the major factor contributing to the huge number of deaths of soldiers of the ARMIR in Russian prisoner of war camps. "It eliminated those who in less extreme conditions could have survived the cold, the discomfort, and the exhaustion. There would have been many; I am referring most of all to the alpini. It was for the aforementioned reasons…that for every 100 soldiers captured, only 14 were able to make it back to Italy."[31]

Epilogue

A SIGN OF HOPE

OPERATION *SORRISO* IN ROSSOSH, 1943–1993[1]

When members of the Italian National Association of Alpini discussed plans to commemorate the fiftieth anniversary of the battle of Nikolaevka, a veteran of that battle suggested that the alpini could build a nursery school for Russian children in the city of Rossosh. This idea received an enthusiastic response, and in October of 1991 initial contacts with various members of the commune of Rossosh began. The Italians and Russians finalized all agreements by March 1992.

Construction of the nursery school began in May 1992, on a site very close to the same building that had once housed the headquarters of the Alpine Corps in 1942–43. About forty alpini comprised the first group of volunteer workers. The group left Italy from Bergamo in a military plane in early June. Every fifteen days a new group of volunteers arrived in Rossosh. Volunteers came from all backgrounds and occupations, regardless of previous military rank or professional qualifications. By the time the construction was finished, 750 alpini had donated their time and energy to build the nursery school.

During this period, numerous veterans of the Russian campaign came to Rossosh with their families to view the progress of construction. Some veterans also wanted to revisit "the places of their youth remaining indelible in their memory." It seemed unbelievable that so many terrifying and painful events had taken place in scorching heat and terrible cold in that same lovely serene and beautiful countryside.

Leonardo Caprioli, the then-president of the Italian National Association of Alpini, and a group of veterans accompanied by an interpreter, had the opportunity to visit a Russian peasant who had helped Caprioli during the withdrawal from the Don. This man still lived in Arnautovo where the alpini had fought so valiantly against tremendous odds. After a friendly handshake and greetings, Caprioli asked, "Do you remember the Italians?"

"The Italians! I remember them well."

"And then, after the battle," Caprioli asked, "Where did the Italians go?"

"They went to Nikolaevka. The Italians were encircled. They were attacked violently."

As Caprioli conversed with the Russian, a woman standing nearby interrupted their conversation. In a loud beseeching voice, she addressed the interpreter: "Dear Doctor, translate this! Those poor soldiers! Their clothing was in rags. I felt such pity. They were all filthy, except for the Germans withdrawing with them. The Germans ignored them. The Italians were great, beautiful, and good. The Germans ignored them. Tell everybody about that! Translate that!"

Following this episode, the veterans moved on to the zone of Nikolaevka, scanning the area after fifty years, re-experiencing the battle etched in their memories. That day, all was peaceful and quiet.

When the nursery school was completed in 1993, it would assume a significant feature: "That of honoring the memories of relationships of humanity between the Italian and Russian population during those very difficult days—for that sense of civility that exists in the hearts of our people and the Russian people."

In the introduction to the film describing the construction of the nursery school, Leonardo Caprioli wrote these words:

This film commemorates the many men who returned from Russia with profound recognition of the Russian population, which with deep humanity offered recovery and help to our wounded during the tragic withdrawal in January 1943.

Thousands and thousands of Italian soldiers walked on Russian soil and had contact with the local population during rare breaks from operations, battle, transfers, and finally during the tragic occurrence of the withdrawal when the horror of death and massacre involved all of us. In those circumstances, Russian civilians gave goodwill, help, and aid to us.

On the occasion of the inauguration of the opening of the nursery school on September 19, 1993, Leonardo Caprioli spoke to the audience of Italians and Russians attending the festivities:

> In a city that was the center of furious battles fifty years ago, the *Casa del sorriso* was born—a space dedicated to life, to serene growth, and games children play. The Italian alpini, 'enemies of that time,' built it brick by brick, to donate it to the population of Rossosh.
>
> It is our contribution to the construction of a new and better future, an opportunity for your children to grow up serenely, a sign of hope for a new generation who will know how to reestablish real values in which they can believe: without hatred, without violence, without thirst for power—in peace.
>
> The hugs Italian and Russian children gave to each other today at the moment of the symbolic handing over of the key of this school are really a sign of a changed world, the hope for a different and better future: a future in which generosity, altruism, and honesty supplants all violence and all meanness.
>
> This is what we wish for the children of the *Casa del sorriso* and all children of the world.

POSTSCRIPT

In the following pages, I have outlined future paths Nello Corti, Veniero Ajmone Marsan, and Carlo Vicentini followed once the war was finished.

While still recuperating from the wound in his arm in September of 1943, Nello was in the village of Cogne in the Valle d'Aosta settling his family in a rented house. His parents and younger brother Marco had returned to Turin from Sala Consilina in August where his father had been serving his sentence of "internal exile" for his anti-Fascist stance. When bombing raids over Turin intensified during late August, the family decided it was too dangerous to remain in the city. Going to Cogne, where they had friends, seemed to be the best choice at that point in time.

Following the signing of the armistice between Italy and the Allies, on September 8, 1943, Nello crossed the Italian Alps to Switzerland to avoid seizure by German or Fascist forces rounding up all Italian soldiers to either send them to German labor camps or enroll them in the newly formed Fascist Republican Army.

While interned in Switzerland, Nello was in touch with a group of Italian patriots who wanted to return to Italy to fight with the partisans against German and Fascist forces. As an accomplished alpinist, Nello went on a mission to scout a safe route across the Alps leading to Valle d'Aosta. He returned to Italy and once he established a route, he escorted the first group of Italians across the mountains. Other partisans then escorted additional groups along the same route. By the early summer of 1944, Nello, his father Alfredo, and younger brother Marco had joined the partisans fighting the Germans and Fascists in Valle d'Aosta.

In October of 1944, Nello accompanied Giulio Einaudi on a partisan military mission to Rome. He and Einaudi crossed the Alps into France. Subsequently they flew to Italy. In November of 1944, General Alexander broadcast a message to the partisans to stand down for the winter months. As a result, Nello was not permitted to return to northern Italy. He remained in Rome and worked in the office of the Italian Ministry of War for Occupied Territories. In the early spring, he was sent to Siena to join a British intelligence unit and began training as a paratrooper, expecting to be dropped behind enemy lines. Fortunately, the war ended before such a mission materialized.

Once the war was over, Nello returned to Turin and continued his university studies, obtaining his degree in Veterinary Science. He remained in Turin where he practiced his profession. In the 1960s, he and his wife and son moved to Rome, and Nello began working for an international consulting firm. This work took him all over the world.

Nello continues to live in Rome. We continue to share a deep and abiding affection for each other and I treasure the time we can spend together.

A few days following his return from Russia, Veniero and Lucia traveled to Madonna di Campiglio in the Dolomite Mountains, where they remained for several weeks. "This was paradise," Lucia said. "We stayed in a small hotel close to a lake. There were very few people in that lovely place. We swam in the lake, we took walks, and we gathered strawberries in the fields. It was there we shared our stories. Veniero wanted to hear all the details of my activities in the Resistance; he kept a small diary in which he wrote all that I told him. Of course I wanted to hear about his time in Russia, but he seemed to be more interested in my activities and those of our families." In fact, during interviews with Veniero over the years, he frequently referred to Lucia's work with the Italian Resistance with great pride.

Lucia and Veniero returned to Milan where she was in the process of setting up a school of social work. Veniero received his discharge from the Alpine Corps in September of 1946. Soon he began to work for IRI—*Instituto Ricostruzione Industriale* (Institute of Industrial

Reconstruction) in Rome. Lucia remained in Milan and he commuted back and forth on weekends until she moved to Rome. Over the years, Veniero rose to the position of Central Co-director of IRI. During those years, Lucia and Veniero raised a family of six children. Veniero retired at the end of 1983.

Already an accomplished linguist, he spoke English, French, and German and had a good command of Latin and Greek. During his retirement, he continued to study and perfect his ability to speak and read Russian. He translated numerous articles from Russian into Italian. Lucia and Veniero traveled extensively after his retirement. Veniero maintained an active lifestyle, was physically fit, and always available and eager to spend time with his family and friends. His affection and warmth was a constant in all that he undertook, and in terms of our relationship, I always felt supported and cared for when in his presence, which now is sorely missed.

In an interview with Carlo Vicentini in 2009, I asked the then ninety-two-year-old if his family in Rome received notification he was a prisoner of war: "My family knew nothing about what had happened to me because the Russians didn't provide any information about prisoners held in Russian prisoner of war camps.

"During the war, Togliatti spoke on Radio Moscow from time to time. In order to get people to listen to his broadcasts in Italy he would mention the names of ten to twenty Italian prisoners of war at the end of his broadcast; he would say these prisoners were alive and well. The Vatican monitored these broadcasts. In December of 1943, my name was one of the names noted. The Vatican sent a letter to my father in January 1944, saying: 'A foreign radio broadcast gave out the news that Lieutenant Vicentini had been captured and was a prisoner.' The Vatican had had to search for my family since no address was given. By the time my family heard this news I had been a prisoner of war for one whole year. No information was given as to where I was being held."

Carlo began his military service after finishing his university studies. While attending the university he had also worked for the Italian railroad system. When he returned from Russia he resumed his job. When asked if it was difficult to adjust to civilian life, he said, "Adjusting wasn't difficult, but it was difficult to share my experiences with others, to have others understand or even believe what I told them. He explained:

"At that time half of the Italians were voting for the hammer and cycle and the socialists. They didn't believe what we the veterans told them about Russia. Even now, many continue to negate our stories. Here is an example. I listen to the TV station RAI-3 every evening. Just the other day a Slovene sent to one of the German concentration camps was interviewed. He had written a book about his experiences and spoke for about half an hour. There seems to be more interest in that sort of thing rather than hearing about the experiences of Italian soldiers who were prisoners of war in Russia."

He continued: "Once we survived the terrible typhus epidemic, three years had passed. I went to work in the Russian villages and slowly the experiences of that terrible first period dissipated. Those of us in prisoner of war camps didn't experience being in combat during the withdrawal, and then re-entering Italy quickly. Soldiers who returned immediately after the withdrawal, had, as their last memory of Russia, the terrible marches, hunger, and the cold, the enemy shooting and bombing them. Their survival was a miracle. Many of them had a very difficult time adjusting once they got home."

We discussed some of Nuto Revelli's interviews with veterans held in Russian prisoner of war camps. In his book *La strada del davai*, Revelli writes about the difficulties these soldiers had when they returned to Italy—the lack of adequate health care, poor job prospects, lack of assistance, difficulties obtaining a pension. Vicentini said, "I was fortunate. When I came home, I had a job waiting for me. However, for example, soldiers who were carpenters, bricklayers, or agricultural workers had to look for work. We officers came from different social strata; many, when they returned, resumed their university studies. They had families who could support them. The ordinary soldier who came home didn't have this support. There was no planning done to assist them. The Communists were in the government and they said that those Italian soldiers went to fight in Russia against our friends! Even ten years ago when I spoke to a group, a fellow in the audience questioned me. He said, 'What were you doing going to Russia?' Well, all you can do is give the fellow a kick in the rear!"

Carlo recalled an experience when invited to speak to a group of high school students about the Russian campaign. During the question and answer period following his presentation, a young student raised his hand, and with a serious face asked Carlo if he had seen Napoleon while he was in Russia! Carlo said, "Ignorance is at the root of the problem; students have lost a sense of history."

In October of 1946, Carlo married his fiancée Lillian. They raised two sons in a beautiful house he built in Monte Porzio Catone near Frascati, surrounded by age-old olive trees. I have visited him there in those beautiful surroundings numerous times.

Upon retiring, Carlo devoted years of work meticulously researching the fate of missing Italian soldiers. His fluency in Russian helped in his work; yet, as noted, answers about the disappearance of so many soldiers who left for the Eastern Front and never returned to Italy remains elusive to this day.

I have translated the last few pages of Carlo's book *Noi Soli Vivi* (first published in 1986) in which he draws a broad picture of a veteran returning home from Russia. His words may well speak for thousands of veterans, illustrating what many discovered as they attempted to integrate back into civil society, realizing their experiences had changed them forever:

> He is a man who is no longer capable of real emotions; no disaster, no massacre, no mournful event rouses him, because he has experienced things and events that are so abnormal there is no possible manner of comparison. This is also true even when he is not involved. The inevitable calamities, illnesses, the setbacks he and his family endure are experienced reluctantly with disappointment, but without distress, because he has learned that real misfortune is something far more serious.
>
> He is a tolerant man, almost indifferent. He doesn't get upset if thieves empty out his house or if he loses his wallet; he doesn't rail against those who dent his car...or if a promotion doesn't arrive, if a holiday ends up as a disaster, if his children don't grow up the way he wishes. Maybe he learned something from the Russians, about their fatalism, and like them, he understands it is a waste of energy not only to object to one's destiny but also to complain about it.
>
> He is a man who doesn't get worked up in a discussion; all of them become somewhat boring after a few rounds. He doesn't give much credit to any political, economic, or even moral theories, because he has learned everything is relative, there are

no real separations between good and evil, between justice and injustice, between truth and falsehood.

He is a man who simply endures; he doesn't tell anyone if he has pains in his stomach, his teeth, or has a fever. After a cut, a burn, a sprain, he doesn't say a word. He is ashamed about complaining, to express any sign of suffering even if the pain is strong or searing. A doctor has a theory that this is caused by an enviable insensibility; instead, it is due to simple pride. When one has seen hundreds of wounded men with their stomach ripped open, with a leg hanging loose, faces devastated by the blast of an explosion, chests resembling a strainer after being hit by a series of shells, hands rotting from frostbite, and has not heard one lament, one entreaty, one complaint, one learns that real physical pain has different dimensions from those that folks attribute to it these days.

He is a man who knows without a doubt what hunger means and knows how to read it in the eyes of others. He understands what "world famine" signifies, but he knows it cannot be eliminated with charity. For him, food comes close to being sacred; wasting it is a crime. He never leaves anything on his plate even if he is full; he prohibits throwing away any leftovers, because they can be eaten the next day, or re-used in hundreds of different ways. He remembers attending an official dinner in a foreign country many years after repatriation and being embarrassed as he conversed with a woman sitting beside him: without realizing it, he had gathered crumbs off the tablecloth and put them in his mouth!

He is a gourmet but is ready to eat any concoction; he doesn't get mad and doesn't push away an overly salted, an under or overcooked meal, or one that reeks of garlic, or a dish messed up by an inexperienced cook.

He doesn't throw anything away; everything might be useful. When in the past a few centimeters of cloth, a piece of paper, a bit of string, a can, or a nail were precious, even in times of abundance, it is still impossible to think they might not be useful. It is a ridiculous habit but the veteran from Russia cannot give it up.

He is a man who with little manual capability and a bit of fantasy has learned how to fix just about anything; he can manage carpentry, masonry, plumbing, electrical work, painting, blacksmithing, or peasantry, because he has seen that a state of real necessity draws unimaginable resources from an individual.

Naturally, this veteran is a special product of a series of exceptional circumstances. He does not try to be an example and doesn't want to teach or model anything. All can judge and classify him as they wish.

He only knows he is a happy man, satisfied with a life that gives little or a lot. Content to be alive, he regards every passing day as a gift when he thinks about the thousands of his comrades who forty years ago ended their youth in a land for a cause that wasn't theirs.[1]

COMPOSITION OF THE
ITALIAN ALPINE CORPS, 1942–43

ITALIAN ALPINE CORPS—GENERAL GABRIELE NASCI

"TRIDENTINA" ALPINE DIVISION—GENERAL L. REVERBERI
    5th ALPINE REGIMENT:
      BATTALIONS: MORBEGNO
                     TIRANO
                     EDOLO
    6th ALPINE REGIMENT:
      BATTALIONS: VESTONE
                     VERONA
                     VAL CHIESE
    2nd ALPINE ARTILLERY REGIMENT:
      GROUPS: VAL CAMONICA
                     VICENZA
                     BERGAMO

"JULIA" ALPINE DIVISION—GENERAL U. RICAGNO
    8th ALPINE REGIMENT:
      BATTALIONS: TOLMEZZO
                     CIVIDALE
                     GEMONA
    9th ALPINE REGIMENT:
      BATTALIONS: VICENZA
                     L'AQUILA
                     VAL CISMON
    3rd ALPINE ARTILLERY REGIMENT:
      GROUPS: CONEGLIANO
                     UDINE
                     VAL PIAVE

"CUNEENSE" ALPINE DIVISION—GENERAL E. BATTISTI
   1st ALPINE REGIMENT:
     BATTALIONS: CEVA
                  MONDOVI`
                  PIEVE DI TECO
   2nd ALPINE REGIMENT:
     BATTALIONS: BORGO S. DALMAZZO
                  SALUZZO
                  DRONERO
   4th ALPINE ARTILLERY REGIMENT:
     GROUPS: VAL PO
                  DRONERO
                  PINEROLO

ACKNOWLEDGMENTS

I am grateful to Nello and Veniero and thank them for the time and effort they contributed, breathing life into this story, as they went back in time, recalling memories of their experiences in Russia. My uncles also assisted with my research, sharing their books, offering suggestions and paths to follow, but most of all, their consistent encouragement helped me complete this work. *Con grande affetto e mille grazie.*

Carlo Vicentini also generously gave of his time and expertise. I am indebted to Carlo for permission to use maps and other resources designed for his own work, and have relied on his copious writings, as well as valuable information obtained in countless interviews. *Con grande ringraziamento per la tua generosita`, fiducia, e amicizia.*

During the course of my work, I have had the unexpected and delightful opportunity to rekindle old friendships and forge new ones. I want to thank all who have participated and helped me along the way.

I thank my former high school classmate Colonel John H. Stokes III (US Army, Retired), who on many occasions helped me understand and unravel unfamiliar military terminology. John read an early draft of my work and offered many timely suggestions drawing upon his military expertise, as well as his rich knowledge of World War II history.

My longtime friends Bea and Tom Roberts also read an early draft of my work. They suggested I forward a copy to their good friend and editor, Lorna Dittmer. Lorna applied her editing skills to my manuscript, offering countless valuable suggestions. She deserves many, many well-earned thanks, not only for her fine editing work but also for her patience, friendship, and humor throughout this process. Many heartfelt thanks go to Bea and Tom for making this valuable connection possible.

My dear friend Florita Botts deserves copious thanks for her generosity. She read an early draft and provided much needed help to unravel "Italianisms" in translations from Italian texts. She also applied her keen critical skills, and offered continuous encouragement to keep writing and to pursue the publishing path. Most of all, I thank her for the many delightful hours of conversation and friendship shared in her bit of paradise in Anguillara Italy on the shore of beautiful Lake Bracciano.

Florita introduced me to Adele Horwitz, an accomplished editor of military books in California. Adele read my manuscript and encouraged me to publish this story, noting the importance of sharing it with an English-speaking readership. My thanks go to Adele for her assistance, encouragement and her friendship.

I want to thank Antony Beevor for generously taking the time to read a draft of my work. His constructive remarks have been a beacon guiding me toward the completion of my manuscript.

Many thanks go to Alexandra Petrova for her help with transliteration of Russian words and place names. I also thank Alexandra and her husband Valter Schiavoni for introducing me to Alarico Rocchi, whose valuable recollections of the time he spent in Russia have enriched this story.

I am indebted to the following individuals and want to thank them for their generosity: the Beraudi family and Museo Storico Italiano della Guerra in Rovereto; Alarico Rocchi; Carlo Vicentini; Paolo Gaspari; Bruno Reverberi; Vincenzo Delmonte, Michele Bellelli and Michele Calandri. *Con grande ringraziamento per la vostra fiducia nel mio lavoro.*

The Beraudi, Ajmone Marsan, Corti families, and Carlo Vicentini deserve many thanks for permission to include their photographs in my work. My appreciation and thanks also goes to Michele Calandri who generously selected photographs from the archives of the Istituto storico della Resistanza e della societa` contemporanea in provincia di Cuneo. The inclusion of these photos adds another important historical dimension to this story.

Evviva la familia! My widespread close-knit family and my partner in life Rudy have all been a solid unwavering force of support throughout the writing of this narrative. You have encouraged me to persevere, reviewing my drafts, offering suggestions, helping me as I struggled with translations from Italian texts. Most of all, you have sustained my belief that the story of the alpini sent to Russia deserves the recognition that I am providing. I could not have completed my book without your unending encouragement, solidarity and love.

Finally, I wish to thank Casemate Publishers for the recognition of the importance of this story. I have experienced consistent support, guidance and encouragement from Steven Smith, Tara Lichterman and Libby Braden throughout the publishing process. Many others among the Casemate staff have contributed their expertise to this book. I offer my heartfelt thanks to all of you.

Grateful acknowledgement is made to the following for permission to quote from the works listed: Penguin Books Ltd. for Antony Beevor, *Stalingrad. The Fateful Siege, 1942–1943* (Viking 1998), reproduced by permission of Penguin Books Ltd. Copyright © Antony Beevor and Artemis Cooper, 1998; Reprinted with the permission of Simon & Schuster, Inc. from *The Rise and Fall of the Third Reich* by William L. Shirer. Copyright © 1959, 1960 William L. Shirer; copyright renewed © 1987, 1988 William L. Shirer; Ugo Mursia Editore S.p.A. for Giulio Bedeschi, *Centomila gavette di ghiaccio* and *Fronte russo: c'ero anch'io*, volume secondo, Egisto Corradi, *La ritirata di Russia*, Carlo Gnocchi, *Cristo con gli alpini*, Marco Innocenti, *L'Italia del 1943, come eravamo nell'anno in cui crollo` il fascismo*, Giovanni Messe, *La guerra al fronte russo, Il corpo di spedizione italiano in Russia*, Carlo Vicentini, *Noi soli vivi, quando settantamila italiani passarono il Don*, and Bruno Zavagli, *Solo un pugno di neve*; the Beraudi family and Rovereto Museo Storico Italiano della Guerra for Gino Beraudi, *Vaina` kaputt, guerra e prigione in Russia (1942–1945)*; Stanislao G. Pugliese, for *Desperate Inscriptions, Graffiti from the Nazi Prison in Rome 1943-1944*; Vincenzo Delmonte, Comune di Cavriago and Michele Bellelli, for *Luigi Reverberi: un soldati, un alpino, un uomo*; William Craig Jr., for William Craig, *Enemy at the Gates*; Michele Calandri, Istituto Storico della Resistenza in Cuneo e Provincia, for *Gli italiani sul front russo*; Giulio Einaudi editore S.p.A. for Nuto Revelli, *La guerra dei poveri*,

Mai tardi. Diario di un alpino in Russia, *La strada del davai*, *Le due guerre, guerra fascista e guerra partigiana*, *L'ultimo fronte*, *Il mondo dei vinti*, and Giorgio Rochat, *Le due guerre italiane 1935–1943. Dall'impero d'Etiopia alla disfatta*; Bruno Reverberi for Luigi Reverberi, "Relazione sulle azioni svolte dalla divisione Tridentina al fronte; Massimo Sani, for *Prigionieri, i soldati italiani nei campi di concentramento, 1940–1947*; Paolo Gaspari editore, for *Il sacrificio della Julia in Russia*; Il Presidente Nazionale Unirr, Centro Studi Unirr, Carlo Vicentini, for *Rapporto sui prigionieri di guerra italiani in Russia*; Carlo Vicentini, for "Le perdite della divisione alpina Cuneense sul fronte russo, inverno 1942–1943," "Dagli archivi russe è arrivata la documentazione sui nostri prigionieri di guerra," and "La campagna di Russia."

We have tried our best to contact all copyright holders of material quoted in this work. In those few individual cases where responses were not forthcoming, the copyright holders are welcome to get in touch with the publisher or author.

NOTES

PREFACE

[1] Rochat, "Mussolini as war leader", in I.C.B.Dear, *The Oxford Companion to World War II*, p. 600.

[2] All translations of Italian texts are mine with the exception of quotes from Mario Rigone Stern's book, *The Sergeant in the Snow*, and Eugenio Corti's book, *Few Returned*.

[3] Beraudi, *Vaina` kaputt, guerra e prigione in Russia, 1942-1945*, p. 9.

[4] Ibid., p. 188.

Chapter 1: THE INVASION OF RUSSIA

[1] General Franz Halder, quoted in Sulzberger, *World War II*, p. 117.

[2] Halder affidavit, Nov. 22, 1945, at Nuremberg, *Nazi Conspiracy and Aggression*, 10 vols. Washington U.S. Government Printing Office, 1946, VII, pp. 645-46, quoted in William Shirer, *The Rise and Fall of the Third Reich*, p. 830.

[3] Ibid.

[4] "The emphasis is in the original order." Keitel's order, July 23, 1941, *Nazi Conspiracy and Aggression*, VI, p. 876 (Nuremberg Document C-52); July 27 order, Ibid., pp. 875-76 (Nuremberg Document C-51), quoted in William Shirer, *The Rise and fall of the Third Reich*, p. 831,

[5] Directive May 13, 1941, *Nazi Conspiracy and Aggression*, Nuremberg documents, III, pp. 409-13, (Nuremberg Document, 447-PS), quoted in William Shirer, *The Rise and Fall of the Third Reich*, p. 832.

[6] Hassell, Ulrich von, "The von Hassell Diaries," London, 1948, 8 Apr. 1941, p. 173, quoted in Antony Beevor, *Stalingrad*, p. 16.

[7] Beevor, *Stalingrad*, p. 15.

[8] Directive May 13, 1941, *Nazi Conspiracy and Aggression*, Nuremberg documents, III, pp. 409-13, (Nuremberg Document, 447-PS), quoted in William Shirer, *The Rise and Fall of the Third Reich*, p. 832.

[9] Text of Rosenberg's instructions, *Nazi Conspiracy and Aggression*, III, pp. 690-93, (Nuremberg Document, 1029, 1030-PS), quoted in William Shirer, *The Rise and Fall of the Third Reich*, p. 833.

[10] Rochat, *Le guerre italiane 1935–1943*, p. 246.

[11] William Shirer, *The Rise and Fall of the Third Reich*, p. 851, and Francesco Valori, *Gli Italiana in Russia*, p. 23.

[12] Rochat, *Le guerre italiane, 1935–1943*, p. 378.

[13] Mussolini was referred to as "*Il Duce*" ("the leader") throughout the Fascist regime.

[14] Innocenti, *L'Italia del 1943*, pp. 65-66.

[15] Ibid.

[16] Ibid., p. 66.

[17] Valori, *Gli italiani in Russia*, p. 39.

[18] Ibid., p. 43. The CSIR (Italian Expeditionary Corps in Russia) consisted of three divisions: Pasubio, Torino and Celere. The Celere Division consisted of the 3rd Bersaglieri, two regiments of cavalry (Savoia and Novara), one regiment of artillery on horseback, and four battalions of Black Shirt Legions (CCnn). The CSIR force included 2,900 officers and 58,000 troops, 4,000 quadrupeds, 5,500 vehicles, 51 fighter planes, 22 reconnaissance planes and 10 transport aircraft.

[19] Ibid., p. 39.

[20] Ibid., p. 41.

[21] Ibid., 41-42.

[22] Messe, *La guerra al fronte russo*, p. 71.

[23] Ibid.

[24] Ibid.

[25] Flower and Reeves, *The War 1939-1945*, p. 209.

[26] Mela e Crespi, "Due diari inediti", quoted in Paola Mocchi, "Dalla Russia con orrore", p. 4.

[27] Ibid.

[28] Ibid, pp. 4-5.

[29] Förster, "Il ruolo dell'8 armata italiana dal punto di vista tedesco," in *Gli italiani sul fronte russo*, Istituto Storico della Resistenza in Cuneo e Provincia, p. 230 and p. 234.

[30] Mocchi, "Dalla Russia con orrore", p. 6.

[31] Shirer, *The Rise and Fall of the Third Reich*, p. 939.

[32] Ibid., 939-40.

[33] Ibid., pp. 937-38.

[34] *Nazi Conspiracy and Aggression*, III, pp. 798-99, quoted in William Shirer, *The Rise and Fall of the Third Reich*, p. 939.

[35] Wendel, "On Leave from Russia," quoted in Flower and Reeves, *The War 1939– 1945*, pp. 223-25.

[36] Deighton, *Blood, Tears and Folly*, p. 473.

[37] Ibid.

[38] Goldhagen, *Hitler's Willing Executioners*, p. 148.

[39] Headland, in Dear, *The Oxford Companion to World War II*, p. 252.
[40] William Shirer, *The Rise and Fall of the Third Reich*, p. 958.
[41] Paladini, "War Diary, July 19, 1941-January 1942," quoted in Stanislao Pugliese, *Desperate Inscriptions, Graffiti from the Nazi Prison in Rome 1943-1944*, p. 9.
[42] Faldella, *Storia delle truppe alpine*, p. 1377.
[43] Porcari, in *Gli italiani sul fronte Russo*, Istituto Storico della Resistenza in Cuneo e Provincia, p. 273.
[44] Ibid.
[45] Messe, *La guerra al fronte russo*, pp. 92-93.
[46] Ibid., p. 91.
[47] Zavagli, *Solo un pugno di neve*, pp. 47-49.
[48] Messe, *La guerra al fronte russo*, p. 91.
[49] Ibid., p. 95.
[50] Ibid., pp. 95-96.
[51] Ibid., p. 96.
[52] Ibid., pp. 96-97.
[53] Ibid., p. 97.
[54] Ibid., p. 96.
[55] Ibid., p. 95.
[56] Ibid., p. 97.
[57] Shirer, *The Rise and Fall of the Third Reich*, p. 909.
[58] Ibid.
[59] Ibid., p. 911.
[60] Ibid.
[61] Messe, *La guerra al fronte russo*, p. 212.
[62] Vicentini, "La campagna di Russia", p. 3, and Valori, *Gli italiani in Russia*, 194.
[63] Messe, *La guerra al fronte russo*, p. 212.
[64] Ibid., p. 214.
[65] Ibid., p. 215.
[66] Ibid., pp. 215-16.
[67] Ibid., 216.
[68] Ibid.
[69] Ibid.

Chapter 2: SUMMER OF 1942

[1] Magnani, "In ricordo della ritirata di Russia," p. 2.
[2] Cucchietti, "Alpini, indossate la maglia di acciaio", in Revelli, *Il mondo dei vinti*, pp. 264-65.
[3] Ajmone Marsan, "1942-1946 Ricordi di guerra e di prigione," p 1.
[4] Ibid.
[5] Revelli, *L'ultimo fronte*, p. XI.
[6] Revelli, "La guerra degli ignorant", p. 4.

[7] Revelli, *La guerra dei poveri*, p. 10.

[8] Ibid.

[9] Revelli, "La guerra degli ignoranti", p. 4.

[10] Revelli, *La guerra dei poveri*, pp. 13-14, and Revelli, "La guerra degli ignoranti", p. 4.

[11] Revelli, "La guerra degli ignorant", p. 4.

[12] Ibid., p. 11.

[13] "Italo Serri" is the pseudonym for Medical Officer Giulio Bedeschi (Julia Division), author of *Centomila gavette di ghiaccio*. Lieutenant Bedeschi served in the 13th battery of the Conegliano Artillery Group of the 3rd Regiment, Julia Division. In his book, Bedeschi substitutes the fictional "26th Battery" for the actual 13th Battery. "Captain Ugo Reitani" is the pseudonym used for Captain D'Amico.

[14] Bedeschi, *Centomila gavette di ghiaccio*, p. 134.

[15] Ibid.

[16] Gallo, in Revelli, *L'ultimo fronte*, 107.

[17] Prina, in Revelli, *L'ultimo fronte*, 199.

[18] Di Michele, *Io prigioniero in Russia*, p. 66.

[19] Ibid.

[20] Beraudi, *Vaina` kaputt*, p. 11.

[21] Ibid.

[22] Ibid., p. 12.

[23] Corradi, *La ritirata di Russia*, pp. 29-30.

[24] Battisti, "La divisione alpina 'Cuneense' al fronte russo", pp. 4-5.

[25] Beevor, *Stalingrad*, pp. 80-81, and Bellamy, *Absolute War*, p. 501.

[26] Faldella, *Storia delle truppe alpine*, p. 1411.

[27] Battisti, "La divisione alpina 'Cuneense' al fronte russo", p. 5.

[28] Cucchietti, "Alpini indossate la maglia di acciaio", in Revelli, *Il mondo dei vinti*, p. 265.

[29] Rochat, *Le guerre italiane, 1935-1943*, p. 379, and footnote 4, p. 379.

[30] Ibid.

[31] Bellamy, *Absolute War*, p. 506, and Davies, *No Simple Victory*, p. 101 (Mt. Elbrus stands at 18,510 feet).

[32] Faldella, *Storia delle truppe alpine*, p. 1409.

[33] Ibid.

[34] Vicentini, *Noi soli vivi*, p. 193.

[35] Faldella, *Storia delle truppe alpine*, p. 1409.

[36] The Italians referred to the Russian PPSh 41 Russian machine pistol as a "parabellum". The PPSh rapid-fire weapons used a pistol cartridge housed in a large drum magazine. (Deighton, *Blood Tears and Folly*, p. 482).

[37] Revelli, *La guerra dei poveri*, p. 15, and p. 22.

[38] Ibid., p. 15.

[39] Faldella, *Storia delle truppe alpine*, p. 1411.

[40] Faldella, *Storia delle truppe alpine*, pp. 1411-12.

[41] Muratti, "Gli alpini del Gemona," in Bedeschi, *Fronte russo: c'ero anch'io*, pp. 280-81.

[42] Faldella, *Storia delle truppe alpine*, pp. 1411-12.

[43] Porcari, "La 'Cuneense' sul fronte di guerra," in *Gli italiani sul fronte russo*, Istituto Storico della Resistenza in Cuneo e Provincia, p. 273.

Chapter 3: THE TREK OF THE ALPINI

[1] Vicentini, *Il sacrificio della Julia in Russia*, p. 14.

[2] Di Michele, *Io prigioniero in Russia*, p. 67.

[3] Cucchetti, "Alpini, indossate la maglia di acciaio", in Revelli, *Il mondo dei vinti*, p. 266.

[4] Di Michele, *Io prigioniero in Russia*, pp. 68-69.

[5] Ibid.

[6] Ibid., p. 67-69.

[7] Di Michele, *Io prigioniero in Russia*, 71.

[8] Ibid.

[9] All temperatures cited in the text are in degrees Celsius.

[10] Bedeschi, *Centomila gavette di ghiaccio*, 152-53.

[11] Magnani, "In ricordo della ritirata di Russia," 4.

[12] Magnani, "In ricordo della ritirata di Russia", p. 5.

[13] Beraudi, *Vaina kaputt*, p. 14.

[14] Revelli, *La guerra dei poveri*, p. 16, and Revelli, "La guerra degli ignorant", p. 1.

[15] Revelli, *La guerra dei poveri*, p. 17.

[16] Battisti, "La divisione alpina 'Cuneense' al fronte russo," p. 8.

[17] Ibid.

[18] Ibid.

[19] Ibid., p. 9.

[20] Bedeschi, *Centomila gavette di ghiaccio*, p. 153.

Chapter 4: ON THE DON LINES

[1] Battisti, "La divisione alpina 'Cuneense' al fronte russo", p. 9, and Bellelli, *Luigi Reverberi*, p. 4.

[2] Bedeschi, *Centomila gavette di ghiaccio*, pp. 155-56.

[3] Cruccu, "Le operazioni italiane in Russia 1941-1943", in *Gli italiani sul fronte russo*, Istituto Storico della Resistenza in Cuneo e Provincia, pp. 215-18.

[4] Ibid., p. 217.

[5] Battisti, "La divisione alpina 'Cuneense' al fronte russo," pp. 9-10.

[6] Sculati, "Pieta` l'e` morta", in Bedeschi, *Fronte russo: c'ero anch'io*, p. 387.

[7] Reverberi, "Relazione", p. 4.

[8] Ibid.

[9] Bedeschi, *Centomila gavette di ghiaccio*, p. 161.

[10] Bedeschi, *Centomila gavette di ghiaccio*, pp. 161-62.

[11] Ibid., pp. 161-66.

[12] Rigone Stern, *The Sergeant in the snow*, p. 1.

[13] Ibid. p. 14.

[14] Sculati, "Pieta` l'e` morta,", in Bedeschi, *Fronte russo: c'ero anch'io*, p. 387.

[15] Grignaschi, "Le isbe – l'amicizia con Platon – la ritirata", in Bedeschi, *Fronte russo: c'ero anch'io*, p. 545.

[16] Faldella, *Storia delle truppe alpine*, pp. 1437-39.

[17] Corradi, *La ritirata di Russia*, pp. 36-37.

[18] Battisti, "La divisione alpina 'Cuneense' al fronte russo", 10-14.

[19] Ibid, and Faldella, *Storia delle truppe alpine* 1433.

[20] Battisti, "La divisione alpina 'Cuneense' al fronte russo", 11-12.

[21] Ibid., 12.

[22] Ibid., 13

[23] Ibid., p. 15.

[24] Ibid.

[25] Ibid., p. 16.

[26] Ibid, pp. 19-20.

[27] Ibid., pp. 20-21

[28] Carbone, in Revelli, *L'ultimo fronte*, pp. 17-18.

[29] Bedeschi, *Centomila gavette di ghiaccio*, p. 158.

[30] Ibid., p. 159.

[31] Cucchietti, "Alpini, indossate la maglia di acciaio", in Revelli, *Il mondo dei vinti*, p. 266.

[32] Ibid.

[33] Bedeschi, *Centomila gavette di ghiaccio*, p.159.

[34] Ibid., pp.159-60.

[35] Trentini, "Per poter salvare vite umane", in Bedeschi, *Fronte russo: c'ero anch'io*, pp. 418-419.

[36] Candela, "Scappate prima che venga il freddo", in Revelli, *La strada del davai*, p. 70.

[37] Ibid., pp. 70-71.

[38] Ibid., pp. 71-72.

[39] Ibid., p. 72.

[40] Battisti, "La divisione alpina 'Cuneense' al fronte russo", p. 21.

[41] Ibid.

[42] Bedeschi, *Centomila gavette di ghiaccio*, pp. 160-61.

[43] Marchisio, "Noi e i prigionieri russi", in Bedeschi, *Fronte russo: c'ero anch'io*, p. 338.

[44] Damini, "Le due ragazze russe 'fucilate' sul posto", in Bedeschi, *Fronte russo: c'ero anch'io*, pp. 415-16.

[45] Gaza, "Ricordi e riflessioni di un 'vecio' della Russia", in Bedeschi, *Fronte russo: c'ero anch'io*, pp. 144-45.

[46] Ibid.

[47] Battisti, "La divisione alpina 'Cuneense' al fronte russo", p. 21.

[48] Gnocchi, *Cristo con gli alpini*, p. 44.

[49] In the spring of 1942, Professor Alfredo Corti was sentenced to five years of "internal exile" (compulsory residence) for voicing his anti-Fascist sentiments. He was sent to the village of Sala Consilina in the region of Campania, one of the most primitive regions of southern Italy. Sentences of internal exile were given to persons considered dangerous or subversive. Professor Corti's wife Helen accompanied him and remained with him throughout the period of his exile, which lasted until Mussolini was overthrown in July 1943.

Chapter 5: GENERAL CONDITIONS ON THE DON FRONT

[1] Battisti, "La divisione alpina 'Cuneense' al fronte russo", pp. 21-22.

[2] Corradi, *La ritirata di Russia*, p. 18.

[3] Battisti, "La divisione alpina 'Cuneense' al fronte russo", p. 22.

[4] Corradi, *La ritirata di Russia*, pp. 17-19.

[5] Revelli, *La guerra dei poveri*, p. 27.

[6] Ibid., pp. 27-28.

[7] Zavaglia, *Un pugno di neve*, p. 99.

[8] Battisti, "La divisione alpina 'Cuneense' al fronte russo", p. 22.

[9] Rochat, *Le guerre italiane 1935-1943*, p. 386.

[10] Revelli, *L'ultimo fronte*, pp. 108-09 and p. 102. Romano Gallo, born in 1915 in Dogliani was a peasant farmer (*contadino*). He completed fifth grade. He was deployed in camp hospital 617, Cuneense Division. He was a veteran of the Greek-Albanian war; declared dispersed on the Russian front. The military used the term "dispersed" when the fate of a missing soldier was unknown.

[11] Ibid., p. 175 and p. 171. Francesco Tortone, Sergeant, 22nd Company, Saluzzo Battalion, Cuneense Division was born in Costigiole Saluzzo in 1914. He was a decorator. Tortone completed fifth grade. He was a veteran of the east African campaign, declared dispersed on the Russian front.

[12] Ibid., pp. 187-88 and p. 182. Giacomo Origlia,15th Company, Borgo San Dalmazzo Battalion, Cuneense Division was a peasant farmer, born in Centallo, 1913. Origlia completed a fifth grade education. Declared dispersed on the Russian front.

[13] Ibid., p. 219 and p. 218. Stefano Rosso was a peasant farmer born in San Pietro Monterosso, 1917. He completed a fifth grade education. Deployed in the Cuneense divisional cannon company declared dispersed on the Russian front.

[14] Ibid., p. 222 and p. 221. Spirito Gonzo born 1921 in Verzuolo was a carpenter. He completed a fifth grade education. Deployed in the Saluzzo Battalion, Cuneense Division, declared dispersed on the Russian front.

[15] Ibid., p. 224 and p 221. Giovanni Gonzo, brother of Spirito, was a carpenter. Born in Verzuolo, 1921, he completed a fifth grade education. Deployed in the Saluzzo Battalion, Cuneense Division, declared, dispersed on the Russian front.

[16] Ibid., p. 254 and p. 251. Bruno Viale was a peasant farmer. Born in Roaschia 1911, he completed a third grade education. He was a veteran of the east African and Greek-Albanian campaigns. Deployed in the Pinorolo Group, Cuneense Division, declared dispersed on the Russian front.

17 Revelli. *L'ultimo fronte*, p. XLVII.
18 Revelli, *La guerra dei poveri*, pp. 32-33.
19 Revelli, "La guerra degli ignorant, p. 5.
20 Revelli, *La guerra dei poveri*, p. 33
21 Ibid., pp. 32-33.
22 Ibid., p. 33.
23 Rigoni Stern, *The Sergeant in the Snow*, p. 25.
24 Battisti, La divisione alpina 'Cuneense' al fronte russo", p. 22.
25 Ibid., p. 23.
26 Ibid., p. 22.
27 Ibid., p. 24.
28 Corradi, *La ritirata di Russia*, p. 58.
29 Battisti, "La divisione alpina 'Cuneense' al fronte Russo", p. 24.
30 Corradi, *La ritirata di Russia*, pp. 20-21.
31 Battisti, "La divisione alpina 'Cuneense' al fronte russo", p. 18-19.
32 Damini, "Le due ragazze russe 'fucilate' sul posto", in Bedeschi, *Fronte russo: c'ero anch'io*, p. 412.
33 Ibid.
34 Ibid, p. 413.
35 Faldella, *Storia delle truppe alpine*, p. 1437.
36 Zilli, "Gli Italiani prigionieri di guerra in URSS", in *Gli italiani sul fronte russo*, Istituto Storico della Resistenza in Cuneo e Provincia, p. 297.
37 Ibid., p. 298.
38 Ibid.
39 Ibid., p. 299.
40 The katyusha was a Russian multiple rocket launcher (BM-13-16), used for the first time July 15, 1942 near Smolensk, Merridale, *Ivan's War*, p. 110.
41 Revelli, *La guerra dei poveri*, p. 34.
42 Bellamy, *Absolute War*, pp. 242-43.
43 Revelli, *La guerra dei poveri*, p. 34.
44 Ibid., pp. 34-35
45 Ibid., p. 35.
46 Castellano, "La guerra e` finita," in Revelli, *La strada del davai*, p. 427.

Chapter 6: THE SOVIET WINTER OFFENSIVE BEGINS
1 Bellamy, *Absolute War*, p. 507.
2 Antill, *Stalingrad 1942*, pp. 51-65.
3 Vicentini, *Il sacrificio della Julia*, p. 19.
4 Ibid.
5 Vicentini, *Noi soli vivi*, pp. 194.
6 Beevor, *Stalingrad*, p. 226–27.
7 Ibid., 225.
8 Corradi, *La ritirata di Russia*, p. 37.
9 Merridale, *Ivan's War*, p. 177.

[10] Antill, *Stalingrad 1942*, pp. 74-75.
[11] Vicentini, *Il sacrificio della Julia*, p. 18.
[12] Vicentini, "La campagna di Russia," p. 5.
[13] Vicentini, *Il sacrificio della Julia*, p. 18.
[14] Ibid.
[15] Ibid., p. 19.
[16] Vicentini, "La campagna di Russia," p. 5-6.
[17] Ibid., P. 6.
[18] Zilli, "Gli Italiani prigionieri di guerra in URSS," in *Gli italiani sul fronte russo*, Istituto Storico della Resistenza in Cuneo e Provincia, pp. 299-300.

Chapter 7: TRANSFER OF THE JULIA DIVISION
[1] Corradi, *La ritirata di Russia*, pp. 43-44.
[2] Ibid., p. 53.
[3] Battisti, "La Divisione alpina 'Cuneense' al fronte russo 1942-43", p. 26.
[4] Vicentini, *Il sacrificio della Julia*, p. 19.
[5] Bedeschi, *Centomila gavette di ghiaccio*, p. 173.
[6] Ibid., pp. 173-77.
[7] Ibid, pp. 177-82.
[8] Ibid., p. 184.
[9] Ibid., pp. 184-85.
[10] Ibid., pp. 187-88.
[11] Ibid., p. 190.
[12] Ibid., pp. 192-200.
[13] Ibid., pp. 203-19.
[14] Ibid., pp. 219-26.
[15] Ibid., pp. 226-32.
[16] Sculati, "Pieta` l'e` morta", quoted in Bedeschi, *Fronte russo: c'ero anch'io*, p. 388.
[17] Faldella, *Storia delle truppe alpine*, p. 1469.
[18] Vicentini, *Il sacrificio della Julia*, p. 37.
[19] Ibid.
[20] Bedeschi, *Centomila gavette di ghiaccio*, pp. 246-49.
[21] "*Ura, Ura*" was the Russian battle cry.
[22] Di Michele, *Io prigioniero in Russia*, pp. 81-82.
[23] Ibid., p. 82.
[24] Ibid.
[25] Ibid., p. 83.
[26] Vicentini, *Il sacrificio della Julia*, p. 44.
[27] Ibid.,
[28] Ibid.
[29] Ibid., pp. 44-45.
[30] Ibid., p. 45.
[31] Ibid.

[32] Bedeschi, *Centomila gavette di ghiaccio*, p. 262.

[33] Ibid., p. 263.

[34] Ibid., pp. 263-64.

[35] Damini, "Le due ragazze russe 'fucilate' sul posto", in Bedeschi, *Fronte russo: c'ero anch'io*, pp. 414-15.

[36] Vicentini, *Il sacrificio della Julia*, p. 56-58.

Chapter 8: ENCIRCLEMENT OF THE ALPINE CORPS

[1] Battisti, "La divisione alpina 'Cuneense' al fronte russo", p. 27.

[2] Corradi, *La ritirata di Russia*, pp. 69.

[3] Reverberi, "Relazione," p. 4-5.

[4] Revelli, *La guerra dei poveri*, p. 36.

[5] Rigoni Stern, *The Sergeant in the Snow*, pp. 16-17.

[6] Ibid., p. 17.

[7] Revelli, *La guerra dei poveri*, pp. 36- 37.

[8] Reverberi, "Relazione", pp. 4-5.

[9] Rigoni Stern, *The Sergeant in the Snow*, pp. 19-20.

[10] Ibid. pp. 22-23.

[11] Ibid., pp. 23.

[12] Ibid., pp. 24-25.

[13] Ibid., pp. 29-30.

[14] Reverberi, "Relazione", pp. 4-5.

[15] Assunto, "Cronaca dei lavori", in *Gli italiani sul fronte russo*, Istituto Storico della Resistenza in Cuneo e Provincia, pp. 501-02.

[16] Ibid.

[17] Rochat, *Le guerre italiane 1935-1943*, p. 393.

[18] Ibid., pp. 392-93.

[19] Battisti, "La divisione alpina 'Cuneense' al fronte russo", pp. 27-28.

[20] Corradi, *La ritirata di Russia*, pp. 69-70.

[21] Faldella, *Storia delle truppe alpine*, pp. 1497-99.

[22] Faldella, *Storia delle truppe alpine*, p. 1500 and Vicentini, *Il sacrificio della Julia in Russia*, pp. 60-61.

[23] Vicentini, *Il sacrificio della Julia*, p. 61.

[24] Corradi, *La ritirata di Russia*, p. 74.

[25] Ibid, pp. 74-75.

[26] Battisti, "La Divisione alpina 'Cuneense' al fronte russo", p. 28.

[27] Vicentini, *Il sacrificio della Julia*, p. 61.

[28] Faldella, *Storia delle truppe alpine*, p. 1501.

[29] Battisti, "La Divisione alpina 'Cuneense' al fronte russo", pp. 28-29.

[30] Ibid., p. 30.

[31] Ibid.

[32] Faldella, *Storia delle truppe alpine*, pp. 1502.

[33] Porcari, "La' Cuneense' sulle fronti di guerra," in *Gli italiani sul fronte russo*, Istituto Storico della Resistenza in Cuneo e Provincia, p. 278.

[34] Ibid.
[35] Ibid.
[36] Faldella, *Storia delle truppe alpine*, p. 1512.

Chapter 9: RETREAT DURING THE HEIGHT OF WINTER
[1] Bedeschi, *Centomila gavette di ghiaccio*, pp. 270-71.
[2] Ibid. p. 272.
[3] Ibid. pp. 278-82.
[4] Corradi, p. 16.
[5] Bedeschi, *Centomila gavette di ghiaccio*, pp. 284-85.
[6] Beraudi refers to Colonel Bellani as "Colonel B" throughout his text.
[7] Beraudi, *Vaina` kaputt*, p. 39.
[8] Lieutenant Beraudi received the rank of Captain during the withdrawal.
[9] Beraudi, Vaina` kaputt, p. 39.
[10] Faldella, *Storia delle truppe alpine*, p. 1515 and Corradi, *La ritirata di Russia*, p. 78.
[11] Faldella, *Storia delle truppe alpine*, p. 1515–16.
[12] Ibid., p. 1515.
[13] Ibid., 1515–16.
[14] Beraudi, *Vaina` kaputt*, p. 47.
[15] Ibid., p. 48.
[16] Ibid., pp. 48-50.
[17] Rigoni Stern, *The Sergeant in the Snow*, p. 32.
[18] Ibid., p. 33.
[19] Ibid., pp. 33-34.
[20] Revelli, *La guerra dei poveri*, pp. 38-41.
[21] Gnocchi, *Christo con gli alpini*, p. 26.
[22] Rigoni Stern, *The Sergeant in the snow*, pp. 36-39.
[23] Ibid., p. 40.
[24] Revelli, *La guerra dei poveri*, p. 45.
[25] Battisti, "La divisione alpina 'Cuneense' al fronte russo", p. 36.
[26] Ibid.
[27] Bedeschi, *Centomila gavette di ghiaccio*, p. 289.
[28] Ibid., p. 290.
[29] Ibid.
[30] Ibid., pp. 290-91.
[31] Ibid., p. 292.
[32] Vicentini, *Il sacrificio della Julia in Russia*, p. 71, and Faldella, *Storia delle truppe alpine*, p. 1529.
[33] Vicentini, *Il sacrificio della Julia in Russia*, pp. 71-73.
[34] Ibid., pp. 71-72, and Bedeschi, *Centomila gavette di ghiaccio*, pp. 295-98.
[35] Faldella, *Storia delle truppe alpine*, p. 1530.
[36] Vicentini, *Il sacrificio della Julia*, p. 73.
[37] Ibid., p. 74.

[38] Ibid.

[39] Ibid., and Bedeschi, *Centomila gavette di ghiaccio*, pp. 298-99.

[40] Vicentini, *Il sacrificio della Julia*, p. 74.

[41] Faldella, *Storia delle truppe alpine*, p. 1536–38.

[42] Corradi, *La ritirata di Russia*, pp. 93-94.

[43] Ibid., p. 92.

[44] Savoia was the Italian royal family name. "*Savoiaaa*" was the battle cry of Italian soldiers.

[45] Bedeschi, *Centomila gavette di ghiaccio*, p. 300.

[46] Corradi, *La ritirata di Russia*, p. 93.

[47] Bedeschi, *Centomila gavette di ghiaccio*, pp. 300-01.

[48] Ibid., p. 301.

[49] Battisti, "La divisione alpina 'Cuneense' al fronte russo", p. 39.

[50] Ibid., p. 40.

[51] Ibid.

[52] Bedeschi, *Centomila gavette di ghiaccio*, pp. 301-02.

[53] Ibid., p. 305.

[54] Ibid., p. 306.

[55] Ibid., pp. 306-10.

[56] Ibid., p. 313, and Faldella, *Storia delle truppe alpine*, p. 1692.

[57] Bedeschi, *Centomila gavette di ghiaccio*, p. 313.

[58] Battisti, "La divisione alpina 'Cuneense' al fronte russo", p. 42.

[59] Faldella, *Storia delle truppe alpine*, p. 1542.

[60] Beraudi, *Vaina`kaputt*, p. 60.

[61] Faldella, *Storia delle truppe alpine*, p. 1544.

[62] Vicentini, *Il sacrificio della Julia in Russia*, p. 75.

[63] Corradi, *La ritirata di Russia*, pp. 99.

[64] Vicentini, *Il sacrificio della Julia in Russia*, pp. 77-78

[65] Ibid., p. 81.

[66] Corradi, *La ritirata di Russia*, p. 100.

[67] Vicentini, *Il sacrificio della Julia in Russia*, p. 73 and p. 81.

[68] Ibid., p. 82.

[69] Ibid., pp. 81-82.

[70] Ibid., p. 82.

[71] Battisti, "La divisione alpina 'Cuneense' al fronte russo," pp. 41-42, and Faldella, *Storia delle truppe alpine*, p. 1596.

Chapter 10: THE CUNEENSE AND JULIA CONTINUE TO WITHDRAW

[1] Faldella, *Storia delle truppe alpine*, p. 1571.

[2] Porcari, "La 'Cuneense' sulle fronti di guerra", in *Gli italiani sul fronte russo*, Istituto Storico della Resistenza in Cuneo e Provincia, pp. 281-82, and Battisti, "La divisione alpina 'Cuneense' al fronte russo", p. 42.

[3] Battisti, "La divisione alpina 'Cuneense' al fronte russo", p. 43.

[4] Ibid, pp. 43-44.

[5] Ibid., p. 44.
[6] Ibid.
[7] Ibid., pp. 44-45.
[8] Ibid., p. 45.
[9] Ibid., p. 45.
[10] Beraudi, *Vaina` kaputt*, pp. 62-63.
[11] Battisti, "La divisione alpina 'Cuneense' al fronte russo", p. 45.
[12] Faldella, *Storia delle truppe alpine*, p. 1604.
[13] Beraudi, *Vaina` kaputt*, p. 61.
[14] Ibid, p. 69.
[15] Vicentini, *Noi Soli Vivi*, pp 33-34.
[16] Ajmone Marsan, unpublished memoir, p. 1.
[17] Battisti, "La divisione alpina 'Cuneense' al fronte russo", p. 46.
[18] Ibid.
[19] Ibid.
[20] Ajmone Marsan, unpublished memoir, p. 1.
[21] Beraudi, *Vaina` kaputt*, p. 65.
[22] Ibid., pp. 70-71.
[23] Ibid.
[24] Ibid., p. 71
[25] Ibid.

Chapter 11: DISASTER ON THE STEPPE
[1] Battisti, "La divisione alpina 'Cuneense' al fronte russo", p. 47.
[2] Ibid.
[3] Ibid.
[4] Ibid., p. 48.
[5] Ibid.
[6] Ibid.
[7] Beraudi, *Vaina` kaputt*, p. 75.
[8] Ibid., p. 77.
[9] Battisti, "La divisione alpina 'Cuneense' al fronte russo", pp. 48-49.
[10] Ibid., p. 49.
[11] Ibid., pp. 49-50.
[12] Porcari, "La 'Cuneense' sulle fronti di guerra", in *Gli italiani sul fronte russo*, Istituto Storico della Resistenza in Cuneo e Provincia, pp. 282-83.
[13] Battisti, "La divisione alpina 'Cuneense' al fronte russo", pp. 50-51.

Chapter 12: WITHDRAWAL OF THE TRIDENTINA DIVISION
[1] Reverberi, "Relazione", 5-6, and Bellelli, *Luigi Reverberi*, p. 27.
[2] Reverberi, "Relazione," p. 6.
[3] Revelli, *La guerra dei poveri*, p. 51.
[4] Fedriga, "Skororib e altro ancora", in Bedeschi, *Fronte russo: c'ero anch'io*, p. 95.

[5] Ibid., p. 95.
[6] Ibid.
[7] Ibid., pp. 96-97.
[8] Ibid., p. 97.
[9] Ibid., p. 97.
[10] Ibid pp. 97-98.
[11] Ibid., p. 98.
[12] Ibid., pp. 98-99
[13] Ibid., p. 99.
[14] Reverberi, "Relazione", pp. 6-7.
[15] Ibid., p. 7
[16] Ibid.
[17] Ibid., pp. 7- 8.
[18] Ibid., p. 8.
[19] Ibid.
[20] Zavagli, *Solo un pugno di neve*, pp. 153-54.
[21] Ibid., pp. 154-55.
[22] Reverberi, "Relazione", p. 8
[23] Ibid., pp. 8-9.
[24] Chierici, "Al commando dell'avanguardia della Tridentina", in Bedeschi, *Fronte russo, c'ero anch'io*, p. 131.
[25] Ibid.
[26] Reverberi, "Relazione", p. 9.
[27] Chierici, "Al commando dell'avanguardia della Tridentina", in Bedeschi, *Fronte russo: c'ero anch'io*, p. 132.
[28] Faldella, *Storia delle truppe alpine*, pp. 1560–61.
[29] Ibid., pp. 1561-63.
[30] Reverberi, "Relazione", p. 11.
[31] Ibid.
[32] Ibid., pp. 11- 12.
[33] Faldella, *Storia delle truppe alpine*, p. 1568–69.
[34] Ibid., p. 1569
[35] Ibid., pp. 1569-70.
[36] Gnocchi, *Cristo con gli alpini*, p. 21.
[37] Ibid., pp. 21-22.
[38] Reverberi, "Relazione", p. 13.
[39] Faldella, *Storia delle truppe alpine*, p. 1571.
[40] Bedeschi, *Centomila gavette di ghiaccio*, pp. 313-14.
[41] Reverberi, "Relazione", pp. 32-33.
[42] Trentini, "Per poter salvare vite umane", in Bedeschi, *Fronte russo: c'ero anch'io*, pp. 421-22.
[43] Gaza, Giorgio, "Ricordi e riflessioni di un 'vecio' della Russia", in Bedeschi, *Fronte russo, c'ero anch'io*, p. 145.
[44] Revelli, *La guerra dei poveri*, p. 71.

[45] Faldella, *Storia delle truppe alpine*, pp. 1619.

[46] Vettorazzo, "A Nikitowka e Nikolajewka, 40 anni fa", in Bedeschi, *Fronte russo, c'ero anch'io*, p. 299.

[47] Zavagli, *Solo un pugno di neve*, pp. 173-74.

[48] Revelli, *La guerra dei poveri*, pp. 70-71.

[49] Bedeschi, *Centomila gavette di ghiaccio*, pp. 314-17.

[50] Revelli, *La guerra dei poveri*, p. 59, and Faldella, *Storia delle truppe alpine*, p. 1634–35.

[51] Bedeschi, *Centomila gavette di ghiaccio*, pp. 339-42.

[52] Zavagli, *Solo un pugno di neve*, p. 206.

[53] Ibid., pp. 206-07.

[54] Ibid., p. 207.

[55] Ibid., pp. 207-08.

[56] Ibid., p. 208.

[57] Faldella, *Storia delle truppe alpine*, pp. 1637-38.

[58] Ibid., p. 1638.

[59] Ibid., pp. 1639–41.

[60] Ibid., pp. 1641–44.

[61] Ibid., p. 1644–46.

[62] Ibid., p. 1647.

[63] Ibid., pp. 1649-50.

[64] Ibid., pp. 1649-51.

[65] Gaza, "Ricordi e riflessioni di un 'vecio' della Russia", in Bedeschi, *Fronte russo: c'ero anch'io*, 146.

[66] Ibid., 146-47.

[67] Bellelli, *Luigi Reverberi*, p. 35.

[68] Faldella, *Storia delle truppe alpine*, 1653.

[69] Pasquale Corti, in Bellelli, *Reverberi*, p. 38.

[70] Candeago, "Così incominciò la grande odissea", in Bedeschi, *Fronte russo: c'ero anch'io*, p. 401.

[71] Faldella, *Storia delle truppe alpine*, p. 1654.

[72] Bedeschi, *Centomila gavette di ghiaccio*, pp. 350-55.

[73] Bellelli, *Reverberi*, pp. 40-41.

[74] Revelli, *La guerra dei poveri*, p. 101.

[75] Corradi, *La ritirata di Russia*, p. 128.

[76] Rigoni Stern, *Il sergente nella neve*, p. 88.

[77] Ibid.

[78] Sculati, "Pietà l'è morta", in Bedeschi, *Fronte russo: c'ero anch'io*, p. 393.

[79] Dalla Rosa, "Il gesto di questi uomini", in Bedeschi, *Fronte russo: c'ero anch'io*, pp. 319-20.

[80] Gaza, "Ricordi e riflessioni di un 'vecio' della Russia", in Bedeschi, *Fronte russo c'ero anch'io*, p. 146.

[81] Bellelli, *Reverberi*, p. 40.

[82] Faldella, *Storia delle truppe alpine*, p. 1655.

[83] Bedeschi, *Centomila gavette di ghiaccio*, pp. 356-57.
[84] Pasquale Corti, in Bellelli, *Reverberi*, p. 40.
[85] Bedeschi, *Centomila gavette di ghiaccio*, p. 357.
[86] Ibid., pp. 357-58.
[87] Ibid., p. 359.
[88] Ibid.
[89] Ibid., p. 360.
[90] Zavagli, *Solo un pugno di neve*, p. 226.
[91] Gnocchi, *Cristo con gli alpini*, p. 13.
[92] Ibid., pp. 13-14.
[93] Marino, Antonio, "Almeno avessimo visto un nostro aereo", in Bedeschi, *Fronte russo: c'ero anch'io*, p. 655.
[94] Bedeschi, *Centomila gavette di ghiaccio*, p. 380.
[95] Ibid., pp. 385-96, and p. 397.
[96] Ibid., pp. 398-99.
[97] Ibid., pp. 399-400.
[98] Ibid., p. 400.
[99] Ibid., p. 401.
[100] Ibid., pp. 402-03.
[101] Faldella, *Storia delle truppe alpine*, p. 1661–62.
[102] Ibid., p. 1661.
[103] Ibid., p. 1662.
[104] Ibid., p. 1664.

Chapter 13: OUT OF THE ENCIRCLEMENT: THE MARCH CONTINUES

[1] Bedeschi, *Centomila gavette di ghiaccio*, p. 405.
[2] Ibid., p. 404.
[3] Ibid., pp. 405-06.
[4] Ibid., p. 407.
[5] Faldella, *Storia delle truppe alpine*, pp. 1665-66.
[6] Ibid and Bedeschi, *Centomila gavette di ghiaccio*, p. 412.
[7] Zavagli, *Solo un pugno di neve*, pp. 247-48.
[8] Ibid., p. 252.
[9] Ibid., p. 253.
[10] Ibid., pp. 255.
[11] Ibid., pp. 256-58.
[12] Ibid., pp. 258-59.
[13] Ibid., p. 259.
[14] Ibid., pp. 259-60.
[15] Ibid., p. 260.
[16] Ibid., pp. 260-61.
[17] Faldella, *Storia delle truppe alpine*, p. 1668, and Vicentini and Resta, *Rapporto sui prigionieri di guerra*, p. 33.
[18] Faldella, *Storia delle truppe alpine*, p. 1668.

[19] Revelli, *Mai tardi*, p. 191.
[20] Ibid., p. 192.
[21] Ibid., p. 193.
[22] Faldella, *Storia delle truppe alpine*, p. 1668.
[23] Ibid., pp. 1668-69, and Vicentini and Resta, *Rapporto sui prigionieri di guerra*, p. 33.
[24] Revelli, *La guerra dei poveri*, p. 100.
[25] Bellelli, *Reverberi*, p. 41.
[26] Revelli, *La guerra dei poveri*, 101.
[27] Bedeschi, *Centomila gavette di ghiaccio* 414-15, and Revelli, *Mai tardi*, 194.

Chapter 14: SURVIVORS OF THE WITHDRAWAL RETURN TO ITALY
[1] Revelli, *La guerra dei poveri*, pp. 104-05.
[2] Ibid., p. 106.
[3] Bedeschi, *Centomila gavette di ghiaccio*, p. 416.
[4] Ibid., p. 420.
[5] Ibid, p. 424.
[6] Ibid., pp. 424-25.
[7] Cucchietti, "Alpini indossate la maglia di acciaio", in Revelli, *Il mondo dei vinti*, p. 268.
[8] Zavagli, *Solo un pugno di neve*, pp. 263-64.
[9] Revelli, *Le due guerre*, p. 123.
[10] Ibid.
[11] Revelli, *La guerra dei poveri*, p. 107.
[12] Ibid., p. 108.
[13] Gnocchi, *Cristo con gli alpini*, p. 15.
[14] Ibid., pp. 15-16.
[15] Revelli, *La guerra dei poveri*, p. 109.
[16] Revelli, *Le due guerre*, p. 123.
[17] Corradi, La ritirata di Russia, pp. 165-66.
[18] Ibid., pp. 167-68.
[19] Corti, *Few Returned*, pp. 138-39.
[20] Ibid., p. 139.
[21] Ibid., p. 25.
[22] Ibid., p. 139.
[23] Corradi, *La ritirata di Russia*, 15.
[24] Revelli, *La guerra dei poveri*, p. 100.
[25] Porcari, "La 'Cuneense' sulle fronti di guerra", (Allegato) in *Gli italiani sul fronte russo*, Istituto Storico della Resistenza in Cuneo e Provincia, p. 291.

Chapter 15: CAPTURE AT VALUIKI
[1] Beraudi, *Vaina` kaputt*, p. 77.
[2] Ibid.

[3] Ibid., p. 78.
[4] Ibid.
[5] Ibid.
[6] Ibid., pp. 78-79.
[7] Ibid., p. 79.
[8] Bellini, "I morti non ritornano", in Sani, *Prigionieri, i soldati italiani nei campi di concentramento, 1940-1947*, p. 68.
[9] Venturini, in Vicentini and Resta, *Rapporto sui prigionieri di guerra italiani in Russia*, p. 45.
[10] Lamberti, "Senza tomba ne` croce", in Sani, *Prigionieri*, i soldati italiani nei campi di concentramento, 1940-1947, p. 65.
[11] Ibid.
[12] Bellini, "I morti non ritornano", in Sani, *Prigionieri, i soldati italiani nei campi di concentramento, 1940-1947*, p. 68.
[13] Beraudi, *Vaina` kaputt*, pp. 79-80.
[14] Ibid., p. 80.
[15] Ibid., pp. 80-81.
[16] Ibid., p. 82.
[17] Ibid., p. 83.
[18] Bellini, "I morti non ritornano", in Sani, *Prigionieri, i soldati italiani nei campi di concentramento, 1940-1947*, p. 68.

Chapter 16: MARCHES OF THE DAVAI
[1] Vicentini, *Noi Soli Vivi*, p. 51.
[2] Vicentini, "Dagli Archivi Russe", p. 4.
[3] Zilli, "Gli Italiani prigionieri di guerra in URSS: vicende, esperienze, testimonianze", in *Gli italiani sul fronte russo*, Istituto Storico della Resistenza in Cuneo e Provincia, p. 305.
[4] Ibid., p. 306.
[5] Vicentini, *Noi Soli Vivi*, p. 69.
[6] Ibid.
[7] Ibid., pp. 69-70.
[8] Ibid.
[9] Ibid., p. 80.
[10] Ibid., p. 82.
[11] Bellini, "I morti non ritornano", in Sani, *Prigionieri, i soldati italiani nei campi di concentramento, 1940-1947*, p. 68.
[12] Ibid.
[13] Ibid.
[14] Ibid, and Bellini, "Amo la patria ancora di piu`", in Revelli, *La strada del davai*, p. 136.
[15] Bellini, "Amo la patria ancora di piu`", in Revelli, *La strada del davai*, p. 136.
[16] Ibid.
[17] Ibid., p. 137.

[18] Ibid.
[19] Ibid.
[20] Ibid.
[21] Ibid., p. 138.

Chapter 17: PRISONER OF WAR TRANSPORTS
[1] Beraudi, *Vaina` kaputt*, p. 87.
[2] Ibid.
[3] Ibid., p. 88.
[4] Ibid., p. 89.
[5] Ibid.
[6] Ibid., p. 90.
[7] Ibid., pp. 90-91.
[8] Ibid., p. 91.
[9] Ibid.
[10] Ibid., p. 93.
[11] Ibid., pp. 93-94.
[12] Ibid., p. 94.
[13] Bongiovanni, "Quante fontane ho sognato in Russia," in Revelli, *La strada del davai*, p. 397.
[14] Lamberti, "Senza Tomba ne` croce", in Sani, *Prigionieri, i soldati italiani nei campi di concentramento, 1940-1947*, pp. 65-66.
[15] Craig, *Enemy at the Gates*, pp. 263-64 and p. 277.
[16] Ibid., pp. 327-28.
[17] Ibid., p. 329.
[18] Vicentini, *Noi soli vivi*, pp. 85-93.

Chapter 18: PRISONER OF WAR CAMPS—THE FIRST MONTHS
[1] Vicentini and Resta, *Rapporto sui prigionieri italiani in Russia*, p. 69.
[2] Ibid., p. 69.
[3] Turla, *7 rubli al cappellano*, p. 91, in Vicentini and Resta, *Rapporto sui prigionieri italiani in Russia*, p. 70.
[4] Craig, *Enemy at the Gates*, p. 392.
[5] Caneva, *Calvario bianco*, p. 94, in Vicentini and Resta, *Rapporto sui prigionieri italiani in Russia*, p. 70.
[6] Bellini, "I morti non ritornano", in Sani, *Prigionieri, i soldati Italiani nei campi di concentramento, 1940-1947*, p. 69.
[7] Vicentini, *Noi soli vivi*, pp. 93-96.
[8] Ibid., p. 97.
[9] Ibid., p. 98.
[10] Ibid., pp. 98-99.
[11] Ibid., p. 100.
[12] Ibid., p. 101.
[13] Ibid., pp. 101-02.

[14] Ibid., pp. 107.

[15] Ibid., pp. 109-11.

[16] Ibid., p. 112.

[17] Ibid., p. 113.

[18] Gambetti, " 'Alba' giornale dei prigionieri di guerra italiani in URSS", in *Gli italiani sul fronte russo*, Istituto Storico della Resistenza in Cuneo e Provincia, p. 335.

[19] Di Michele, *Io, prigioniero in Russia*, p. 96.

[20] Zilli, "Gli italiani prigionieri di guerra in URSS vicende, esperienze, testimonianze", in *Gli italiani sul fronte russo*, Istituto Storico della Resistenza in Cuneo e Provincia, p. 307.

[21] Di Michele, *Io prigioniero in Russia*, p. 99.

[22] Zilli, "Gli italiani prigionieri di guerra in URSS: vicende, esperienze, testimonianze", in *Gli italiani sul fronte russo*, Istituto Storico della Resistenza in Cuneo e Provincia, p. 309.

[23] Gambetti, " 'L'Alba' giornale dei prigionieri di guerra italiani in URSS", in *Gli italiani sul fronte russo*, Istituto Storico della Resistenza in Cuneo e Provincia, p. 336.

[24] Di Michele, *Io prigioniero in Russia*, p. 101.

[25] Ibid.

[26] Gambetti, " 'L'Alba' giornale dei prigionieri di guerra italiani in URSS", in *Gli italiani sul fronte russo*, Istituto Storico della Resistenza in Cuneo e Provincia, p. 336.

[27] Ibid., pp. 336-37.

[28] Ibid., p. 337.

[29] Beraudi, *Vaina` kaputt*, p. 95.

[30] Zilli, "Gli italiani prigionieri di guerra in URSS: vicende, esperienze, testimonianze", in *Gli italiani sul fronte russo*, Istituto Storico della Resistenza in Cuneo e Provincia, p. 307.

[31] Beraudi, *Vaina` kaputt*, p. 97.

[32] Ibid.

[33] Ibid., pp. 104-05.

[34] Ibid., p. 105.

[35] Craig, *Enemy at the Gates*, pp. 362-63.

[36] Ibid., p. 393.

[37] Ibid., pp. 390-92.

[38] Beraudi, *Vaina` kaputt*, 108.

[39] Vicentini, *Noi soli vivi*, pp. 115-18.

[40] Ibid., pp. 119-20.

[41] Ibid., p. 121.

[42] Ibid., p. 129.

[43] Ibid., pp. 133-35.

[44] DeMaria, "I russi sono gente giusta", in Revelli, *La strada del davai*, p. 206.

[45] Vicentini and Resta, *Rapporto sui prigionieri di guerra italiani in Russia*, p. 85.

[46] Ibid.

[47] Ibid.

[48] Serale, Andrea, "Forza, se passiamo torniamo a casa", in Revelli, *La strada del davai*, p. 124.

[49] Vicentini and Resta, *Rapporto sui prigionieri di guerra italiani in Russia*, p. 105, and Di Michele, *Io prigioniero in Russia*, p. 116.

[50] Di Michele, *Io prigioniero in Russia*, pp. 116-17.

[51] Ibid., p. 118.

[52] Ibid., pp. 119-20.

[53] Ibid., p. 120.

[54] Ibid., pp. 120-21.

[55] Ibid., p. 121.

[56] Ibid., pp. 123-24.

Chapter 19: CAMPS SUZDAL AND KRASNOGORSK

[1] Ajmone Marsan, unpublished memoir, p. 2.

[2] Vicentini and Resta, *Rapporto sui prigionieri di guerra in Russia*, p. 105.

[3] Vicentini, *Noi soli vivi*, p. 170-71.

[4] Ibid.

[5] Ibid., p. 172.

[6] Ibid., pp. 177-78.

[7] Ibid., pp. 179-81.

[8] Ibid., pp. 190.

[9] Ajmone Marsan, unpublished memoir, p. 2.

[10] Vicentini, *Noi soli vivi*, pp. 198-201.

[11] Ibid., p. 215.

[12] Ibid.

[13] Zilli, "Gli italiani prigionieri di guerra in URSS", in *Gli italiani sul fronte Russo*, Istituto Storico della Resistenza in Cuneo e Provincia, p. 310.

[14] Ajmone Marsan, unpublished memoir, p. 2.

[15] Lamberti, "L'importanza del giornale "L' Alba"", in *Gli italiani sul fronte Russo*, Istituto Storico della Resistenza in Cuneo e Provincia, p. 326.

[16] Zilli, "Gli italiani prigionieri di guerra in URSS", in *Gli italiani sul fronte Russo*, Istituto Storico della Resistenza in Cuneo e Provincia, pp. 310-11.

[17] Ajmone Marsan, unpublished memoir, p. 2.

[18] Vicentini, *Noi soli vivi*, p. 216.

[19] Ibid., p. 217.

[20] Ibid.

[21] Lamberti, "L'importanza del giornale "L'Alba"", in *Gli italiani sul fronte Russo*, Istituto Storico della Resistenza in Cuneo e Provincia, p. 327.

[22] Ajmone Marsan, unpublished memoir, p. 2.

[23] Vicentini, *Noi soli vivi*, p. 218.

[24] Ibid., p. 219.

[25] Ibid.

[26] Beraudi, *Vaina` kaputt*, pp. 126-27.

[27] Ibid., pp. 127-28.
[28] Ibid., p. 128.
[29] Vicentini, *Noi soli vivi*, p. 221.
[30] Ibid.
[31] Ibid.
[32] Ajmone Marsan, unpublished memoir, p. 3.
[33] Beraudi, *Vaina` kaputt*, p. 129.
[34] Ibid., pp. 129-30.
[35] Ibid., p. 130
[36] Ibid., p. 131.
[37] Ibid., p. 132
[38] Ibid.
[39] Ibid., p. 133.
[40] Ibid.
[41] Ibid., p. 134.
[42] Ibid.
[43] Ibid.
[44] Ibid., p. 135.
[45] Ibid., pp. 135-36.
[46] Ibid., p. 140.
[47] Ibid., pp. 140-41.
[48] Ibid., p. 141.
[49] Ibid., p. 143.
[50] Ibid., p. 144.
[51] Ibid., p. 146.
[52] Ibid., pp. 147-48.
[53] Ibid., p. 148
[54] Ajmone Marsan, pp. 2-3.
[55] Beraudi, *Vaina` kaputt*, p. 149.
[56] Ibid., p. 154.
[57] Ibid., p. 155.
[58] Ibid., p. 157, and Ajmone Marsan, unpublished memoir, p. 2-3.
[59] Beraudi, *Vaina` kaputt*, pp. 156-57.
[60] Ibid., pp. 157-58.
[61] Vicentini, *Noi Soli Vivi*, pp. 239-40.
[62] Ibid., pp. 242-43.
[63] Ibid., pp. 243-44.
[64] Beraudi, *Vaina` kaputt*, p. 158.
[65] Ibid., p. 160.
[66] Ibid., pp. 160-61.
[67] Ibid., p. 161.
[68] Ibid., p. 162.
[69] Ajmone Marsan, unpublished memoir, p. 3.
[70] Ibid., p. 2.

[71] Ibid.
[72] Ibid., p. 1.
[73] Ibid.
[74] Ibid., p. 3
[75] Ibid.
[76] Ibid.
[77] Ibid., p. 4.
[78] Beraudi, *Vaina` kaputt*, pp. 162-63.
[79] Ibid., p. 163.
[80] Ibid., pp. 163-64.
[81] Ibid., pp. 170-71.
[82] Ibid., p. 172.
[83] Ibid., pp. 173-74.
[84] Ibid., p. 174.
[85] Ibid., p. 175.
[86] Ibid., p. 176.
[87] Ibid.
[88] Novikov, (trans. Ajmone Marsan), "Come gli italiani salvarano Cerniz dalla fame", p. 1.
[89] Ibid., pp. 2-3.
[90] Ibid., p. 1.
[91] Ibid., p. 3.
[92] Ibid., p. 5.
[93] Ibid.
[94] Ibid., p. 3.
[95] Ibid., p. 2.
[96] Ibid., p. 4.
[97] Ibid.

Chapter 20: THE HOMEWARD JOURNEY
[1] Beraudi, Vaina` kaputt, pp. 176-77
[2] Ibid., p. 179.
[3] Ibid., p. 180.
[4] Ibid.
[5] Ibid., pp. 180-81.
[6] Ibid., p. 181.
[7] Ibid., pp. 181-82.
[8] Ibid., p. 182.
[9] Ibid., p. 183.
[10] Ibid., p. 184.
[11] Ibid.
[12] Ibid., p. 185.
[13] Ibid.
[14] Ibid., p. 186.

[15] Ibid.

[16] Ibid., pp. 186-87.

[17] Ibid., p. 187.

[18] Gallo, *For Love and Country*, p. 98.

[19] Vicentini and Resta, *Rapporto sui prigionieri italiani di guerra in Russia*, p. 161.

[20] Revelli, *La strada del davai*, p. XXXIII.

[21] Belmondo et. al., "La "campagna" di Russia nella stampa e nella pubblicistica piemontese ed in particolare della provincia di Cuneo", in *Gli italiani sul fronte russo*, Istituto Storico della Resistenza in Cuneo e Provincia, p. 458.

[22] Vicentini and Resta, *Rapporto sui prigionieri di guerra italiani in Russia*, pp. 161-62.

[23] Viale, "Hai una famiglia, forza, resisti", in Revelli, *La strada del davai*, p. 33.

[24] Ibid., p. 34.

[25] Castellano, "La guerra e` finita", in Revelli, *La strada del davai*, pp. 437-38.

[26] Zilli, "Gli italiani prigionieri di guerra in URSS", in *Gli Italiani sul fronte russo*, Istituto Storico della Resistenza in Cuneo e Provincia, p. 316-17.

[27] Vicentini, *Noi soli vivi*, pp. 303-04

[28] Ibid., p. 304.

[29] Ibid., p. 306.

[30] Ibid., p. 308.

[31] Lamberti, "Senza tomba ne` croce", in Sani, *Prigionieri, i soldati italiani nei campi di concentramento*, p. 67.

[32] Lamberti, "Un altra volta anch'io vi rompero` la testa", in Revelli, *La strada del davai*, pp. 376-77.

[33] Ibid.

[34] Turla, Guido, *7 rubli al cappellano*, in Vicentini and Resta, *Rapporto sui prigionieri di guerra italiani in Russia*, p. 169.

[35] Ibid.

[36] Vicentini, *Noi soli vivi*, p. 311.

[37] Ibid., p. 314.

[38] Ibid.

[39] Ibid., p. 315.

[40] Ibid.

[41] Ibid.

[42] Ibid., p. 316.

[43] Ibid.

[44] Ibid.

[45] Ibid., p. 317.

[46] Ibid.

[47] Ibid., p. 318.

[48] Ibid.

[49] Ibid., pp. 318-19.

[50] Ibid., p. 319.

[51] Ibid.

[52] Lamberti, "Senza tomba ne` croce", in Sani, *Prigionieri, i soldati Italiani nei campi di concentramento*, p. 67.

[53] Vicentini and Resta, *Rapporto sui prigionieri di guerra italiani in Russia*, p. 162.

[54] Ibid., p. 166.

[55] Ibid.

[56] Revelli, *La strada del davai*, p. XXXII.

[57] Isoardi, in Revelli, *L'ultimo fronte*. p. 138.

[58] Rovera, in Revelli, *L'ultimo fronte*, p. 33.

[59] Carbone, in Revelli, *L'ultimo fronte*, pp. 12-13.

[60] Origlia, in Revelli, *L'ultimo fronte*, p. 182.

[61] Ibid., pp. 182-83.

[62] Prina, in Revelli, *L'ultimo fronte*, p. 198.

Chapter 21: *LE PERDITE*— THE LOSSES

[1] Revelli, *La strada del davai*, p. XXXI.

[2] Ibid, and Belmondo et. al., "La 'campagna' di Russia nella stampa e nelle pubblicistica piemontese ed in particolare della provincia di Cuneo", in *Gli italiani sul fronte russo*, Istituto Storico della Resistenza in Cuneo e Provincia, pp. 454-55.

[3] Revelli, *La strada del davai*, p. XXX.

[4] Vicentini, *Il sacrificio della Julia in Russia*, p. 10.

[5] Vicentini and Resta, *Rapporto sui prigionieri di guerra in Russia*, p. 17.

[6] Giusti, "Il rimpatrio dei prigionieri italiani dall'Urss", p. 45, and Vicentini and Resta, *Rapporto sui prigionieri di guerra italiani in Russia*, p. 161, and Vicentini, "Dagli archivi russe e` arrivata la documentazione sui nostri prigionieri di guerra", p. 2.

[7] Vicentini and Resta, *Rapporto sui prigionieri di guerra italiani in Russia*, p. 18.

[8] Ibid.

[9] Vicentini, "La campagna di Russia", p. 6.

[10] Vicentini, "Dagli archivi russe e` arrivata la documentazione sui nostri prigionieri di guerra", p. 1.

[11] Ibid.

[12] Ibid.

[13] Ibid.

[14] Vicentini, "Dagli archivi russe e` arrivata la documentazione sui nostri prigionieri di guerra", pp. 1-2.

[15] Giusti, "Il rimpatrio dei prigionieri italiani dall'Urss", p. 44.

[16] Vicentini, "Dagli archivi russe e` arrivata la documentazione sui nostri prigionieri di guerra", p. 2.

[17] Ibid.

[18] Ibid.

[19] Ibid., p. 3.

[20] Ibid.
[21] Ibid., p. 3.
[22] Ibid., p. 4.
[23] Ibid.
[24] Riba, "C'e` nessuno di Valgrana?", in Revelli, *La strada del davai*, p. 236.
[25] Tosello, "Nel campo 101 'La norma' ", in Sani, *Prigionieri*, p. 70.
[26] Riba, "C'e` nessuno di Valgrana?", in Revelli, *La strada del davai*, p. 236.
[27] Vicentini, "Dagli archivi russe e` arrivata la documentazione sui nostri prigionieri di guerra", p. 5.
[28] Ibid.
[29] Ibid.
[30] Ibid.
[31] Ibid.

EPILOGUE

[1] The material presented in this portion of the text is based on a film produced by the Italian National Association of Alpini. Other than quotes attributed to Leonardo Caprioli, the then president of the association, the source of all other quoted material originates from the unnamed narrator of the film.

POSTSCRIPT

[1] Vicentini, *Noi Soli Vivi*, pp. 324-26.

BIBLIOGRAPHY

Antill, Peter. *Stalingrad 1942*. New York: Osprey Publishing Ltd., 2007.

Ajmone Marsan, Veniero. "Unpublished Memoir."

Ajmone Marsan, Veniero. "1942–1946 Ricordi di guerra e di prigione," "Unpublished Memoir."

Assunto, Bianco. "Cronaca dei lavori." In *Gli italiani sul fronte russo*. Istituto Storico della Resistenza in Cuneo e Provincia, pp. 485–511.

Battisti, Emilio (General). "La divisione alpina 'Cuneense' al fronte russo 1942–43." Archivio dell'Ufficio Storico dello Stato Maggiore dell'Esercito.

Bedeschi, Giulio. *Centomila gavette di ghiaccio*. Milano: Mursia, 1994.

_____. *Fronte russo: c'ero anch'io*. Volume secondo. Milano: Mursia, 1983.

Beevor, Anthony. *Stalingrad. The Fateful Siege: 1942–1943*. New York: Penguin Books, 1999.

Bellamy, Chris. *Absolute War, Soviet Russia in the Second World War*. New York: Vintage Books, 2008.

Bellelli, Michele. *Luigi Reverberi: un soldato, un alpino, un uomo*. Centro Culturale Comunale, Comune di Cavriago: 2009.

Bellini, Vittorio. "I morti non ritornano." In Massimo Sani, *Prigionieri, i soldati italiani nei campi di concentramento, 1940–1947*, pp. 67–69.

_____. "Amo la patria ancora piu` di prima." In Nuto Revelli, *La strada del davai*, pp. 127–43.

Belmondo, Rosalba, Luciano Bertello, Piermario Bologna, Michele

Calandri, Alberto Cavaglion, Emma Mana. "La 'campagna' di Russia nella stampa e nelle pubblicistica piemontese ed in particolare della provincia di Cuneo". In *Gli italiani sul fronte russo*. Istituto Storico della Resistenza in Cuneo e Provincia, pp. 425–64.

Beraudi, Gino. *Vaina` kaputt, guerra e prigionia in Russia (1942–1945)*. Rovereto: Museo Storico Italiano della Guerra, 1996.

Blumentritt, Gunther (General). "Advance." In *The War 1939–1945*. Eds. Desmond Flower and James Reeves, p. 209.

Bongiovanni, Grato. "Quante fontane ho sognato in Russia." In Nuto Revelli, *La strada del davai*, pp. 388–409.

Calvocoressi, Peter, Guy Wint, and John Pritchard. *Second World War*. London: Penguin Books, 1995.

Candeago. Mose`. "Cosi incomincio` la grande odissea." In Giulio Bedeschi, *Fronte russo: c'ero anch'io*, pp. 395–402.

Candela, Battista. "Scappate prima che venga il freddo." In Nuto Revelli, *La strada del davai*, pp. 68–97.

Caneva, Carlo. *Calvario bianco*. Grafica Friulana, 1967.

Carbone, Rocco G.B. In Nuto Revelli, *L'ultimo fronte*, pp. 16–19.

Castellano, Guido. "La guerra e` finita." In Nuto Revelli, *La strada del davai*, pp. 425–38.

Chierici, Policarpo. "Al commando dell'avanguardia della Tridentina." In Giulio Bedeschi, *Fronte russo: c'ero anch'io*, pp. 129–39.

Corradi, Egisto. *La ritirata di Russia*. Milano: Mursia, 2009.

Corti, Eugenio. *Few Returned. Twenty-eight Days on the Russian Front, Winter 1942–1943*. (Peter Edward Levy, trans.). Columbia, Missouri: University of Missouri Press, 1997.

Corti, Nello. "Unpublished Diary."

Corti, Pasquale. *La disfatta, la tragedia degli Alpini in Russia (1942–1943)*. T&M: Reggio Emilia, 2007.

Craig, William. *Enemy at the Gates*. London: Penguin Books, 2001.

Cruccu, Rinaldo. "Le operazioni italiane in Russia 1941–1943." In *Gli italiani sul fronte russo*. Istituto Storico della Resistenza in Cuneo e Provincia, pp. 209–27.

Cucchietti, Vincenzo. "Alpini indossate la maglia di acciaio." In Nuto Revelli, *Il mondo dei vinti*, pp. 262–68.

Dalla Rosa, Sergio. "Il gesto di questi uomini." In Giulio Bedeschi, *Fronte Russo: c'ero anch'io*, pp. 318–20.

Damini, Angelo. "Le due ragazze russe 'fucilate' sul posto." In Giulio Bedeschi, *Fronte russo: c'ero anch'io*, pp. 412–16.

Davies, Norman. *No Simple Victory, World War II in Europe, 1939–1945*. New York: Penguin Group: 2006.

Dear, I.C.B., and M.R.D. Foot (eds), *The Oxford Companion to World War II*. New York: Oxford University Press, 2005.

Deighton, Len. *Blood, Tears and Folly*. Edison, NJ: Castle Books, 1999.

Demaria, Giuseppe. "I russi sono gente giusta." In Nuto Revelli, *La strada del davai*, pp. 201–09.

Di Michele, Vincenzo. *Io prigioniero in Russia*. Firenze: MEF – L'Autore Libri, 2008.

Faldella, Emilio. *Storia delle truppe alpine 1872–1972*, vol. 3: edita sotto gli auspici della Associazione Nazionale Alpini: Milano: Cavalotti Landoni, 1972.

Flower, Desmond, and James Reeves, eds. *The War 1939–1945*. New York: Da Capo Press Inc. 1997.

Förster, Jürgen, "Il ruolo dell 8 armata italiana dal punto di vista tedesco." In *Gli italiani sul fronte russo*. Istituto Storico della Resistenza in Cuneo e Provincia, pp. 229–59.

Gallo, Patrick. *For Love and Country*. Lanham, Maryland: University Press of America, Inc., 2003.

Gallo, Romano. In Nuto Revelli, *L'ultimo fronte*, pp. 102–11.

Gambetti, Fidia. "'L'Alba' giornale dei prigionieri di guerra italiani in URSS." In *Gli italiani sul fronte russo*. Istituto Storico della Resistenza in Cuneo e Provincia, pp. 331–45.

Gaza, Giorgio. "Ricordi e riflessioni di un 'vecio' della Russia." In Giulio Bedeschi, *Fronte russo: c'ero anch'io*, pp. 143–49.

Ghibaudo, Bartolomeo. In Nuto Revelli, *L'ultimo fronte*, pp. 124–28.

Giusti, Maria Teresa. "Il Rimpatrio dei prigionieri italiani dall'Urss (1941–1946)." Milano: Studi e ricerche, F. Angeli, 2000.

Gnocchi, Carlo. *Cristo con gli alpini*. Milano: Mursia, 2008.

Goldhagen, Daniel Jonah. *Hitler's Willing Executioners, Ordinary Germans and the Holocaust*. New York: Alfred A. Knopf, 1996.

Grignaschi, Pasquale. "Le isbe – l'amicizia con Planton – la ritirata." In Giulio Bedeschi, *Fronte russo: c'ero anch'io*, pp. 539–51.

Hassell, Ulrich von. *The von Hassell Diaries*. London, 1948, 8 Apr. 1941, p. 173. In Antony Beevor, *Stalingrad*, p. 15.

Hart, B.H. Liddell. *History of the Second World War*. Old Saybrook,

CT: Konecky and Konecky, 1970.

Headland, R. "Messages of Murder." London 1992. In I.C.B. Dear, *The Oxford Companion to World War II*, p. 252.

Innocenti, Marco. *L'Italia del 1943, come eravamo nell'anno in cui crollo` il fascismo*. Milano: Mursia, 1993.

Isoardi, Claudio. In Nuto Revelli, *L'ultimo fronte*, pp. 138–48.

Istituto Storico della Resistenza in Cuneo e Provincia. *Gli Italiani sul fronte russo*. Prefazione di Guido Quazza, ed. De Donato. Bari: 1982.

Lamberti, Giuseppe. "Senza tomba ne` croce." In Massimo Sani, *Prigionieri, i soldati italiani nei campi di concentramento, 1940-1947*, pp. 65–67.

_____. "Un'altra volta anch'io vi rompero` la testa." In Nuto Revelli, *La strada del davai*, pp. 361–79.

_____. "L'importanza del giornale 'L'Alba' per l'evoluzione democratica dei prigionieri italiani in Urss a seguito del secondo conflitto mondiale." In Istituto Storico della Resistenza in Cuneo e provincia, pp. 323-30.

Magnani, Ugo. "In ricordo della ritirata di Russia di Ugo Magnani:" [online]. Available: Seconda Guerra Mondiale – Italia – Ritirata in Russia: http://www.cronologia.it 2000.

Marchisio, Pietro. "Noi e i prigionieri russi." In Giulio Bedeschi, *Fronte russo: c'ero anch'io*, pp. 337–39.

Marino, Antonio. "Almeno avessimo visto un aereo." In Giulio Bedeschi, *Fronte russo: c'ero anch'io*, pp. 650–61.

Mela, Luciano and Pietro Crespi, "Dosvidania" and "Savoia Cavalleria dal fronte russo alla resistenza." Due diari inediti, Edizioni Vita e Pensiero. In Paola Mocchi, "Dalla Russia con orrore", [online]. Available: Seconda Guerra Mondiale – Italia – Ritirata in Russia: http://www.cronologia.it 2006.

Merridale, Catherine. *Ivan's War*. New York: Picador, 2006.

Messe, Giovanni (General), *La guerra al fronte russo, Il corpo di spedizione italiano in Russia (CSIR)*. Milano: Mursia, 2005.

Mocchi, Paola. "Dalla Russia con orrore:" [online].Available: Seconda Guerra Mondiale– Italia – Ritirata in Russia: http://www.cronologia.it 2000.

Muratti, Bonaldo. "Gli alpini del Gemona." In Giulio Bedeschi, *Fronte russo: c'ero anch'io*, pp. 276–81.

Natkiel, Richard. *Atlas of World War II*. New York: Barnes & Noble, Inc., 2000.

Novikov, N. "Come gli italiani salvarono Cerniz dalla fame." Translated by Veniero Ajmone Marsan. Suzdal: Vecerni Zvon, 4, 1991.

Origlia, Giacomo. In Nuto Revelli, *L'ultimo fronte*, pp. 182–91.

Paladini, Arrigo. "War diary, July 19, 1941–January 1942." In Stanislao G. Pugliese, *Desperate Inscriptions, Graffiti from the Nazi Prison in Rome 1943–1944*, p. 9.

Porcari, Libero (General). "La 'Cuneense' sulle fronti di guerra." In *Gli italiani sul fronte russo*. Istituto Storico della Resistenza in Cuneo e Provincia, pp. 261–91.

Prina, Antonio Votero. In Nuto Revelli, *L'ultimo fronte*, pp. 198–204.

Pugliese, Stanislao G. *Desperate Inscriptions, Graffiti from the Nazi Prison in Rome 1943–1944*. Bordighera Press, 2002.

Revelli, Nuto. *La guerra dei poveri*. Torino: Einaudi, 1993.

_____ . *Mai tardi. Diario di un alpino in Russia*. Torino: Einaudi: 2001.

_____ . *La strada del davai*. Torino: Einaudi, 1966.

_____ . *Le due guerre, guerra fascista e guerra partigiana*. Torino: Einaudi, 2003.

_____ . *L'ultimo fronte*. Torino: Einaudi, 2009.

_____ . *Il mondo dei vinti*, Torino: Einaudi, 1997.

_____ ."La guerra degli ignoranti Available [online] http://www.alpcub/ GuerraIgnoranti.pdf

Reverberi, Luigi (General). "Relazione sulle azioni svolte dalla divisione Tridentina al fronte." (Dott. Ing. Bruno Reverberi, archivio).

Rochat, Giorgio. *Le due guerre italiane 1935–1943. Dall'impero d'Etiopia alla disfatta*. Torino: Einaudi, 2005.

_____ . "Mussolini as war leader". (John Gooch trans). In I.C.B. Dear, *The Oxford Companion to World War II*, pp. 598–01.

Rovera, Rocco G.B. In Nuto Revelli, *L'ultimo fronte*, pp. 12–13, and pp. 16–19.

Riba, Giovanni. "C'e` nessuno di Valgrana?" In Nuto Revelli, *La strada del davai*, pp. 230–40.

Rigone Stern, Mario. *The Sergeant in the Snow*. Translated by Archibald Colquhoun, Evanston, Illinois: The Marlboro Press/ Northwestern, Northwestern University Press, 1998.

————. *Il sergente nella neve, ritorno sul Don.* Torino: Einaudi, 1990.

Sani, Massimo. *Prigionieri, i soldati italiani nei campi di concentramento, 1940–1947.* Torino: ERI, Edizioni RAI, 1987.

Sculati, Eraldo. "Pieta` l'e` morta." In Giulio Bedeschi, *Fronte russo: c'ero anch'io*, pp. 383–93.

Serale, Andrea. "Forza, se passiamo torniamo a casa." In Nuto Revelli, *La strada del davai*, pp. 120–26.

Shirer, William L. *The Rise and Fall of the Third Reich.* New York: Simon & Schuster Paperbacks, 1990.

Smith, Denis Mack. *Mussolini's Roman Empire.* New York: The Viking Press, 1976.

Sulzberger, C.L. *World War II.* New York: Houghton Mifflin Company, 1969.

Tosello, Adolfo. "Nel campo 101: 'La norma.' In Massimo Sani, *Prigionieri, i soldati nei campi di concentramento, 1940–1947*, pp. 70–71.

Trentini, Vittorio. "Per poter salvare vite umane." In Giulio Bedeschi, *Fronte russo: c'ero anch'io*, pp. 417–22.

Turla, Guido. *7 rubli al cappellano*, Milano: ITE, 1965.

Valori, Francesco. *Gli italiani in Russia, la campagna dello C.S.I.R. e dell'A.R.M.I.R.* Milano: Casa Editrice Bietti, 1967.

Venturini, Luigi. In Carlo Vicentini, and Paolo Resta, Unione Nazionale Italiana Reduci di Russia, p. 45.

Vetturazzo, Guido. "A Nikitowka e Nikolajewka, 40 anni fa." In Giulio Bedeschi, *Fronte russo, c'ero anch'io*, pp. 292–301.

Viale, Giuseppe. "Hai una famiglia, forza resisti." In Nuto Revelli, *La strada del davai*, pp. 20–34.

Vicentini, Carlo. *Noi soli vivi, quando settantamila italiani passarono il Don.* Milano: Mursia, 1997.

————. *Il sacrificio della Julia in Russia.* Udine: Fondazione CRUP, Gaspari editore, 2006.

————. "Le perdite della divisione alpina Cuneense sul fronte russo, inverno 1942–1943." Centro Studi U.N.I.R.R. Unione Nazionale Italiana Reduci di Russia, 1998.

————."Dagli archivi russe e` arrivata la documentazione sui nostri prigionieri di guerra". Intervento al convegno di studio, "La deportazione italiana durante la seconda guerra mondiale," organizato dall'Istituto Bergamasco per la storia della resistenza e dell'eta` contemporanea, Bergamo,1997.

─────── . "La Campagna di Russia." unpublished, 1987.

Vicentini, Carlo, and Paolo Resta. *Rapporto sui prigionieri di guerra italiani in Russia.* Unione Nazionale Italiana Reduci di Russia, Seconda Edizione. Milano: 2005.

Wendel, Else, "On Leave from Russia." In *The War 1939–1945*, eds. Desmond Flower and James Reeves, pp. 223–25.

Winchester, Charles D. *Hitler's War On Russia.* USA: Osprey Direct c/o House Distribution Center, Maryland: 2007.

Zavagli, Bruno. *Solo un pugno di neve.* Milano: Mursia & C., 1966.

Zilli, Valdo. "Gli italiani prigionieri di guerra in URSS: vicende, esperienze, testimonianze." In *Gli italiani sul fronte russo.* Istituto Storico della Resistenza in Cuneo e Provincia, 1982, pp. 295–321.

PUBLISHED DOCUMENTARY MATERIAL

Directive May 13, 1941, *Nazi Conspiracy and Aggression,* III, pp. 409–13 (Nuremberg Document 447-PS). In William Shirer, *The Rise and Fall of the Third Reich*, p. 832.

Halder affidavit, Nov. 22, 1945, at Nuremberg, *Nazi Conspiracy and Aggression*, VIII, pp. 645–46. In William, Shirer, *The Rise and Fall of the Third Reich*, p. 830.

Keitel's order, July 23, 1941. *Nazi Conspiracy and Aggression*, VI, p. 876 (Nuremberg Document C-52); July 27 order, *ibid.*, pp 875–76 (Nuremberg Document C-51). In William Shirer, *The Rise and Fall of the Third Reich*, p.831.

Nazi Conspiracy and Aggression, III, pp. 798–99. In William Shirer, *The Rise and Fall of the Third Reich*, p. 939.

Rosenberg Instructions, *Nazi Conspiracy and Aggression*, III, pp. 690–93 (Nuremberg Document 1029, 1030-PS), and Text, *Nazi Conspiracy and Aggression*, III, pp. 716–17 (Nuremberg Document 1058-PS). In William Shirer, *The Rise and Fall of the Third Reich*, p. 833.

FILM

Associazione Nazionale Alpini: *La "Casa del sorriso" un segno di speranza*, realizzata da DIFI INFORFILM ITALIA, Edizioni R.V.R. Romana Videoriversamenti, Roma, 1993.

INDEX